The Mortal Messiah
From Bethlehem to Calvary
Book IV

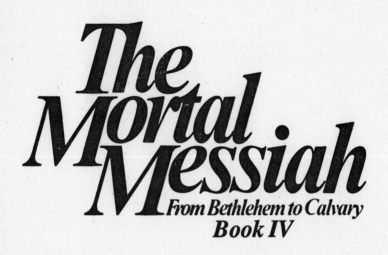

The Mortal Messiah

From Bethlehem to Calvary
Book IV

Bruce R. McConkie

Deseret Book Company
Salt Lake City, Utah

©1981 Deseret Book Company
All rights reserved
Printed in the United States of America
Vol. 4 ISBN 0-87747-856-2

No part of this book may be reproduced in any
form or by any means without permission in writing
from the publisher, Deseret Book Company,
P.O. Box 30178, Salt Lake City, Utah 84130.

First printing March 1981
Second printing March 1983
Third printing August 1985
Fourth printing July 1987
Fifth printing July 1988

Library of Congress Cataloging-in-Publication Data (Revised)

McConkie, Bruce R.
    The mortal Messiah.

    Includes index.
    1. Jesus Christ—Biography.   2. Christian
biography—Palestine.   3. Judaism—History—Post-
exilic period, 586 B.C.-210 A.D.   I. Title.
BT301.2.M16   232.9'01   79-19606
ISBN 0-87747-784-1   (Vol. 1)

THE MESSIANIC TRILOGY

The forerunner of this work is *The Promised Messiah: The First Coming of Christ*, which deals with the Messianic Prophecies. This work, *The Mortal Messiah: From Bethlehem to Calvary*, is a Life of Christ published in four books. This is Book IV.

BOOK IV

The other books on the Life of Christ are published separately as follows:

BOOK I

BOOK II

BOOK III

The concluding work in this whole series will be *The Millennial Messiah: The Second Coming of the Son of Man.*

ABBREVIATIONS

Scriptural references are abbreviated in a standard and self-identifying way. Other books are cited by author and title except for the following:

Commentary 1   Bruce R. McConkie, *Doctrinal New Testament Commentary.* Vol. 1, *The Gospels.* Bookcraft, 1965.

Edersheim   Alfred Edersheim, *The Life and Times of Jesus the Messiah.* 1883.

Farrar   F. W. Farrar, *The Life of Christ.* London: Cassell & Co., Ltd., 1874.

Geikie   Cunningham Geikie, *The Life and Words of Christ.* 1886.

Hymns   *Hymns, The Church of Jesus Christ of Latter-day Saints.* 1948.

JST   Joseph Smith Translation (Inspired Version) of the Bible.

Mormon Doctrine   Bruce R. McConkie, *Mormon Doctrine,* 2nd ed. Bookcraft, 1966.

Sketches   Alfred Edersheim, *Sketches of Jewish Social Life in the Days of Christ.* 1876.

Talmage   James E. Talmage, *Jesus the Christ.* 1915.

Teachings   Joseph Fielding Smith, comp., *Teachings of the Prophet Joseph Smith.* 1938.

Temple   Alfred Edersheim, *The Temple: Its Ministry and Services As They Were at the Time of Jesus Christ.*

CONTENTS

Chapter 98

Chapter 99

Chapter 100

Chapter 101

Chapter 102

Chapter 107

Chapter 108

Chapter 109

SECTION XIII

HE RISETH; HE MINISTERETH; HE ASCENDETH

Chapter 110

Chapter 111

Chapter 112

Chapter 113

Chapter 114

Chapter 115

Chapter 116

Chapter 117

Chapter 118

Chapter 119

Chapter 120

Chapter 121

Chapter 122

SECTION XI

THE PASCHAL FEAST, THE PRIVATE PRAYERS AND SERMONS, AND GETHSEMANE

THE PASCHAL FEAST, THE PRIVATE PRAYERS AND SERMONS, AND GETHSEMANE

Salvation was, and is,
and is to come,
in and through the atoning blood
of Christ, the Lord Omnipotent.
(Mosiah 3:18.)
If we walk in the light,
as he is in the light,
we have fellowship one with another,
and the blood of Jesus Christ
his Son
cleanseth us from all sin.
(1 Jn. 1:7.)

Jesus who is called Christ—and blessed be his name!—is preparing himself to die, and his disciples to accept that divine destiny which is his.

He takes the Twelve apart by themselves and tells them in plain words what is about to be—his betrayal and crucifixion.

Then Judas leaves their presence to conspire, plot, and bargain; he sells his soul for the price of a slave.

3

Peter and John make ready the Passover, which with Jesus and the rest they eat in an upper chamber in the house of a disciple.

At the Paschal table Jesus washes the feet of the disciples and names Judas as his betrayer; after that unworthy one has gone out into the night, the Master institutes the sacrament of the Lord's Supper in remembrance of his own death.

That blessed night he commands the disciples to love one another; discourses on the Two Comforters—one the Holy Ghost, the other he himself; and proclaims himself as the Way, the Truth, and the Life.

"If ye love me, keep my commandments," he says, and gives the grandest of all the allegories: that of the Vine, the Husbandman, and the Branches.

He speaks at length of love, of the persecutions ahead, and of the Holy Ghost who will guide his saints into all truth.

Then comes the greatest of all the recorded prayers— the Intercessory Prayer in which he defines eternal life and pleads for the Twelve and all of the saints, that they may be one as he and the Father are one.

Then it is Gethsemane! Alone, in the greatest ordeal ever borne by man or God, in agony beyond compare, sweating great drops of blood from every pore, in a way beyond mortal comprehension, he takes upon himself the sins of all men on condition of repentance.

The infinite and eternal atonement, in large measure, is accomplished. Jesus has done what none but he could do.

After that, the betrayal and the arrest. Judas earns his thirty pieces of silver and loses his own soul. The Son of God chooses to bow to the will of wicked men—and the cross is just ahead.

Chapter 94

PREPARING FOR THE CRUCIFIXION

They shall consider him a man,
and say that he hath a devil,
and shall scourge him,
and shall crucify him.
(Mosiah 3:9.)
He came into the world, even Jesus,
to be crucified for the world,
and to bear the sins of the world,
and to sanctify the world,
and to cleanse it
from all unrighteousness.
(D&C 76:41.)
I came into the world
to do the will of my Father,
because my Father sent me.
And my Father sent me
that I might be lifted up
upon the cross.
(3 Ne. 27:13-14.)

Preparing the Disciples for His Death
(Matthew 26:1-2)

Steadily, ominously, borne by a tide that no man can stop—that neither God nor his Son in their infinite wisdom will stop—Jesus is going to his death. He came into the world to die upon the cross for the sins of the world, to die that men might live; and die he will and die he must. And in death he will gain his greatest victory.

Two days of life remain. He is with the Twelve and perhaps others who are beloved by him. We suppose he is in Bethany; if not, he is in that immediate vicinity. The last words we heard him speak came forth on the Mount of Olives as a lowering dusk ended the same day on which he bore the final public witness of his own divine Sonship. He and his friends rested somewhere that night near the Mount of Ascension. We like to think that he, at least, found peace and companionship within those hallowed walls in Bethany where the beloved sisters dwelt.

But now it is Wednesday, April 5, 13th Nisan, A.D. 30, and tomorrow is the day for the slaying of thousands of Paschal lambs. It must be early in the day, a day that Jesus is devoting to his intimate friends. Of all that transpired on this day only one sentence has come down to us, but oh, what a significant declaration it is:

Ye know that after two days is the feast of the passover, and the Son of man is betrayed to be crucified.

Specifying that it is two days before the Passover preserves for us the chronology and continuity of the events of the week of his passion; the statement about his betrayal and crucifixion reveals the subject that was uppermost in the minds of all of them as the climax of the one perfect ministry approached.

As to the day on which Jesus spoke these words, Edersheim says: "The day before that on which the Paschal Lamb [that is, he himself] was to be slain, with all that was to follow, would be one of rest, a Sabbath to His Soul before its Great Agony. He would refresh Himself, gather Himself up for the terrible conflict before Him. . . . Only two days more, as the Jews reckoned them—that Wednesday and Thursday—and at its Even the Paschal supper! And Jesus knew it well, and He passed that day of rest and preparation in quiet retirement with His disciples—perhaps in some hollow of the Mount of Olives, near the home of Bethany—speaking to them of His Crucifixion on the near Passover." (Edersheim 2:468-69.)[1]

As to his betrayal and crucifixion, we have somewhat more to say. We are speaking of the death of a God. God himself—the Great Creator, "the Lord Omnipotent who reigneth, who was, and is from all eternity to all eternity," who had "come down from heaven among the children of men" (Mosiah 3:5)—God himself, subjecting himself to the will of the Father in all things, was appointed to die. He who was born in a lowly stable is about to die upon a cruel cross.

Yea, he is to do more than die in the manner and way common to all mankind. As he came into mortality in the lowliest circumstances—born in a stable, cradled in a manger, crooned to by braying asses and lowing cattle—so he is to depart this life in the most ignominious way then known in a cruel and merciless world. Roman nails driven by Jewish hands will tear his flesh. As he hangs, like a common criminal, between two thieves, a Roman spear, hurled with pharisaic zeal, will rend his side; then his marred body will be placed in a borrowed grave, and the seal of death and failure will be placed, by unbelieving zealots, upon his life and mission.

Though the Twelve and others have been with him through his whole ministry, even they must be further conditioned to accept that which is about to be. Any remaining slivers of false Jewish tradition must be swept from their minds. Their Deliverer is to die; their God is to be

7

crucified; their Messiah is to fail—as far as the Jewish concept is concerned. Everything that is about to happen in his life will run counter to all that the scribes and Pharisees have supposed and believed and taught. Jesus, as we assume, has set apart this day to counsel and strengthen his chosen ones with reference to his coming demise and the glorious resurrection that will result therefrom.

That the Promised Messiah was appointed unto death, unto an agonizing death on a crucifier's cross, was something of which the prophets of old had spoken freely. They had said in plain words, and in many similitudes, that death and crucifixion awaited the mortal Son of the immortal Father. Of all this, fervent and extended witness is elsewhere borne. (*The Promised Messiah*, pp. 527–36.) For our present purposes we need only recount some of the numerous occasions of which we know, and there must have been many others, when the Mortal Messiah spoke of his coming crucifixion—all preparatory to this day on which, we cannot doubt, he taught and explained the coming reality in fulness.

1. *At the first Passover.*

Three years before, at the Passover, as he began his early Judean ministry, Jesus made the first such declaration of which we know. After the first cleansing of the temple, and in answer to the Jewish demands as to his authority for so doing, he said: "Destroy this temple"—as John says, "he spake of the temple of his body"—"and in three days I will raise it up." It was not, however, until after "he was risen from the dead" that the full significance of this pronouncement dawned upon his disciples. (John 2:13-22.) Yet it was the beginning; he was commencing the process of indoctrination that one day would leave them with a perfect knowledge of his death and resurrection.

2. *To Nicodemus.*

In the great Born-Again Sermon, delivered, as we suppose, in the home of John in Jerusalem, Jesus told

Nicodemus, a friendly Sanhedrist: "As Moses lifted up the serpent in the wilderness, even so must the Son of man be lifted up." (John 3:14.) How apt are the figures and how plain the similitudes that bear record of Him!

3. *To the disciples of John.*

When these worthies asked Jesus why his disciples did not fast often, as was the case with them and the Pharisees, our Lord replied: "Can the children of the bride-chamber mourn, as long as the bridegroom is with them? but the days will come, when the bridegroom shall be taken from them, and then shall they fast." (Matt. 9:14-15.) In keeping with the Jewish custom of pondering and discussing religious questions morning, noon, and night, seven days a week, how often thereafter must the disciples of John have thought and spoken of this reply.

4. *To the sign-seeking scribes and Pharisees.*

"For as Jonas was three days and three nights in the whale's belly; so shall the Son of man be three days and three nights in the heart of the earth," he said as he excoriated them for their evil and adulterous lives. (Matt. 12:38-40.) Again, we are left to suppose that many people thereafter saw in the miraculous experience of Jonah a sign and a type of their Messiah.

5. *To the Twelve.*

At the time of the sending forth of the Twelve, and as a part of a statement about losing one's life for Jesus' sake, our Lord said: "And he that taketh not his cross, and followeth after me, is not worthy of me." (Matt. 10:38-39.) The allusion is clear and the portent ominous.

6. *In the sermon on the bread of life.*

All those whose hearts were open, familiar as they were with the usage of Jewish figures and symbolism, saw in his declarations that he was the Bread of Life who came down from heaven, a reaffirmation of his divine Sonship. When he said, "And the bread that I will give is my flesh, which I will give for the life of the world," they knew he meant he

9

would be slain, so that, figuratively, all men might eat his flesh and drink his blood. (John 6:48-56.)

7. *Following Peter's testimony near Caesarea Philippi.*

After Peter's solemn and Spirit-born confession, Matthew says: "From that time forth began Jesus to shew unto his disciples, how that he must go unto Jerusalem, and suffer many things of the elders and chief priests and scribes, and be killed, and be raised again the third day." (Matt. 16:21.) From this it appears that both then and on many subsequent occasions Jesus spoke in plainness to his chosen and favored ones of his death and resurrection.

8. *On the Mount of Transfiguration.*

Though at the time the knowledge of such was reserved for Peter, James, and John only, Jesus discussed "his decease which he should accomplish at Jerusalem" with Moses and Elias, when those translated beings ministered to him on the Mount of Transfiguration. (Luke 9:28-31.)

9. *To the disciples in Galilee.*

After they came down from the Holy Mount—hallowed forever because of the Transfiguration—and returned to Galilee, the scripture says: "And while they abode in Galilee, Jesus said unto them, The Son of man shall be betrayed into the hands of men: And they shall kill him, and the third day he shall be raised again. And they were exceeding sorry." (Matt. 17:22-23.)

10. *En route to Jerusalem.*

Again we but need to quote the scripture: "And Jesus going up to Jerusalem took the twelve disciples apart in the way, and said unto them, Behold, we go up to Jerusalem; and the Son of man shall be betrayed unto the chief priests and unto the scribes, and they shall condemn him to death, And shall deliver him to the Gentiles to mock, and to scourge, and to crucify him: and the third day he shall rise again." (Matt. 20:17-19.)

11. *In the teachings about the good shepherd.*

How could he have spoken more plainly or with greater

clarity than when he said: "I am the good shepherd: the good shepherd giveth his life for the sheep. . . . As the Father knoweth me, even so know I the Father: and I lay down my life for the sheep. . . . Therefore doth my Father love me, because I lay down my life, that I might take it again. No man taketh it from me, but I lay it down of myself. I have power to lay it down, and I have power to take it again. This commandment have I received of my Father." (John 10:11-18.)

12. *In the parable of the wicked husbandmen.*

"They will reverence my son," said the householder whose servants had been beaten, stoned, and killed. But instead, when the wicked "husbandmen saw the son, they said among themselves, This is the heir; come, let us kill him, and let us seize on his inheritance. And they caught him, and cast him out of the vineyard, and slew him." Jesus then announced himself as the Stone which the builders rejected, and the chief priests and Pharisees knew that "he spake of them" as the slayers of the Son. (Matt. 21:33-46.)

We cannot believe that all these sayings—given as allusions, as similitudes, and in plain words—constituted a tithe, or a hundredth, or a thousandth part of what the Blessed One said of his coming death and crucifixion and of his resurrection on the third day. Nor can we think that the people generally were unaware of his teachings; friends and foes alike had fixed in their minds that such was his announced course. That few truly envisioned the import and glory of it all, there is no doubt. Even the Twelve needed yet added teachings about his atoning sacrifice. And we conclude that on this day, alone with them and others of like spiritual stature, he taught them all that they were then able to receive about his coming ordeal and the glory and exaltation—for himself and for the faithful—which would result therefrom.

11

Judas and the Jews Plot His Death
(Matthew 26:3-5, 14-16; Mark 14:1-2, 10-11;
JST, Mark 14:1-3, 31-32; Luke 22:1-6)

If a God is to die, what circumstances shall attend his demise? If the Great Deliverer is to be destroyed, how can the deed be done? If the Jewish Messiah is to be murdered—in cold blood, with malice aforethought, by evil men—how shall it be brought to pass?

As with all else that unto this mortal probation doth appertain, the awful act will come about by seemingly normal means. It will grow out of the social, political, and religious milieu of the moment. And those who do the evil deed will justify themselves in their own sinful and knavish minds. Satan always has an explanation for wickedness— even the murder of a God!—which will suffice for those who love darkness rather than light because their deeds are evil.

And so it was on this dark day. "It was inevitable that the burning words of indignation which Jesus had uttered on this last great day of His ministry should exasperate beyond all control the hatred and fury of the priestly party among the Jews. Not only had they been defeated and abashed in open encounter in the very scene of their highest dignity, and in the presence of their most devoted adherents; not only had they been forced to confess their ignorance of that very Scripture exegesis which was their recognised domain, and their incapacity to pronounce an opinion on a subject respecting which it was their professed duty to decide; but, after all this humiliation, He whom they despised as the young and ignorant Rabbi of Nazareth—He who neglected their customs and discountenanced their traditions—He on whose words, to them so pernicious, the people hung in rapt attention—had suddenly turned upon them, within hearing of the very Hall of Meeting, and had pronounced upon them—upon *them* in the odour of their sanctity—upon *them* who were accustomed to breathe all their lives the incense of unbounded

12

adulation—a woe so searching, so scathing, so memorably intense, that none who heard it could forget it forevermore.

"It was time that this should end. Pharisees, Sadducees, Herodians, Priests, Scribes, Elders, Annas the astute and tyrannous, Caiphas the abject and servile, were all now aroused; and, dreading they knew not what outburst of religious anarchy, which would shake the very foundations of their system, they met together"—probably while Jesus was in quiet seclusion with his loved ones at or near Bethany—"in the Palace of Caiaphas, sinking all their differences in a common inspiration of hatred against that long-promised Messiah in whom they only recognised a common enemy. It was an alliance for His destruction, of fanaticism, unbelief, and worldliness; the rage of the bigoted, the contempt of the atheist, and the dislike of the utilitarian; and it seemed but too clear that from the revengeful hate of such a combination no earthly power was adequate to save.

"Of the particulars of the meeting we know nothing; but the Evangelists record the two conclusions at which the high conspirators arrived—the one a yet more decisive and emphatic renewal of the vote that He must, at all hazards, be put to death without delay; the other, that it must be done by subtilty, and not by violence, for fear of the multitude; and that, for the same reason—*not* because of the sacredness of the Feast—the murder must be postponed, until the conclusion of the Passover had caused the dispersion of the countless pilgrims to their own homes." (Farrar, pp. 588–89.)

Their plan was to slay their Savior after the Passover; after the Galilean patriots had returned to their rugged homeland; after any sympathetic souls from outlying areas had departed for their dwelling places. But Jesus had named the Passover as the time when the Lamb of God should pour out his soul unto death in the supreme atoning sacrifice. And as he had spoken, so must it be.

Accordingly, Judas, one of the Twelve, believed to be

13

the only Judean among them, left the Holy Party and aligned himself with the unholy alliance of wicked men whose hearts were hardened by priestcrafts and iniquities; and he—a traitor—then "promised" to betray Jesus and deliver him up "in the absence of the multitude." If he could be arrested, tried, sentenced, and slain without such a tumult as to arouse their Roman overlords or permit him to be rescued by a mob, then let his death come soon; he could not die too soon to please his implacable foes.

Judas, be it realized, took the initiative in the betrayal; his was a willful act; he went to the evil-hearted Sanhedrists—to the sin-hardened Satanists—to tell them how he would place his Master into their hands. But he would do it for a price. The price of a slave? Nay, the price of his soul! Yet the words spoken by the mouth of Zechariah must not fail; not one jot or tittle must fall short of the prophetic mark. They must weigh for the price of their King "thirty pieces of silver"! (Zech. 11:12.) "What greedy chafferings took place we are not told, nor whether the counter-avarices of these united hatreds had a struggle before they decided on the paltry blood-money. If so, the astute Jewish priests beat down the poor ignorant Jewish Apostle. For all that they offered and all they weighed to him was thirty pieces of silver—about three pounds, sixteen shillings—the ransom-money of the meanest slave. For this price he was to sell his Master, and in selling his Master to sell his own life, and to gain in return the execration of the world for all generations yet to come." (Farrar, p. 529.)

Thirty pieces of silver! (Ex. 21:28-32.) "They 'weighed out' to him from the very Temple-treasury those thirty pieces of silver. . . . It was surely as much in contempt of the seller as of Him Whom he sold, that they paid the legal price of a slave. Or did they mean some kind of legal fiction, such as to buy the Person of Jesus at the legal price of a slave, so as to hand it afterwards over to the secular authorities? Such fictions, to save the conscience by a

14

logical quibble, are not so uncommon—and the case of the Inquisitors handing over the condemned heretic to the secular authorities will recur to the mind. But, in truth, Judas could not now have escaped their toils. They might have offered him ten or five pieces of silver, and he must still have stuck to his bargain. Yet none the less do we mark the deep symbolic significance of it all, in that the Lord was, so to speak, paid for out of the Temple-money which was destined for the purchase of sacrifices, and that He, Who took on Him the form of a servant, was sold and bought at the legal price of a slave." (Edersheim 2:477.)

Why did Judas become a traitor and seek to betray Jesus? Mark says, "He turned away from him, and was offended because of his words." Luke says simply: "Then entered Satan into Judas." And Matthew preserves for us the words spoken by this evil apostle to the chief priests: "What will ye give me, and I will deliver him unto you?" John said of him: "He was a thief." (John 12:1-6.) In all of this Judas displays disbelief, a rejection of the gospel, personal offense against the word—all because of the gospel truism: "The guilty taketh the truth to be hard, for it cutteth them to the very center." (1 Ne. 16:2.) In all this there is selfishness, avarice, dishonesty, and a grasping after worldly things that resulted in a satanic domination of his soul. Satan can have no power over human souls unless it is given to him by them. People are subject to him only when they hearken to his enticements. In other words, Judas was an evil traitor because of personal wickedness, because he preferred to live after the manner of the world, because he "loved Satan more than God." He truly had become "carnal, sensual, and devilish" by choice.[2]

It is common, almost classical, to ask: What were the motives of this man? Who can attempt to fathom the unutterable abyss, to find his way amid the weltering chaos, of a heart agitated by unresisted and besetting sins?

From such a launching pad, every self-appointed theologian and every pseudo-doctrinaire who writes about the

15

life of Christ seems to feel an obligation—almost a compulsion—to explain Judas and to tell why he planted the traitor's kiss on the cheek of Him who did no sin. The act in itself is so revolting and is looked upon with such abhorrence that writers and expounders seek for some explanation other than the obvious one. They point to avarice, of course, but then seek to probe what must have been in the mind of one who would turn the Son of God over to his enemies. They speculate as to what all-consuming passion must have burned in the soul of one who would betray the Sinless One into the hands of sinful men.

Having named avarice as the ruling passion in the life of Judas, Farrar speculates in this way: "Doubtless other motives mingled with, strengthened—perhaps to the self-deceiving and blinded soul substituted themselves for—the predominant one. 'Will not this measure,' he may have thought, 'force Him to declare His Messianic kingdom? At the worst, can He not easily save Himself by miracle? If not, has He not told us repeatedly that He will die; and if so, why may I not reap a little advantage from that which is in any case inevitable? Or will it not, perhaps, be meritorious to do that of which all the chief priests approve?' A thousand such devilish suggestions may have formulated themselves in the traitor's heart, and mingled with them was the revulsion of feeling which he suffered from finding that his self-denial in following Jesus would, after all, be apparently in vain; that he would gain from it not rank and wealth, but only poverty and persecution. Perhaps, too, there was something of rancour at being rebuked [this in regard to his views relative to selling Mary's ointment for three hundred pence]; perhaps something of bitter jealousy at being less loved by Jesus than his fellows; perhaps something of frenzied disappointment at the prospect of failure; perhaps something of despairing hatred at the consciousness that he was suspected.

"Alas! sins grow and multiply with fatal fertility, and

blend insensibly with hosts of their evil kindred. 'The whole moral nature is clouded by them; the intellect darkened, the spirit stained.' Probably by this time a turbid confused chaos of sins was weltering in the soul of Judas—malice, worldly ambition, theft, hatred of all that was good and pure, base ingratitude, frantic anger, all culminating in this foul and frightful act of treachery—all rushing with blind, bewildering fury through this gloomy soul.''

But Farrar, whose gift is to wield the witchery of words, also points to the basic and obvious reason for Judas's act. It was sin—evil, wicked, soul-blackening sin. In this—and let there be no mistake on this point—Judas was no different from the thousands and millions of sinners who preceded him and the billions who have come after. Why does any traitor betray his friends? Why are there crimes and murders and wars? "From whence come wars and fightings among you?" James asks. His declarative answer, though given in the form of a question, is: "Come they not hence, even of your lusts that war in your members?" (James 4:1.) The world has been cursed with Judases without number, and one is no different from any of the others; yet one does stand out above them all because he happened to betray *the Greatest of All.* Similarly, the world has suffered from Pilates without end at whose word innocent men have gone to their graves, and one is no different from any of the others; yet one stands out above them all because he chanced to stand at the crossroads of history and authorized the legal murder of the one who was *the Innocent above All.*

And so, with proper insight, Farrar says, in answer to his question about the motive of Judas: "The commonest observance of daily facts which come before our notice in the moral world, might serve to show that the commission of crime results as frequently from a motive that seems miserably inadequate, as from some vast temptation. . . . The sudden crisis of temptation might seem frightful, but its

17

issue was decided by the entire tenor of the traitor's previous life; the sudden blaze of lurid light was but the outcome of that which had long burnt and smouldered deep within his heart." (Farrar, pp. 592-94.)

Thus Judas—traitorous, evil, wicked, as he was—was in reality no different from his Jewish forebears of whom Jehovah said: "They sold the righteous for silver, and the poor for a pair of shoes." (Amos 2:6; 8:6.) Nor was he any different from those anciently who, "for handfuls of barley and for pieces of bread," slew "the souls that should not die." (Ezek. 13:19.) Judas betrayed the Son of Man himself, but is it not written: "Inasmuch as ye have done it unto one of the least of these my brethren, ye have done it unto me"? (Matt. 25:40.) It is sad to contemplate how many Judases there really are among the hosts of men.

And on this note ends the day of conspiracy; the day on which Jesus taught the eleven who were righteous about the glory and wonder of his death and resurrection; the day on which the one of the Twelve who was evil became an incarnate devil to plan the very death out of which life for all men would come—and in that act Judas sold his soul to another master whose disciple and follower he thus became.

This night the Son of Man will lay down his head in sleep "for the last time on earth." On the Thursday morning he will awake "never to sleep again." (Farrar, p. 595.)

NOTES

1. As to the way the Jews reckoned days, "the day always belonged to the previous night. . . . The day lasted till three stars became visible. . . . In regard to the Passover, it is distinctly stated that it began with the darkness on the 14th Nisan." (Edersheim 2:468-69, footnote 2.)

2. The quoted words are taken from earliest days. After Adam and Eve had "made all things" that God had revealed to them "known unto their sons and their daughters," the scripture says: "And Satan came among them, saying: I am also a son of God; and he commanded them, saying: Believe it not; and they believed it not, and they loved Satan more than God. And men began from that time forth to be carnal, sensual, and devilish." (Moses 5:12-13.)

18

Chapter 95

THE PASCHAL SUPPER

In the fourteenth day
of the first month
at even [between the two evenings]
is the Lord's passover. (Lev. 23:5.)
Your lamb shall be without blemish, . . .
And ye shall keep it up
until the fourteenth day of the same month:
and . . . shall kill it
in the evening [between the two evenings].
. . . And they shall eat the flesh in that night,
roast with fire, and unleavened bread;
and with bitter herbs they shall eat it. . . .
It is the Lord's passover.
(Ex. 12:5-11.)

Peter and John Make Ready the Passover[1]
(Matthew 26:17-19; Mark 14:12-16; Luke 22:7-13)

It is the time of the Lord's Passover!

Nay, more, it is the Passover of Passovers. In Jehovah's House, in Jerusalem the Holy City, on this very day—April 6, A.D. 30—calculating on the basis of one yearling lamb for each ten persons, some two hundred and sixty thousand

19

lambs will be slain. And then on the Passover morrow the Lamb of God himself will be sacrificed; he in whose name and honor countless lambs have had their blood sprinkled on the holy altar will himself have his blood shed that its saving power may be sprinkled upon believing souls forever.

From that dark Egyptian night a millennium and a half before, when two million of their fathers were prepared to march out of bondage, to this bright Palestinian day, when, though still subject to a Gentile yoke, they were free to worship and rejoice in a long and glorious history—from then until now, there had never been such a Passover as this. This was to be the climax and the end. Never again would any Passover meet with divine approval; and, indeed, a few years hence, with the destruction of the temple, the sacrificial parts of the feast would cease. But now, "Everyone was going to Jerusalem, or had those near and dear to them there, or at least watched the festive processions to the Metropolis of Judaism. It was a gathering of universal Israel, that of the memorial of the birth-night of the nation, and of its Exodus, when friends from afar would meet, and new friends be made; when offerings long due would be brought, and purification long needed be obtained—and all [would] worship in that grand and glorious Temple, with its gorgeous ritual. National and religious feelings were alike stirred in what reached far back to the first, and pointed far forward to the final Deliverance. On that day a Jew might well glory in being a Jew." (Edersheim 2:479-80.)

Jesus' disciples felt the fervor of the festive season. They knew that on Nisan 14, *between the two evenings*— for so the revealed rubric reads in Hebrew—their Paschal lamb must be slain. And Nisan 14 had begun on the *evening* before, on Wednesday the 13th, when the first of three stars appeared; and it will end the *evening* of this Thursday when the same three heavenly luminaries make their reappearance. Then before the midnight that will follow, their Paschal lamb, properly roasted, with the bitter herbs and all else appertaining to the Paschal supper must be eaten. Any of the lamb that remains until morning must be burned in the fire.

And so, on Thursday morning, knowing that the preparations must be made to eat the Passover meal, the disciples ask Jesus: "Where wilt thou that we go and prepare that thou mayest eat the passover?" Will it be in blessed Bethany, which was designated by Rabbinical authority as part of Jerusalem for the purposes of the feast, or back in the city proper? Only a few hours remain in which the needed lamb could be slain in the temple; what arrangements, therefore, shall they make?

Then Jesus, using seeric power—the power to see beforehand the happenings that shall be—calls Peter and John and says: "Go and prepare us the passover, that we may eat." They ask: "Where wilt thou that we prepare?" Jesus answers: "Behold, when ye are entered into the city, there shall a man meet you, bearing a pitcher of water; follow him into the house where he entereth in. And ye shall say unto the goodman of the house, The Master saith unto thee, Where is the guestchamber, where I shall eat the passover with my disciples? And he shall shew you a large upper room furnished: there make ready."

From this we can draw no conclusion except that a favored disciple had foreknowledge that Jesus and the Twelve desired to eat the Passover in his house. Whether this knowledge came by the spirit of inspiration or in some other way, we are not told. This we know: A man bearing a pitcher of water did in fact go out to meet them; he led them to the house; obviously they conversed en route; upon arrival they told the homeowner that the Master—thus identifying Jesus—asked for a guestchamber in which he and his disciples could eat the Passover; he then took them to an upper room that was already "furnished and prepared." The table was set; the couches were arranged; the dinnerware was in place; the cups and herbs and bowls and wine were there; cakes of unleavened bread were at hand; food was available; the goodman of the house had prepared for thirteen guests. It was his blessed privilege to host Him who should make an end to the Passover and in its place institute the sacrament of the Lord's Supper; and his house—clearly it was a large and commodious one—was the chosen place. What loving care must have attended the preparation that preceded the arrival of Peter and John!

Drawing on our learned friend Edersheim, we now note a most remarkable coincidence; or, rather, we discover a marvelous example of that divine attention to detail which ever delights the souls of those who ponder the words of holy writ. By combining the accounts of the three Synoptists, the message spoken by Peter and John to the goodman of the house comes out thus: 'The Master saith, My time is at hand—with thee [that is, in thy house: the emphasis is on this] I hold the Passover with my disciples. Where is my hostelry [or hall], where I shall eat the Passover with my disciples?'

The Hebrew word used here for hostelry or hall is *Katalyma;* and it is used only one other place in the whole New Testament. It is the word used to designate the inn or hostelry in Bethlehem where the Lord Jesus was born of Mary; where he drew his first mortal breath; where he began the mortal life that was destined to end at this very Passover time. As we are aware, Jesus was born in an open *Khan,* among the beasts, because there was no room in any of the inns or guestchambers that surrounded and opened upon the open courtyard. And this day in Jerusalem, the disciples did not ask for the upper chamber, but for a hostelry or hall that opened upon the *Khan* of the house. This Khan was the place in the house where, as in the open Khan, the beasts of burden were unloaded, and where shoes and staff, and dusty garments and burdens were put down. Apartments or guestchambers opened upon it. "He Who was born in a 'hostelry'—*Katalyma*—was content to ask for His last meal in a *Katalyma*." Born in the humblest of circumstances, he was prepared to remain in them all his days.

But now at this Passover, he made one provision with reference to the guest chamber; it was to be "my Katalyma." His purpose was to eat his last meal alone with his apostles. None of his other followers were to be present—not even his Blessed Mother, nor Mary Magdalene, who had so often traveled with the Twelve in their missionary journeys, nor Mary who worshipped at his feet in Bethany. He and the Twelve were more than the minimum of ten needed for the Passover meal, and he and they had sacred ordinances to perform before he went to Gethsemane to take upon himself the combined weight of all the sins of all men.

But as we have seen—and as Jesus foreknew—the goodman of the house took Peter and John to "a large upper room," "perhaps the very room where three days afterwards [as we shall note shortly] the sorrow-stricken Apostles first saw their risen Saviour—perhaps the very room where, amid the sound of a rushing mighty wind, each meek brow was first mitred with Pentecostal flame." (Farrar, p. 598.)

Who was the homeowner whose gracious preparations so well served the needs of Jesus on this memorable occasion? He is not named, and we do not know. No doubt Jesus withheld his name for two reasons: so that Peter and John, following his instructions, would learn anew of his seeric powers, and also to keep the knowledge from Judas. That unworthy one, who by now had returned from conspiring with the chief priests, must not be able to lead them to Jesus until after all things had been accomplished at the Passover meal and in the Garden of Gethsemane. The traitor must first go with the others to eat the Paschal meal, and then he must be told to leave and carry out his evil work.

As to the identity of the disciple who hosted the Lord Jesus in his last meal in mortality, many have speculated that it was the father of John Mark. The reasoning involved is to this effect: From the account in Acts relative to the freeing of Peter from prison we know that the family home of John Mark was a large one where the saints were wont to gather. (Acts 12:1-17.) From the fact that Mark alone tells about the young man who was accompanying Christ as he was led away captive, and who himself escaped arrest by fleeing naked as his captors tore from him his sole article of apparel, a loose linen garment—this has led to the universal assumption that Mark himself was the young man. (Mark 14:51-52.) What, then, is more natural than to conclude that Judas returned to the Passover-home with the arresting soldiers, only to find that Jesus and the other apostles had departed for Gethsemane; that in the commotion at the home young John Mark was aroused from sleep and hastily put on a loose tunic and followed the soldiers to the garden; that there he was a witness and an unwilling observer of the betrayal and arrest; and that he lost his own garment in fleeing from those who held captive his Lord? Someday it will be gratifying to know all things relative to these memorable days and to acclaim those disciples who then laid their all on the altar as they confessed before men Him who has since confessed them before his Heavenly Father.

But back to the Passover preparations. Certain ritualistic performances were an essential part thereof. One of these, the solemn search for leaven—for this also was the Feast of Unleavened Bread—had already occurred under the direction of the homeowner. On the evening of Nisan 13, as Nisan 14 commenced, this search was made in each house. Any leaven that had been hidden or lost must be found, put in a safe place, and later destroyed. From midday on the 14th nothing leavened might be eaten, and it was, in fact, the custom to fast on that day preparatory to eating the Paschal supper.

Further: The ordinary evening service and sacrifice in the temple must precede the supper. On this feast day this service began an hour early, or at about 1:30 P.M., with the evening sacrifice itself being offered at about 2:30 P.M. This was the time for the slaying of the Paschal lambs by their owners and the sprinkling of their blood upon the altar by the priests. Both Mark and Luke say that Peter and John were to "make ready" the Passover meal, and they both record that "they made ready the passover." Of necessity this means that the two apostles, rather than the home-owner or some other person, were required to and did attend the temple services for the formal slaying and prepa-ration of the lamb; and to this assumption there is a certain fitness and propriety: two of the chief apostles, for them-selves and on behalf of their Lord and their brethren, were complying to the full to the letter of the law on the last day on which its provisions were in force. When, on the mor-row, the true Paschal Lamb was slain, the old order would be over and the new covenant only would have binding efficacy and force.

And so we can envision Peter and John in the temple courts, amid the massive throngs of worshippers, submit-ting for the last time in this respect to the law of Moses, and there witnessing and participating in the ceremonial per-formances so familiar to them. We cannot leave this scene without singling out certain of the scriptural words chanted that day by the Levites. The language is recorded in Psalm 81, and as there and then given—"broken three times by the threefold blast from the silver trumpets of the priests"—it included a promise and a call to Israel to serve their God and also a prophecy of their fate if they did not do so. This is the call and the promise:

Hear, O my people, and I will testify unto thee: O

Israel, if thou wilt hearken unto me; There shall no strange god be in thee; neither shalt thou worship any strange god. I am the Lord thy God, which brought thee out of the land of Egypt: open thy mouth wide, and I will fill it.

Then came the seeric and prophetic pronouncement— and what sad and mournful significance it must have had to apostolic ears on this day:

But my people would not hearken to my voice; and Israel would [have] none of me. So I gave them up unto their own hearts' lust: and they walked in their own counsels. Oh that my people had hearkened unto me, and Israel had walked in my ways!

And further, as the blood of thousands of lambs was sprinkled on the altar, the Levites chanted the *Hallel* (Psalms 113 to 118), with the people responding with cries of Hallelujah (praise Jehovah) at the proper places, and with the people, also at the proper place, saying:

Save now, I beseech thee, O Lord: O Lord, I beseech thee, send now prosperity. Blessed be he that cometh in the name of the Lord.

This chant—the same one shouted amid cries of Hosanna by the exultant throngs, as Jesus rode triumphantly into the Holy City—was thus here given for the last authorized time by the legal administrators of the Mosaic order. Its recitation here could not have done other than relight in the breasts of Peter and John those fires of testimony and rejoicing which burned so brightly on that triumphal day.

After attending to all that was incumbent upon them, Peter and John—with their lamb flayed and cleansed, and with the required parts left on the altar for burning— returned to the appointed home to meet Jesus and the others, there to partake of the crowning Paschal supper of the ages. The two appointed apostles had done their work well; the Paschal supper was made ready; all things had happened as Jesus foretold—such being in itself a witness that all things he had said of his coming betrayal, crucifixion, and resurrection would also come to pass.

Jesus and the Twelve Recline at the Paschal Table
(Matthew 26:20; Mark 14:17; Luke 22:14)

Peter and John have now done their work; they and the homeowner have made ready the guest chamber. The lamb has been roasted on a pomegranate spit; the unleavened cakes, the bitter herbs, the dish with vinegar—all are in place. Such items of food as needed are on the movable table; the festive lamps are lit; it is eventime, and the meal is ready.

"It was probably as the sun was beginning to decline in the horizon that Jesus and the other ten disciples descended once more over the Mount of Olives into the Holy City. Before them lay Jerusalem in her festive attire. All around pilgrims were hastening towards it. White tents dotted the sward, gay with the bright flowers of early spring, or peered out from the gardens or the darker foliage of the olive plantations. From the gorgeous Temple buildings, dazzling in their snow-white marble and gold, on which the slanting rays of the sun were reflected, rose the smoke of the altar of burnt-offering. These courts were now crowded with eager worshippers, offering for the last time, in the real sense, their Paschal lambs.

"The streets must have been thronged with strangers, and the flat roofs covered with eager gazers, who either feasted their eyes with a first sight of the Sacred City for which they had so often longed, or else once more rejoiced in view of the well-remembered localities. It was the last day-view which the Lord had [free and unhindered] of the Holy City—till His resurrection! Only once more in the approaching night of His betrayal was he to look upon it in the pale light of the full moon. He was going forward to 'accomplish His death' in Jerusalem; to fulfil the type and prophecy, and to offer Himself up as the true Passover

27

Lamb—'the Lamb of God, which taketh away the sin of the world.'

"They who followed Him were busy with many thoughts. They knew that terrible events awaited them, and they had only a few days before been told that these glorious Temple-buildings, to which, with a national pride not unnatural, they had directed the attention of their Master, were to become desolate, not one stone being left upon the other. Among them, revolving his dark plans, and goaded on by the great Enemy, moved the betrayer. And now they were within the city. Its Temple, its royal bridge, its splendid palaces, its busy marts, its streets filled with festive pilgrims, were well known to them, as they made their way to the house where the guestchamber had been prepared for them. Meanwhile the crowd came down from the Temple-mount, each bearing on his shoulders the sacrificial lamb, to make ready for the Paschal Supper." (*Temple,* pp. 226–28.)

The Holy Party (one of whom was unholy) entered the chosen house and ascended the stairs to the appointed upper chamber. Assuming it to be the house of Mark, Edersheim asks: "Was this [the] place of Christ's last, also that of the Church's first, entertainment; that, where the Holy Supper was instituted with the Apostles, also that, where it was afterwards first partaken of by the Church; the Chamber where He last tarried with them before His death, that in which He first appeared to them after His resurrection; that, also, in which the Holy Ghost was poured out, even as (if the Last Supper was in the house of Mark) it undoubtedly was that in which the Church was at first wont to gather for common prayer?" His answer (and ours): "We know not, and can only venture to suggest, deeply soul-stirring as such thoughts and associations are." (Edersheim 2:490.)

We do feel, however, that we can with measurable certainty reach some conclusions relative to the Paschal supper and all that it means in the eternal scheme of things.

The Lord Jesus, in the more than a dozen years of his mature life, may have presided over other Paschal suppers, thus being the One who offered the slain lamb in similitude of his own coming sacrifice. The likelihood, however, is that such was not the case. At any prior Passover spent in Jerusalem, where alone the sacrificial lambs could be offered, he would have been a guest at someone else's table. At each table a minimum of ten diners was required, and the host was the one who made the offering.

It is pleasant to suppose that this is the one Paschal supper over which Jesus presided, and that, therefore, he offered *the last symbolic sacrifice* preparatory to his offering of *the only real sacrifice* which would free men from their sins. If this is the case, the only sacrifices in which he involved himself (and there is a certain reverential fitness about such being the case) would be the symbolical one on Thursday whose emblems betokened the infinite and eternal one on Friday. Thus he would endorse and approve all of the similitudes of the past and announce their fulfillment in him. Thus also would the past, the present, and the future all be tied together in him, with the assurance held out to all the faithful of all ages, that all who look to him and his atoning sacrifice shall be saved.

Two of the ordinances given of God to his people, without which accountable men cannot be saved, are baptism and the sacrament of the Lord's Supper; and with one Jesus commenced, and with the other he concluded his ministry. Both ordinances bear record of his death, burial, and resurrection. The faithful, buried with him in baptism and thereby dying unto sin, then come forth from the watery grave in a newness of life and in the likeness of his resurrection. Similarly when they partake of his Holy Supper—made efficacious because the Lamb of God shed his own blood in an eternal Passover—they remember anew that death out of which comes life.

On this Passover night, in the home of Mark, the Lord of Life is prefiguring his own death, even as he had done at

Bethabara when he was baptized of John. And he is now testifying that all the righteous sacrifices and baptisms of the past have his approval, even as all the righteous sacramental ordinances of the future shall find eternal efficacy in him. The old and the new—all things—center in him.

Thus there is, in reality, only one sacrifice—the sacrifice of the Lord Jesus Christ. All of the symbolisms are swallowed up in him. As Paul said, "Christ our passover is sacrificed for us: Therefore let us keep the feast"—and in this sense we shall keep the Feast of the Passover forever—"not with old leaven, neither with the leaven of malice and wickedness; but with the unleavened bread of sincerity and truth." (1 Cor. 5:7-8.)

The Passover is not the child of the Mosaic law. As part of the gospel, which the Lord first gave to Israel's ancient lawgiver, it was administered under the Mosaic system until the coming of Christ. It was given before the law, and its truths remain after the law. "It was not of the Law, for it was instituted before the Law had been given or the Covenant ratified by blood; nay, in a sense it was the cause and foundation of all the Levitical Sacrifices and of the Covenant itself. And it could not be classed with either one or the other of the various kinds of sacrifices, but rather combined them all, and yet differed from them all. Just as the Priesthood of Christ was real, yet not after the order of Aaron, so was the Sacrifice of Christ real, yet not after the order of Levitical sacrifices but after that of the Passover. And as in the Paschal supper all Israel were gathered around the Paschal Lamb in commemoration of the past, in celebration of the present, in anticipation of the future, and in fellowship in the Lamb, so has the Church been ever since [when it has been on earth] gathered together around its better fulfilment in the Kingdom of God." (Edersheim 2:492.)

One other matter of considerable interest is the seating arrangement at the Paschal table, or, rather, the reclining positions assumed by the partakers of the meal. With refer-

30

ence to that first Passover night in Egypt, the divine word was: "And thus shall ye eat it; with your loins girded, your shoes on your feet, and your staff in your hand; and ye shall eat it in haste." (Ex. 12:11.) But in Jesus' day it was different; the Rabbinic decree then was that all who ate should recline at a table, to indicate rest, safety, and liberty. Low, moveable tables were used—sometimes they even hung from the ceiling so as not to touch the floor and be defiled—and it was the custom for each person to occupy a separate divan or pillow, to lie on his left side and lean on his left hand, the feet stretching back towards the ground. The couches upon which the diners reclined were set on two sides and one end of the table so as to leave about a third of the table free for serving trays and dishes. Needless to say, the reality had no resemblance to the paintings of Leonardo da Vinci and others whose genius has memorialized this event through the ages.

It is interesting, based on the scriptural allusions and inferences, to place Jesus and at least three of the Twelve in the positions they may have occupied at the table. This we shall now do, reserving for more extended recitation the specific matters that bear upon our suggestive conclusions.

As the Twelve began to take selected positions at the table, a contention arose, evidently over precedence in seating. By instinct we feel Judas—who was out of harmony with his brethren, and who at this late date was manifesting none of the Christian attributes of tolerance, charity, or concern for the comfort and well-being of his associates—we feel instinctively that Judas was at the root of the trouble. Various inferences and allusions found in the general setting and set forth in the scriptural accounts bear this out.

Among the Pharisees this matter of rank and precedence, of what place each person occupied at the table, was a matter of great concern; and Judas—influenced, nay, dominated by the prince of this world, who is Lucifer—was more of a Pharisee than a Christian. He, by training and

31

inclination, would follow the Pharisaic custom and seek for himself the seat of honor. John speaks, in connection with the supper, of the devil having entered into Judas; and as Jesus said, in another connection, "He that hath the spirit of contention is not of me, but is of the devil, who is the father of contention, and he stirreth up the hearts of men to contend with anger, one with another." (3 Ne. 11:29.)

We reason, thus, that Judas's acts caused the contention in which he gladly participated. With whom would he contend? Obviously with Peter, who was in fact the chief apostle and who knew his place was at the Lord's side in the position of honor and precedence. When Jesus rebuked the contention, a very natural thing would happen: impetuous Peter would go and take the lowest seat, while spiritually hardened Judas, immune to feelings of conscience and decency, would maintain his claim and take the seat of honor at the side of Jesus. This suggests the position of two of the Twelve.

As to the Beloved John, he leaned on the Master's bosom, which could only be done if he were on Jesus' right side. It was the custom for the chief personage at a feast to have someone on either side. Thus, starting on one side of the table, we would have John, then Jesus, and then Judas; the others would place themselves where they chose, but Peter would go across from John at the foot of the semicircle. Thus when Christ told John the sign by which the traitor would be known, none of the others would hear him. Thus Jesus, as part of the Paschal ceremony, could give the sop first to Judas, who sat in the seat of honor at his left hand. Thus when Judas asked if his treachery was known, and received an affirmative answer, none of the others knew what was involved. And thus Peter, having placed himself at the foot, would have to beckon to John to ask who it was who should betray the Lord. At least that is the reasoning involved; and, once again, we say this is something that someday we shall know with certainty. All that will be required is for the Lord to show one of his servants, in a vision or a dream, what happened that Passover night two millennia ago.

NOTE

1. The Jewish customs, practices, and traditions relative to Paschal matters are digested and summarized from Edersheim, whose life's work it was to search them out from the abundant and voluminous original sources.

Chapter 96

THE LAST SUPPER

We'll wash and be washed,
   and with oil be anointed,
Withal not omitting the washing of feet;
For he that receiveth his penny appointed
Must surely be clean at the harvest of wheat.[1]

Strife Erupts at the Passover Table
(Luke 22:24-30; JST, Luke 22:26-27, 30)

As the Holy Party prepare to recline on the couches around the Passover table, the flaring fires of strife are ignited, as we suppose, by Judas, whose spirit is evil and whose judgment is warped. It is over the age-old question, raised anew, that has caused strife and contention from the beginning of time. Who among them shall be accounted the greatest? Who shall have the place of honor at the table? For all such things do the Pharisees seek; and does not Judas have the same spirit as those with whom he is conspiring to shed innocent blood?

But a short time before, when James and John and their mother sought to have Zebedee's two sons chosen—to the indignation of the other disciples—to sit on Jesus' right and left hand in his kingdom, our Lord had severely rebuked such strivings. It seems sad that at this solemn hour, when the precedence of the cross, if so it may be called, is coming into view, such a contention should arise again. Well might their feelings have been: Who will take precedence in suffering for His name now, that they may be named by him before his Father hereafter? Yet, where there is an evil spirit, contention is ever found; and so Jesus patiently rehearses the old gospel verities over again:

The kings of the Gentiles exercise lordship over them, and they that exercise authority upon them are called benefactors. But it ought not to be so with you; but he who is greatest among you, let him be as the younger; and he who is chief, as he who doth serve.

For whether is he greater, who sitteth at meat, or he who serveth? I am not as he who sitteth at meat, but I am among you as he who serveth.

The servants of the Lord in all ages, even as with Him whom they serve, are to forget the honors of men and the glories of the world. Where now is the grandeur that was Greece and the glory that was Rome? Are those who held sway in any of the ancient empires anything more than handfuls of dead dust? What will it matter a few years hence what earthly honors were conferred by mortals on their fellows? Who will even remember tomorrow who sat where at what table? With the Lord's servants, all strife over precedence must cease; theirs is a ministry of service and not of rulership. To this Jesus' whole life and ministry attested. And yet even those who serve tables in his earthly kingdom shall not go unrewarded. As also he has said aforetime, he now repeats:

Ye are they who have continued with me in my temptations. And I appoint unto you a kingdom, as my Father hath appointed unto me; That ye may eat and drink at my table in my kingdom; and sit on twelve thrones, judging the twelve tribes of Israel.

What more can they ask than to have eternal association with their Lord, even to eating and drinking at his table forever? And how few will hold greater positions in eternity than those Twelve who return in glory with the Son of Man, and who are then appointed to sit on twelve thrones judging the whole house of Israel?

Jesus Washes the Feet of His Disciples
(John 13:1-17; JST, John 13:8, 10)

After reclining at the Passover table, Jesus and his apostolic friends ate the Passover meal with such portion of its rites and ceremonies as then suited their purposes. Then he introduced the gospel ordinance of the washing of feet, identified Judas as the one who would betray him, sent the traitor out into the night, and gave the ordinance of the sacrament. Since the sacramental rites grew out of the Passover procedures, we shall reserve our consideration of the Passover meal itself until we take up the sacrament of the Lord's Supper. To keep things in proper perspective, however, it is important to emphasize that the washing of feet came in the course of the meal, not at the beginning, and it was not simply an illustration of Godly humility, devised by Jesus to demonstrate his teachings about precedence, but was in fact the introduction of a new gospel ordinance.

John alone records such portions of what transpired relative to the foot-washing ordinance as have come down to us from biblical sources; our more extended knowledge relative thereto comes from latter-day revelation. The Beloved Disciple begins his Passover recitations by saying that "before the feast of the passover"—and what he is about to say is something of which we too are aware—"when Jesus knew that his hour was come that he should depart out of this world unto the Father," there yet remained something of great concern to him. "Having loved his own which were in the world," he must yet, incident to the Passover meal, manifest to them how "he loved them unto the end." And the two ordinances about to be revealed—those of the washing of feet and of the partaking of the emblems of his flesh and blood—these two become an eternal manifestation of the grace and goodness and love of the Lord for the Twelve and for all who believe and obey his gospel, thereby making themselves worthy to receive each of these ordinances.

And so, John says, "supper being ended," or, rather 'during supper,' "the devil having now put into the heart of Judas Iscariot, Simon's son, to betray him" (these words read like a formal indictment) and "Jesus knowing that the Father had given all things into his hands, and that he was come from God, and went to God; He riseth from supper, and laid aside his garments; and took a towel, and girded himself. After that he poureth water into a basin, and began to wash the disciples' feet, and to wipe them with the towel wherewith he was girded."

This appears to be a general summary of all that transpired. What then follows are some of the particulars. As to these particulars, John says: "Then cometh he to Simon Peter: and Peter saith unto him, Lord, dost thou wash my feet?" Jesus replied: "What I do thou knowest not now; but thou shalt know hereafter." That is: 'You assume that I am acting only as any slave or host might, which is far from the case. I am about to perform a sacred ordinance, the meaning of which I will explain, and in due course you will know its true meaning.' Still impulsive and reticent, the Chief Apostle said: "*Thou*"—our Master and Lord!— "*Thou*," of all people, "needest not to wash my feet." 'Even though it be a sacred ordinance, let someone else do it instead!'

If we judge aright, Peter was the first one to have his feet washed, as he should have been, he being the senior apostle and the future president of the Church. John's phrase, "Then cometh he to Simon Peter," means, not that he came to him after the others, but either that he came to him from across the table or from the place where the basin and water for purification had stood. It would have been quite inappropriate, a self-serving assertion of excessive humility on his part, if Peter had first seen Jesus wash the feet of others and had then objected to the performance of the same act on his behalf. Since it was common for slaves and servants to wash the feet of guests, Peter's objection was to the Lord of heaven, as though he were merely a slave, washing the feet of one so unworthy as he deemed himself to be. It compares with previous like reactions on the part of the man Simon. "Depart from me; for I am a sinful man, O Lord" was his cry when, though he had toiled all night and caught nothing, yet, casting once again at Jesus' command, in one sweep the net became so full that it brake. (Luke 5:1-11.) "Be it far from thee, Lord: this shall not be unto thee," was his reaction when Jesus told the disciples that he must suffer many things of the elders and chief priests and scribes, and be killed, and be raised again the third day. (Matt. 16:21-23.) After hearing the conversation with Peter, and learning somewhat the meaning and import of the ordinance, none of the others would have objected.

Jesus then said: "If I wash thee not, thou hast no part with me." Catching a partial glimpse of the cleansing power of the new ordinance, Peter, ever impetuous, ever desiring to do all and more than need be, exclaimed: "Lord, not my feet only, but also my hands and my head." Jesus replied: "He that has washed his hands and his head, needeth not save to wash his feet, but is clean every whit; and ye are clean, but not all."

At this point, with reference to the ordinance itself, John explains: "Now this was the custom of the Jews under their law; wherefore, Jesus did this that the law might be fulfilled." The full significance of this is not apparent to the casual reader, nor should it be, for the washing of feet is a sacred ordinance reserved to be done in holy places for those who make themselves worthy. It is evident, however, that the Jews also had sacred ordinances performed in their temple, a knowledge of which has not been preserved, nor could it be, in any literature that has come down to us.

As to Jesus' statement that the Twelve were "clean, but not all," John explains: "For he knew who should betray him; therefore said he, Ye are not all clean. So after he had washed their feet, and had taken his garments, and was set down again, he said unto them, Know ye what I have done to you?"

What had he done? He had instituted—nay, reinstituted, for "the order of the house of God has been, and ever will be, the same"[2]—he had reinstituted one of the holy ordinances of the everlasting gospel. Those who have been washed in the waters of baptism, who have been freed from sin and evil through the waters of regeneration, who have come forth thereby in a newness of life, and who then press forward with a steadfastness in Christ, keeping the commandments and walking in paths of truth and righteousness, qualify to have an eternal seal placed on their godly conduct. They are thus ready to be endowed with power from on high. Then, in holy places, they cleanse their hands and their feet, as the scripture saith, and become "clean from the blood of this wicked generation." (D&C 88:74-75, 137-141.) Then, as the scripture also saith, they receive anointings and washings and conversations and statutes and judgments. (D&C 124:37-40.) Then they receive what Jesus here gave the Twelve, for as the Prophet said: "The house of the Lord must be prepared, . . . and in it we must attend to the ordinance of washing of feet. It was never intended for any but official members. It is calculated to unite our hearts, that we may be one in feeling and sentiment, and that our faith may be strong, so that Satan cannot overthrow us, nor have any power over us here." (*Commentary* 1:709.)

Did the Twelve then know what Jesus had done in their behalf? Perhaps in part, with the full significance to come to them after receiving that pentecostal endowment from on high which is the Holy Ghost. No doubt, also, Jesus then said more to them than John chose to record, for many things relative to these holy things are too sacred to publish to the world. It should be clear to all, however, that just as the act of immersion in water only hints at the true significance and power of baptism, so the act of the washing of feet is far more than the cleansing and refreshing of dusty and tired pedal extremities. It is an eternal ordinance, with eternal import, understood only by enlightened saints. That it might be continued by those having divine authorization to perform it, Jesus said:

Ye call me Master and Lord: and ye say well; for so I am. If I then, your Lord and Master, have washed your feet; ye also ought to wash one another's feet. For I have given you an example, that ye should do as I have done to you.

Verily, verily, I say unto you, The servant is not greater than his lord; neither he that is sent greater than he that sent him. If ye know these things, happy are ye if ye do them.

Jewish proverbial expressions that give added depth and meaning to Jesus' words are set forth for us by Edersheim. "He, Who really was Lord and Master, had rendered this lowest service to them as an example that, as He had done, so should they do. No principle [was] better known, almost proverbial in Israel, than that a servant was not to claim greater honour than his master, nor yet he that was sent than he who had sent him. . . .

"The Greek word for 'the towel,' with which our Lord girded Himself, occurs also in Rabbinic writings, to denote the towel used in washing and at baths (*Luntith* and *Aluntith*). Such girding was the common mark of a slave, by whom the service of footwashing was ordinarily performed. And, in a very interesting passage, the Midrash contrasts what, in this respect, is the way of man with what God had done for Israel. For, He [God] had been described by the prophet as performing for them [Israel] the service of washing, and others usually rendered by slaves." It scarcely needs to be here interjected that such a Jewish concept is purely Messianic in nature.

"The idea, that if a man knows (for example, the Law) and does not do it, it were better for him not to have been created, is not unfrequently expressed. But the most interesting reference is in regard to the relation between the sender and the sent, and a servant and his master. In regard to the former, it is proverbially said, that while he that is sent stands on the same footing as he who sent him, yet he must expect less honour. And as regards Christ's statement that 'the servant is not greater than his Master,' there is a passage in which we read this, *in connection with the sufferings of the Messiah:* 'It is enough for the servant that he be like his Master.' " (Edersheim 2:501-2.)

And in conclusion, well might we ask: If true disciples are to wash each other's feet, where among the sects of Christendom is this done? And how could it be done except by revelation? Who would know all that is involved unless God revealed it? Is not this holy ordinance one of the many signs of the true Church?

Jesus Names Judas as His Betrayer
(John 13:18-30; JST, John 13:19; Matthew 26:21-25; Mark 14:18-21; JST, Mark 14:30; Luke 22:21-23)

The blessed Twelve, their feet washed in an holy ordinance, their whole bodies being thereby cleansed from the blood and sins of that evil and adulterous generation in which they lived—the blessed Twelve were clean, "clean every whit"—"but not all." Judas yet sat in their circle; his deed of shame and infamy lay ahead; he must yet raise the standard of betrayal and sin round which all the traitors of all the ages might rally. "The hands of the Lord of Life had just washed the traitor's feet. Oh, strange unfathomable depth of human infatuation and ingratitude! that traitor, with all the black and accursed treachery in his false heart, had seen, had known, had suffered it; had felt the touch of those kind and gentle hands, had been refreshed by the cleansing water, had seen that sacred head bent over his feet, stained as they yet were with that hurried secret walk which had taken him into the throng of sanctimonious murderers over the shoulder of Olivet. But for him there had been no purification in that lustral water; neither was the devil within him exorcised by that gentle voice, nor the leprosy of his heart healed by that miracle-producing touch.'' (Farrar, p. 602.) Truly all ordinances must be sealed by the Holy Spirit of Promise, else they are not binding on earth and sealed everlastingly in the heavens! And none are so sealed and ratified except for those who are just and true.

I speak not of you all: I know whom I have chosen: but that the scripture may be fulfilled, He that eateth bread with me hath lifted up his heel against me. Now I tell you before it come, that, when it is come to pass, ye may believe that I am the Christ.

King David—whose son, now reclining at the Passover table, has inherited the ancient throne—using his own experiences as a base, wrote these Messianic words: "All that hate me whisper together against me: against me do they devise my hurt. . . . Yea, mine own familiar friend, in whom I trusted, which did eat of my bread, hath lifted up his heel against me. But . . . as for me, thou upholdest me in mine integrity, and settest me before thy face for ever." (Ps. 41:7-12.) [3] In these words, David declaimed both his own betrayal by his counselor, Ahithopel, and the betrayal of his Lord by Judas in the coming day. Both Judas and Ahithopel, their conspiracies not unfolding as they had supposed, went and hanged themselves, that the ancient promise might be a perfect type of the evil deed to be done in the Messianic day. (2 Sam. 15:10-12; 17.) At this point Jesus said:

Verily, verily, I say unto you, He that receiveth whomsoever I send receiveth me; and he that re-

ceiveth me receiveth him that sent me.

"Soon should they know with what full foreknowledge He had gone to all that awaited Him; soon should they be able to judge that, just as the man who receives in Christ's name His humblest servant receiveth Him, so the rejection of Him is the rejection of His Father, and that this rejection of the Living God was the crime which at this moment was being committed in their very midst." (Farrar, p. 603.) Having so spoken, Jesus "was troubled in spirit"—not, as we suppose, because of what lay ahead for him, but for the evil deed spawned in the heart of his "own familiar friend." He said:

Verily, verily, I say unto you, that one of you shall betray me.

One of you which eateth with me shall betray me.

But, behold, the hand of him that betrayeth me is with me on the table.

"And they were exceeding sorrowful," Matthew says. Indeed, "a deep unspeakable sadness had fallen over the sacred meal. Like the sombre and threatening crimson that intermingles with the colours of sunset, a dark omen seemed to be overshadowing them—a shapeless presentiment of evil—an unspoken sense of dread. If all their hopes were to be thus blighted—if at this very Passover, He for whom they had given up all, and who had been to them all in all, was indeed to be betrayed by one of themselves to an unpitied and ignominious end—if *this* were possible, *anything* seemed possible. Their hearts were troubled." (Farrar, p. 604.)

One by one, eleven of the Twelve, "doubting of whom he spake," each asked in turn, "Is it I?" Their consciences were clear, and yet none dared ask, "Is it he?" "Better the penitent watchfulness of a self-condemning humility than the haughty Pharisaism of censorious pride. The very horror that breathed through their question, the very trustfulness which prompted it, involved their acquittal." (Farrar, p. 604.)

43

John, at this point, was leaning on Jesus' bosom. Peter beckoned to him to ask Jesus who it was; he asked, and Jesus answered:

He it is, to whom I shall give a sop, when I have dipped it.

It is one of the twelve, that dippeth with me in the dish.

The Son of man goeth as it is written of him: but woe unto that man by whom the Son of man is betrayed! it had been good for that man if he had not been born.

Better for Judas if he had never been born! Yea, and better for all those who knowingly and willfully reject the truth and defy the Christ, better for them also if they had never been born! Their position in preexistence—in the presence of God—limited though their progression could be in the spirit state, was better than to be consigned to that state of which it is written: "Where God and Christ dwell they cannot come, worlds without end." (D&C 76:112.) Judas is not alone as an inheritor of the awesome wo here pronounced, as this Book of Mormon language reveals: "And wo be unto him that will not hearken unto the words of Jesus, and also to them whom he hath chosen and sent among them; for whoso receiveth not the words of Jesus and the words of those whom he hath sent receiveth not him; and therefore he will not receive them at the last day; And it would be better for them if they had not been born. For do ye suppose that ye can get rid of the justice of an offended God, who hath been trampled under feet of men, that thereby salvation might come?" (3 Ne. 28:34-35.)

As to the sign by which the traitor might be known—dipping with Jesus in the common bowl and the taking of the sop from his hand—such was neither designed nor intended to identify Judas with clarity and certainty, and it did not have such an effect. All who sat at the table dipped their hands in the bowl, and all received a sop from Jesus' hand as part of the Passover rituals, as we shall see shortly, though it would appear that Judas was the first so served, or, perhaps, that he received an additional sop. In any event Jesus then "dipped the sop" and gave it to Judas, and then, and then only, did Judas ask, "Master, is it I?" Jesus answered: "Thou hast said," apparently whispering the reply only to Judas, without making the others aware in words who the traitor was.

Of Judas John tells us that after the sop, "Satan entered into him." Thus—"As all the winds, on some night of storm, riot and howl through the rent walls of some desecrated shrine, so through the ruined life of Judas envy and avarice, and hatred and ingratitude, were rushing all at once. In that bewildering chaos of a soul spotted with mortal guilt, the Satanic had triumphed over the human; in that dark heart earth and hell were thenceforth at one; in that lost soul sin had conceived and brought forth death." (Farrar, p. 605.)

Jesus then said: "What thou doest, do quickly; but beware of innocent blood." John notes that none of them at the table "knew for what intent he spake this unto him." Some thought the keeper of the bag was being sent to buy provisions for the continuing period of the feast, others that he was being sent to give alms to the poor who even then, this being a day of festivity, were still mingling in the courts of the temple. But Judas, "having received the sop went immediately out." "And so from the lighted room, from the holy banquet, from the blessed company, from the presence of his Lord, he went immediately out, and—as the beloved disciple adds, with a shudder, letting the curtain of darkness fall for ever on that appalling figure—'and it was night.' " (Farrar, pp. 605–6.)

NOTES

1. This is a verse from the hymn "The Spirit of God Like a Fire Is Burning," by W.W. Phelps, as that glorious hymn of praise and exultation was sung at the dedication of the Kirtland Temple, March 27, 1836.

2. The quoted phrase is from the Prophet Joseph Smith and was spoken in connection with the holy endowment and the ordinance of the washing of feet. For a full discussion, including the Prophet's explanations, see *Commentary* 1:707-10.

3. There is "a terrible literality about this prophetic reference to one who ate his bread," as is seen from the fact that "Judas, like the rest, lived of what was supplied to Christ, and at that very moment sat at His table." (Edersheim 2:503, footnote 1.)

Chapter 97

THE SACRAMENT OF THE LORD'S SUPPER

He that eateth this bread
eateth of my body to his soul;
and he that drinketh of this wine
drinketh of my blood to his soul;
and his soul shall never
hunger nor thirst,
but shall be filled.
(3 Ne. 20:8.)

Jesus Saith: 'Love One Another'
(John 13:31-35)

Jesus has more to say—much, much more—about his love for his disciples, about their love for him, and about their love for each other. He will say it this night in this upper room in the home of John Mark. And his own beloved John will preserve for us a digest of his sayings in which we shall rejoice forever.

Already we have pondered John's own summary of Jesus' feelings as he reclined with his friends to partake of the Passover. "Now before the feast of the passover," our apostolic colleague wrote, "when Jesus knew that his hour was come that he should depart out of this world unto the Father, having loved his own which were in the world, he loved them unto the end." (John 13:1.) As death approached, love was uppermost in the divine mind. O if they could but love him as he loved them; O if they would but love each other as his law required; O if they would but love the Lord their God with all their heart, might, mind, and strength—then all would be well with them in time and in eternity!

And, as we have seen, the ordinance of the washing of feet was a manifestation of Jesus' eternal love for his own, a love that impelled the Loving One to do all in his power to seal his friends up unto eternal life in his Father's kingdom. Now we shall see how the sacrament of the Lord's Supper, for the same reason, is also a message of love to all mankind. And so, with Judas out groping in the boundless night that enveloped his sin-blackened soul, Jesus can turn to the law of love as a prelude to instituting the sacrament of love.

"No sooner had Judas left the room, than, as though they had been relieved of some ghastly incubus, the spirits of the little company revived. The presence of that haunted soul lay with a weight of horror on the heart of his Master, and no sooner had he departed than the sadness of the feast seems to have been sensibly relieved. The solemn exultation which dilated the soul of their Lord—that joy like the sense of a boundless sunlight behind the earth-born mists—communicated itself to the spirits of His followers. The dull clouds caught the sunset colouring. . . . Now it was that, conscious of the impending separation and fixed unalterably in His sublime resolve, He opened His heart to the little band of those who loved Him, and spoke among them those farewell discourses." (Farrar, pp. 609–10.)

Now is the Son of man glorified, and God is glorified in him. If God be glorified in him, God shall also glorify him in himself, and shall straightway glorify him.

Let the Twelve be reassured—no matter that Judas has left to play his ill and evil part; let that be as it may—what truly matters is that the Son of Man is true and faithful in all things. Shortly he shall be glorified; he shall "receive power, and riches, and wisdom, and strength, and honour, and glory, and blessing." (Rev. 5:12.) And even God is glorified in him, for the glory and honor and dominion and kingdoms gained by the Son are added to those of the Father, thus glorifying him.[1] Indeed, the Father "glorifieth himself" whenever any of his children gain exaltation, and the added kingdoms thereby brought into being constitute "the continuation" of his works. (D&C 132:29-31.) And— " 'If the Father is glorified and exalted to a higher station because of the works and triumphs of the Son, then the Father will further reward the Son with the Father—and the hour for all this is at hand; it shall straightway take place.' " (*Commentary* 1:726.)

Little children, yet a little while I am with you. Ye shall seek me: and as I said unto the Jews, Whither I go, ye cannot come; so now I say to you.

"The time which remained for Him to be with them was short; as He had said to the Jews, so now he said to them, that whither He was going they could not come. And in telling them this, for the first and last time, he calls them 'little children.' In that company were Peter and John, men whose words and deeds should thenceforth influence the whole world of man until the end—men who should become the patron saints of nations—in whose honour cathedrals should be built, and from whom cities should be named; yet their greatness was but a dim, faint reflection from His risen glory, and a gleam caught from that Spirit which He would send. Apart from Him they were nothing, and less than nothing—ignorant Galilean fishermen, unknown and unheard of beyond their native village—having no intellect and no knowledge save that He had thus regarded them as his 'little children.' And though they could not follow Him whither he went, yet he did not say to them, as He had said to the Jews, that they should seek Him and not find Him. [John 7:34; 8:21.] Nay, more, He gave them a new commandment, by which, walking in His steps, and

49

being known by all men as His disciples, they should find Him soon." (Farrar, p. 610.)[2]

A new commandment I give unto you, That ye love one another; as I have loved you, that ye also love one another. By this shall all men know that ye are my disciples, if ye have love one for another.

A new commandment! Love one another! Yea, and an old commandment, one in force from the beginning, one that dwelt with God in eternity before ever the foundations of the earth were laid! Indeed, it was a new and an everlasting commandment—new each time it fell from divine lips; everlasting because it had lain at the root of all saving fellowship from the beginning, from the day when Adam first gloried in the name of Christ, to that present moment. Thus saith Jehovah to Moses: "Thou shalt love thy neighbour as thyself: I am the Lord." (Lev. 19:18.) "For this is the message that ye heard from the beginning, that we should love one another," John said. (1 Jn. 3:11.) But it came then to the Twelve, as it always comes, with a new emphasis, a new prominence, a new influence. They were true disciples and had become such in the waters of baptism. If now they would manifest, one toward another, that love upon which the everlasting gospel is founded, then all men would recognize them for what they were: apostles of the Lord Jesus Christ.

They Eat the Passover Meal
(Luke 22:15-20; JST, Luke 22:16)

This night in the Passover meal and in the sacrament of the Lord's Supper all of the sacrificial similitudes of all the ages combined to bear testimony of the infinite and eternal atoning sacrifice—the sacrifice of the Lamb of God who taketh away the sins of the world. The heart and center and core of revealed religion is that the Son of God will shed his blood, in a garden and on a cross; that he will take upon himself the sins of all men on conditions of repentance; that he will ransom men from the temporal and spiritual death brought into the world by the fall of Adam; that he will abolish death and bring life and immortality to light through his gospel; that through him all men will be raised in immortality, while those who believe and obey will ascend unto eternal life—all because of his atoning sacrifice.

From the day of the first Adam (the first man, the first flesh, the first mortal) to the day of the Second Adam (who will be the first to rise in immortality, the first to gain eternal life)—for all these four thousand years, the Lord's people have offered the firstlings of their flocks in sacrifice in similitude of the coming sacrifice of the Son of God.[3] From the Exodus to this hour the annual Feast of the Passover has been one of the chief occasions on which these sacrifices, with all that they typify, have been performed. A few hours hence and Jesus will be lifted up upon the cross; sacrifices by the shedding of blood will cease among the faithful;[4] and in their place the saints of the Most High will pay their devotions by partaking of the sacramental emblems in remembrance of the torn flesh and spilt blood of the Atoning One. Jesus and the Twelve are about to end the old similitudes of the past and institute the new symbolisms of the future. This very night they shall perform the ordinance which *looks forward* to the sacrifice of God's Son, and also the ordinance performed *in remembrance* of his death. In this setting—portentous, momentous, of eternal importance—it is no wonder, then, that we hear Jesus say to the Twelve:

With desire I have desired to eat this passover with you before I suffer; For I say unto you, I will not any more eat thereof, until it be fulfilled which is written in the prophets concerning me. Then I will partake with you, in the kingdom of God.

This night in Gethsemane, and tomorrow before the rulers of this world and on Calvary, he will suffer, suffer as none other has ever done, either before or since. But first—the Passover! They must eat it together, for they will

51

not do so again—note it well!—until the Messianic prophecies concerning his death are fulfilled; until, in resurrected glory, they keep the feast in the kingdom of God. Jesus and the Twelve are going to eat the Passover meal again incident to his glorious return, a return when the kingdom of God, in all its glorious perfection, will be set up on the millennial earth! But first, in the course of this Passover in the upper room this night, "he took the cup, and gave thanks," as the Passover ritual required, and said:

Take this, and divide it among yourselves: For I say unto you, I will not drink of the fruit of the vine, until the kingdom of God shall come.

Again it is the Passover of which he speaks. He will not drink again of the wine of the feast until the latter-day kingdom comes, until He rules whose right it is. At this point, as Luke recounts, he breaks and blesses the bread and blesses the wine, identifies them as the sacramental emblems, and gives them to the Twelve. Then, as we shall see, he repeats—this time with reference to the sacramental wine—that he will not drink it again until that same blessed day when he shall also eat and drink the Passover meal again.

In summary, then, the sacrificial performances pointed men's minds forward to the future death of their Savior, and the sacramental emblems are partaken in remembrance of a death that is past. Sacrifices were performed until he came; the sacrament is the new order that serves the same purpose since he came—except that there was at least one sacramental ordinance before he came, and there shall be certain sacrificial performances after his coming.

In an ordinance prefiguring the sacrament, as Abraham returned from the slaughter of the kings, he was met by that great high priest from whom the Father of the Faithful himself had received the priesthood. At this time "Melchizedek, king of Salem"—the same to whom Abraham paid tithes—"brought forth bread and wine; and he break bread and blest it; and he blest the wine, he being the priest of the most high God, And he gave to Abram." (JST, Gen. 14:17-18.) Such was the prefiguring of the sacramental ordinance. And in a yet future day, to complete the restitution of all things, the sacrifices that were part of the gospel, and that antedated the law of Moses, will again be performed.[5] Since Jesus says he will eat of the Passover again with the Twelve, as well as partake of the sacrament with them, we can well suppose he may do both things again, at the same time, even as he did them this night in the upper room. As to his partaking of the sacrament at his coming, we will have more to say as we consider the institution of the sacramental ordinance itself. First, however, it will profit us to recount the Passover performances so as to see how easily and naturally the sacrament grew out of them.

The Passover procedures have varied through the ages. It is common to speak of the Egyptian Passover that Israel kept in her early years as a nation, and of the permanent Passover kept in later generations. In each the symbolisms and performances were geared to the assumed needs of the respective days. In spite of extensive source material, we cannot with absolute certainty define each rite and step as it prevailed in Jesus' day, and it may be that some of these varied and changed even in the short span of his life. From reliable sources we suggest something to the following effect took place in thousands of Jewish homes in Jerusalem on this April 6, A.D. 30. We will concern ourselves particularly with what took place in the upper room.

1. The head of the company—in this case Jesus—took the first of four cups of wine, said two benedictions over it, and then all present drank of the cup. It will help us feel the spirit of the solemn occasion to quote the two benedictions customarily spoken, both of which are accepted as having been in use in Jesus' day. One was in these words: "Blessed art Thou, Jehovah our God, who hast created the fruit of the vine!" The other was more extended and self-exulting: "Blessed art Thou, Jehovah our God, King of the Universe, who hast chosen us from among all people, and

53

exalted us from among all languages, and sanctified us with Thy commandments! And Thou hast given us, O Jehovah our God, in love, the solemn days for joy, and the festivals and appointed seasons for gladness; and this the day of the feast of unleavened bread, the season of our freedom, a holy convocation, the memorial of our departure from Egypt. For us hast Thou chosen; and us hast Thou sanctified from among all nations, and Thy holy festivals with joy and with gladness hast Thou caused us to inherit. Blessed art Thou, O Jehovah, who sanctifiest Israel and the appointed seasons! Blessed art Thou, Jehovah, King of the Universe, who hast preserved us alive and sustained us and brought us to this season!''

As we have seen, Luke tells us Jesus took the first cup, "gave thanks," and passed it to the Twelve. In so stating Luke is speaking of the Passover cup, not the sacramental cup, which he mentions later. We cannot, however, believe that Jesus used the words of these prayers. It probably was common for individuals to exercise freedom in what they said, and certainly the Giver of the feast would not have been bound by the Rabbinic rituals. All we know is that he did offer a blessing of some sort over the cup, and that he and the Twelve drank therefrom.

2. Next came the washing of his own hands by the head of the company, as he recited these words: "Blessed art Thou, Jehovah our God, who hast sanctified us with thy commandments, and hast enjoined us concerning the washing of our hands." Later, after the meal proper, all present would wash their hands. We cannot believe that Jesus performed this act of washing; we have heretofore heard him excoriate the Jewish formalists for their adherence to the washing traditions of the elders. It is probable that at this point he did wash the feet of the disciples; and we know that he said to Peter, "He that has washed his hands and his head, needeth not save to wash his feet, but is clean every whit." John's comment on this was that Jesus so acted because it "was the custom of the Jews under their

54

law," and that he did it "that the law might be fulfilled." Of this we have already taken note.

3. A table was then brought in upon which were placed the bitter herbs, the unleavened bread, the *charoseth* (a dish made of dates, raisins, and vinegar), the Paschal lamb, and the flesh of the *chagigah* (a festive sacrifice in addition to the Paschal lamb). The head of the company, usually the father, dipped a piece of herb in the *charoseth,* ate it, offered a benediction, and distributed a similar morsel to all. Then the second cup was filled but not drunk.

4. Then came the inquiries from a son or the youngest person present. 'Why is this night different from all others? Why do we eat only unleavened bread, bitter herbs and roasted lamb? Why are the herbs dipped twice rather than only once?' Then the officiating head recounted the history of Israel, beginning with Abraham and with particular emphasis on the deliverance from Egypt and the giving of the law.

5. Next the items used in the feast were explained and the head of the company offered a prayer that included these words: "We are bound to thank, praise, laud, glorify, extol, honour, bless, exalt, and reverence Him, because He hath wrought for our fathers, and for us all these miracles. He brought us forth from bondage into freedom, from sorrow into joy, from mourning to a festival, from darkness to a great light, and from slavery to redemption. Therefore let us sing before Him: Hallelujah!" Thereupon they sang the first part of the Hallel (Psalms 113 and 114) and offered this benediction: "Blessed art Thou, Jehovah our God, King of the Universe, who hast redeemed us and redeemed our fathers from Egypt."

6. Then the second cup was drunk, hands were washed a second time, with the same prayer as before, one of the unleavened cakes was broken, and a thanks was given. The thanksgiving followed the breaking of the bread, rather than preceded it, as was the case with the sacrament soon to be instituted.

7. "Pieces of the broken cake with bitter herbs between them, and dipped in the *Charoseth,* were next handed to each in the company. This, in all probability, was 'the sop' which, in answer to John's inquiry about the betrayer, the Lord 'gave' to Judas. The unleavened bread with bitter herbs constituted, in reality, the beginning of the Paschal Supper, to which the first part of the service had only served as a kind of introduction. But as Judas, after 'having received the sop, went immediately out,' he could not even have partaken of the Paschal lamb, far less of the Lord's Supper." It was the practice in the day of Jesus for this sop to consist of flesh from the Paschal lamb, a piece of unleavened bread, and bitter herbs.

8. At this point the Paschal supper itself was eaten.

9. "Immediately afterwards the third cup was drunk, a special blessing having been spoken over it. There cannot be any reasonable doubt that this was the cup which our Lord connected with His own Supper. It is called in Jewish writings, just as by St. Paul, 'the cup of blessing,' partly because it and the first cup required a special 'blessing,' and partly because it followed on the 'grace after meat.' "

10. The service ended with the drinking of the fourth cup, the singing of the second part of the Hallel (Psalms 115, 116, 117, and 118), and the giving of two more prayers of the same general type as already quoted.

Thus was the Paschal supper conducted in the day of the Lord Jesus. Since he was, in fact, celebrating the supper and fulfilling the law, we must conclude that he followed, insofar as they did not violate true principles, the successive steps in the general format set forth. And building on this foundation he then brought into being the sacramental ordinance itself.

Whether the cups drunk at the Paschal supper were also in similitude of the coming decree that men must drink his blood, we cannot say. Certain it is, however, that the sacrificial lamb, and all that appertained to its offering, was in

56

similitude of the sacrifice of the Only Begotten of the Father.

An interesting Messianic sidelight to this whole procedure is the fact that "to this day, in every Jewish home, at a certain part of the Paschal service—just after the third cup, or the cup of blessing, has been drunk—the door is opened to admit Elijah the prophet as forerunner of the Messiah, while appropriate passages are at the same time read which foretell the destruction of all heathen nations."[6]

But now let us turn to the Lord's Supper itself.

Jesus Giveth Them the Sacrament

(3 Nephi 18:1-14, 27-33; 20:1-9; Moroni 4:1-3; 5:1-2;
Matthew 26:26-29; JST, Matthew 26:22-25; Mark 14:22-25;
JST, Mark 14:20-25; Luke 22:15-20; JST, Luke 22:16;
1 Corinthians 11:20-34; D&C 20:75-79; 27:1-14)

No single account of the institution of the sacrament of the Lord's Supper, standing alone, contains enough to let us know the reality and the glory and the wonder of what happened in that upper room as the Paschal supper died and the sacramental supper was born. Nor for that matter do all the biblical accounts taken together reveal the glorious mystery of it all.

John does not preserve a single word on the subject, though he is the one who recorded the great sermon on the bread of life, which includes the statements about eating the flesh and drinking the blood of the One who came down from heaven. Luke confines his account to two sentences, which scarcely do more than announce that the new ordinance came into being; Matthew and Mark each give a partial account, from which, however, the full significance of what then transpired cannot be discerned; and Paul, who learned either by revelation or from the testimonies of the participants of what then occurred, does not shed any great additional flood of light upon the blessed events. Providentially the Nephite accounts do contain portions of what

57

Jesus said to the American Hebrews as he instituted the same sacramental services among them. Even they, however, do not record the words of blessing spoken by the Lord over the bread and over the wine, though we know such words were preserved at the time, for, nearly four hundred years later, Moroni copied them into his inspired writings. We also have received them by revelation, as well as an account of the drinking of the sacramental wine in the millennial day. It is our privilege now to weave all these accounts into one unified whole and catch for ourselves a vision of what Jesus did that April night and what it has meant ever since to the saints of the Most High.

"And as they were eating"—no doubt as they neared the end of the Paschal supper—"Jesus took bread and brake it, and blessed it, and gave to his disciples, and said":

Take, eat; this is in remembrance of my body which I give a ransom for you. (Matthew.)

Take it, and eat. Behold, this is for you to do in remembrance of my body; for as oft as ye do this ye will remember this hour that I was with you. (Mark.)

This is my body which is given for you: this do in remembrance of me. (Luke.)

Take, eat: this is my body, which is broken for you: this do in remembrance of me. (Paul.)

In the Nephite setting, "Jesus commanded his disciples," the Nephite Twelve, whom he had called and chosen for a like apostolic ministry to that of the Jerusalem Twelve, "that they should bring forth some bread and wine unto him. And while they were gone for bread and wine, he commanded the multitude that they should sit themselves down upon the earth. And when the disciples had come with bread and wine, he took of the bread and broke and blessed it; and he gave unto the disciples and commanded that they should eat. And when they had eaten and were filled, he commanded that they should give unto the multitude. And when the multitude had eaten and were filled, he said unto the disciples'':

Behold there shall one be ordained among you, and to him will I give power that he shall break bread and bless it and give it unto the people of my church, unto all those who shall believe and be baptized in my name.

And this shall ye always observe to do, even as I have done, even as I have broken bread and blessed it and given it unto you.

And this shall ye do in remembrance of my body, which I have shown unto you. And it shall be a testimony unto the Father that ye do always remember me. And if ye do always remember me ye shall have my Spirit to be with you. (Nephi the Disciple.)

To this account we need only append the words of thanks and blessing spoken by Jesus and the picture will be complete. And we cannot doubt that the words spoken— thereby becoming the pattern for use among the Lord's people in all places and in all ages—conformed, at least in substance and thought content, to the following:

O God, the Eternal Father, we ask thee in the name of thy Son, Jesus Christ, to bless and sanctify this bread to the souls of all those who partake of it; that they may eat in remembrance of the body of thy Son, and witness unto thee, O God, the Eternal Father, that they are willing to take upon them the name of thy Son, and always remember him, and keep his commandments which he hath given them, that they may always have his Spirit to be with them. Amen. (Moroni.)

All these accounts, woven into one majestic tapestry to hang in the halls of the heart of every true saint, enable us to understand what the Master does for his saints in the sacrament. From them we learn: (1) He gave himself, his body, the very flesh of which he was composed, to ransom men. His was a supreme sacrifice—that of his own life, his own body. The ransom paid delivers his brethren from the temporal and spiritual death brought into the world by the fall of Adam. (2) "In memory of the broken flesh, We eat the broken bread; And witness with the cup, afresh, Our faith in Christ, our Head."[7] We eat in remembrance—in remembrance of that Paschal hour, in remembrance of Gethsemane, of Calvary, of an open tomb. (3) The sacrament must be administered by legal administrators; it is a holy ordinance; those who break and bless the bread must be ordained unto that very power; it is not a prerogative men can assume without divine approval. (4) It is administered only to those who believe and have been baptized (except in the case of little children, who need no baptism); indeed, it is the very ordinance whereby the saints renew the covenants made in the waters of baptism. (5) It is a perpetual, continuing, everlasting ordinance; the faithful always observe its rites and provisions. (6) Those who partake testify to the Father that they will always remember his Son. (7) They also repeatedly renew their covenant to take upon them the name of the Son, to be the Lord's own peculiar people, to set themselves apart from the world, to live as becometh saints, to hold his name in everlasting reverence. (8) In this ordinance the solemn promise is made to keep the commandments of God. (9) In consequence of all this the worthy partakers of this blessed and sanctified emblem receive the promise that they will always have the Lord's Spirit to be with them. (10) And as we shall hereafter note, if any partake unworthily, they thereby eat and drink damnation to their souls.

"And he took the cup, and when he had given thanks, he gave it to them; and they all drank of it. And he said unto them":

This is in remembrance of my blood which is shed for many, and the new testament which I give unto you; for of me ye shall bear record unto all the world. (Mark.)

60

Drink ye all of it. For this is in remembrance of my blood of the new testament, which is shed for as many as shall believe on my name, for the remission of their sins. (Matthew.)

This cup is the new testament in my blood which is shed for you. (Luke.)

This cup is the new testament in my blood: this do ye, as oft as ye drink it, in remembrance of me. For as often as ye eat this bread, and drink this cup, ye do shew the Lord's death till he come. (Paul.)

Among the Nephites, "he commanded his disciples that they should take of the wine of the cup and drink of it, and that they should also give unto the multitude that they might drink of it. And it came to pass that they did so, and did drink of it and were filled; and they gave unto the multitude, and they did drink, and they were filled. And when the disciples had done this, Jesus said unto them":

Blessed are ye for this thing which ye have done, for this is fulfilling my commandments, and this doth witness unto the Father that ye are willing to do that which I have commanded.

And this shall ye always do to those who repent and are baptized in my name; and ye shall do it in remembrance of my blood, which I have shed for you, that ye may witness unto the Father that ye do always remember me. And if ye do always remember me ye shall have my Spirit to be with you. (Nephi the Disciple.)

Again to complete the beauteous tapestry, we append the words of blessing and thanks similar to those that must have fallen from Jesus' lips on these sacred occasions:

O God, the Eternal Father, we ask thee, in the name of thy Son, Jesus Christ, to bless and sanctify this wine to the souls of all those who drink of it, that they may do it in remembrance of the blood of thy Son, which was shed for them; that they may witness unto thee, O God, the Eternal Father, that they

*do always remember him, that they may have his
Spirit to be with them. Amen.* (Moroni.)

Again, all these accounts, becoming part of our tapestry
of love and faith and triumph, enable us to understand what
Jesus has done for us. Again we learn of a ransom that was
paid—paid in blood, paid in the spilt blood of the Lamb.
This blood is a new testament—a new covenant!—a testament that replaces the old covenant of Moses. Of it—the
new covenant, the gospel covenant—the saints bear record
to the world. They drink in remembrance of the blood of
the new covenant, the blood shed by Jesus the Mediator of
the new covenant, which is shed for those who believe.
They gain "the remission of their sins"—through baptism
and through the renewal of the baptismal covenant as they
partake worthily of the sacrament. And again, as often as
the saints do these things, they show the Lord's death till
he come. Their acts are the fulfilling of the commandment
and a witness before the Father that they will keep the
commandments of his Son. The same covenant of obedience that appertains to the broken bread is made anew with
the wine, and the glorious promise comes again to the
saints—for only those who have repented and been baptized are involved—that they shall always have his Spirit to
be with them.

*And as oft as ye do this ordinance, ye will remem-
ber me in this hour that I was with you, and drank
with you of this cup, even the last time in my ministry.* (Mark.)

*And I give unto you a commandment, that ye shall
observe to do the things which ye have seen me do,
and bear record of me even unto the end.* (Matthew.)

*And I give unto you a commandment that ye shall
do these things. And if ye shall always do these
things blessed are ye, for ye are built upon my rock.
But whoso among you shall do more or less than
these are not built upon my rock, but are built upon
a sandy foundation; and when the rain descends,*

and the floods come, and the winds blow, and beat upon them, they shall fall, and the gates of hell are ready open to receive them.

Therefore blessed are ye if ye shall keep my commandments, which the Father hath commanded me that I should give unto you. (Nephi the Disciple.)

The true saints, remembering the Lord Jesus—and to most of us the remembrance is rooted in what we have read in holy writ—are commanded to do all the things he has done and to bear record of him all their days. Those who so act, being thus built upon the gospel rock, are blessed. Those who do either more or less than he has commanded, either with reference to the sacramental ordinance itself or to any other gospel verity, are built on a sandy foundation; their house shall fall, and they shall be welcomed in the gates of hell. And oh, how many there are in so-called Christendom, where the sacramental ordinance itself is concerned, who even now do either more or less than the Lord Jesus ordained.[8] And oh, how many there are even among the saints who have partaken unworthily of the sacred emblems when the ordinance was administered according to the divine standard.[9] And so, continuing his instruction to the Nephites, Jesus said:

Behold verily, verily, I say unto you, I give unto you another commandment. . . . And now behold, this is the commandment which I give unto you, that ye shall not suffer any one knowingly to partake of my flesh and blood unworthily, when ye shall minister it;

For whoso eateth and drinketh my flesh and blood unworthily eateth and drinketh damnation to his soul; therefore if ye know that a man is unworthy to eat and drink of my flesh and blood ye shall forbid him.

Nevertheless, ye shall not cast him out from among you, but ye shall minister unto him and shall pray for him unto the Father, in my name; and if it so be that he repenteth and is baptized in my name, then shall ye receive him, and shall minister unto him of my flesh and blood.

But if he repent not he shall not be numbered among my people, that he may not destroy my people, for behold I know my sheep, and they are numbered.

Nevertheless, ye shall not cast him out of your synagogues, or your places of worship, for unto such shall ye continue to minister; for ye know not but what they will return and repent, and come unto me with full purpose of heart, and I shall heal them; and ye shall be the means of bringing salvation unto them.

Therefore, keep these sayings which I have commanded you that ye come not under condemnation; for wo unto him whom the Father condemneth. (Nephi the Disciple.)

Gross perversions of the true meaning and intent of the sacrament of the Lord's Supper crept into the Church itself even in Paul's day. Apparently, patterning their actions too literally after what Jesus and the Twelve did at the Paschal supper, the Corinthian saints were assembling together and banqueting themselves before partaking of the blessed emblems. The apostle directed them to cease this practice, to eat at home, and when they came together, to partake only of the emblems of the body and blood of their Lord. This they must do in worthiness.

Wherefore whosoever shall eat this bread, and drink this cup of the Lord, unworthily, shall be guilty of the body and blood of the Lord.

But let him examine himself, and so let him eat of that bread, and drink of that cup. For he that eateth and drinketh unworthily, eateth and drinketh damnation to himself, not discerning the Lord's body. (Paul.)

But to return to the upper room, the concluding sacramental expressions of which we have record were these:

But I say unto you, I will not drink henceforth of this fruit of the vine, until that day when I drink it new with you in my Father's kingdom. (Matthew.)

Verily I say unto you, Of this ye shall bear record; for I will no more drink of the fruit of the vine with you, until that day that I drink it new in the kingdom of God. (Mark.)

Were it not for latter-day revelation, no one would know the significance of this promise. In the revelation authorizing the use of water or other liquids besides wine, the word of the Lord Jesus Christ to his prophet, Joseph Smith, was: "It mattereth not what ye shall eat or what ye shall drink when ye partake of the sacrament, if it so be that ye do it with an eye single to my glory—remembering unto the Father my body which was laid down for you, and my blood which was shed for the remission of your sins." Then, with reference to the use of wine, the direction was: "You shall partake of none except it is made new among you; yea, in this my Father's kingdom which shall be built up on the earth."

With reference to the very words spoken in the upper room, the same voice, heard again in latter days, promised: "Marvel not, for the hour cometh that I will drink of the fruit of the vine with you on the earth." Having so announced, the Lord named others who would be present to partake of the blessed emblems in the great assemblage that is to come together at Adam-ondi-Ahman incident to the return of the Son of Man to rule and reign in righteousness among men on earth. Those named were: Moroni, Elias of the restoration, who is also identified as being Gabriel or Noah; John the Baptist, Elijah, Joseph who was sold into Egypt, Jacob, Isaac, Abraham, Michael who is Adam, and Peter, James, and John. The New Testament promise was that Jesus would partake of the sacrament with the eleven who first ate the bread and drank the wine in the upper room. To all of this the latter-day word adds: "And also with all those whom my Father hath given me out of the world," which is to say that the righteous saints of all ages, from Adam down to that hour, will all assemble with the Lord Jesus in that great congregation just before the great and dreadful day of the Lord arrives.

Such, then, is the law of the sacrament—the system ordained in the infinite wisdom of God to aid in the cleansing and perfecting of human souls, the system that manifests the infinite love of an infinite being to all us finite creatures here below. And so we conclude our consideration of this part of our Lord's ministry with these words, spoken by him when, for a second time, he administered the sacrament to the Nephites:

He that eateth this bread eateth of my body to his soul; and he that drinketh of this wine drinketh of my blood to his soul; and his soul shall never hunger nor thirst, but shall be filled.

NOTES

1. In this connection, Joseph Smith said: "What did Jesus do? Why; I do the things I saw my Father do when worlds came rolling into existence. My Father worked out his kingdom with fear and trembling, and I must do the same; and when I get my kingdom, I shall present it to my Father, so that he may obtain kingdom upon kingdom, and *it will exalt him in glory.* He will then take a higher exaltation, and I will take his place, and thereby become exalted myself. So that Jesus treads in the tracks of his Father, and inherits what God did before; and *God is thus glorified and exalted in the salvation and exaltation of all his children.*" (*Teachings,* pp. 347–48. Italics added.)

2. Using a similar tender approach, the Lord addressed his latter-day servants in like manner. "Fear not, little children," he said, "for you are mine, and I have overcome the world, and you are of them that my Father hath given me." (D&C 50:40-41; 78:17-18.)

3. Of the sacrifices offered by Adam, who had been commanded so to do, the angelic ministrant said: "This thing is a similitude of the sacrifice of the Only Begotten of the Father, which is full of grace and truth." (Moses 5:5-8.)

4. "It is expedient that there should be a great and last sacrifice," Amulek taught, "and then shall there be, or it is expedient there should be, a stop to the shedding of blood; then shall the law of Moses be fulfilled; yea, it shall be all fulfilled, every jot and tittle, and none shall have passed away. And behold, this is the whole meaning of the law, every whit pointing to that great and last sacrifice; and that great and last sacrifice will be the Son of God, yea, infinite and eternal." (Alma 34:13-14.) The Risen Lord himself said to the Nephites: "Ye shall offer up unto me no more the shedding of blood; yea, your sacrifices and your burnt offerings shall be done away, for I will accept none of your sacrifices and your burnt offerings. And ye shall offer for a sacrifice unto me a broken heart and a contrite spirit." (3 Ne. 9:19-20.)

5. From Joseph Smith we quote: "It is generally supposed that sacrifice was entirely done away when the Great Sacrifice, the sacrifice of the Lord Jesus was offered up. . . . [But] the offering of sacrifices has ever been connected and forms a part of the duties of

66

the Priesthood. It began with the Priesthood, and will be continued until after the coming of Christ, from generation to generation. We frequently have mention made of the offering of sacrifice by the servants of the Most High in ancient days, prior to the law of Moses; which ordinances will be continued when the Priesthood is restored with all its authority, power and blessings. . . .

"These sacrifices, as well as every ordinance belonging to the Priesthood, will, when the Temple of the Lord shall be built, and the sons of Levi be purified, be fully restored and attended to in all their powers, ramifications, and blessings. This ever did and ever will exist when the powers of the Melchizedek Priesthood are sufficiently manifest; else how can the restitution of all things spoken of by the Holy Prophets be brought to pass. It is not to be understood that the law of Moses will be established again with all its rites and variety of ceremonies; this has never been spoken of by the Prophets; but those things which existed prior to Moses' day, namely, sacrifice, will be continued." (*Teachings*, pp. 172–73.)

6. The data summarized and the quotations given are from Edersheim, Farrar, and Dummelow, who are in agreement on the basics but disagree on some details. Edersheim may be taken as the most authoritative in cases where views are divergent. (*Temple*, pp. 229–48; Edersheim 2:490-512; Farrar, pp. 596–608; Dummelow, pp. 710–12.) Extensive other literature is also available for those desiring to pursue the matter further.

7. Eliza R. Snow, "How Great the Wisdom and the Love," *Hymns*, no. 68.

8. Speaking of those who have done "more" than Jesus commanded, Farrar comments: "The 'transubstantiation' and 'sacramental' controversies which have raged for centuries round the Feast of Communion and Christian love are as heart-saddening as they are strange and needless. They would never have arisen if it had been sufficiently observed that it was a characteristic of Christ's teaching to adopt the language of picture and of emotion. But to turn metaphor into fact, poetry into prose, rhetoric into logic, parable into systematic theology, is at once fatal and absurd. It was to warn us against such error that Jesus said so emphatically, *'It is the spirit that quickeneth; the flesh profiteth nothing: the words that I speak unto you, they are spirit and they are life.'* (John 6:63.)" (Farrar, p. 608, footnote 2.)

9. "See that ye are not baptized unworthily; see that ye partake not of the sacrament of Christ unworthily; but see that ye do all things in worthiness, and do it in the name of Jesus Christ, the Son of the living God; and if ye do this, and endure to the end, ye will in nowise be cast out." (Morm. 9:29.)

Chapter 98

THE DISCOURSE ON THE TWO COMFORTERS

I now send upon you another Comforter,
even upon you my friends,
that it may abide in your hearts,
even the Holy Spirit of promise;
which other Comforter is the same
that I promised unto my disciples,
as is recorded in the testimony of John.
This Comforter is the promise
which I give unto you of eternal life,
even the glory of the celestial kingdom;
Which glory is that
of the church of the Firstborn,
even of God, the holiest of all,
through Jesus Christ his Son.
(D&C 88:3-5.)

"In My Father's House Are Many Mansions"
(John 13:36-38; 14:1-6; JST, John 14:3)

Jesus and the Twelve (minus Judas) have now finished
the Paschal feast with its Jewish rituals and performances,
except that they must yet drink the fourth cup and sing the
remaining part of the Hallel. Both of these they shall do

shortly. The holy party has also partaken, for the first time, of the sacramental emblems, in remembrance of spilt blood and broken flesh of the One who then instituted this new ordinance in his earthly kingdom. The appointed hour for the Atoning One to walk the short distance to Gethsemane, there to take upon himself the sins of the world, is almost at hand. There remain only the private sermons, the Intercessory Prayer, and some conversations with Peter (and the others) about the testing to which they also are being subjected. Then the dread hour of infinite agony will begin.

It is out of Peter's solemn assertion—"I will lay down my life for thy sake"—that the private sermons come. We have already heard Jesus tell the apostles that he will soon be glorified and that where he is going they cannot come. It is this that causes Peter to ask, "Lord, whither goest thou?" Jesus replies: "Whither I go, thou canst not follow me now; but thou shalt follow me afterwards." To this Peter asks, "Lord, why cannot I follow thee now?" and makes the rash promise that he is prepared to lay down his life for Jesus' sake. "Wilt thou lay down thy life for my sake?" Jesus asks, and then says: "Verily, verily, I say unto thee, The cock shall not crow, till thou hast denied me thrice." We shall consider the import of this conversation—here placed by John (and Luke) in the upper room—when we come to similar and more extended statements made, as recorded by Matthew and Mark, when Jesus and the apostles were en route to Gethsemane. For the present we refer to them simply as the basis for the discourse and discussion that followed. Jesus then said:

Let not your heart be troubled: ye believe in God, believe also in me.

Truly, the Son of Man will soon depart; he will be separated from them for a season; they shall follow him at a later time. But why should this worry them? They believe in God and know of his overruling providences in the lives of men; they must continue to believe in Jesus. He is the

Son, and it is as easy to believe that the Father has a son as to believe in the Father alone. Indeed, how can God be a father unless he has a son? How can there be a son of God unless God is the father? It is as easy to believe in one as in the other.

In my Father's house are many mansions: if it were not so, I would have told you. I go to prepare a place for you.

Jesus endorses the Jewish concept that there are degrees of reward in eternity; that those who enter the kingdoms of glory shall have different abodes; that they will be rewarded as they merit. It is true that in his Father's house there are many kingdoms. Such is implicit in the eternal scheme of things. If mortality is a testing and probationary estate, if men are to be judged according to the deeds done in the flesh, and if there are as many degrees of righteousness here on earth as there are men, then a just God could not do other than have an infinite number of kingdoms and rewards in the realms ahead. "If it were not so, I would have told you." That is: All men should by instinct know there are different degrees of glory and many levels of reward in the hereafter. If such were not the case, Jesus would have so stated. And he was going to prepare a place in the highest heaven for the faithful saints.

And if I go and prepare a place for you, I will come again, and receive you unto myself; that where I am, there ye may be also.

Theirs is to be a place in the presence of their Lord; the disciple shall be as his Master, and the servant as his Lord; they shall be even as he is, and he is even as the Father. Though it would not be their privilege to follow him immediately, yet he gave them this assurance: "And whither I go ye know, and the way ye know." Thomas responded: "Lord, we know not whither thou goest; and how can we know the way?" This brought forth from Jesus one of the greatest divine proclamations of his entire ministry:

I am the way, the truth, and the life: no man cometh unto the Father, but by me.

Salvation is in Christ! The plan of salvation is the gospel of God; it is the system ordained by the Father to enable his spirit children, Christ included, to advance and progress and become like him. But Christ is the Redeemer of men, the Savior of the world, the one by whom all men are raised in immortality, and by whom those who believe and obey may gain eternal life. He has abolished death, as the scriptures say, and brought life and immortality to light through the gospel. He is the Resurrection and the Life. He is the way: he charts the course; he invites all men to follow him. He is the truth, the embodiment and personification of this holy attribute: his word is truth, and truth alone saves. He is the life: life exists because of him; he is the Creator. No man cometh unto the Father but by him. He redeemeth from the fall; he raiseth men from death; he maketh eternal life possible. He is our Advocate with the Father: without him we are nothing; because of him we can attain all things. Truly, salvation was, and is, and is to come, in and through his holy name, and in no other way.

"He That Hath Seen Me Hath Seen the Father"
(John 14:7-14)

God was in Christ manifesting himself to the world. The Great God, the Almighty Father, the Creator, Upholder, and Preserver of all things, revealed himself to all men by sending his Son who is in the express image of his Father's person. Both holy beings now have tangible bodies of flesh and bones; both eat and digest food; both occupy space, travel from place to place, and possess the fulness of all good things. Both are exalted and perfected Men, Holy Men, Men in whose image mortals are made. While he was on earth, Jesus was in the image and likeness of the Father. He came to reveal the Father. By knowing the Son men thereby knew the Father.

71

If ye had known me, ye should have known my Father also: and from henceforth ye know him, and have seen him.

But Philip, not satisfied to see Christ only, and in that way to envision who and what the Father is, asked: "Lord, shew us the Father, and it sufficeth us." 'Let us see him as well as his Prototype and it will suffice us.' But Jesus said:

Have I been so long time with you, and yet hast thou not known me, Philip? he that hath seen me hath seen the Father; and how sayest thou then, Shew us the Father?

" 'Philip, after all your association with me, have you not come to know that I am the Son of God, and that the Father is manifesting himself to the world through me? Surely by this time you should know that he who hath seen me hath seen the Father, as it were, for I am so fully and completely like him. Why, then, do you ask for that which you are not now ready to receive, by saying, Show us the Father also?' " (*Commentary* 1:731.)

Believest thou not that I am in the Father, and the Father in me? the words that I speak unto you I speak not of myself: but the Father that dwelleth in me, he doeth the works. Believe me that I am in the Father, and the Father in me: or else believe me for the very works' sake.

The Father and the Son dwell in each other in that they both think the same thoughts, say the same words, and do the same acts. The words that fall from the lips of the Son, and the works that his arm performs, are the very words the Father would speak and the identical works the Father would perform, if he personally were present. They are thus one and dwell in each other. If men cannot believe and know that Christ is in the Father, and the Father in him, then they should believe in Christ because of his works, works that none but God could do.

Verily, verily, I say unto you, He that believeth on me, the works that I do shall he do also; and greater

works than these shall he do; because I go unto
my Father.

This night Jesus designs to reveal to his disciples some of the mysteries of his kingdom, some of the deep and hidden doctrines, some things that can be understood only by the power of the Spirit. His answer to Peter about the many mansions, his explanation to Philip about the indwelling of the Father and the Son in each other, and now this pronouncement that believing disciples will do not only the same works he has done, but even greater works "because" he went unto the Father—all of these are numbered with the mysteries of the kingdom.

That the disciples by faith—for by faith all things are possible and nothing is too hard for the Lord—can do among men what their Master had done is self-evident. The same measure of faith always has borne and always will bear the same fruit. But what of the greater works? Are the disciples to surpass the mighty miracles of their Lord? Yes—in eternity! No ministry shall ever equal his on earth, but that ministry was only a small foretaste of the miraculous powers to be wielded by all the faithful in the oncoming ages yet to be. "The greater works which those that believed on his name were to do were to be done in eternity, where he was going and where they should behold his glory."[1]

And whatsoever ye shall ask in my name, that
will I do, that the Father may be glorified in the Son.
If ye shall ask any thing in my name, I will do it.

Ask in my name! Ask and ye shall receive; ask in faith and receive an answer; but ask in the name of Christ. Pray unto the Father; pray in faith and God will grant the petition; but pray in the name of Christ. His is the name that the saints take upon them in the waters of baptism; his is the name by which the faithful are called; in his name are miracles wrought, prophecies made, and salvation gained. "Thou shalt do all that thou doest in the name of the Son." (Moses 5:8.) "And whatsoever ye shall ask the Father in

73

my name, which is right, believing that ye shall receive, behold it shall be given unto you." (3 Ne. 18:20.)

I will do it! Prayers are made to the Father; answers come from the Son, who is the Mediator between God and man. All things are committed into his hands, and God the Father "hath highly exalted him, and given him a name which is above every name." (Philip. 2:9-11.)

Jesus Speaks of the Two Comforters
(John 14:15-26)

"If ye love me, keep my commandments."

Through this whole night—a night of blessing and of agony—the Blessed Lord, whose coming agony will redeem his brethren, repeatedly centers the hearts of his disciples on the rock foundation of love. Nowhere is this more evident than in the forthcoming words about the two Comforters. The disciples must love one another or they are not his; his Father so loved the world that he sent his Only Begotten Son to work out, this night, the infinite and eternal atoning sacrifice; he himself came to do the will of the Father because of his infinite love for mankind; and the disciples must love him and signify the same by obedience and service. Nay, more: unless they kept his commandments and do his will and serve their fellowmen, they do not in fact love him to the degree and in the way they must to gain an everlasting inheritance with him in that kingdom which he is about to prepare.[2]

And I will pray the Father, and he shall give you another Comforter, that he may abide with you for ever; Even the Spirit of truth; whom the world cannot receive, because it seeth him not, neither knoweth him: but ye know him; for he dwelleth with you, and shall be in you.

As long as Jesus has been with them, he has been their Comforter; he has spoken peace to their souls; those who were heavy laden with the sorrows and sufferings and

74

struggles of the world came to him and found rest for their souls. He comforted the widow and was a father to the fatherless. His words lifted believing souls to new heights of serenity and peace. Now he is leaving, but he will send another Comforter—the Holy Ghost—to abide with the faithful forever.

For all men except those few who heard his voice in mortality, the Holy Ghost is the first Comforter. This member of the Godhead speaks peace to the souls of the righteous in all ages. The Holy Ghost "is the gift of God unto all those who diligently seek him, as well in times of old as in the time that he should manifest himself unto the children of men" (1 Ne. 10:17), and, as well also, in times to come. He is the Spirit of truth—as also is Christ—but the world cannot receive the Holy Ghost because the Spirit will not dwell in unclean tabernacles.

Further, the Spirit cannot be seen by mortal eyes. "The wind bloweth where it listeth, and thou hearest the sound thereof, but canst not tell whence it cometh, and whither it goeth," as Jesus said to Nicodemus, "so is every one that is born of the Spirit." (John 3:8.) But the disciples know the Spirit; they hear the whisperings of the still small voice; they feel the sanctifying influence he sends forth; they receive the revelations of truth that he broadcasts out into all immensity—all because he dwells in them. They have the gift of the Holy Ghost, which is the right to the constant companionship of that member of the Godhead based on faithfulness.[3]

I will not leave you comfortless: I will come unto you.

For the faithful saints who receive the Holy Ghost, which is the first Comforter, there is more—much, much more—ahead. The Lord Jesus himself will come to them. Though he has ascended to his Father, yet will he return to show himself to each individual who abides the law which enables men to rend the heavens and see the visions of eternity.

75

Yet a little while, and the world seeth me no more;
but ye see me: because I live, ye shall live also.

The disciples shall see their resurrected Lord, and because he lives—has both immortality and eternal life—so shall they also inherit that fulness of life which is both immortality and eternal life.

At that day ye shall know I am in my Father, and
ye in me, and I in you. He that hath my command-
ments, and keepeth them, he it is that loveth me:
and he that loveth me shall be loved of my Father,
and I will love him, and will manifest myself to him.

Even as the Father and the Son dwell in each other, so do the faithful saints, by the power of the Holy Ghost, dwell in both the Father and the Son, and so also do the Gods of heaven dwell in men. It is figurative, symbolic language. All those who think the same thoughts, speak the same words, and do the same deeds dwell in each other; and all who are as Christ is shall surely, while dwelling as mortals, see his face and converse with him as one friend speaketh with another.[4]

Such wondrous doctrine, comprehensible only to those whose souls are afire with the enlightening power of the Spirit, was too much for the disciples at that point in time. Judas Thaddeus, otherwise known as Lebbeus, asked: "Lord, how is it that thou wilt manifest thyself unto us, and not unto the world?" Jesus replied:

If a man love me, he will keep my words: and my
Father will love him, and we will come unto him,
and make our abode with him.

With reference to these words our revelations recite: "The appearing of the Father and the Son, in that verse, is a personal appearance; and the idea that the father and the Son dwell in a man's heart is an old sectarian notion, and is false." (D&C 130:3.)

And with reference to the whole concept of the Second Comforter, we have these words of divine and eternal truth given to us by the Prophet Joseph Smith: "There are two

76

Comforters spoken of. One is the Holy Ghost, the same as given on the day of Pentecost, and that all saints receive after faith, repentance, and baptism. This first Comforter or Holy Ghost has no other effect than pure intelligence. . . .

"After a person has faith in Christ, repents of his sins, and is baptized for the remission of his sins and receives the Holy Ghost (by the laying on of hands), which is the first Comforter, then let him continue to humble himself before God, hungering and thirsting after righteousness, and living by every word of God, and the Lord will soon say unto him, Son, thou shalt be exalted. When the Lord has thoroughly proved him, and finds that the man is determined to serve Him at all hazards, then the man will find his calling and his election made sure, then it will be his privilege to receive the other Comforter, which the Lord hath promised the Saints, as is recorded in the testimony of St. John. . . .

"Now what is this other Comforter. It is no more nor less than the Lord Jesus Christ Himself; and this is the sum and substance of the whole matter; that when any man obtains this last Comforter, he will have the personage of Jesus Christ to attend him, or appear unto him from time to time, and even He will manifest the Father unto him, and they will take up their abode with him, and the visions of the heavens will be opened unto him, and the Lord will teach him face to face, and he may have a perfect knowledge of the mysteries of the Kingdom of God; and this is the state and place the ancient Saints arrived at when they had such glorious visions—Isaiah, Ezekiel, John upon the Isle of Patmos, St. Paul in the three heavens, and all the Saints who held communion with the general assembly and Church of the Firstborn." (*Teachings*, pp. 149–51.)

He that loveth me not keepeth not my sayings: and the word which ye hear is not mine, but the Father's which sent me. These things have I spoken unto you, being yet present with you.

But the Comforter, which is the Holy Ghost, whom the Father will send in my name, he shall teach you all things, and bring all things to your remembrance, whatsoever I have said unto you.

Though Thaddeus and the others could not then envision in full the import of the divine words, yet there would be a day, after Pentecost, when, as the fire of the Spirit burned in their souls, they would know for themselves of the marvels here taught. The Holy Spirit of God would bring the words back into their minds and would impress upon their hearts and souls the true meanings and significance of the language used. The Holy Ghost would teach them all things.[5]

"My Father Is Greater than I"
(John 14:27-31; JST, John 14:29-31; Matthew 26:30; Mark 14:26; JST, Mark 14:26-27; Luke 22:39)

Their time together in the upper room—a sacred, blessed period, of infinite worth to them and to us—is drawing to its close. The deep doctrine of the Second Comforter has saluted their ears, and some fifty days hence, after Pentecost, it will begin to burn in their hearts. Now Jesus says:

Peace I leave with you, my peace I give unto you: not as the world giveth, give I unto you. Let not your heart be troubled, neither let it be afraid.

Gospel peace! The peace possessed by the saints! What a marvelous blessing this is! "He who doeth the works of righteousness shall receive his reward, even peace in this world, and eternal life in the world to come." (D&C 59:23.) Christ is the Prince of Peace, the revealer and dispenser of that inner serenity known only to those who have received the gift of the Holy Ghost. Peace is one of the gifts of the Spirit. Thus, Jesus speaks not of the worldly salutation, "Peace be with you," which was commonly spoken among the Jews, but of that inner serenity reserved for those who have entered into the rest of the Lord and who know of the truth and divinity of the Lord's earthly kingdom.

Ye have heard how I said unto you, I go away, and come again unto you. If ye loved me, ye would rejoice, because I said, I go unto the Father: for my Father is greater than I.

If all faithful saints envisioned the glories that lie ahead for them, they would rejoice at the prospects of going where God and Christ and holy beings are. And as to Jesus himself, he is going to eternal glory with his Father who—and again we catch a glimpse of one of the mysteries of the kingdom—is greater than he is.

Jesus' Father is greater than he! "Are they not one? Do they not both possess all power, all wisdom, all knowledge, all truth? Have they not both gained all godly attributes in their fulness and perfection? Verily, yes, for the revelations so announce and the Prophet so taught. And yet our Lord's Father is greater than he, greater in kingdoms and dominions, greater in principalities and exaltations. One does and shall rule over the other everlastingly. Though Jesus is himself God, he is also the Son of God, and as such the Father is his God as he is ours. 'I ascend unto my Father, and your Father; and to my God, and your God,' he is soon to say.

"Joseph Smith, with inspired insight, tells how Jesus is God's heir; how he receives and possesses all that the Father hath, and is therefore (as Paul said) 'equal with God' and yet at the same time is subject to and less than the Father. These are his words: 'What did Jesus do? Why; I do the things I saw my Father do when worlds came rolling into existence. My Father worked out his kingdom with fear and trembling, and I must do the same; and when I get my kingdom, I shall present it to my Father, so that he may obtain kingdom upon kingdom, and it will exalt him in glory. He will then take a higher exaltation, and I will take his place, and thereby become exalted myself. So that Jesus treads in the tracks of his Father, and inherits what God did before; and God is thus glorified and exalted in the salvation and exaltation of all his children.' "[6]

And now I have told you before it come to pass, that, when it is come to pass, ye might believe. Hereafter I will not talk much with you; for the prince of darkness, who is of this world, cometh, but hath no power over me, but he hath power over you. And I tell you these things, that ye may know that I love the Father; and as the Father gave me commandment, even so do I. Arise, let us go hence.

Jesus has overcome the world. The prince of darkness, who opposes the Prince of peace and of light, has no power over him. The disciples, however, are still subject to the world and all its evils and darkness. But Jesus—blessed be his name—is fulfilling the Father's will. He is prepared to go to Gethsemane. And so, having first "sung a hymn," undoubtedly the latter part of the Hallel, as Mark says, the disciples "were grieved, and wept over him." Then they arose from the Paschal table to go forth to "the mount of Olives."

It will help us better to gain for ourselves a feeling of what then was in the hearts of the Twelve if we ponder some of the words of the hymn then sung. Included, as we suppose, for they were following the Passover format, were these Davidic expressions, which must have enveloped the disciples like a gloomy mist:

I love the Lord, because he hath heard my voice and my supplications. . . .

The sorrows of death compassed me, and the pains of hell gat hold upon me: I found trouble and sorrow. Then called I upon the name of the Lord; O Lord, I beseech thee, deliver my soul. . . .

What shall I render unto the Lord for all his benefits toward me? I will take of the cup of salvation, and call upon the name of the Lord. . . .

Precious in the sight of the Lord is the death of his saints. . . .

The Lord is on my side; I will not fear: what can man do unto me? . . .

Thou hast thrust sore at me that I might fall: but the Lord helped me. The Lord is my strength and song, and is become my salvation. . . .

The stone which the builders refused is become the head stone of the corner. This is the Lord's doing; it is marvellous in our eyes. . . .

Blessed be he that cometh in the name of the Lord. . . .

God is the Lord. . . .

Thou art my God, and I will praise thee: thou art my God, I will exalt thee. O give thanks unto the Lord; for he is good: for his mercy endureth for ever. (Psalms 116-118.)

With these thoughts and upon this tone the Paschal feast ends. Jesus will now speak a few more words to the chosen Twelve and then go to Gethsemane and the cross.

NOTES

1. The words are those of Joseph Smith as recorded in the *Lectures on Faith,* pp. 64–66. Additional explanations on the point involved are found in *Commentary* 1:732-33.

2. "If thou lovest me thou shalt serve me and keep all my commandments." (D&C 42:29.) For more extended commentary on this point and the other matters forming part of this discourse on the two Comforters, see *Commentary* 1:734-41.

3. "The Holy Ghost has not a body of flesh and bones, but is a personage of Spirit. Were it not so, the Holy Ghost could not dwell in us. A man may receive the Holy Ghost, and it may descend upon him and not tarry with him." (D&C 130:22-23.) "Therefore it is given to abide in you; the record of heaven; the Comforter; the peaceable things of immortal glory; the truth of all things; that which quickeneth all things, which maketh alive all things; that which knoweth all things, and hath all power according to wisdom, mercy, truth, justice, and judgment." (Moses 6:61.)

4. "Verily, thus saith the Lord: It shall come to pass that every soul who forsaketh his sins and cometh unto me, and calleth on my name, and obeyeth my voice, and keepeth my commandments, shall see my face and know that I am." (D&C 93:1.) "Because of the knowledge of this man," the Book of Mormon says with reference to the brother of Jared, "he could not be kept from beholding within the veil; and he saw the finger of Jesus, which, when he saw, he fell with fear; for he knew that it was the finger of the Lord; and he had faith no longer, for he knew, nothing doubting. Wherefore, having this perfect knowledge of God, he could not be kept from within the veil; therefore he saw Jesus; and he did minister unto him." (Ether 3:19-20.)

5. "And by the power of the Holy Ghost ye may know the truth of all things." (Moro. 10:5.)

6. *Commentary* 1:743; *Mormon Doctrine*, pp. 492–93; John 20:17; *Teachings*, pp. 347–48.

81

Chapter 99

THE DISCOURSE ON THE LAW OF LOVE

Beloved, let us love one another;
for love is of God;
and every one that loveth
is born of God, and knoweth God.
He that loveth not, knoweth not God;
for God is love.
In this was manifested
the love of God toward us,
because that God sent his only begotten Son
into the world, that we might live
through him. Herein is love,
not that we loved God, but that he loved us,
and sent his Son to be the propitiation
for our sins.
Beloved, if God so loved us,
we ought also to love one another.
No man hath seen God at any time,
except them who believe. If we love one another,
God dwelleth in us, and his love
is perfected in us. . . .
And we have known and believed the love
that God hath to us. God is love;

and he that dwelleth in love
dwelleth in God, and God in him.
Herein is our love made perfect,
that we may have boldness
in the day of judgment; because as he is,
so are we in this world.
There is no fear in love;
but perfect love casteth out fear;
because fear hath torment.
He that feareth is not made perfect in love.
We love him, because he first loved us.
If a man say, I love God,
and hateth his brother,
he is a liar;
for he that loveth not his brother
whom he hath seen, how can he love God
whom he hath not seen?
And this commandment have we from him,
That he who loveth God love his brother also.
(JST, 1 Jn. 4:7-21.)[1]

"I Am the Vine, Ye Are the Branches"
(John 15:1-8)

Jesus and eleven of the Twelve—the holy party—have now finished the Paschal meal; the last legal performances of the law, given by Jehovah to Moses, have been performed by Him who gave the law; new emblems, symbolical of the sacrifice of God's Son, have been introduced into the New Order; the washing of feet has been attended to; the disciples have risen from their couches; and the musical chanting of the Hallel is over. But "before they started for their moonlight walk to the Garden of Gethsemane, perhaps while yet they stood around their Lord when the Hallel was over, He once more spoke to them." (Farrar, p. 116.)[2]

I am the true vine, and my Father is the husbandman.

Every branch in me that beareth not fruit he taketh away: and every branch that beareth fruit, he purgeth it, that it may bring forth more fruit. Now ye are clean through the word which I have spoken unto you.

The allegory of the vine, the husbandman, and the branches! "A grander analogy is not to be found in the world's literature. Those ordained servants of the Lord were as helpless and useless without Him as is a bough severed from the tree. As the branch is made fruitful only by virtue of the nourishing sap it receives from the rooted trunk, and if cut away or broken off withers, dries, and becomes utterly worthless except as fuel for the burning, so those men, though ordained to the Holy Apostleship, would find themselves strong and fruitful in good works, only as they remained in steadfast communion with the Lord. Without Christ what were they, but unschooled Galileans, some of them fishermen, one a publican, the rest of undistinguished attainments, and all of them weak mortals? As branches of the Vine they were at that hour clean and healthful, through the instructions and authoritative ordinances with which they had been blessed, and by the reverent obedience they had manifested." (Talmage, pp. 604–5.)

Abide in me, and I in you. As the branch cannot bear fruit of itself, except it abide in the vine; no more can ye, except ye abide in me.

I am the vine, ye are the branches: He that abideth in me, and I in him, the same bringeth forth much fruit: for without me ye can do nothing.

If a man abide not in me, he is cast forth as a branch, and is withered; and men gather them, and cast them into the fire, and they are burned.

"By their fruits ye shall know them." (Matt. 7:20.) And whatever else—as a foul fungus, or some spongy excrescence, or other parasitic or morbid growth—whatever else may grow on a dead vine, it is not the fruit of eternal life. Only those living branches, into whose vascular tissues flow revelation from the Vine and heavenly power from on high—only such living branches can bear fruit unto eternal life. And any man, be he the highest apostolic minister or the lowest branch in the living Church—any man who does not abide in Christ shall wither away and be cast into eternal fire in the dread day of burning that is to be.

If ye abide in me, and my words abide in you, ye shall ask what ye will, and it shall be done unto you.

There are no limits to the power of faith. By it the worlds were made; by it all things are; by it the heavens and the earth shall pass away. Faith is the supreme, ruling power in the universe; it is the power of God; it is infinite and eternal. If the earth itself, the universe, the sidereal heavens—all things—were created and are preserved and upheld by faith, who is to say that the little things of this life shall not be governed by that same infinite power? There is nothing the Twelve shall seek—in faith—that shall not be granted! "But no man is possessor of all things except he be purified and cleansed from all sin. And if ye are purified and cleansed from all sin, ye shall ask whatsoever you will in the name of Jesus and it shall be done. But know this, it shall be given you what you shall ask." (D&C 50:28-30.)

Herein is my Father glorified, that ye bear much fruit; so shall ye be my disciples.

God is glorified, as we have seen, when his children gain exaltation, with resultant kingdoms of their own, for all such are added to his dominions.

Such, then, is the grandest allegory of them all. How better could Jesus have taught that he and his prophets are one; that the life-giving power comes from the Vine; but that the branches must bear the fruit? How better could he have shown that true ministers must receive their power from him? Or that " 'every apostle, prophet, and legal administrator whom I have commissioned to offer the fruit of eternal life to men shall be cut off by my Father unless he carries forward my work; and every minister who is faithful in my service shall be pruned of dead foliage (divested of worldly distractions) and given power to bring forth more fruit.' " (*Commentary* 1:745.)

Truly—and how often have we said it—never man spake as this Man!

"*The Royal Law: Love Thy Neighbour*"[3]
(John 15:9-17)

"Which is greater and more to be desired, to love God or be loved by him? In his providences the one grows out of the other, for Deity reciprocates in full and abundant measure the love his children confer upon him. And Jesus here speaks, not of the divine decree that men should love God, but of the special and preferential love bestowed by the Lord upon those who love and serve him. Such are singled out by Deity to receive special grace and goodness because they are in process of becoming one with him." (*Commentary* 1:747.)

As the Father hath loved me, so have I loved you: continue ye in my love. If ye keep my command- ments, ye shall abide in my love; even as I have kept my Father's commandments, and abide in his love.

Love is the child of obedience, and the greater the obedience the greater the love. As Jesus follows the Father, so must we follow the Son; as the Father loves the Son, so the Son loves us. As the Father's love for the Son comes because of the obedience of the Son, so Jesus' love for us comes because we keep his commandments.

These things have I spoken unto you, that my joy might remain in you, and that your joy might be full.

As a father has joy and rejoicing in his righteous chil- dren, so Jesus finds—and here expresses—his joy in the obedient Twelve. To them he holds out the hope that they may have a fulness of joy, for "Men are, that they might have joy" (2 Ne. 2:25), and both he and his Father, being no respecters of persons, desire to reward all men with the choicest blessings of time and eternity. To others of his apostolic witnesses, three of the Twelve on the American continent, he will soon give an even greater promise. "Ye have desired that ye might bring the souls of men unto me, while the earth shall stand," he will say. "And for this cause ye shall have fulness of joy; and ye shall sit down in the kingdom of my Father; yea, your joy shall be full, even as the Father hath given me fulness of joy; and ye shall be even as I am, and I am even as the Father; and the Father and I are one." (3 Ne. 28:9-10.) This is a promise of exaltation, and to gain exaltation is to have a fulness of joy..

This is my commandment, That ye love one another, as I have loved you. Greater love hath no man than this, that a man lay down his life for his friends.

Love is a commandment! Thou shalt love the Lord thy God; thou shalt love thy neighbor as thyself; thou shalt love thy wife and family; thou shalt love one another. Christ is the Prototype; as he loved us, so we must love one another. And he will soon lay down his life in the atonement of love, the supreme manifestation of his love for his brethren.

Ye are my friends, if ye do whatsoever I command you. Henceforth I call you not servants; for the servant knoweth not what his lord doeth: but I have called you friends; for all things that I have heard of my Father I have made known unto you.

As Abraham was the Friend of God, so the Twelve are the friends of Jesus; and as it was with those worthies, so shall it be with all who are on intimate terms with their Maker. Friends hold each other in high regard and associate on terms of intimacy and love. Their aims and goals are similar; they walk arm in arm; and, if need be, they are prepared to die for each other.[4]

Friends confide in each other, and Jesus has told his

intimates among the Twelve all things they are able to understand. Peter, James, and John are the only ones, for instance, who know what transpired on the Mount of Transfiguration, though the eternal verities there revealed will in due course be given to all of them. And shortly, this very night, Jesus will say to them that there are many things they cannot yet bear that will be manifest to them when they receive the gift of the Holy Ghost.

Ye have not chosen me, but I have chosen you, and ordained you, that ye should go and bring forth fruit, and that your fruit should remain: that whatsoever ye shall ask of the Father in my name, he may give it you.

These things I command you, that ye love one another.

Jesus, the Lord, chooses his own friends; he calls his own servants; he names whom he will to stand as his agents. True ministers do not call themselves to apostolic positions, nor to serve as elders or in any ministerial capacity. Jesus came in his Father's name, bearing his Father's power and authority, doing and saying what his Father commanded. The servants of the Son act similarly. They are called by Christ; he endows them with power from on high; they go forth, duly commissioned, in his name; and they do and say what he commands. They are ordained; they hold Aaronic or Melchizedek authority; they have the gift of the Holy Ghost so they can receive direction from their Lord and Master and Friend.

All other would-be servants are false ministers, false apostles, false prophets. Such do not preach the fulness of the everlasting gospel in all its glory, beauty, and perfection; such cannot perform the ordinances of salvation so they are binding on earth and in heaven. Whatever they may do, so be it; whatever ethical principles they may teach, let them stand; whatever improvements their exhortations may make in the lives of ungodly men, it is all to the good—but theirs can never be more than a preparatory work. Only those called of God, by his own voice, or by angelic ministrations, or by the gift of the Holy Ghost— such only are true apostles and true ministers. Theirs only is the prerogative to seal men up unto eternal life. They are the ones whose fruit will endure. They are the ones who shall ask the Father in the name of Christ for whatsoever they will, and it shall be given them. They are the ones who love one another, thereby testifying before the world that they are true disciples.

God's Enemies Hate Christ and His Work
(John 15:18-27; 16:1-4)

According to the eternal law of opposites—the law which recites: "It must needs be, that there is an opposition in all things" (2 Ne. 2:11)—according to this law, if there is love, there must be hate. Neither of these attributes can exist without the other. Unless there is darkness, there can be no light; unless there is vice, there can be no virtue; unless there is hate, there can be no love. Love is of God and is manifest in the lives of the friends of God; hate is of the world and is manifest in the lives of the enemies of God. And so, having spoken of love and the blessings that flow therefrom, the Lord of love now speaks of hate and the cursings that attend this evil-given attribute.

If the world hate you, ye know that it hated me before it hated you. If ye were of the world, the world would love his own: but because ye are not of the world, but I have chosen you out of the world, therefore the world hateth you.

The world—what is it? It is the state of carnality and evil that dwells in the hearts of those who live on the earth and who have become, since the fall of Adam, "carnal, sensual, and devilish, by nature." (Alma 42:10.) It is the sum total of the social conditions created by carnal men, on a fallen earth, which conditions will continue to prevail until "the end of the world, or the destruction of the wicked, which is the end of the world." (JS-H 1:4.) Of course the world loves its own and hates the saints. How could it be otherwise? The worldly forces, the forces of worldliness, are but the armies of Lucifer, who first fought against God in preexistence and who now continue, here on earth, that primeval war. "Know ye not that the friendship of the world is enmity with God?" James asks. His answer: "Whosoever therefore will be a friend of the world is the enemy of God." (James 4:4.)

Remember the word that I said unto you, The servant is not greater than his lord. If they have persecuted me, they will also persecute you; if they have kept my saying, they will keep yours also.

As with the Master, so with his servants. If persecution is the heritage of the Son of God, will not those who have taken upon them the name of Christ, those who are thus members of his family, will not they also be persecuted? If Christ be scourged, will not his servants feel the biting lash? If Christ be crucified, what if his disciples lay down their lives for the testimony of Jesus and the joy reserved for the saints? And the few among the many who would give heed to the words of Jesus, should he personally minister among them—such are the ones who will receive his servants and give heed to their words.

But all these things will they do unto you for my name's sake, because they know not him that sent me.

Everywhere—on every hand, among all sects, parties, and denominations; everywhere—among every nation, and kindred, and tongue, and people; everywhere—from one end of the earth to the other—everywhere those who hate and persecute the saints do it because they reject Christ. No matter that they may give lip service to his holy name; no matter that they think he is their God; no matter that they follow what they falsely suppose is his plan of salvation—they in fact are rejecting the living Christ when they reject and persecute those whom he hath called and sent forth to preach his word. And all of this is because, regardless of what false assumptions they may make as to their own forms of worship, they know not the One who sent Christ into the world.

If I had not come and spoken unto them, they had not had sin: but now they have no cloke for their sin.

He that hateth me hateth my Father also.

If I had not done among them the works which none other man did, they had not had sin: but now have they both seen and hated both me and my Father.

But this cometh to pass, that the word might be fulfilled that is written in their law, They hated me without a cause.

How awful and fearful it is to reject light and truth! "For of him unto whom much is given much is required; and he who sins against the greater light shall receive the greater condemnation." Men "become transgressors," when otherwise they would have been blameless, because they receive added light and knowledge from on high and do not walk in its blazing glory. (D&C 82:3-4.) The Son of God walks among men, speaks as never man spake, and performs miracles that none else have ever done. Those who reject him thereby become sinners; they can no longer cloak their sins, and they are damned for choosing to walk in darkness at noonday. In Christ they have seen and heard both him and his Father. They have hated both of them without a cause.

But when the Comforter is come, whom I will send unto you from the Father, even the Spirit of truth, which proceedeth from the Father, he shall testify of me: And ye also shall bear witness, because ye have been with me from the beginning.

However much the world may hate and deny and reject both the Father and the Son; however much carnality may reign in the hearts of the enemies of God; however much the saints may be persecuted and slain—yet Jesus will send the Comforter, from the Father, to the faithful. Then this testator will testify to those whose hearts are contrite; he will proclaim to them the divinity of God's Son and bear record of the saving truths that are in Christ. The faithful then shall raise their voices in the congregations of the wicked, for all who receive the Holy Ghost become living witnesses of the truth and divinity of the Lord's person and work.

These things have I spoken unto you, that ye should not be offended. They shall put you out of the synagogues: yea, the time cometh, that whosoever killeth you will think that he doeth God service.

And these things will they do unto you, because they have not known the Father, nor me. But these things have I told you, that when the time shall come, ye may remember that I told you of them. And these things I said not unto you at the beginning, because I was with you.

Saul of Tarsus thought he did God's service when, assenting to the death of Stephen, he held the cloaks of those who hurled the stones. "Indeed, according to Jewish Law, 'a zealot' might have slain without formal trial those caught in flagrant rebellion against God—or in what might be regarded as such, and the Synagogue would have deemed the deed as meritorious as that of Phinehas." (Edersheim 2:524.)

And in this connection, well might it be said: "Sincerity has almost nothing to do with gaining salvation. Men who slay the saints can be just as sincere as those who thus become martyrs. Men can believe so devoutly in falsehood that they will even lay down their own lives for it. What does it matter that those who killed the prophets, either ancient or modern, thought they did God service? The thing that counts is truth, pure God-given truth." (*Commentary* 1:752.)

NOTES

1. The disciple whom Jesus loved, called by us John the Beloved, and who alone has

preserved for us Jesus' words about love as spoken on this Passover day, is also the author of these transcendentally beautiful words.

2. "The Discourse of Christ recorded in St. John 16, and His prayer [recorded in John 17], were certainly uttered *after* they had risen from the Supper, and *before* they crossed the brook Kidron [en route to Gethsemane]. In all probability they were, however, spoken before the Saviour left the house. We can scarcely imagine such a Discourse, and still less such a Prayer, to have been uttered while traversing the narrow streets of Jerusalem on the way to Kidron." (Edersheim 2:513. Italics added.)

3. James 2:8.

4. Similar divine affirmations have been made by the same Lord to his latter-day disciples. "As I said unto mine apostles, even so I say unto you, for you are mine apostles, even God's high priests; ye are they whom my Father hath given me; ye are my friends; . . . for from henceforth I shall call you friends." (D&C 84:63, 77.) Also: "Verily, I say unto my servant Joseph Smith, Jun., or in other words, I will call you friends, for you are my friends, and ye shall have an inheritance with me—I called you servants for the world's sake, and ye are their servants for my sake." (D&C 93:45-46.)

Chapter 100

THE DISCOURSE ON THE HOLY GHOST

And the twelve did teach the multitude;
and behold, they did cause
that the multitude should kneel down
upon the face of the earth,
and should pray unto the Father
in the name of Jesus.
And the disciples did pray unto the Father
also in the name of Jesus. . . .
And they did pray
for that which they most desired;
and they desired that the Holy Ghost
should be given unto them.
And when they had thus prayed
they went down unto the water's edge,
and the multitude followed them.
And it came to pass that
Nephi went down into the water
and was baptized.
And he came up out of the water
and began to baptize. And he baptized
all those whom Jesus had chosen.
And it came to pass

when they were all baptized and had come up
out of the water,
the Holy Ghost did fall upon them,
and they were filled with the Holy Ghost
and with fire. (3 Ne. 19:6-13.)

"The Comforter Knoweth All Things"[1]
(John 16:5-15)

There is a certain fitness of things—or, better, a divine, controlling providence—about what lies ahead for Jesus. Our Blessed Lord has climbed one majestic peak after another; his mortal life is coming not simply to an end, but to an awesome climax of triumph and glory. His miracles, save only the crowning miracle of the atonement and the resurrection, are part of the tapestry of the past. His teachings have been shown forth upon one mountain crest after another. After such sermons as the one on the Second Comforter and on love, what is there left to say? There remains only—and this is the divine fitness of which we speak—the discourse on the Holy Ghost, a few remaining words about his coming death and resurrection, the great Intercessory Prayer with its assurance of eternal life for the faithful, and then Gethsemane, Calvary, an open tomb, a resurrected ministry, and the ascension on Olivet.

After all that he has said, through three and a half years of ministerial service, what can he now do better than to speak of the gift of the Holy Ghost and of the atonement which assures the saints that they may receive that divine and heavenly gift? Eternal life itself is the greatest of all the gifts of God, for it consists of receiving, inheriting, and possessing the same glorious exaltation enjoyed by the Father himself. It is to be like God, to be one with the Father and the Son. But eternal life is gained only in eternity.

The greatest gift known to and enjoyed by mortals is the gift of the Holy Ghost, which is the right to the constant companionship of that member of the Godhead based on righteousness. This gift, given by the laying on of hands, is enjoyed by those who love God with all their hearts. Into their lives flow revelations of eternal truth; they see the visions of eternity and entertain the angels of heaven; they are in tune with the Infinite, as were their kindred spirits of old who held apostolic offices and served in the majesty of their prophetic callings. The Holy Ghost is a revelator. And into their lives comes the sanctifying and cleansing power that perfects the lives of men, so they become fit friends and companions of Gods and angels. The Holy Ghost is a sanctifier. And so, what is more natural at this point—with all that has been said and all that has been done during the greatest ministry ever performed—what is more natural than to hear Jesus say:

But now I go my way to him that sent me; and none of you asketh me, Whither goest thou? But because I have said these things unto you, sorrow hath filled your heart.

Their Lord and Friend is about to return to his Father. Sorrow fills their hearts; the prospects of his death and their separation from him are not pleasant. He chides them gently: " 'Instead of being sorrowful and silent because I said I am going to the Father, why don't you ask me more about it and learn the great gospel truths which are involved.' " (*Commentary* 1:753.)

Nevertheless I tell you the truth; It is expedient for you that I go away: for if I go not away, the Comforter will not come unto you; but if I depart, I will send him unto you.

'Though I am the Son of God and have been with you this long time—teaching, admonishing, guiding, giving to you all that you have been able to receive—yet there is something even more wondrous which awaits you. I will send the Comforter. As long as I have been with you, this

96

right to the constant companionship of the Holy Spirit of God has not been yours. My word has sufficed on all matters. Now I shall work out the atoning sacrifice—for which purpose I came into the world—and you shall receive, from the Holy Ghost, the cleansing power that will prepare your souls for celestial rest.'

And when he is come, he will reprove the world of sin, and of righteousness, and of judgment:

Of sin, because they believe not on me;

Of righteousness, because I go to my Father, and ye see me no more;

Of judgment, because the prince of this world is judged.

" 'When you receive the companionship of the Spirit, so that you speak forth what he reveals to you, then your teachings will convict the world of sin, and of righteousness, and of judgment. The world will be convicted of *sin* for rejecting me, for not believing your Spirit-inspired testimony that I am the Son of God through whom salvation comes. They will be convicted for rejecting your testimony of my *righteousness*—for supposing I am a blasphemer, a deceiver, and an imposter—when in fact I have gone to my Father, a thing I could not do unless my works were true and righteous altogether. They will be convicted of false *judgment* for rejecting your testimony against the religions of the day, and for choosing instead to follow Satan, the prince of this world, who himself, with all his religious philosophies, will be judged and found wanting.' " (*Commentary* 1:754.)

I have yet many things to say unto you, but ye cannot bear them now.

Howbeit when he, the Spirit of truth is come, he will guide you into all truth: for he shall not speak of himself; but whatsoever he shall hear, that he shall speak; and he will shew you things to come.

Though they had been with him during his whole ministry; though they had heard unnumbered sermons and seen more healing miracles than any mortals from the beginning; though they knew more than all the scribes and Pharisees combined, ten thousand times over—yet it was but the beginning. After the receipt of the gift of the Holy Ghost, then their days of learning would really begin.

"He will guide you into all truth." First comes a testimony of the truth and divinity of the Lord's earthly work, of the fact that he gives to men the power to keep his commandments and gain eternal life; then the doctrines of salvation are revealed in plainness; then all things pertaining to God and man and the universe will be shown forth. Whence came God? How was creation possible? What of man, and all forms of life upon the earth, to say nothing of the sidereal heavens and the endless creations of the Endless One? How can we learn redemption's mystery? Or how the resurrection is brought to pass? Or how the great God in heaven speaks to his lowly creatures on earth by the power of his Spirit? The questions are endless; the answers are eternal; and the power of the Holy Ghost, which makes them manifest, is infinite.

As Jesus said a few moments before, the world cannot receive the Comforter; this blessed gift is reserved for the saints, and he will abide in the faithful forever. True it is that honest truth seekers come to know of the truth and divinity of the Lord's work by the power of the Holy Ghost: they receive a flash of revelation telling them that Jesus is the Lord, that Joseph Smith is his prophet, that the Book of Mormon is the mind and will and voice of the Lord, that The Church of Jesus Christ of Latter-day Saints is the only true and living Church upon the face of the whole earth. They gain a testimony before baptism. But it is only after they pledge their all in the cause of Christ that they receive the gift of the Holy Ghost, which is the heavenly endowment of which Jesus spoke. Then they receive a fulfillment of the promise: "By the power of the Holy Ghost ye may know the truth of all things." (Moro. 10:5.) Then they receive "the spirit of revelation," and the Lord tells them in their heart and in their mind whatsoever he will. (D&C 8:1-3.)[2]

"He shall not speak of himself." Rather, he is Christ's minister; his commission is to bear record of the Father and the Son; he is appointed to reveal the truths of eternity to receptive souls. Jesus is going away, and the Holy Ghost is coming to act in the place and stead of the Lord, to say what Jesus wants said, to say what Jesus would say if he were personally present. The Holy Ghost speaks what he has heard from the Father and the Son for he is one with them and knows all things. And thus it is that the Lord's mortal agents have this promise: "And as ye shall lift up your voices by the Comforter, ye shall speak and prophesy as seemeth me good; For, behold, the Comforter knoweth all things, and beareth record of the Father and the Son." (D&C 42:16-17.)

"He will shew you things to come." He is a revelator. That which is past, that which is present, that which is future—all are known to him. "God shall give unto you knowledge by his Holy Spirit, yea, by the unspeakable gift of the Holy Ghost"—is the voice of the Lord to his saints—knowledge "that has not been revealed since the world was until now." (D&C 121:26-32.)[3] To all those who serve him in righteousness and in truth, the Lord Jesus says:

To them will I reveal all mysteries, yea, all the hidden mysteries of my kingdom from days of old, and for ages to come, will I make known unto them the good pleasure of my will concerning all things pertaining to my kingdom.

Yea, even the wonders of eternity shall they know, and things to come will I show them, even the things of many generations.

And their wisdom shall be great, and their understanding reach to heaven; and before them the wisdom of the wise shall perish, and the understanding of the prudent shall come to naught.

For by my Spirit will I enlighten them, and by my power will I make known unto them the secrets of my will—yea, even those things which eye has not seen, nor ear heard, nor yet entered into the heart of man. (D&C 76:1-10.)

Knowing, as we do, that the New Testament accounts are wont to digest the words of Jesus and to set forth only selected gems from the rich treasure house of his sayings, we may not be far off in suggesting that these very words—those afore quoted—or their equivalent may have been spoken to the ancient Twelve. But back to John's account of what Jesus then said:

He shall glorify me: for he shall receive of mine, and shall shew it unto you.

In the same sense in which the Father is glorified when his children gain eternal life, thus adding to his kingdoms and dominions, so it is with the Son. He is glorified because souls are saved, because his brethren enlist in his cause, because great numbers sit down with him and with his Father in the kingdom of God to go no more out. And the Holy Ghost receives from Christ that which will lead souls to salvation and gives it to men.

All things that the Father hath are mine: therefore said I, that he shall take of mine, and shall shew it unto you.

It is the Father's kingdom, but he has given it to the Son, and therefore the Son, who is exalted with the Father, can give these things, by the power of the Spirit, to the disciples.[4]

Jesus Shall Die and Rise Again
(John 16:16-33; JST, John 16:23)

His discourse on the Holy Ghost being ended—and how grateful we are for that portion which has been preserved for us—Jesus then, somewhat enigmatically, said: "A little while, and ye shall not see me: and again, a little while, and ye shall see me, because I go to the Father." To us, in retrospect, the message is clear. He was about to leave them in death; they would not then see him in mortality. But he would rise from the grave, that he might return in glorious immortality to his Father; then, after the resurrection, they would see him again. To the disciples, however, the statement was not immediately clear. They said among themselves: "What is this that he saith unto us, A little while, and ye shall not see me: and again, a little while, and ye shall see me: and, Because I go to the Father?" They also said: "What is this that he saith, A little while? we cannot tell what he saith." It is evident that Jesus gave them time to ponder and wonder so that when he revealed the full import of his saying, it would sink with greater force into their hearts.

Knowing they desired to ask him the meaning of his statement, Jesus said: "Do ye inquire among yourselves of that I said, A little while, and ye shall not see me: and again, a little while, and ye shall see me?" The teaching moment had arrived; their minds were ready to receive the message. Jesus said:

Verily, Verily, I say unto you, That ye shall weep and lament, but the world shall rejoice: and ye shall be sorrowful, but your sorrow shall be turned into joy.

A woman when she is in travail hath sorrow, because her hour is come: but as soon as she is delivered of the child, she remembereth no more the anguish, for joy that a man is born into the world.

And ye now therefore have sorrow: but I will see you again, and your heart shall rejoice, and your joy no man taketh from you.

How better could he have stated it? For a brief moment he will go away to visit the spirits in prison. Because they live together in love, they shall weep at his death. But when he appears again—resurrected, glorified, perfected—their joy will be unbounded. Death is but the birth

101

pang of life; as a man child is born through travail, so immortality is the child of death. Sorrow is for a moment; joy is eternal.

And in that day ye shall ask me nothing but it shall be done unto you. Verily, verily, I say unto you, Whatsoever ye shall ask the Father in my name, he will give it you.

Hitherto have ye asked nothing in my name: ask, and ye shall receive, that your joy may be full.

"*In my name.*" 'Let your prayers now be perfected. As long as I have been with you—teaching, guiding, leading—you have not received the gift of the Holy Ghost; my presence and words sufficed. As long as I have been with you, your petitions have come to me or you have prayed to the Father according to the traditions of your fathers. Now as I leave you, having worked out my own salvation by doing all that my Father sent me to do, now your prayers are always to be in my name. I am the Savior, the Redeemer; salvation comes by me. I am the Way, the Truth, and the Life; no man cometh unto the Father but by me. Ye shall always use my name in your prayers. Pray always to the Father, and to none other; pray always in my name, and in none other. My name is the only name given under heaven whereby salvation cometh. "Ye must pray always, and not faint; . . . ye must not perform any thing unto the Lord save in the first place ye shall pray unto the Father in the name of Christ, that he will consecrate thy performance unto thee, that thy performance may be for the welfare of thy soul." ' (2 Ne. 32:9.)

These things have I spoken unto you in proverbs: but the time cometh, when I shall no more speak unto you in proverbs, but I shall shew you plainly of the Father.

Proverbs were used to hide the truth, or, at least, they limited the extent of the understanding of the disciples. However, after they received the companionship and enlightenment of the Holy Spirit of God, then—and then only—could they receive the mysteries of the kingdom in plainness. Then—and then only—could Jesus manifest to them the Father.

At that day ye shall ask in my name: and I say not unto you, that I will pray the Father for you: For the Father himself loveth you, because ye have loved me, and have believed that I came out from God.

Their prayers in Jesus' name are to begin after his resurrection. Then they will no longer need to rely upon him to pray to the Father for them. The Father loves them and they have direct access to him. Having the Holy Ghost, they then will be able to formulate their own Spirit-guided petitions; then they will feel secure in coming boldly "unto the throne of grace," that they "may obtain mercy, and find grace to help in time of need." (Heb. 4:16.)

I came forth from the Father, and am come into the world: again, I leave the world, and go to the Father.

To all this the disciples responded: "Lo, now speakest thou plainly, and speakest no proverb. Now are we sure that thou knowest all things, and needest not that any man should ask thee: by this we believe that thou camest forth from God." That is, their faith had been strengthened; they believed Jesus came from God, and they were willing to direct their petitions to the Father, as he directed. To their response, Jesus asked, "Do ye now believe?" It is as though he were saying: 'I am glad you believe, for there are hard times ahead for you.'

Behold, the hour cometh, yea, is now come, that ye shall be scattered, every man to his own, and shall leave me alone: and yet I am not alone, because the Father is with me.

Until, at Pentecost, they receive the gift of the Holy Ghost, they will remain weak and wayward and will be scattered before the persecutor's sword. After Pentecost, when the Holy Spirit will burn in their hearts like fire, they will be gathered again, never to depart from the truth, never to do aught save that which He commands them.

These things I have spoken unto you, that in me ye might have peace. In the world ye shall have tribulation: but be of good cheer; I have overcome the world.

Jesus' words bring peace; the preaching of the word to believing souls brings peace; the gospel is a message of peace, of peace on earth and good will to men. Peace is one of the gifts of the Spirit. No matter that there is tribulation in the world; no matter that there is persecution and sorrow and evil; the war cry of the saints is, "Be of good cheer," for Jesus has overcome the world. And because he overcame the world—overcame carnality and evil to the full— he is now ready to be offered. There remains, then, only the Intercessory Prayer, and then he and the disciples will depart for Gethsemane and the atoning ordeal.

NOTES

1. D&C 42:17.
2. "A person may profit by noticing the first intimation of the spirit of revelation; for instance, when you feel pure intelligence flowing into you, it may give you sudden strokes of ideas, so that by noticing it, you may find it fulfilled the same day or soon; that is, those things that were presented unto your minds by the Spirit of God, will come to pass; and thus by learning [to recognize] the Spirit of God and understanding it, you may grow into the principle of revelation, until you become perfect in Christ Jesus." (*Teachings*, p. 151.)
3. This passage names with particularity some of the marvels to be revealed in the dispensation of the fulness of times.
4. In this connection, the Lord Jesus has promised "all that my Father hath" to all of his brethren who keep the terms and conditions of the covenant of the Holy Priesthood. (D&C 84:33-44.)

Chapter 101

THE INTERCESSORY PRAYER

Listen to him who is the advocate
with the Father,
who is pleading your cause before him—
Saying: Father, behold the sufferings and death
of him who did no sin,
in whom thou wast well pleased;
behold the blood of thy Son which was shed,
the blood of him whom thou gavest
that thyself might be glorified;
Wherefore, Father, spare these my brethren
that believe on my name,
that they may come unto me
and have everlasting life. (D&C 45:3-5.)

The Prayer for Eternal Life
(John 17:1-5)

If holy writ contains—and Jehovah be praised, it does!—a prayer that truly merits the designation "The Lord's Prayer," that divine litany of praise and communion is in the 17th chapter of the Gospel of the Beloved John. At least therein we have a digest of what Jesus then said to his Father, what he said as he was about to go to Gethsemane to pray again as the burdens of all the sins of all the ages fell upon him. We know that on other occasions—two, at least, of which we have knowledge—he offered greater prayers than the one preserved for us by John; and even on this occasion he may have uttered words too sacred and holy to be recorded for the spiritually untutored to read. What pleases us beyond any measure of expression is that we have what we have. If his sermons—filled with eternal truths—reached their peak in his pronouncements about the Comforter, who would lead the faithful into all truth, surely his recorded prayers attained the summit of summits when he interceded with the Father for the Twelve and for the faithful of all ages in the Intercessory Prayer.[1]

The only two prayers of which we are aware that were intended to be heard by mortal ears, and that were greater than the Intercessory Prayer, were given among the Nephites. When he prayed alone the night before the calling of the Twelve or in Gethsemane on the night of his agony, the prayers were his own, as they were, no doubt, on many occasions during his prayer-filled life. Of such prayers we cannot speak; no doubt they were like or greater than his expressions made in the presence of the Nephite multitude.

As to the Nephite prayers, the scripture saith: "He himself also knelt upon the earth; and behold he prayed unto the Father, and the things which he prayed cannot be written, and the multitude did bear record who heard him. And after this manner do they bear record: The eye hath never seen, neither hath the ear heard, before, so great and marvelous things as we saw and heard Jesus speak unto the Father; And no tongue can speak, neither can there be written by any man, neither can the hearts of men conceive so great and marvelous things as we both saw and heard Jesus speak; and no one can conceive of the joy which filled our souls at the time we heard him pray for us unto the Father. And it came to pass that when Jesus had made an end of praying unto the Father, he arose; but so great was the joy of the multitude that they were overcome." (3 Ne. 17:15-18.)

Also: "And it came to pass that he went again a little way off and prayed unto the Father; And tongue cannot speak the words which he prayed, neither can be written by man the words which he prayed. And the multitude did hear and do bear record; and their hearts were open and they did understand in their hearts the words which he prayed. Nevertheless, so great and marvelous were the words which he prayed that they cannot be written, neither can they be uttered by man. And it came to pass that when Jesus had made an end of praying he came again to the disciples, and said unto them: So great faith have I never seen among all the Jews; wherefore I could not show unto them so great miracles, because of their unbelief. Verily I say unto you, there are none of them that have seen so great things as ye have seen; neither have they heard so great things as ye have heard." (3 Ne. 19:31-36.)

But now, still in the home of John Mark, as we have supposed, Jesus "lifted up his eyes to heaven, and said":

Father, the hour is come; glorify thy Son, that thy Son also may glorify thee: As thou hast given him power over all flesh, that he should give eternal life to as many as thou hast given him.

This was Jesus' appointed hour—the hour for which he came into the world; the hour when he would take upon himself the sins of the world. For this purpose was he born; for this purpose had he lived. And because he would accomplish the appointed purpose, he would soon rise in immortal glory—for which glory he now prayed. 'Glorify me, Father, and I will glorify thy name.' Jesus is asking for eternal life. Prayers should fit the needs of the hour; the petitions they contain should be expressive of present needs; but there are two things that may, with propriety, be included in all prayers and on all occasions. They are (1) that God will give us his Spirit here and now in this mortal sphere, and (2) that he will save us in his kingdom in the world to come. Salvation is eternal life, and—we repeat—Jesus now prays that he may have eternal life. He is God's Son, God's Almighty Son. His mortal probation is drawing to its close; he has done all things well, and with him the Father is well pleased. All this he knows, and yet his prayer, for himself, is: 'O Father, grant me eternal life with thee in thy kingdom.' Can there be a more perfect pattern in prayer than this?

Jesus has power over all flesh; all things are subject to him. He is the Creator and Redeemer; he judges all men. He is "the Lord Omnipotent who reigneth, who was, and is from all eternity to all eternity." (Mosiah 3:5.) He can give, in his Father's name, eternal life to all who believe and obey; he rewards all men. The Father has placed all things in his hands; salvation and eternal life come because of him. "There is no flesh that can dwell in the presence of God, save it be through the merits, and mercy, and grace of the Holy Messiah." (2 Ne. 2:8.) And since there is no greater gift than eternal life, no greater gift that can be gained by men or Gods, it is the very reward that he himself seeks. Of what does such a high reward consist that it is even the desire of the heart of a God? Jesus continues:

And this is life eternal, that they might know thee the only true God, and Jesus Christ, whom thou hast sent.

Eternal life is God's life; it is the name of the kind of life he lives. The Father has eternal life for two reasons: (1) He has all power in heaven and on earth; he is omnipotent, omniscient, and, by the power of his Spirit, omnipresent; all things are subject to him; he possesses what, in summary, is called the fulness of the Father, or the fulness of the glory of the Father. (2) He lives in the family unit; he has eternal increase; he has a continuation of the seeds and of the lives forever and ever.

Eternal life thus comes only to those who know the Father and the Son, and who know them in the sense of doing and experiencing what it is their eternal lot to do and experience. In this sense, no one can know God without possessing the knowledge and exercising the power vested in Deity, without creating as he creates, without fathering spirit children as he fathers his eternal progeny, without doing all that he does. Since eternal life is the name of the kind of life God lives, no man can possess it unless and until he becomes like his Eternal Father and has the same eternal powers that are resident in the Eternal One. Of those so obtaining it is written: "Then shall they be gods, because they have no end; therefore shall they be from everlasting to everlasting, because they continue; then shall they be above all, because all things are subject unto them. Then shall they be gods, because they have all power, and the angels are subject unto them." (D&C 132:20.)[2]

I have glorified thee on the earth: I have finished the work which thou gavest me to do. And now, O Father, glorify thou me with thine own self with the glory which I had with thee before the world was.

Speaking of things to come as though they already were, Jesus announces the completion of his work on earth and asks for a return of that glory which was his in preexistence. In his spirit state, he was the Firstborn of the Father, the Beloved and Chosen from the beginning, the Creator of all things, the Lord Jehovah, the God of Israel, the Lord God Almighty. Now that his mortal work is over he seeks—and is assured of—all that once was his. And is not this a pattern of what shall be with all of the noble and great? Will not Adam and Enoch and Abraham and all the rest return to receive that glory which was theirs before the world was? And will not they, as with Jesus after the resurrection, receive all power in heaven and on earth, which is eternal life?

The Prayer for the Apostles
(John 17:6-19; 3 Nephi 19:19-36)

Having laid the foundation by holding out the hope of eternal life to all who come unto him and his Father, Jesus now begins to plead the cause of the faithful ones who have been with him in the days of his ministry.

I have manifested thy name unto the men which thou gavest me out of the world: thine they were, and thou gavest them me; and they have kept thy word.

What a tribute this is! The Twelve are Jesus' special friends! They marched under his banner before the world was; they were foreordained as he himself was; they were noble and great sons of the Father whom he gave to Christ to be his mortal companions. To them Jesus has manifest the Father's doctrine, and they have kept his word.

Now they have known that all things whatsoever thou hast given me are of thee. For I have given them the words which thou gavest me; and they have received them, and have known surely that I came out from thee, and they have believed that thou didst send me.

These apostles—all of them—believed in Christ; they knew he came from the Father; they accepted the Father as the source of that pure religion which was theirs. It is neither fitting nor proper to belittle or demean them in any way; their mortal shortcomings, which they freely announced, existed because they had not yet received the Comforter. If ever there were spiritual giants among men, such were these friends of Jesus.

In the comparable prayer, given among the Nephites after the Nephite Twelve had received the Holy Ghost, Jesus said:

Father, I thank thee that thou hast given the Holy Ghost unto these whom I have chosen; and it is because of their belief in me that I have chosen them out of the world.

110

Father, I pray thee that thou wilt give the Holy Ghost unto all them that shall believe in their words.

Father, thou hast given them the Holy Ghost because they believe in me; and thou seest that they believe in me because thou hearest them, and they pray unto me; and they pray unto me because I am with them.

The Nephite Twelve, the Jewish Twelve—all men—are blessed and favored on the same basis. The Gods of heaven are no respecters of persons, and the gifts of the Spirit are available for the faithful on all continents and in all worlds. Let us return to the Twelve in Jerusalem. Jesus continues his prayer:

I pray for them: I pray not for the world, but for them which thou hast given me; for they are thine. And all mine are thine, and thine are mine; and I am glorified in them.

Jesus pleads the cause of the Twelve—and all the saints—in the courts above. He is their Mediator, Advocate, and Intercessor. He makes intercession for them, because they have forsaken the world and come unto him; he advocates their cause, for their cause is his cause and they have received his gospel; he performs a divine service of mediation, reconciling fallen man to his Maker, because the fallen ones choose now to associate with those who are not of this world. Jesus prays, thus, not for the world, but for those who have kept his commandments; who have reconciled themselves to God through faith and repentance; who are preparing themselves for an abode with him and his Father. And his interceding petitions are always available for all men, if they will but believe his word and obey his law.[3]

And now I am no more in the world, but these are in the world, and I come to thee. Holy Father, keep through thine own name those whom thou hast given me, that they may be one, as we are.

Among the Nephite Hebrews—they having received

the gift of the Holy Ghost, which did not come to the Twelve in Jerusalem until Pentecost—among the Nephite Hebrews, Jesus' words of intercession and his prayer for unity were even more express.

Father, I thank thee that thou hast purified those whom I have chosen, because of their faith, and I pray for them, and also for them who shall believe on their words, that they may be purified in me, through faith on their words, even as they are purified in me.

Father, I pray not for the world, but for those whom thou hast given me out of the world, because of their faith, that they may be purified in me, that I may be in them as thou, Father, art in me, that we may be one, that I may be glorified in them.

Jesus here introduces into his Jewish prayer—and in this instance the prayer is also a sermon—the theme of unity; he speaks of the perfect oneness that should prevail among the saints and between them and those divine beings whose they are. We shall hear more on this shortly. For the moment we note only the great need for the Twelve to be one while they are yet in the world, where they are subject to all the tuggings and temptations that might drive a wedge among them, and between them and their Lord, who is departing to his Father. In the Nephite account the Twelve, having received the Holy Ghost, are already purified, and Jesus' petitions are that all who believe may attain a like purity of person and become, like the Twelve, one with him and his Father. With reference to the Jewish Twelve he continues:

While I was with them in the world, I kept them in thy name: those that thou gavest me I have kept, and none of them is lost, but the son of perdition; that the scripture might be fulfilled.

Jesus' ministry where the Twelve are concerned has succeeded. He has cared for the spiritual well-being of the souls entrusted to him. Only Judas has been lost; and even he, though a son or follower of Satan, who is perdition, as we have heretofore seen, is probably not a son of perdition in the sense of eternal damnation. Judas, of course, is not with them as these words are spoken. He departed from the upper room some time ago that he might conspire with the chief priests and bargain for the life of his Lord.

And now come I to thee; and these things I speak in the world, that they might have my joy fulfilled in themselves.

Jesus' words—spoken to the Father, heard by the Twelve—are designed to give them the joy he himself possesses. Those who are "sanctified from all sin," as the scripture saith, "enjoy the words of eternal life in this world, and eternal life in the world to come, even immortal glory." (Moses 6:59.)

I have given them thy word; and the world hath hated them, because they are not of the world, even as I am not of the world.

Why does the world hate and persecute the saints? With what insight Jesus goes to the heart of the matter! Sinners hate righteous people because they are righteous. Sinners love sinners and hate the obedient. Misery loves company. Lucifer was cast out of heaven and became "miserable forever"; accordingly, he now seeks to make "all mankind" miserable like unto himself. (2 Ne. 2:18.) So also do all those who are of the world; they follow their exemplar, who is the prince of this world, and seek to pull all men down to their low and carnal state.

I pray not that thou shouldst take them out of the world, but that thou shouldst keep them from the evil. They are not of the world, even as I am not of the world.

Jesus and his disciples are in the world, but are not of the world. They live in the midst of carnality and evil, but do not partake of the ever-present wickedness. Such is the divine purpose and intent: this life is a probationary estate, and all men must be subject to the lusts and enticements of

113

the flesh; if they shun that which is evil and cleave unto that which is good, they thereby overcome the world and gain salvation.

Sanctify them through thy truth: thy word is truth.

As thou hast sent me into the world, even so have I also sent them into the world. And for their sakes I sanctify myself, that they also might be sanctified through the truth.

To be sanctified is to be cleansed from all sin; it is to stand pure and spotless before the Lord; it is to overcome the world and be a fit candidate for a celestial inheritance. The "sanctified" are "them of the celestial world." (D&C 88:2.) The Holy Ghost is a sanctifier. His baptism of fire burns dross and evil out of repentant souls as though by fire. Sanctification comes only to the obedient; it is the truth of heaven—the very word of God, his everlasting gospel—which sanctifies the souls of men. As the Father sent Jesus to proclaim his gospel, so Jesus sent the Twelve to proclaim the same word of truth; and as Jesus sanctified himself by obedience to the words of the Father, so the Twelve may sanctify themselves through the truth Jesus has given them.

The Prayer for the Saints
(John 17:20-26)

Deity, in his infinite wisdom, presents the truths of salvation to his children on earth in the most graphic and plain manner they are able to bear. One of his standard approaches is to hold up his prophets and apostles as examples before their fellows, and then to say to other men: 'Go and be thou as these are.' He has the practice of rewarding the noble and great for their spiritual achievements, and then of saying: 'All men can achieve as these favored ones have done.' "Take, my brethren, the prophets, who have spoken in the name of the Lord," James says, "for an example of suffering affliction, and of

114

patience." They are your patterns. "Ye have heard of the patience of Job, and have seen the end of the Lord; that the Lord is very pitiful, and of tender mercy." (James 5:10-11.) And nowhere is this divine practice of selecting certain patterns, and inviting all men to be as they are, set forth in a better way than in the Intercessory Prayer. Jesus has extolled and honored the Twelve. He has spoken of their mission and sanctification; now he is going to extend out to every faithful person all that he has given or promised the Twelve.

Neither pray I for these alone, but for them also which shall believe on me through their word; That they all may be one; as thou, Father, art in me, and I in thee, that they also may be one in us: that the world may believe that thou hast sent me.

Such were Jesus' words in Jerusalem. In the land Bountiful, among a kindred people, for whom another Twelve had been ordained, he said:

And now Father, I pray unto thee for them, and also for all those who shall believe on their words, that they may believe in me, that I may be in them as thou, Father, art in me, that we may be one. (3 Ne. 19:23.)

Jesus prays for all the saints; he is their Intercessor, Mediator, and Advocate, as well as he is for the Twelve. And all who believe are to be one—one in belief, one in godly attributes, one in good works, one in righteousness. He is as his Father, and he and the Father are one; the Twelve are as he is, and he and the Twelve are one; all the saints are as the Twelve, and they are all one. And Jesus dwells in the Father, because they are one; the Twelve dwell in Jesus, because they are one; and all the saints dwell in the Twelve, because the same perfect unity prevails in their hearts. "The Lord our God is one Lord" (Deut. 6:4), and his command to all his disciples is: "Be one; and if ye are not one ye are not mine" (D&C 38:27).

115

*And the glory which thou gavest me I have given
them; that they may be one, even as we are one: I in
them, and thou in me, that they may be made perfect in one; and that the world may know that thou
hast sent me, and hast loved them, as thou hast
loved me.*

God gave his glory to the Son; Jesus gave that same
glory to the Twelve; and the Twelve, in turn, make the same
eternal fulness, the same glory, the same eternal life, available to all the saints. All of the Lord's people may thus
become one with the Gods of heaven. To Adam the Lord
said: "Behold, thou art one in me, a son of God; and thus
may all become my sons." (Moses 6:68.) And as with
Adam—for he is but the pattern and the type—all who live
the perfect law of unity "become the sons of God, even one
in me as I am one in the Father, as the Father is one in me,
that we may be one." (D&C 35:2.) The unity and oneness
of the saints is one of the great evidences of the truth and
divinity of the Lord's work on earth.

*Father, I will that they also, whom thou hast given
me, be with me where I am; that they may behold my
glory, which thou hast given me: for thou lovedst me
before the foundation of the world.*

The intercessory pleadings continue: 'Father, wilt thou
give these my brethren eternal life; may they reign in everlasting glory with me in my kingdom, for they are as I am,
and I am as thou art. Thou lovedst me and them before the
foundation of the world, and as it was in the beginning so
shall it be everlastingly.'

*O righteous Father, the world hath not known
thee: but I have known thee, and these have known
that thou hast sent me. And I have declared unto
them thy name, and will declare it: that the love
wherewith thou hast loved me may be in them, and I
in them.*

Again Jesus bears witness that the Twelve know he was
sent by his Father; they know he is the Son of God. Jesus

has taught them of the Father, and the Father loveth them as he loves his own Son, for they are in the Son and he is in them. And as with the Twelve, so with all the saints, of whom the scripture saith: "Know ye not your own selves, how that Jesus Christ is in you, except ye be reprobates?" (2 Cor. 13:5.)

And so ends the Intercessory Prayer, or in other words these are the last words of the prayer preserved for us by the Beloved John. And so Jesus and the Twelve leave the Holy City to find a hallowed spot in the Garden of Sorrow and Anguish where the miracle of the atonement will take place.

NOTES

1. The Intercessory Prayer is also called the High-Priestly Prayer because, as commentators have chosen to conclude, it was offered by Jesus in his capacity as the Great High Priest, whatever that may be deemed to mean. Of this prayer, Farrar summarized: "He lifted up His eyes to heaven, and uttered His great High-Priestly prayer; first, that His Father would invest His voluntary humanity with the eternal glory of which He had emptied Himself when He took the form of a servant; next, that He would keep through His own name these His loved ones who had walked with Him in the world; and then that He would sanctify and make perfect not these alone, but all the myriads, all the long generations, which should hereafter believe through their word." (Farrar, p. 617.)

2. Two other passages have a significant bearing on the matters here considered. "If you keep my commandments and endure to the end you shall have eternal life, which gift is the greatest of all the gifts of God." (D&C 14:7.) And: "This is eternal lives—to know the only wise and true God, and Jesus Christ, whom he hath sent." (D&C 132:24.)

3. Any concept that others than Jesus can mediate between man and his Maker is not of God. Paul says: "There is one God, and one mediator between God and men, the man Christ Jesus." (1 Tim. 2:5.) And the Nephite Jacob testifies: "He shall make intercession for all the children of men; and they that believe in him shall be saved. And because of the intercession for all, all men come unto God; wherefore, they stand in the presence of him to be judged of him according to the truth and holiness which is in him." (2 Ne. 2:9-10.)

Chapter 102

IN GETHSEMANE

I command you to repent—
repent, lest I smite you by the rod
of my mouth, and by my wrath,
and by my anger,
and your sufferings be sore—
how sore you know not,
how exquisite you know not,
yea, how hard to bear you know not.
For behold, I, God, have suffered these things
for all, that they might not suffer
if they would repent;
But if they would not repent
they must suffer even as I;
Which suffering caused myself, even God,
the greatest of all, to tremble
because of pain, and to bleed
at every pore, and to suffer
both body and spirit—
and would that I might not drink
the bitter cup, and shrink—
Nevertheless, glory be to the Father,
and I partook and finished my preparations
unto the children of men.
(D&C 19:15-19.)

The Trial of Peter's Faith
(Luke 22:31-38; JST, Luke 22:21-36; John 13:36-38; Matthew 26:31-35; Mark 14:27-31; JST, Mark 14:33)

As nearly as we can determine from the sacred accounts, while Jesus and his friends were yet in the upper room, finishing their Paschal ceremonies and partaking of the sacrament of the Lord's Supper, some conversations began about the tests that lay ahead for all of them, and of the allegiance they would manifest to their Lord. The colloquy then commenced was interrupted by the discourse on the two comforters, by that on the law of love, and then by that on the Holy Ghost, and also by the offering of the Intercessory Prayer. Then as the holy party left the city, crossed the wadi called Kidron, and came near the Mount of Olives, the same theme was picked up again.

Through it all it is evident that the tests now facing his apostolic associates were of deep concern to Jesus, and that he desired to encourage and strengthen them so they would come off triumphant. It was not his purpose to stay the tempter's power nor to shelter his chosen ones from the onslaught of evil. They must overcome the world even as he had done, if they were to be with him and partake of his glory. He would, however, do all in his power to strengthen their faith that they might be victorious in the warfare with Satan. How true it is that the Lord "scourgeth every son whom he receiveth." (Heb. 12: 6.) Let the lash fall; let their flesh be cut; let their faith be tested—but let them bear up under it all.

If Abraham must be willing to offer Isaac, if Isaac and Jacob and all the holy prophets must lay their all on the altar, not even withholding their lives in many cases—then those who would dwell everlastingly with faithful Abraham, those who would sit down in the kingdom of God with Abraham, Isaac, and Jacob, and all the holy prophets, must also pass the same tests of faith and devotion as did their faithful forebears. And next to the agonies about to engulf Jesus himself, the greatest tests ahead were for Peter. What

119

they were we are not told, nor does it matter, for every man's tests—in the wisdom of Him who ordained all things well—are those which are suited to him and him alone. But we do know that in principle the higher one of the Lord's servants stands in the hierarchy of righteousness, the more severe are the tests to which his faith will be subjected. Jesus is about to carry the greatest burdens ever placed upon a mortal soul. Shall the Twelve, who stand next to him—with Peter at their head—escape their share of the tests and burdens ahead?

And so, Jesus, while they were yet in the upper room, said to Peter: "Simon, Simon, behold, Satan hath desired you, that he may sift the children of the kingdom as wheat." Satan sought the soul of Simon. Every lost soul adds to the revelry and rebellion in the lower realms. Satan seeks to harvest all the souls of men, to sift the saints as wheat is harvested on the threshing floor, so that both the wheat and the tares may be garnered into his granary. And oh, if he can only topple Peter from his high place; if only the chief apostle can be destroyed spiritually; if only the defenders of Zion can be destroyed—how much easier it will be to harvest the then unprotected fields.

"But I have prayed for you," Jesus says to Peter, "that your faith fail not; and when you are converted strengthen your brethren." Peter has a testimony; he knows that Jesus is the Christ, the Son of the living God; he has preached and baptized other believing souls; he has wrought many mighty miracles in the name of Christ; he has been valiant, true, and obedient. But he is not as yet converted. He has not yet become a new creature by the power of the Holy Ghost; he has not as yet put off the natural man, and put on Christ, and become "as a child, submissive, meek, humble, patient, full of love, willing to submit to all things which the Lord seeth fit to inflict upon him, even as a child doth submit to his father." (Mosiah 3:19.) All this can be his only after Pentecost; only after the descent of the Holy Spirit; only after he receives the gift of the Holy Ghost.

But Peter, "being aggrieved" at Jesus' words to him, said: "Lord, I am ready to go with you, both into prison, and unto death." 'Surely I am converted and will stand by thee in all things, though it cost me my life.' Jesus replied: "I tell you, Peter, that the cock shall not crow this day, before that you will thrice deny that you know me."

Then, by way of reassurance, to remind them all that a Divine Providence would preserve them in the tests ahead, Jesus asked: "When I sent you without purse and scrip, or shoes, lacked ye any thing?" Their answer: "Nothing." Jesus continued: "I say unto you again, He who hath a purse, let him take it, and likewise his scrip; and he who hath no sword, let him sell his garment and buy one." In the troublesome times ahead, when the hands of all men would be against them, they would need to provide their own food, clothing, and shelter, and for their own protection.[1]

Whatever lay ahead for the disciples, however— whether they were to be preserved by Divine Providence or by means of their own wise planning and defense, as the varying situations might require—they must not overlook the great reality that their Lord was about to leave them in death. They must not take his passing upon the cross as a sign of defeat. Lest they do so, he reminds them of the Messianic prophecies which speak of his death, and, indeed, he quotes one of them. "For I say unto you," Jesus continues, "This that is written must yet be accomplished in me, And he was reckoned among the transgressors; for the things concerning me have an end." The reference, of course, is to Isaiah's Messianic pronouncement that he should "pour out his soul unto death" and in that hour be "numbered with the transgressors." (Isa. 53:12.) To this the disciples respond, "Lord, behold, here are two swords," falsely assuming that he is asking for a means of defense for himself, rather than telling them they may defend themselves in the treacherous days ahead. Their offer is waved aside by the Lord: "It is enough," he says,

121

meaning, 'Enough of this kind of talk; it is not my purpose to be defended by the arm of flesh.'

For the continuation of this theme—and how heavily it must have weighed on the mind of Jesus—we go now with him and the Twelve toward the Mount of Olives. In "that night" when "the fierce wind of hell was allowed to sweep unbroken over the Saviour, and even to expend its fury upon those that stood behind in His Shelter" (Edersheim 2:535), we hear him say to his friends, "All ye shall be offended because of me this night: for it is written, I will smite the shepherd, and the sheep of the flock shall be scattered." "What a dreadful thing it is to call for a sword against God; and yet it is part of the plan. Jesus is to die; the Shepherd is to be slain; the sheep are to be scattered." (*Commentary* 1:769.) Did not Jehovah by the mouth of Zechariah foretell what was to be in this dark hour? "Awake, O sword, against my shepherd, and against the man that is my fellow, saith the Lord of hosts," is the prophetic word; and "smite the shepherd, and the sheep shall be scattered: and I will turn mine hand upon the little ones." (Zech. 13:7.) But through it all—and this they must never forget—the Lord Jesus, risen in glorious immortality, shall go before them into Galilee; there they will meet again and their joy will be full.

Once again Peter, still brooding over what he esteems to be his total devotion to his Lord, says: "Though all men shall be offended because of thee, yet will I never be offended." Again the prophetic word falls from the lips of the Chief Prophet: "Verily I say unto thee, That this day, even in this night, before the cock crow twice, thou shalt deny me thrice." And still Peter persists: "Though I should die with thee, yet will I not deny thee." And Matthew adds: "Likewise also said all the disciples," for all, in one degree or another, were also being tested.

Jesus Prays and Suffers in Gethsemane
(Matthew 26:36-46; JST, Matthew 26:43; Mark 14:32-42;

JST, Mark 14:36-38, 40, 42-43, 47; Luke 22:40-46;
JST, Luke 22:45; John 18:1-2)

Outside Jerusalem's walls, across the wadi Kidron, part-way up the slopes of Olivet, in (as we suppose) a secluded vale, was the Garden of the Oil Press—the Garden of Gethsemane. Thither "Jesus ofttimes resorted . . . with his disciples." Surely the site, known to Judas, was the possession of some worthy believer who rejoiced that the Lord often chose his spot of earth as a place to pray and ponder and teach and rest. Though often dry, the wadi, with its precipitous sides, was in April the host of a surging stream. The gentle slopes of Olivet were familiar land to the little party of spiritual giants who were now pondering the truths they had been taught and sorrowing over the separation of which they had been told.

Mark says: "They came to a place which was named Gethsemane, which was a garden; and the disciples began to be sore amazed, and to be very heavy, and to complain in their hearts, wondering if this be the Messiah." Though they all knew, as Jesus himself attested in the private sermons and prayer just delivered, that he was the Son of God, yet he did not fit the popular pattern for the Jewish Messiah, and the disciples, of course, had not yet received the gift of the Holy Ghost, which means they did not have the constant companionship of that member of the Godhead. "And Jesus knowing their thoughts, said to his disciples"—that is, to eight of them—"Sit you here, while I shall pray." Also: "Pray that ye enter not into temptation."

Then he took Peter, James, and John with him on into the Garden. As they went he "rebuked them"—apparently for the doubt that arose in their hearts that he was the Messiah—and said: "My soul is exceeding sorrowful, even unto death; tarry ye here and watch." Then he withdrew from them "about a stone's cast, and kneeled down, and prayed." The statement that he "kneeled" is Luke's; Mark says he "fell on the ground [that is, prostrated himself], and

123

prayed." Matthew says he "fell on his face." No doubt he did all of these things, over a long period and in the course of repeated prayers.

We cannot recount with surety the order in which each thing happened, nor reconstruct with certainty the sequence of Jesus' spoken words, this night in this garden— in this "other Eden, in which the Second Adam, the Lord from heaven, bore the penalty of the first, and in obeying gained life." (Edersheim 2:534.) What has been preserved for us is only a sliver from a great tree, only a few sentences of what was said, only a brief glimpse of what transpired. It would appear that Jesus and the disciples spent some hours there in Gethsemane; that one (or many!) angels were present; and that Jesus poured out his soul in agony as he interceded for the faithful and felt the weight of the world's sins upon his own sinless soul. There is no mystery to compare with the mystery of redemption, not even the mystery of creation. Finite minds can no more comprehend how and in what manner Jesus performed his redeeming labors than they can comprehend how matter came into being, or how Gods began to be. Perhaps the very reason Peter, James, and John slept was to enable a divine providence to withhold from their ears, and seal up from their eyes, those things which only Gods can comprehend. We do know, however, that these words were included in Jesus' prayer:

O my Father, if it be possible, let this cup pass from me: nevertheless not as I will, but as thou wilt. (Matthew.)

Abba, Father, all things are possible unto thee; take away this cup from me; nevertheless, not my will, but thine be done. (Mark.)

Father, if thou be willing, remove this cup from me: nevertheless not my will, but thine, be done. (Luke.)

Then, as nearly as we can determine, and as Luke records: "There appeared an angel unto him from heaven, strengthening him." The angelic ministrant is not named. We know that on the Mount of Transfiguration "Moses and Elias . . . appeared in glory, and spake of his decease which he should accomplish at Jerusalem" (Luke 9:30-31); and if we might indulge in speculation, we would suggest that the angel who came into this second Eden was the same person who dwelt in the first Eden. At least Adam, who is Michael, the archangel—the head of the whole heavenly hierarchy of angelic ministrants—seems the logical one to give aid and comfort to his Lord on such a solemn occasion. Adam fell, and Christ redeemed men from the fall; theirs was a joint enterprise, both parts of which were essential for the salvation of the Father's children.

But back to Luke. "And being in an agony he prayed more earnestly: and his sweat was as it were great drops of blood falling down to the ground." The Son of God who did all things well—whose every thought and act and deed was perfect; whose every prayer pierced the firmament and ascended to his Father—the Son of God himself (note it well) "prayed more earnestly." Even he reached a pinnacle of perfection in prayer that had not always been his. And as to the blood that oozed from his pores, we cannot do better than recall the words of the angelic ministrant, spoken to the Nephite Hebrew, Benjamin: "And lo, he shall suffer temptations, and pain of body, . . . even more than man can suffer, except it be unto death; for behold, blood cometh from every pore, so great shall be his anguish for the wickedness and the abominations of his people." (Mosiah 3:7.)

"And when he rose up from prayer," Luke continues, "and was come to his disciples"—meaning Peter, James, and John—"he found them sleeping; for they were filled with sorrow; And he said unto them, Why sleep ye? rise and pray, lest ye enter into temptation." This same occurrence as recorded by Mark happened this way: "Simon, sleepest thou? Couldest not thou watch one hour? Watch ye and pray, lest ye enter into temptation." At this point, they—the three of them—answered: "The spirit truly is ready, but the flesh is weak."

Jesus then left the chosen three and prayed again: "O my Father, if this cup may not pass away from me, except I drink it, thy will be done." Returning, Jesus found them sleeping again, which presupposes he had been away some time and had offered many petitions to his Father. This time they knew not how to answer him. Jesus went away and prayed the third time, "saying the same words." Returning this last time, he said, "Sleep on now, and take your rest." Then, as Mark has it, "After they had finished their sleep, he said, Rise up, let us go; lo, he who betrayeth me is at hand."

Thus ends such accounts as we have of Jesus' suffering in Gethsemane. It is now over and he has won the victory; the atonement, in large measure, has been worked out, and he is now ready for the shame and humiliation and pain of the cross. Then will come the resurrection and the crown.

As he went into Gethsemane, it was with a total awareness of what lay ahead. "Jesus knew that the awful hour of His deepest humiliation had arrived—that from this moment till the utterance of that great cry with which He expired, nothing remained for Him on earth but the torture of physical pain and the poignancy of mental anguish. All that the human frame can tolerate of suffering was to be heaped upon His shrinking body; every misery that cruel and crushing insult can inflict was to weigh heavy on His soul; and in this torment of body and agony of soul even the high and radiant serenity of His divine spirit was to suffer a short but terrible eclipse. Pain in its acutest sting, shame in its most overwhelming brutality, all the burden of the sin and mystery of man's existence in its apostasy and fall— this was what He must now face in all its most inexplicable accumulation." (Farrar, pp. 622–23.)

There is no language known to mortals that can tell what agony and suffering was his while in the Garden. Of it Farrar says: "A grief beyond utterance, a struggle beyond endurance, a horror of great darkness, a giddiness and stupefaction of soul overmastered Him, as with the sinking swoon of an anticipated death. . . . How dreadful was that paroxysm of prayer and suffering through which He passed." (Farrar, p. 624.)

And as to the prayer in the Garden—repeating, as it did, his divine promise made in the councils of eternity when he was chosen for the labors and sufferings of this very hour; the divine prayer in which he said, "Father, thy will be done, and the glory be thine forever" (Moses 4:2)—as to the prayer in the Garden, "That prayer in all its infinite reverence and awe was heard; that strong crying and those tears were not rejected. We may not intrude too closely into this scene. It is shrouded in a halo and a mystery into which no footstep may penetrate. We, as we contemplate it, are like those disciples—our senses are confused, our perceptions are not clear. We can but enter into their amazement and sore distress. Half waking, half oppressed with an irresistible weight of troubled slumber, they only felt that they were dim witnesses of an unutterable agony, far deeper than anything which they could fathom, as it far transcended all that, even in our purest moments, we can pretend to understand. The place seems haunted by presences of good and evil, struggling in mighty but silent contest for the eternal victory. They see Him, before whom the demons had fled in howling terror, lying on His face upon the ground. They hear that voice wailing in murmurs of broken agony, which had commanded the wind and the sea, and they obeyed Him. The great drops of anguish which fall from Him in the deathful struggle, look to them like heavy gouts of blood." (Farrar, p. 624.) And so they were.

And as he came out of the Garden, delivering himself voluntarily into the hands of wicked men, the victory had been won. There remained yet the shame and the pain of his arrest, his trials, and his cross. But all these were overshadowed by the agonies and sufferings in Gethsemane. It was on the cross that he "suffered death in the flesh," even as many have suffered agonizing deaths, but it was in Gethsemane that "he suffered the pain of all men, that all men might repent and come unto him." (D&C 18:11.)

The first Adam brought death, both temporal and spiritual, into the world and was cast out of the first Eden. The second Adam (Paul says he is the Lord from heaven) brought life—spiritual life, eternal life—into the world when he bore the sins of all men on that awesome night in a second Eden. Let God be praised that Adam fell; let Gods and angels rejoice that the Messiah came in the meridian of time to ransom men from the effects of the fall! In part the ransom was paid on a cross—having particular reference to the immortality that passes upon all men because Jesus rose from the dead. But primarily the ransom was paid in a garden—for there eternal life was won for the obedient—in the Garden of the Oil Press, where Judas now stands, strengthened by the arm of flesh, ready to betray the Atoning One.

The Betrayal and the Arrest
(Matthew 26:47-56; JST, Matthew 26:47-48; Mark 14:43-52; JST, Mark 14:52-53, 56-57; Luke 22:47-53; John 18:3-12)

That which Jesus himself had foretold—"how . . . he must go unto Jerusalem, and suffer many things of the elders and chief priests and scribes, and be killed, and be raised again the third day" (Matt. 16:21)—is now coming to pass. Every detail is taking place; every jot and tittle is being fulfilled; the cruel deeds of a cruel week are unfolding—all with a power and vengeance that no human hand can stay; all with a hatred and malignity that should have made even the demons of the deep shudder in their hellish home. The agonies of Gethsemane have seen the blood of a God fall in oozing drops from every pore to hallow forever that sacred spot, where, among the olive trees, apart even from his intimate friends, he took upon himself that weight which none other could bear. His blood, the choicest blood on earth, the atoning blood of God's Son, is now dried on the rocks and mingled with the soil of the Garden where the greatest miracle of the ages has been wrought.

Even now Judas—"mine own familiar friend, in whom I trusted, which did eat of my bread, hath lifted up his heel against me" (Ps. 41:9), as the Psalmist described him—has arrived to plant the traitor's kiss and supervise the arrest. Judas, into whom Satan has entered, is the one to whom the world—the Gentile world, of which Rome is the symbol, and the ecclesiastical world, of which the Jewish hierarchy are the leaders—Judas is the one upon whom the god of this world now depends to bring to pass his nefarious purposes.

Judas, standing in Satan's stead, is at the head of a motley band composed of the servants of the chief priests and many elders and Pharisees, of the temple guards with their officers, and of a contingent of Roman soldiers from the tower of Antonia, under the command of a tribune. They are armed with swords and staves—with swords to slay their opponents, if need be; with staves to quiet any tumult or disperse any bellicose rabble. They are carrying lanterns and torches, lest he whom they seek slip away from their iron grasp into the darkness of the night. Probably there are six hundred armed men in the arresting force, for this is no small thing they are undertaking; at last their Galilean enemy, who subverts their religion and rebels against their traditions, is to be done away with. A great multitude of the curious and of those whose sympathies are with the arresting cohort also dog the steps of the fierce Romans and the vengeful Jews sent to arrest the Son of Man. That such an army—at Passover time, when the watchful eye of Rome kept her soldiers on alert to quell disturbances—could not have moved without the prior approval of the Roman procurator, one Pontius Pilate, is perfectly clear. Indeed, a prior authorization of the arrest by Pilate accounts for his subsequent readiness to participate in the events of this dread night.

Having conspired beforehand with the chief priests and Pharisees—"Whomsoever I shall kiss, that same is he: hold him fast," was his promise—Judas must first have led the evil band to the house in Jerusalem where the holy party celebrated the Feast of the Passover. Finding them gone, and, as we suppose, rousing John Mark in the process, Judas then led those under his command to Gethsemane which he knew was the place to which they commonly resorted. Finding Jesus and the Eleven, Judas called out "Hail master"—'Hail Rabbi'—and kissed him; or, better, as the Greek text conveys, "not only kissed but covered Him with kisses, kissed Him repeatedly, loudly, effusively." (Edersheim 2:543.) There must be no mistake made as to the identity of Jesus; the promised sign must be clear and certain. It was the custom to greet friends and guests with a kiss; Jesus himself had condemned his host, Simon the Pharisee, by saying, "Thou gavest me no kiss." (Luke 7:45.) There must be absolute certainty in the kiss of betrayal, and so Judas showered Jesus with kisses, which but makes the traitorous act all the more repulsive. Jesus then said: "Judas, betrayest thou the Son of man with a kiss?" And then: 'Friend'—for so Judas is identified in the Messianic prophecy—'do that for which thou art come.'

Judas had made the identification. But the armed cohort—whose daily business it was to quell riots, subdue disturbers of the peace, and arrest malefactors—stood in awe. The Presence was more than they were ready to face. Jesus stepped forward, voluntarily and without hesitation, and asked: "Whom seek ye?" They answered, "Jesus of Nazareth," to which Jesus rejoined, "I am he." At this the arresting soldiers, who many times before had arrested criminals and faced armed foes without fear, "went backward, and fell to the ground." No more could Jesus be arrested without his consent than could his life be taken unless he willed it. Even though all the armies of all the nations of men had come to take him—no matter—he was master of all things. But as he would soon choose to die, so now he chose to be arrested. Again he asked the powers of this world: "Whom seek ye?" and again they answered, "Jesus of Nazareth." Then Jesus said: "I have told you that I am he: if therefore ye seek me, let these go their way."

This "last remark had reference to the apostles, who were in danger of arrest; and in this evidence of Christ's solicitude for their personal safety, John saw a fulfilment of the Lord's then recent utterance in prayer, 'Of them which thou gavest me have I lost none.' It is possible that had any of the Eleven been apprehended with Jesus and made to share the cruel abuse and torturing humiliation of the next few hours, their faith might have failed them, relatively immature and untried as it then was; even as in succeeding years many who took upon themselves the name of Christ yielded to persecution and went into apostasy." (Talmage, pp. 615-16.)

"Then came they, and laid hands on Jesus, and took him." He consented to the arrest; he permitted himself to be taken; the Son of God was then bound as a common criminal by men. "The Great Prophet had voluntarily resigned Himself; He was their helpless captive. No thunder had rolled; no angel flashed down from heaven for His deliverance; no miraculous fire devoured amongst them. They saw before them nothing but a weary unarmed man, whom one of His own most intimate followers had betrayed, and whose arrest was simply watched in helpless agony by a few terrified Galileans." (Farrar, p. 634.)

Seeing this turn of events, the disciples asked: "Lord, shall we smite with the sword?" Not waiting for an answer, Peter drew his sword and slashed off the right ear of Malchus, the servant of the high priest.

Then, turning to Peter, Jesus said: "Put up thy sword into the sheath: the cup which my Father hath given me, shall I not drink it?" And also: "He who taketh the sword shall perish with the sword." And yet further: "Thinkest thou that I cannot now pray to my Father, and he shall presently give me more than twelve legions of angels? But how then shall the scriptures be fulfilled, that thus it must be?" Eleven weak mortals—as mortals—were as nothing before this assembled army; and he who could command twelve legions of angels, and more, would make no move to stay the course he must pursue to fulfill all of the Messianic prophecies about his death and resurrection. Having so spoken—and shall we not say he was planning another evidence of his own divinity, of which the high priest shall soon hear?—Jesus asked for the sufferance of the arresting soldiers, while "he put forth his finger and healed the servant of the high priest."

Then Jesus, bound securely and subject to them, spoke to "the chief priests, and captains of the temple, and the elders"—that is, to the leaders of the Jews, through whose evil machinations he had been taken—and asked: "Are ye come out, as against a thief, with swords and with staves to take me? I was daily with you in the temple teaching, and ye took me not: but the scriptures must be fulfilled." And as Luke adds, he also said: "But this is your hour"—your hour of trial and evil—when for the moment "the power of darkness" shall seem to prevail.

"And the disciples, when they heard this saying, all forsook him and fled," thus fulfilling his word that the sheep should be scattered. That their danger was real is seen from the fact that there was then present "a certain young man, a disciple, having a linen cloth cast about his naked body," whom the soldiers attempted to arrest. But he—and we assume he was John Mark—"left the linen cloth and fled from them naked, and saved himself out of their hands."

NOTE

1. "When faced with persecution, do the Lord's ministers turn the other cheek or raise the sword in their own defense? Do they go forth supplying their own needs or do they rely for their daily wants upon the generosity of those among whom they minister? Who but God can answer such questions, for the answers depend on a full knowledge both of present conditions and of the future. Jesus counseled one course at one time and the opposite at another. There is, thus, no sure guide for the Lord's people except present day revelation." (*Commentary* 1:771.)

SECTION XII

THE TRIALS,
THE CROSS,
AND THE TOMB

THE TRIALS, THE CROSS, AND THE TOMB

Let him be crucified. . . .
Let him be crucified.
(Matt. 27:22-23.)
Crucify him. . . . Crucify him.
(Mark 15:13-14.)
Crucify him, crucify him.
(Luke 23:21.)
Away with him, away with him,
crucify him. (John 19:15.)
Jesus of Nazareth,
a man approved of God among you
by miracles and wonders and signs,
which God did by him
in the midst of you, . . .
Him, being delivered by
the determinate counsel and foreknowledge
of God, ye have taken,
and by wicked hands
have crucified and slain.
(Acts 2:22-23.)

From Gethsemane they take Him to evil Annas—an adulterous Jew; a one-time high priest; the father-in-law of Caiaphas—and there He is examined and smitten. This is their hour—the hour of darkness.

In all Israel there is not a more wicked or influential man than Annas, who commits himself to see that Jesus is put to death.

They take him before Caiaphas and the Sanhedrin. They plot a judicial murder, seek false witnesses, find him guilty of blasphemy, and say: "He is worthy of death."

He is maltreated by the guards as they await the morning trial. Peter, before the cock crows twice, thrice denies that he knows him.

Then he is hailed before the Sanhedrin in formal session, where he testifies that he is the Son of God, and "the whole council condemned him" and sent him bound to Pilate.

Pilate, whose hands reek with blood, yet seeks to free him. Jesus testifies that he is a king, but that his kingdom is not of this world.

As a Galilean he is sent to Herod to be examined and derided. There he remains silent.

Before Pilate again he is charged with sedition and treason. Pilate seeks to release him, but the people demand Bar-Abbas instead and shriek, "Crucify him, crucify him."

He is scourged, mocked, derided, and sentenced to be crucified.

Iscariot commits suicide.

Jesus carries his cross for a ways, and then Simon of Cyrene is impressed into service.

They crucify their King.

Pilate places a superscription over his head in Latin, and in Greek, and in Aramaic, reading: "JESUS OF NAZARETH, THE KING OF THE JEWS."

The soldiers cast lots for his garments. The Sanhedrists incite mockery and derision against him.

He ministers from the cross, promising the penitent thief, "This day shalt thou be with me in paradise," and committing the care of the Blessed Virgin to the Beloved Disciple.

He hangs on the cross for six hours, during the last three of which darkness covers the land, and he suffers again the pains of Gethsemane. The atonement is complete. His work is finished. He voluntarily lays down his life.

A Roman spear pierces his side, but no bone of his body is broken.

Pilate permits Joseph of Arimathea to have the body, and he and Nicodemus prepare it for burial. They place it in the Arimathean's tomb.

Jesus meanwhile enters paradise, preaches to the righteous dead there assembled, organizes the work, and declares liberty to the captives and the opening of the prison doors to them that are bound.

Chapter 103

THE JEWISH PRE-TRIALS

There is save one Messiah
spoken of by the prophets,
and that Messiah is he who should be rejected
of the Jews. (2 Ne. 25:18.)
The Jews at Jerusalem sought to kill Jesus,
according to his word. (4 Ne. 1:31.)
Believe in Jesus Christ,
that he is the Son of God,
and that he was slain by the Jews.
(Morm. 7:5.)

Jesus Is Examined and Smitten before Annas
(John 18:12-14, 19-23)

"This is your hour," saith the Lord Jesus, the hour of "the power of darkness"! And if it was true in Gethsemane, how much more does the message tingle in every ear with reference to the unjudicial court procedures of the night and the day that followed.

From Gethsemane—a sacred place, hallowed by the blood of Jesus, sweat in agonizing drops from every pore—to the palace of Annas—an evil, wicked, adulterous Jew—Jesus was taken, bound and subservient, by the Roman soldiers and the temple guards. The alien power

141

and the Jewish rulers were placing the Judge of all the earth into the custody of wicked men to be judged by an evil and apostate court system.

The account of the false and blasphemous travesty that swept him from Annas to Caiaphas to Pilate to Herod and back to Pilate is preserved for us by all four of the Evangelists. Each Gospel recitation is fragmentary; each supplements the others; and from them all we gain such a vision of the sad happenings of that doleful night and day as a divine providence has seen fit to preserve for us. That there are gaps and discrepancies in the account, which cause reputable scholars to disagree on the details of the trials, is of no moment. There is no divine *ipse dixit,* no voice from an archangel, and as yet no revealed latter-day account of all that transpired when God's own Son suffered himself to be judged by men so that he could voluntarily give up his life upon the cross. Needless to say, however, the overall picture that we shall paint—allowing for divergence of views as to details—is true, eternally true. Jesus was judged of men that the scriptures might be fulfilled, that the atonement might be completed, that immortality might pass upon all men, and that the saints of the Most High might be inheritors of eternal life in the Everlasting Presence.[1] We shall draw freely upon the words and phrases of some of Christianity's ablest apologists as we recite what happened, and—what is equally important— seek to *feel* the ignominy and the victory interlaced with the balance of the life of Him of whom we testify.

Jesus was subjected to three Jewish trials. The first, before Annas, though unofficial in the strict sense, was the one that assured the ultimate Roman-imposed penalty of death. It was the crowning act of conspiratorial evil; the authoritative prejudging of him who, according to their law, should have been presumed to be innocent. It was the practical trial; the one before the *de facto* high priest; before the recognized source of Jewish power; before the one who wielded the real power of the Jewish people.

The second trial, before Caiaphas, though involved primarily with preliminary questioning, was the occasion when the real or formal determination was made that the Guiltless One, the Sinless One, was worthy of death. And the third trial, before the Sanhedrin, constituted a ratification of the illegal procedures before Annas and Caiaphas; in it the formal decision was pronounced; strictly speaking it was the only real and legal trial, though, as we shall see, it too violated almost every basic and established rule, order, and law set down for Sanhedrinic operation.

As to the trial before Annas, a brief comment about him and his influence in the Jewish social structure will show why the cunning conspirators would choose first to take Jesus before his bar. Under his guidance Caiaphas and the whole Sanhedrin would nod, almost as a reflex action, a firm approval of the plot that would only succeed when Jesus' body lay in the grave.

Who was Annas, as he is called by the Evangelists? He was the best known, one of the wealthiest, and certainly the most influential Jew of his day; and if wickedness be measured by evil opposition to the truth and by a desire to shed innocent blood, he ranks with Judas among the abominable of the earth. He was Hanan, the son of Seth, the Ananus of Josephus. He had been the actual high priest for some seven years, and since being deposed by the Procurator Valerius Gratus, he had been the power behind the priestly throne. In his degenerate day, when the high priests were appointed and deposed by Gentile overlords; when the office was more of a political than a religious one; when, in spite of the general moral decay, the office did require "a certain amount of external dignity and self-denial which some men would only tolerate for a time" (Farrar, p. 639)—under these circumstances, to appoint and control a high priest was greater and more to be desired than to be one.

"The Jewish historian calls this Hanan the happiest man of his time, because he died at an advanced old age, and because both he and five of his sons in succession—not to mention his son-in-law [and a grandson]—had enjoyed the shadow of the High Priesthood; so that, in fact, for nearly half a century he had practically wielded the sacerdotal power. But to be admired by such a renegade as Josephus is a questionable advantage. In spite of his prosperity Hanan seems to have left behind him but an evil name, and we know enough of his character, even from the most unsuspected sources, to recognize in him nothing better than an astute, tyrannous, worldly Sadducee, unvenerable for all his seventy years, full of a serpentine malice and meanness which utterly belied the meaning of his name [Clement or merciful], and engaged at this very moment in a dark, disorderly conspiracy, for which even a worse man would have had cause to blush. It was before this alien and intriguing hierarch that there began, at midnight, the first stage of that long and terrible inquisition. . . .

"If there were one man who was more guilty than any other of the death of Jesus, that man was Hanan. His advanced age, his preponderant dignity, his worldly position and influence, as one who stood on the best terms with the Herods and the Procurators, gave an exceptional weight to his prerogative decision. . . . If we may believe not a few of the indications of the Talmud, that Sanhedrin was little better than a close, irreligious, unpatriotic confederacy of monopolizing and time-serving priests—the Boethusim, the Kamhits, the Phabis, the family of Hanan, mostly of non-Palestinian origin—who were supported by the government, but detested by the people, and of whom this bad conspirator was the very life and soul." (Farrar, pp. 639–41. Italics added.)[2]

We can see on every hand reasons why the scribes and Pharisees would seek the death of Jesus. From the beginning of his ministry, day in and day out, in one setting after another, it had been his unvarying practice to deride and defame their cherished Mosaic traditions and to hurl bolts of divine wrath upon them for their ignorance and selfish self-exultation. We can scarcely count the times he has called them hypocrites, liars, adulterers, a generation of vipers, a people fit only for the burning fires of Gehenna. In much of this anathema the Sadducees took secret delight, for they too ignored the strict formalities of the law, and could not have been other than gratified to see both their scribal and their Pharisaic foes repeatedly routed by this rustic Galilean and his Rabbinically unschooled friends.

But why the Saducean rage against him? Why did Judas and the temple guards make sure Jesus was delivered into Sadducean hands to be tried by a Sadducean Sanhedrin? Why would anyone who felt the pulse of the people know that Annas would lead out in opposition to Jesus?

We cannot doubt that the underlying reason for the rebellion of all sects, parties, and groups—the Sadducees included—was religious. Though as sects they fought among themselves, their one common point of agreement was opposition to Jesus. But there was something more. To the Sadducees, Jesus was an economic threat. Their crafts were in danger. He was destroying the thriving business enterprises that poured the wealth of the world into their rapacious pockets. We cannot escape the conclusion that "the rage of these priests was mainly [or, at least, in large measure] due to our Lord's words and acts concerning that House of God which they regarded as their exclusive domain, and, above all, to His second public cleansing of the Temple. . . . The first cleansing might have been passed over as an isolated act of zeal, to which little importance need be attached, while the teaching of Jesus was mainly confined to despised and far-off Galilee; but the second had been more public, and more vehement, and had apparently kindled a more general indignation against the gross abuse which called it forth. Accordingly, in all three Evangelists we find that those who complained of the act are not distinctively Pharisees, but 'Chief Priests and Scribes,' who seem at once to have derived from it a fresh stimulus to seek His destruction.

"But, again, it may be asked, Is there any reason beyond this bold infraction of their authority, this indignant repudiation of an arrangement which *they* had sanctioned, which would have stirred up the rage of these priestly families? Yes—for we may assume from the Talmud that it tended *to wound their avarice, to interfere with their illicit and greedy gains*. Avarice—the besetting sin of Judas—the besetting sin of the Jewish race—seems also to have been the besetting sin of the family of Hanan. It was they who had founded the *chanujoth*—the famous four shops under the twin cedars of Olivet—in which were sold things legally pure, and which they had manipulated with such commercial cunning as artificially to raise the price of doves to a gold coin apiece, until the people were delivered from this gross imposition by the indignant interference of a grandson of Hillel. There is every reason to believe that the shops which had intruded even under the Temple porticoes were not only sanctioned by their authority, but even managed for their profit. To interfere with these was to rob them of one important source of that wealth and worldly comfort to which they attached such extravagant importance. There was good reason why Hanan, the head representative of 'the viper brood,' as a Talmudic writer calls them, should strain to the utmost his cruel prerogative of power to crush a Prophet whose actions tended to make him and his powerful family at once wholly contemptible and comparatively poor." (Farrar, pp. 641–42.)

Thus Jesus is hailed before a gold-bloated usurper, who exercises the power of an office he does not hold, and who has already determined what judgment should be rendered. Jesus had been arrested at night and on the testimony of an accomplice, both of which acts were illegal under Jewish law. Now he is before Annas—who is sitting as a sole judge, and it is still night, both of which conditions make the hearing itself illegal. Though he has been arrested, there is as yet no charge lodged against him. Annas, therefore, questions him about two things: his disciples and his doctrine. Perhaps some charge of sedition can be lodged against his followers; perhaps there is some doctrinal statement that can be construed as false or blasphemous. As far as the record goes, Jesus ignored the attempt to involve his followers; he, not they, was to suffer and die at this time; their day of martyrdom lay ahead. As to the doctrinal inquisition, he said: "I spake openly to the world; I ever taught in the synagogue, and in the temple, whither the Jews always resort; and in secret have I said nothing. Why askest thou me? ask them which heard me, what I have said unto them: behold, they know what I said." Such a reply by the Prisoner was proper; he was entitled to be confronted by his accusers; there was nothing for him to confess; if they wanted to try him, let them present their case. "Even the minions of Annas felt the false position of their master under this calm rebuke; they felt that before the transparent innocence of this youthful Rabbi of Nazareth the hypocrisy of the hoary Sadducee was abashed. 'Answerest thou the High Priest so?' said one of them with a burst of illegal insolence; and then, unreproved by this priestly violator of justice, he profaned with the first infamous blow the sacred face of Christ. Then first that face which, as the poet-preacher says, 'the angels stare upon with wonder as infants at a bright sunbeam,' was smitten by a contemptible slave." (Farrar, p. 643.) Jesus answered simply: "If I have spoken evil, bear witness of the evil: but if well, why smitest thou me?"[3]

Jesus before Caiaphas and the Council
(Matthew 26:57-66; JST, Matthew 26:59-61, 67; Mark 14:53-64; JST, Mark 14:65; Luke 22:54; John 18:24)

Joseph Caiaphas, the legal high priest—the son-in-law of that evil and avaricious Annas, and himself also of like nature and disposition—was the next Jewish ruler to hurl his anathematizing curse upon the Son of God. He was, John says, "the high priest that same year," which we cannot do other than accept as an ironical slur against the apostate system under which the life-long office of high priest was passed around among the family of Annas, as though they were designating which steward should care for their interests for the year.

"Now Caiaphas was he"—as John is also careful to mention at this point—"which gave counsel to the Jews, that it was expedient that one man should die for the people." (John 18:14.) As we are aware, this counsel of Caiaphas was a prophetic utterance. God had used him as he used Baalam's ass to proclaim a message to his people, and that message did not carry the meaning and intent that was in the evil heart of the wicked man whose tongue was then guided in what he said. With reference to Jesus' work and miracles, other members of the Supreme Council had then said: "If we let him thus alone, all men will believe on him: and the Romans shall come and take away both our place and nation." Intending to concur with this view and seeking to incite bitterness against Jesus, Caiaphas had then said: "Ye know nothing at all, Nor consider that it is expedient for us, that one man should die for the people, and that the whole nation perish not." Thus he "had been the first to enunciate in plain words what seemed to him *the political necessity for the judicial murder of Christ*. There had been no pretense on his part of religious motives or zeal for God; he had cynically put it in a way to override the scruples of those old Sanhedrists by raising their fears. What was the use of discussing about forms of Law or about that Man? it must in any case be done; even the friends of Jesus in the Council, as well as the punctilious observers of [the] Law, *must regard His Death as the less of two evils*. He spoke as the bold, unscrupulous, determined man that he was; Sadducee in heart rather than by conviction: a worthy son-in-law of Annas." (Edersheim 2:546. Italics added.) But a divine power decreed other-

wise, and his words—John says "he prophesied"—became an announcement that Jesus would die as the Deliverer of the Jews, "And not for that nation only, but that
also he should gather together in one the children of God
that were scattered abroad." (John 11:49-52.) That, like
Baalam's ass, Caiaphas knew no more after the divine
word fell from his lips than he did before is evident from the
course he is now pursuing. He is still bent on finding a way
to bring death to Him by whom life comes.

Having failed to elicit any incriminating evidence
against Jesus, Annas "sent him"—not "had sent," as a
poor biblical translation has it, but "sent him bound unto
Caiaphas the high priest."[4] And it stretches the bounds of
credulity to suppose that Annas himself remained aloof
from the continuing inquisition; certain it is that he went
with the guards and their prisoner, that he might add his
influence and prestige and be a personal witness of the
hoped-for triumph over his enemy. The leading elders,
scribes, and chief priests—alerted as they were that Jesus
would be arrested that night—were already assembled; and
Peter and John, having overcome the first flush of panic
that swept over them in Gethsemane, were also present as
sorrowing observers.

There, in the palace of Caiaphas, then "took place the
second private and irregular stage of the trial. There—for
though the poor Apostles could not watch for one hour in
sympathetic prayer, these nefarious plotters could watch
all night in their deadly malice—a few of the most desperate enemies of Jesus among the Priests and Sadducees were
met." (Farrar, pp. 643–44.) At least twenty-three members
of the Great Sanhedrin were present, the number required
for a quorum, for both Matthew and Mark call the meeting
one of the council which is the Sanhedrin.

They had before them a prisoner charged with no crime.
Innocent of all crimes, as he was, even these conspiring
Satanists had not been able to come up with an offense for
which he could be arraigned. Annas had failed in his at-

tempt to charge the disciples with sedition and Jesus with teaching false and apostate doctrines. Their dilemma was real, for they themselves were sharply divided on all major issues save one—that the man Jesus must die. "If they dwelt on any supposed opposition to civil authority, *that* would rather enlist the sympathies of the Pharisees in His favour; if they dwelt on supposed Sabbath violations or the neglect of traditional observances, that would accord with the views of the Sadducees. The Sadducees dared not complain of His cleansing of the Temple: the Pharisees, or those who represented them, found it useless to advert to His denunciations of tradition. But Jesus, infinitely nobler than His own noblest Apostle, would not foment these latent animosities, or evoke for His own deliverance a contest of these slumbering prejudices. He did not disturb the temporary compromise which united them in a common hatred against Himself." (Farrar, pp. 645–46.)

Since a charge must be lodged to justify Jesus' arrest, since they themselves were not sufficiently united to bring up any of their old doctrinal objections, and since the charge must be one that the Romans would consider to be a capital offense, "the chief priests, and elders, and all the council" (after counseling with Satan whose servants they were) chose the most evil of all possible courses. They "sought false witness"!

Read it again, for it is forever inscribed in the records of eternity—they sought not witnesses, but *false witnesses.* Let none come forward but those who will perjure their souls; who will condemn the Holy One and the Just; who will cry, 'Away with him. Crucify him, crucify him.' No voice must be raised in his defense; no lie must be refuted; no falsehood shall be denied. This is God's Son (oh, the shame of it all!) and the leaders of his own people—acting for their constituents; reflecting the feelings that smoldered like the fires of hell in the breasts of all recalcitrant Jewry of the time—these leaders "sought false witness against Jesus, to put him to death." He must not live; let him die the death, and whatever perjured word is needed to nail him to a Roman cross, so be it!

Nor was it difficult to find those to whom Jehovah's word spoken to Moses the man of God, amid the fires and thunders of Sinai—"Thou shalt not bear false witness against thy neighbour" (Ex. 20:16)—was as alien gibberish. Search was made only among the rabble who followed the arresting party, who followed in the hopes of seeing one whom they hated suffer an ignominious death. And "though many false witnesses came," Matthew says, "they found none that could accuse him." None could devise a charge that would stand up before the Roman law. "For many bare false witness against him," as Mark records it, "but their witness agreed not together." "Though the agents of these priests were eager to lie, yet their testimony was *so* false, so shadowy, so self-contradictory, that it all melted to nothing, and even those unjust and bitter judges could not with any decency accept it." (Farrar, p. 646.)

Finally, "there arose certain"—meaning, apparently, that there arose some from among their own number; from among the priests themselves; from among those who were present when Jesus first cleansed the temple—"there arose certain" to "bear false witness against him" that would cause Roman ears to listen. It will be remembered that on the occasion of the first Passover, Jesus drove from the temple the moneychangers and those who sold oxen and sheep and doves; that he thus made a shamble of the bazaars of the sons of Annas; and that when asked for a sign as to his authority for so doing, he told them that if they would destroy the temple of his body, he would raise it up again in three days. There was to be no sign given to that wicked and adulterous generation except the sign of the prophet Jonas, the sign of his resurrection. Now, three years later, his words are to be twisted and perverted by false witnesses. We suppose Annas and Caiaphas, who suffered financially on the first purgation of Jehovah's house, were the ones who now saw the possibility of using what Jesus then said as a basis for a criminal charge against him.

The perjured words of the false priests included such statements as, "We heard him say, I will destroy this temple that is made with hands, and within three days I will build another made without hands." That there were other perversions of his word is clear from Mark's conclusion, "But neither so did their witness agree together." This charge that Jesus would first destroy and then rebuild, in three days, the most magnificent building of their age; that stone for stone he would put back together, in three days, what had been under construction for forty-six years, and was far from finished; that in a moment of time, as it were, he would bring into being what thousands of workers had spent scores of years to build—this fantastic claim (which he had never made) would indicate to the Romans that he was a dangerous seducer of the people with magical pretensions. He thus would be one who would rally the people around him in a revolt that would destroy the peace of the land. And, be it remembered, "The purpose of the High-Priest was not to formulate a capital charge in *Jewish* Law, since the assembled Sanhedrists had no intention so to try Jesus, but to formulate a charge which would tell before the Roman Procurator. And here none other could be so effective as that of being a fanatical seducer of the ignorant populace, who might lead them on to wild tumultuous acts." (Edersheim 2:559.)

Through all this "Jesus listened in silence while His disunited enemies hopelessly confuted each other's testimony. . . . But that majestic silence troubled, thwarted, confounded, maddened them. It weighed them down for the moment with an incubus of intolerable self-condemnation. They felt, before that silence, as if *they* were the culprits, He the judge. And as every poisoned arrow of their carefully-provided perjuries fell harmless at His feet, as though blunted on the diamond shield of His white

152

innocence, they began to fear lest, after all, their thirst for His blood would go unslaked, and their whole plot fail. Were they thus to be conquered by the feebleness of their own weapons, without His stirring a finger, or uttering a word? Was this Prophet of Nazareth to prevail against *them,* merely for lack of a few consistent lies? Was His life charmed even against calumny confirmed by oaths? It was intolerable.

"Then Caiaphas was overcome with a paroxysm of fear and anger. Starting up from his judgment-seat, and striding into the midst—with what a voice, with what an attitude we may well imagine!"—he would set this court proceeding on its proper course. Their own false witnesses—carefully selected, screened, and coached, that their every word would be dipped in the poison of death—their own appointed perjurers, though they skirted the truth and gave a devilish twist to what Jesus had said—they, nonetheless, could arouse no response from Him who had spoken only the truth; the lips of innocence were closed against their calumnies. But Caiaphas himself would hurl the question: "Answerest thou nothing?" How can a man be silent when, knowing his life is at stake, he hears others lie about him? "Knowest thou what these witness against thee?" 'Their false words will cost thee thy life, and yet thou sayest nothing.' "Had not Jesus been aware that these His judges were wilfully feeding on ashes and seeking lies, He might have answered; but now His awful silence remained unbroken.

"Then, reduced to utter despair and fury, this false High Priest—with marvellous inconsistency, with disgraceful illegality—still standing as it were with a threatening attitude over his prisoner, exclaimed, 'I adjure Thee by the living God to tell us'—what? whether Thou art a malefactor? whether Thou *hast* secretly taught sedition? whether Thou hast openly uttered blasphemy?—no, but (and surely the question showed the dread misgiving which lay under all their deadly conspiracy against Him)—'WHETHER THOU

ART THE CHRIST, THE SON OF GOD?' " (Farrar, pp. 646–47.)

How intense was the hatred of that hour! How many unseen demons must have laughed in the background as the legal high priest in Israel, speaking in Jehovah's name, adjured Jehovah himself to proclaim his own divine Sonship! No doubt the prince of devils himself was there; what is more natural than to expect the master of all evil to come face to face with Him that is the embodiment of all that is good? "Tell us whether thou be the Christ, the Son of God!" Suppose, just suppose he was, what then of Caiaphas, and the Sanhedrin, and the Jewish nation? Would they be buffeted and scattered and scourged and hated of all men until the times of restitution?

"Strange question to a bound, defenceless, condemned criminal; and strange question from such a questioner—a High Priest of His people! Strange question from the judge who was hounding on his false witnesses against the prisoner! Yet so adjured, and to such a question, Jesus could not be silent; on such a point He could not leave Himself open to misinterpretation. In the days of His happier ministry, when they would have taken Him by force to make Him a King—in the days when to claim the Messiahship in *their* sense would have been to meet all their passionate prejudices half way, and to place himself upon the topmost pinnacle of their adoring homage—in *those* days He had kept His title of Messiah utterly in the background: but now, at this awful decisive moment, when death was near—when, humanly speaking, nothing could be gained, everything *must* be lost, by the avowal—there thrilled through all the ages—thrilled through that Eternity, which is the synchronism of all the future, and all the present, and all the past—the solemn answer, 'I AM: *and ye shall see the Son of Man sitting on the right hand of power, and coming in the clouds of heaven.*' " (Farrar, pp. 647–48.)

'Art thou the Messiah? Art thou the Son of God?' 'I AM; I AM THAT I AM: I am the Eternal One; I am the Lord Jehovah; I am Jesus Christ the Son of the living God; I am the Son of that Holy Man who is your Father in heaven. Ye shall reject me now and do with me as ye will; but I shall come again, in all the glory of my Father's kingdom. Then shall ye see me sitting on the right hand of power, and coming in the clouds of heaven; then shall ye know that I am he of whom Moses and all the prophets spake. I am the Christ. I am the Son of God.'

"In that answer the thunder rolled—a thunder louder than at Sinai, though the ears of the cynic and the Sadducee heard it not then, nor hear it now. In overacted and ill-omened horror, the unjust judge who had thus supplemented the failure of the perjuries which he had vainly sought—the false High Priest rending his linen robes before the True [High Priest]—demanded of the assembly His instant condemnation.

" 'BLASPHEMY!' he exclaimed; 'what further need have we of witnesses? See, *now* ye *heard* his blasphemy! What is your decision?' And with the confused tumultuous cry, 'He is *ish maveth,*' 'A man of death,' 'Guilty of death,' the dark conclave was broken up, and the second stage of the trial of Jesus was over." (Farrar, p. 648.)

"He is guilty of death." Thus saith the Sanhedrin.

"And they all condemned him to be guilty of death." Thus saith the Sanhedrin.

We do not say this was a sentence of death, for the Sanhedrin had no such power in that day. Rather, it was their heartfelt, devil-inspired pronouncement: 'He is *worthy* of death; he *ought* to die, according to our law, for he is a blasphemer.' "And yet is it not after all true—that He was either the Christ, the Son of God, or a blasphemer? This Man, alone so calm and majestic among those impassioned false judges and false witnesses; majestic in His silence, majestic in His speech; unmoved by threats to speak, undaunted by threats when He spoke; Who saw it all—the end from the beginning; the Judge among His judges, the Witness before His witnesses: which was He—the Christ or a blaspheming imposter? Let history decide; let the heart and conscience of mankind give answer. If He had been what Israel said, He deserved the death of the Cross; if He is what the Christmas-bells of the Church, and the chimes of the Resurrection-morning ring out, then do we rightly worship Him as the Son of the Living God, the Christ, the Saviour of men." (Edersheim 2:561–62.)

Yea, and let more than history record; let more than the heart and conscience of mankind speak out—for though history turn into myth and legend, and though the conscience of mankind be seared with a hot iron, yet He remains true and faithful. Let the answer then come from the lips of those to whom he has revealed himself anew in the latter days. We are they, and we say: He is God's Son, the true Messiah; he spake no blasphemy; and all who would live and reign with him and his Father must believe the witness he bore of himself. He is the Son of God.

NOTES

1. Along this line Farrar testifies: "After repeated study, I declare, quite fearlessly, that though the slight variations are numerous—though the lesser particulars cannot in every instance be rigidly and minutely accurate—though no one of the narratives taken singly would give us an adequate impression—yet, so far from their being, in this part of the Gospel story, any irreconcilable contradiction, we can see how one Evangelist supplements the details furnished by another, and can understand the true sequence of the incidents by combining into one whole the separate indications which they furnish. It is easy to call such combinations arbitrary and baseless; but they are only arbitrary in so far as we cannot always be absolutely *certain* that the succession of facts was exactly such as we suppose; and so far are they from being baseless, that, to the careful reader of the Gospels, they carry with them a conviction little short of certainty. If we treat the Gospels as we should treat any other authentic documents recording all that the authors know, or all that they felt themselves commissioned to record, of the crowded incidents in one terrible and tumultuous day and night, we shall, with care and study, see how all that they tell us falls accurately into its proper position in the general narrative, and shows us a sixfold trial, a quadruple derision, a triple acquittal, a twice-repeated condemnation of Christ our Lord." (Farrar, p. 637.)

2. "No figure is better known in contemporary Jewish history than that of Annas; no person deemed more fortunate or successful, but none also more generally execrated than the late High-Priest. He had held the Pontificate for only six or seven years; but it was filled by not fewer than five of his sons, by his son-in-law Caiaphas, and by a grandson. And in those days it was, at least for one of Annas' disposition, much better to have been than to be the High-Priest. He enjoyed all the dignity of the office, and all of its influence also, since he was able to promote to it those most closely connected with him. And, while they acted publicly, he really directed affairs, without either the responsibility or the restraints which the office imposed. His influence with the Romans he owed to the religious views which he professed, to his open partisanship of the foreigner, and to his

enormous wealth. The Sadducean Annas was an eminently safe Churchman, not troubled with any special convictions nor with Jewish fanaticism, a pleasant and a useful man also, who was able to furnish his friends in the Praetorium with large sums of money. We have seen what immense revenues the family of Annas must have derived from the Temple-booths, and how nefarious and unpopular was the traffic. The names of those bold, licentious, unscrupulous, degenerate sons of Aaron were spoken with whispered curses. Without referring to Christ's interference with that Temple-traffic, which, if His authority had prevailed, would, of course, have been fatal to it, we can understand how antithetic in every respect a Messiah, and such a Messiah as Jesus, must have been to Annas. He was as resolutely bent on His death as his son-in-law, though with his characteristic cunning and coolness, not in the hasty, bluff manner of Caiaphas. It was probably from a desire that Annas might have the conduct of the business, or from the active, leading part which Annas took in the matter, . . . [and] that it was desirable to dismiss the Roman soldiery as quickly as possible—that Christ was first brought to Annas, and not to the actual High-Priest." (Edersheim 2:547.)

3. Our King James Version says the officer struck Jesus "with the palm of his hand." The Revised Version says "with a rod." Edersheim comments and speculates: "We are almost thankful that the text leaves it in doubt, whether it was with the palm of the hand, or the lesser indignity—with a rod. Humanity itself seems to reel and stagger under this blow. In pursuance of His Human submission, the Divine Sufferer, without murmuring or complaining, or without asserting His Divine Power, only answered in such tone of patient expostulation as must have convicted the man of his wrong, or at least have left him speechless. May it have been that these words and the look of Christ had gone to his heart, and that the now strangely-silenced malefactor became the confessing narrator of this scene to the Apostle John?" (Edersheim 2:550.)

4. This change in a verb tense in John 18:24 is one of the reasons we know there was a separate examination before Annas, the high priest in fact, before Jesus was taken to Caiaphas, the titular high priest.

Chapter 104

THE FORMAL JEWISH TRIAL

I gave my back to the smiters,
and my cheeks to them
that plucked off the hair:
I hid not my face from shame and spitting.
(Isa. 50:6.)
It pleased the Lord to bruise him;
he hath put him to grief.
(Isa. 53:10.)

They Maltreat Jesus
(Matthew 26:67-68; Mark 14:65; Luke 22:63-65)

Annas and Caiaphas had done their work well. As the high priests in Israel—one the real, the other the titular high priest—they had guided the Sadducean-dominated Sanhedrin, representative of the hosts of the people, to find Jesus guilty of blasphemy because he said he was the Son of God. And the garments of Caiaphas had been rent in everlasting witness that the blasphemer before them was worthy of death. They had spoken; the council had spoken; and through them, as the representative leaders of all Jewry, the whole nation had spoken; the collective judgment of the Jews (though yet to be formally ratified) had nonetheless been given. "And this was how the Jews at last received their promised Messiah—longed for with passion-

158

ate hopes during two thousand years; since then regretted in bitter agony for well-nigh two thousand more! From this moment He was regarded by all the apparitors of the Jewish Court as a heretic, liable to death by stoning; and was only remanded into custody to be kept till break of day, because by daylight only, and in the *Lishcat Haggazzith,* or Hall of Judgment, and only by a full session of the entire Sanhedrin, could He be legally condemned. And since now they looked upon Him as a fit person to be insulted with impunity, He was haled through the court-yard to the guard-room with blows and curses, in which it may be that not only the attendant menials, but even the cold but now infuriated Sadducees took their share."[1]

Then, "in the guard-room to which He was remanded to await the break of day"—or in whatever place his captors kept their prisoner—"all the ignorant malice of religious hatred, all the narrow vulgarity of brutal spite, all the cold innate cruelty which lurks under the abjectness of Oriental servility, was let loose against Him. His very meekness, His very silence, His very majesty—the very stainlessness of His innocence, the very grandeur of His fame—every divine circumstance and quality which raised Him to a height so infinitely immeasurable above His persecutors—all these made Him an all the more welcome victim for their low and devilish ferocity. They spat in His face; they smote Him with rods; they struck Him with their closed fists and with their open palms. In the fertility of their furious and hateful insolence, they invented against Him a sort of game. Covering His eyes, they hit Him again and again, with the repeated question, 'Prophesy to us, O Messiah, who it is that smote thee.' So they wiled away the dark cold hours till the morning, revenging themselves upon His impassive innocence for their own present vileness and previous terror; and there, in the midst of that savage and wanton varletry, the Son of God, bound and blindfold, stood in His long and silent agony, defenceless and alone. It was His first derision—His derision as the

Christ, the Judge attainted, the Holy One a criminal, the Deliverer in bonds." (Farrar, p. 654.)

This night, as time seemed to stand still, the prince of devils worked his will through those mortal devils who submitted their wills to his. It seems clear enough that among those degenerate humans who so reveled in their base and evil sport were members of the Sanhedrin itself. Matthew records that the members of that council said, "He is guilty of death," and his very next words are: "Then did *they* spit in his face, and buffeted him; and *others* smote him with the palms of their hands." That is, the members of the Great Council, the legal lights and leaders of the people, spurted their foul spittle into the face of their Messiah, while others, their servants and menials, struck him with physical force. Mark also seems to differentiate between those who did the spitting and the buffeting and "the servants" who did the striking. Luke speaks as though the soldiers—"the men that held Jesus"—were the ones who mocked and smote him. This truly was their hour, and they were enveloped in darkness!

Peter Denies Knowing Who Jesus Is
(Matthew 26:69-75; Mark 14:66-72; JST, Mark 14:81-82; Luke 22:55-62; John 18:15-18, 25-27)

Peter and John—blessed brethren of infinite valor and faith—recovering quickly (sooner than any of the other apostles) from that panic which swept over them in Gethsemane, set out to follow Jesus and the soldiers who held him bound. One or both of them may have been present when Annas began the Jewish inquisition that was designed to find a legal reason to slay the man whose death was already a foregone conclusion in their minds. We know that both were present at the palace of Caiaphas. John was known to the high priest, and apparently to his servants; he gained ready admittance. "Peter stood at the door without," unable to gain entrance; strict security measures were in force on this evil night, for one of the followers of

Jesus, with a flashing sword, had, in Gethsemane, already slashed off the ear of Malchus; there must be no further dissension or uproar. But John, apparently not without some influence in high places, went out and persuaded the portress who kept the gate, and who also must have known him, to admit his fellow apostle.

John hastened into the palace where Jesus stood arraigned before the Sanhedrin, or such portion of it as was assembled at this dread hour; Peter, discreetly or of necessity, remained in the hall or courtyard where he mingled with the servants and court followers and warmed himself over a coal fire. As Peter sat among these rowdies and malcontents, listening to the accounts of the arrest and hearing the predictions of what lay ahead for his Master, the damsel who had admitted him realized who he was. "Art not thou also one of this man's disciples?" she first asked. He replied, "I am not." She persisted: "Thou also wast with Jesus of Nazareth." To the others present she said, "This man was also with him." But Peter continued to disassociate himself from his Lord. "I know not, neither understand I what thou sayest," he affirmed. And also: "Woman, I know him not." Disconcerted by this challenge to his presence, Peter left the fire, "And he went out into the porch; and the cock crew."

While Peter was out on the porch, another maid—perhaps a replacement for the portress who had admitted him—said to those there assembled: "This fellow was also with Jesus of Nazareth." Again Peter denied, this time with an oath, saying, "I do not know the man." A man standing by agreed with the maid and said, "Thou art also of them." Peter said, "Man, I am not." All of this, as nearly as we can tell, may be counted the second denial.

About an hour then elapsed—such quite likely being the time during which Caiaphas held his hearing and issued his blasphemous adjuration—and it appears that Peter was back, standing beside the fire, warming himself with the others, for it was cold. One of those who stood by them said, "Surely thou also art one of them; for thy speech bewrayeth thee," as Matthew has it; or: "Surely thou art one of them: for thou art a Galilean, and thy speech agreeth thereto," as Mark has it; or: "Of a truth this fellow also was with him: for he is a Galilean," as Luke has it. Or, as John's account says, "Art not thou also one of his disciples?" to which he said, "I am not." At this point a kinsman of Malchus recognized Peter and said, "Did not I see thee in the garden with him?" To all of this came firm denials. Peter cursed and swore with an oath, "I know not the man." Also: "I know not this man of whom ye speak." And: "Man, I know not what thou sayest." All this may be accounted the third denial. And immediately, for the second time, the cock crew.

At this point, "the Lord turned, and looked upon Peter." Peter then remembered the prophecy, "Before the cock crow twice, thou shalt deny me thrice." Then he went out and wept bitterly.

Such is the sparsely worded account of Peter's so-called denial of his Lord, a denial that was rather a failure to stand up and testify of the divine Sonship when an occasion afforded than a denial of any divinity resident in the Son of Man.[2]

Two eloquent passages deserve preservation in our present record, for both help us to *feel* as well as to *know* what happened in Peter's life this night.

"The Lord in the agony of His humiliation, in the majesty of His silence—'*the Lord turned and looked upon Peter.*' Blessed are those on whom, when He looks in sorrow, the Lord also looks with love! It was enough. Like an arrow through his inmost soul, shot the mute eloquent anguish of that reproachful glance. As the sunbeam smites the last hold of snow upon the rock, ere it rushes in avalanche down the tormented hill, so the false self of the fallen Apostle slipped away. It was enough: 'he saw no more enemies, he knew no more danger, he feared no more

162

death.' Flinging the fold of his mantle over his head, he too, like Judas, rushed forth into the night. Into the night, but not as Judas; into the unsunned outer darkness of miserable self-condemnation, but not into the midnight of remorse and of despair; into the night, but, as has been beautifully said, it was 'to meet the morning dawn.' If the angel of Innocence had left him, the angel of Repentance took him gently by the hand. Sternly, yet tenderly, the spirit of grace led up this broken-hearted penitent before the tribunal of his own conscience, and there his old life, his old shame, his old weakness, his old self was doomed to that death of godly sorrow which was to issue in a new and spiritual birth." (Farrar, pp. 653–54.)

"The Lord turned round and looked upon him—yes, in all that assembly, upon Peter! His eyes spake His Words; nay, much more; they searched down to the innermost depths of Peter's heart, and broke them open. They had pierced through all self-delusion, false shame, and fear: they had reached the man, the disciple, the lover of Jesus. Forth they burst, the waters of conviction, of true shame, of heart-sorrow, of the agonies of self-condemnation; and, bitterly weeping, he rushed from under those suns that had melted the ice of death and burnt into his heart—out from that cursed place of betrayal by Israel, by its High Priest—and even by the representative Disciple.

"Out he rushed into the night. Yet a night lit up by the stars of promise—chiefest among them this, that the Christ up there—the conquering Sufferer—had prayed for him. God grant us in the night of our conscious self-condemnation the same star-light of His Promises, the same assurance of the intercession of the Christ, that so, as Luther puts it, the particularness of the account of Peter's denial, as compared with the briefness of that of Christ's Passion, may carry to our hearts this lesson: 'The fruit and use of the sufferings of Christ is this, that in them we have the forgiveness of our sins.' " (Edersheim 2:564.)

Jesus before the Sanhedrin
(Luke 22:66-71; 23:1; Matthew 27:1-2; Mark 15:1; JST, Mark 15:1-2)

"Gather unto me seventy men of the elders of Israel, whom thou knowest to be the elders of the people, and officers over them," the Lord commanded Moses, "and they shall bear the burden of the people with thee, that thou bear it not thyself alone." (Num. 11:16-17.) Thus was the Lord's system of government perfected in ancient Israel. Moses served as the prophet, seer, and revelator; at his side were "the princes of Israel," twelve in number, comparable to the Twelve Apostles, one of whom presided over each of the tribes (Num. 7); then came the Seventy—holy and noble men who also sat in judgment and regulated the affairs of the people. And a millennium and a half later, the Jews still maintained the form of their ancient order; the Great Sanhedrin—either patterned after or descended from the Quorum of Seventy called by Moses—still attempted to rule over the people. Albeit, to their sorrow, those of whom it was composed in time's meridian were no longer the spiritual giants who were qualified to go up into the Holy Mount and see "the God of Israel," as had been their predecessors in office. (Ex. 24:9-11.)

At the time the Great Sanhedrin, in its apostate and fallen state, chose to seek out and sit in judgment on that God who himself had called their predecessors, the tribunal was composed of seventy-one persons. Their traditional meeting place had been in one of the temple chambers—the *Lishkath haGazith* (*Lishcat Haggazzith*) or Chamber of Hewn Stones—but now it was common for them to meet in the merchandising booths of the sons of Annas. Their members were ordained and set apart by the laying on of hands, and twenty-three of their number constituted a quorum for the transaction of business. There is some confusion and uncertainty as to the powers and place of the Sanhedrin in that day; probably these varied from year to year depending upon the political climate. The council, as a stabilizing influence, operated with Roman approval and the Procurator appointed the high priests. Its authority was limited to religious matters, and it did not have the power to inflict the death penalty, though in fact the Roman authorities seemed to overlook some judicial murders made on religious grounds. Stephen was convicted before the Sanhedrin on suborned testimony and suffered death by stoning. (Acts 6-7.) Paul would have been killed by act of the Council had he not been rescued by Roman soldiers. (Acts 23.) And the Jews, without reference to Rome, had sought on previous occasions to kill Jesus. (John 5:18; 7:25.)

But let us return to the Jewish trials of Jesus. Caiaphas and the Sanhedrin had "condemned him to be guilty of death." (Mark 14:64.) But—"The law and the practice of the time required that any person found guilty of a capital offense, after due trial before a Jewish tribunal, should be given a second trial on the following day; and at this later hearing any or all of the judges who had before voted for conviction could reverse themselves; but no one who had once voted for acquittal could change his ballot. A bare majority was sufficient for acquittal, but more than a majority [two more, in fact] was required for conviction. By a provision that must appear to us most unusual, if all the judges voted for conviction on a capital charge the verdict was not to stand and the accused had to be set at liberty; for, it was argued, a unanimous vote against a prisoner indicated that he had had no friend or defender in court, and that the judges might have been in conspiracy against Him. Under this rule in Hebrew jurisprudence the verdict against Jesus, rendered at the illegal night session of the Sanhedrists, was void, for we are specifically told that 'they all condemned him to be guilty of death.'

"Apparently for the purpose of establishing a shadowy pretext of legality in their procedure, the Sanhedrists adjourned to meet again in early daylight. Thus they techni-

165

cally complied with the requirement—that on every case in which the death sentence had been decreed the court should hear and judge a second time in a later session—but they completely ignored the equally mandatory provision that the second trial must be conducted on the day following that of the first hearing. Between the two sittings on consecutive days the judges were required to fast and pray, and to give the case on trial calm and earnest consideration." (Talmage, pp. 627–28.)[3]

And so the continued happenings of that doleful night were these: "At last the miserable lingering hours were over"—the hours before Annas and Caiaphas, during which he was derided, mocked, slapped, cursed, and showered with spittle—"and the grey dawn shuddered, and the morning blushed upon that memorable day. And with the earliest dawn, . . . the Sanhedrin had been summoned, for His third actual, but His first formal and legal trial. It was now probably about six o'clock in the morning, and a full session met. Well-nigh all—for there were the noble exceptions at least of Nicodemus and of Joseph of Arimathea, and we may hope also of Gamaliel, the grandson of Hillel—were inexorably bent upon His death. The Priests were there, whose greed and selfishness He had reproved; the Elders, whose hypocrisy He had branded; the Scribes, whose ignorance He had exposed; the worse than all, the worldly, skeptical, would-be philosophic Sadducees, always the most cruel and dangerous of opponents, whose empty sapience He had so grievously confuted. All these were bent upon His death; all filled with repulsion at that infinite goodness; all burning with hatred against a purer nature than any which they could even conceive in their loftiest dreams. And yet their task in trying to achieve his destruction was not easy. . . . The fact was that the Sanhedrists had not the power of inflicting death, and even if the Pharisees might have ventured to usurp it in a tumultuary sedition, as they afterwards did in the case of

Stephen, the less fanatic and more cosmopolitan Sadducees would be less likely to do so.

"Not content, therefore, with the *cherem,* or ban of greater excommunication, their only way to compass His death was to hand Him over to the secular arm. At present they had only against Him a charge of constructive blasphemy, founded on an admission forced from Him by the High Priest, when even their own suborned witnesses had failed to perjure themselves to their satisfaction. There were many old accusations against Him, on which they could not rely. His violations of the Sabbath, as they called them, were all connected with miracles, and brought them, therefore, upon dangerous ground. His rejection of oral tradition involved a question on which Sadducees and Pharisees were at deadly feud. His authoritative cleansing of the Temple might be regarded with favour both by the Rabbis and the people. The charge of esoteric evil doctrines had been refuted by the utter publicity of His life. The charge of open heresies had broken down, from the total absence of supporting testimony. The problem before them was to convert the ecclesiastical charge of constructive blasphemy into a civil charge of constructive treason. But how could this be done? Not half the members of the Sanhedrin had been present at the hurried, nocturnal, and therefore illegal, session in the house of Caiaphas; yet if they were all to condemn him by a formal sentence, they must all hear something on which to found their vote. In answer to the adjuration of Caiaphas, He had solemnly admitted that He was the Messiah and the Son of God. The latter declaration would have been meaningless as a charge against Him before the tribunal of the Romans; but if He would repeat the former, they might twist it into something politically seditious. But He would not repeat it, in spite of their insistence, because He knew that it was open to their wilful misinterpretation, and because they were evidently acting in flagrant violation of their own express rules and traditions, which demanded that every arraigned criminal should be regarded and treated as innocent until his guilt was actually proved." (Farrar, pp. 654–56.)

Thus Caiaphas, now before the whole council, demanded: "Art thou the Christ? tell us." Perhaps he would say something that the Romans would interpret as being seditious. After all, the Jewish concept of a Messiah was one of a Deliverer, a Deliverer from all alien yokes, Rome included. But Jesus: "If I tell you, ye will not believe." "How sad and how true! Gospel truth is taught by testimony: the spiritually alive, believe; the spiritually sick, question; the spiritually dead, deny and reject. And here stands the Lord Omnipotent, the being by whose hands all things are, the being through whom salvation comes, ready to testify again of his divine Sonship with full knowledge that his testimony will avail his hearers nothing." (*Commentary* 1:796.)

Jesus continued: "And if I also ask you, ye will not answer me, nor let me go. Hereafter shall the Son of man sit on the right hand of the power of God." Thus was the foundation laid for the question of the whole council: "Art thou then the Son of God?" To this Jesus replied: "Ye say that I am," which they all understood to mean: 'It is as ye have said, I am.' Then as Caiaphas had done earlier, they all cried out, "What need we any further witnesses? for we ourselves have heard of his own mouth." This man was a blasphemer worthy of death!

"And the whole council condemned him, and bound him," Mark said, "and carried him away, and delivered him to Pilate."

NOTES

1. Farrar, pp. 649–50. It is, of course, the speculative license of an author to say Jesus was taken from the place where he had been judged to a guardroom. There is nothing in the inspired account to indicate where or in what place the maltreatment took place. All we know for certain is that, from whatever place he was kept, Jesus was able to look upon Peter when that apostle made his third denial. Further, as shall be seen hereafter, the so-called formal trial of Jesus in all probability took place in the palace of

Caiaphas and not in the Hall of Judgment, though, as Farrar indicates, that is the only place it could have been held legally.

2. "Peter failed on this occasion to testify as becometh one who is a special witness of the Lord, but so in effect had all the disciples, for they all forsook him and fled. But Peter was not yet the man he was to be, for about fifty days hence, at Pentecost, he and all the saints were to receive the gift of the Holy Ghost. Perhaps, then, the great lesson to be learned from this experience of the chief apostle is this: if men are to resist and overcome the world; if they are to stand valiantly in the Cause of Christ; if they are to be faithful and true in all things—they must have the gift of the Holy Ghost." (*Commentary* 1:794.)

3. Edersheim argues—falsely, we are confident to assert—that Jesus was never formally tried by the Sanhedrin. In so doing he gives an instructive recitation of the illegalities that would have existed had the procedures of the night been a trial. That they were, in fact, a trial Talmage and many others assert with confidence, and so it seems to us. "Alike Jewish and Christian evidence establish the fact, that Jesus was not formally tried and condemned by the Sanhedrin," Edersheim contends. "It is admitted on all hands, that forty years before the destruction of the Temple the Sanhedrin ceased to pronounce capital sentences. This alone would be sufficient. But, besides, the trial and sentence of Jesus in the Palace of Caiaphas would (as already stated) have outraged every principle of Jewish criminal law and procedure." (And so it did!) "Such causes could only be tried, and capital sentence pronounced, in the regular meeting-place of the Sanhedrin, not, as here, in the High-Priest's Palace; no process, least of all such an one, might be begun in the night, not even in the afternoon, although if the discussion had gone on all day, sentence might be pronounced at night. Again, no process could take place on Sabbaths or Feastdays, or even on the eves of them, although this would not have nullified [the] proceedings, and it might be argued on the other side, that a process against one who had seduced the people should preferably be carried on, and sentence executed, at the great public Feasts, for the warning of all. Lastly, in capital causes there was a very elaborate system of warning and cautioning witnesses, while it may safely be affirmed, that at a regular trial Jewish judges, however prejudiced, would *not* have acted as the Sanhedrists and Caiaphas did on this occasion." (This, as we view it, is exactly what these prejudiced and hate-filled judicial officers did.)

"But as we examine it more closely, we perceive that the Gospel-narratives do not speak of a formal trial and sentence by the Sanhedrin. . . . The four Gospels equally indicate that the whole proceedings of that night were carried on in the Palace of Caiaphas, and that during that night no formal sentence of death was pronounced. . . . And when in the morning, in consequence of a fresh consultation, also in the Palace of Caiaphas, they led Jesus to the Praetorium, it was not as a prisoner condemned to death of whom they asked the execution, but as one against whom they laid certain accusations worthy of death, while, when Pilate bade them judge Jesus according to Jewish Law, they replied, not: that they had done so already, but, that they had no competence to try capital causes." (All of this ignores the condemnation of guilt imposed for blasphemy, the penalty for which, under Jewish law, was death by stoning. For Jesus to have died by stoning, as in the case of Stephen, would have nullified the Messianic word about the cross. Hence the divine providence that guided his foes to seek a Roman death sentence for a Roman offense, such as for sedition or treason. Jesus must die, not by Jewish stoning, but by Roman crucifixion. Thus it was written, and thus it must be.)

"But although Christ was not tried and sentenced in a formal meeting of the Sanhedrin, there can, alas! be no question that His Condemnation and Death were the work, if not of the Sanhedrin, yet of the Sanhedrists—of the whole body of them ('all the council'), in the sense of expressing what was the judgment and purpose of all the Supreme Council and Leaders of Israel, with only very few exceptions. We bear in mind, that the resolution to sacrifice Christ had for some time been taken. Terrible as the proceedings of that night were, they even seem a sort of concession—as if the Sanhedrists would fain have found some legal and moral justification for what they had determined to do." (Edersheim 2:556-58.)

Chapter 105

THE FIRST TWO ROMAN TRIALS

He is despised and rejected of men;
a man of sorrows, and acquainted with grief:
and we hid as it were our faces from him;
he was despised, and we esteemed him not. . . .
We did esteem him stricken,
smitten of God, and afflicted. . . .
He was oppressed, and he was afflicted,
yet he opened not his mouth:
he is brought as a lamb to the slaughter,
and as a sheep before her shearers is dumb,
so he openeth not his mouth. . . .
Yet it pleased the Lord to bruise him;
he hath put him to grief.
(Isa. 53:3-10.)

Jesus before Pilate
*(John 18:28-38; Matthew 27: 2, 11-14; JST, Matthew 27:12, 15;
Mark 15:2-5; JST, Mark 15:4; Luke 23:2-5; JST, Luke 23:3)*

Jesus who is called Christ—the same whom all Israel
had for ages worshipped as the Lord Jehovah, the one Holy
Being who was incapable of falsely ascribing divinity to
himself—has now been convicted by the Great Sanhedrin
of that very blasphemous offense, and by them con-

demned, according to Jewish law, to pay the supreme penalty; this Man of Galilee, bound and with a cord around his neck (Matthew says: "When they had bound him, they led him away"), is led, like a common criminal, to Pontius Pilate, the Roman Procurator. It would surprise us if Annas and Caiaphas and the Sanhedrin did not lead the tumultuous Jewish mob as the temple guards delivered their Jewish prisoner to the Gentile ruler. By these Jewish leaders the prisoner was taken to the magnificent palace of Herod, occupied at Passover time by Pilate, whose normal residence was Caesarea Palestina.

Pontius Pilate—into whose hands the Lord of Life is being delivered, that the penalty of death decreed by the Sanhedrin may be ratified—this ignoble Roman governor was, as were all the Gentile overlords of the day, a murderous, evil despot who ruled with the sword and was a master at political intrigue. He was neither better nor worse than others of his ilk, but his name is engraved forever in Christian memory because he sent the Son of God to the cross. This act of infamy on his part required preparation. No ruler—however supreme and autocratic; however subject to the political pressures and passions of the populace; however prejudiced toward a race and a people—no ruler knowingly and willfully sends an innocent man to death unless prior sins have seared his conscience, tied his hands, and buried his instinct to deal justly. Through all his length of days, Pilate had been and then was an evil man, inured to blood and hardened against violence.

"What manner of man was this in whose hands were placed, by power from above, the final destinies of the Saviour's life? . . . In Judea he had acted with all the haughty violence and insolent cruelty of a typical Roman governor. Scarcely had he been installed as Procurator, when, allowing his soldiers to bring with them by night the silver eagles and other insignia of the legions from Caesarea to the Holy City, he excited a furious outburst of Jewish feeling against an act which they regarded as idolatrous profanation. For five days and nights—often lying prostrate on the bare ground—they surrounded and almost stormed his residence at Caesarea with tumultuous and threatening entreaties, and could not be made to desist on the sixth, even by the peril of immediate and indiscriminate massacre at the hands of soldiers whom he sent to surround them. He had then sullenly given way, and this foretaste of the undaunted and fanatical resolution of the people with whom he had to deal, went far to embitter his whole administration with a sense of overpowering disgust."[1]

On another occasion, to build an aqueduct to bring water from the Pools of Solomon, Pilate confiscated money from their sacred treasury. "The people rose in furious myriads to resent this secular appropriation of their sacred fund. Stung by their insults and reproaches, Pilate disguised a number of his soldiers in Jewish costume, and sent them among the mob, with staves and daggers concealed under their garments, to punish the ringleaders. Upon the refusal of the Jews to separate quietly, a signal was given, and the soldiers carried out their instructions with such hearty good-will, that they wounded and beat to death not a few both of the guilty and the innocent, and created so violent a tumult that many perished by being trodden to death under the feet of the terrified and surging mob."

And on yet another occasion, a "seditious tumult" arose which "must still more have embittered the disgust of the Roman Governor for his subjects, by showing him how impossible it was to live among such a people—even in a conciliatory spirit—without outraging some of their sensitive prejudices. In the Herodian palace at Jerusalem, which he occupied during the festivals, he had hung some gilt shields dedicated to Tiberius." Whether this was done out of wanton malice or as part of a harmless work or ornamentation is not clear. But he felt he could not remove them "without some danger of offending the gloomy and suspicious Emperor to whose honour they were dedicated. Since he would not give way, the chief men of the nation wrote a letter of complaint to Tiberius himself. It was a part of Tiberius's policy to keep the provinces contented, and his masculine intellect despised the obstinacy which would risk an insurrection rather than sacrifice a whim. He therefore reprimanded Pilate, and ordered the obnoxious shields to be transferred from Jerusalem to the Temple of Augustus at Caesarea. . . .

"Besides these three outbreaks, we hear in the Gospels of some wild sedition in which Pilate had mingled the blood of the Galileans with their sacrifices. [Luke 13:1.] . . . Such was Pontius Pilate, whom the pomps and perils of the great yearly festival had summoned from his usual residence at Caesarea Phillipi to the capital of the nation which he detested, and the head-quarters of a fanaticism which he despised."

And yet—be it noted—"of all the civil and ecclesiastical rulers before whom Jesus was brought to judgment, Pilate was the least guilty of malice and hatred, the most anxious, if not to spare His agony, at least to save His life." It is to the conspiratorial evils of this day of judgment and of crucifixion to which we now turn our attention.

After a dread and evil night—whenever was there such a night as this, a night when God himself was spit upon and cursed and smitten?—Jesus is led by his captors into the Hall of Judgment of the palace of Herod. It is a Gentile house where there might be some crust of unleavened bread. Hence: "The great Jewish hierarchs, shrinking from ceremonial pollution, though not from moral guilt—afraid of leaven, though not afraid of innocent blood—refused to enter the Gentile's hall, lest they should be polluted, and should consequently be unable that night" to continue their Paschal celebration. Pilate, no doubt annoyed and condescending, but willing for the moment to placate their superstitions, thus went out to them. An experienced ruler, and probably having personally authorized Jesus' arrest the night before, the Roman Procurator asked, abruptly: "What accusation bring ye against this man?"

Taken by surprise—they had come to receive a ratifying approval of their already imposed death penalty; they had come to gain Roman approval for Jesus' death, so that none of his friends could raise a tumult; they had come to arrange a Roman crucifixion, which was more demeaning than a Jewish stoning; they had come to gain a license to kill, an approval to perform a judicial murder—thus, taken by surprise at Pilate's apparent intent to assume original jurisdiction and hold a Roman trial, they responded: "If he were not a malefactor, we would not have delivered him up unto thee." 'We have found him guilty; he has broken our law; he should be punished.'

"But Pilate's Roman knowledge of law, his Roman instinct of justice, his Roman contempt for their murderous fanaticism, made him not choose to act upon a charge so entirely vague, nor give the sanction of his tribunal to their dark disorderly decrees. He would not deign to be an executioner where he had not been a judge." Accordingly, Pilate said: "Take ye him, and judge him according to your law."[2] Their response: "It is not lawful for us to put any man to death." This reply, John says, was given, "That the saying of Jesus might be fulfilled, which he spake, signifying what death he should die." And thus, "they are forced to the humiliating confession that, having been deprived of the 'right of the sword,' they cannot inflict the death which alone will satisfy them; for indeed it stood written in the eternal councils that Christ was to die, not by Jewish stoning or strangulation, but by that Roman form of execution which inspired the Jews with a nameless horror, even by crucifixion; that He was to reign from His cross—to die by that most fearfully significant and typical of deaths—public, slow, conscious, accursed, agonising—worse even than burning—the worst type of all possible deaths, and the worst result of that curse which He was to remove for ever."

Caiaphas and his conspiring confederates—though they had hoped it might be otherwise—dropped the charge of blasphemy and raised the cry of sedition and treason. Under Roman law all the gods of all the nations of all the earth were revered and accepted; even the emperors deified themselves that they might be worshipped; any charge of blasphemy against this Jewish Jehovah would have been as empty nothingness, to Pilate. And so new charges were hurled. They said—Caiaphas, as we suppose, being voice—"We found this fellow perverting the nation, and forbidding to give tribute to Caesar, saying that he himself is Christ a King."

As to any perverting of the nation, Pilate could not care less; the Jews were already a benighted mob of religious fanatics in his view—let them be what they were. As to giving tribute to Caesar, that charge was idle rhetoric; grasping publicans and Roman steel saw to the taxes of the day. But a would-be king, that was another matter. Thereupon Pilate went into the Judgment Hall, called Jesus, and asked: "Art thou the King of the Jews?" "Thou poor, friendless, wasted man, in thy poor peasant garments, with thy tied hands, and the foul traces of the insults of thine enemies on thy face, and on thy robes—thou, so unlike the fierce magnificent Herod, whom this multitude which thirsts for thy blood acknowledged as their sovereign—art *thou* the King of the Jews?"

Jesus' answer will depend on what Pilate means. Is he speaking temporally or spiritually? Yes, this Suffering Servant is the king of the Universe; before him every knee shall one day bow, while every tongue acclaims him Lord of all. No, he is not the temporal Messiah, the Deliverer of Jewish expectation, the kind of a king who would lead an armed assault against a Roman fortress. "Sayest thou this thing of thyself," Jesus asks, "or did others tell it thee of me?"

Pilate's response is disdainful. "Am I a Jew?" he says. "Thine own nation and the chief priests have delivered thee unto me." As with the priests, so with the people; the derision, declaiming, and denunciation of Christ is not an isolated act of a few rabid partisans; the nation and its leaders have delivered him up to their Gentile overlord. Even without hearing Jesus' answer, it is hard for Pilate to envision him as a temporal ruler, and so he asks: "What hast thou done?" What indeed! 'I have preached the gospel to the poor, proclaimed liberty to the captives, and opened the prison door to those who were bound. I have opened blind eyes, unstopped deaf ears, and given strength to lame legs; I have cast out devils and called back rotting corpses from their graves; I have fed multitudes, stilled storms, walked on raging waves; I have been and am the manifestation among men of the Father who is in heaven. I am his Son.'

My kingdom is not of this world: if my kingdom were of this world, then would my servants fight, that I should not be delivered to the Jews: but now is my kingdom not from hence.

His was no Jewish Messianic kingdom; no political dominion ruled from palaces with floors of agate and lazuli; no kingdom that wages war with its neighbors and makes slaves of the conquered. His kingdom was not of this world; not one comprised of carnal, sensual, and devilish souls; not a kingdom of revelry and lust and wickedness. Rather, his kingdom on earth was made up of the saints of the Most High; and his kingdom in heaven was the everlasting kingdom of his Eternal Father. His royalty was the royalty of holiness, of righteousness, of eternal life. "Art thou a king then?" Pilate marvels. 'Can one who speaks of ruling in spiritual realms, as you do, really be a king!' Jesus answered:

Thou sayest that I am a king. To this end was I born, and for this cause came I into the world, that I should bear witness unto the truth. Every one that is of the truth heareth my voice.

Or, as Matthew has it, "Thou sayest truly; for thus it is written of me." 'And not only am I an eternal king, but my

176

kingly mission is to proclaim the truth—the truth that makes men free; the truth that saves and exalts eternally; the truth which brings peace to the souls of men in my earthly kingdom, and then assures them of eternal life in my eternal kingdom. Everyone who seeks truth and loves righteousness believes my words.'

"Yes!" Jesus was a king, "but a king not in this region of falsities and shadows, but one born to bear witness unto the truth, and one whom all who were of the truth should hear. 'Truth,' said Pilate impatiently, 'what is *truth*?'[3] What had he—a busy, practical Roman governor—to do with such dim abstractions? what bearing had they on the question of life and death? what unpractical hallucination, what fairyland of dreaming phantasy was this? Yet, though he contemptuously put the discussion aside, he was touched and moved. A judicial mind, a forensic training, familiarity with human nature which had given him some insight into the characters of men, showed him that Jesus was not only wholly innocent, but infinitely nobler and better than His raving sanctimonious accusers. He wholly set aside the floating idea of an unearthly royalty; he saw in the prisoner before his tribunal an innocent and high-souled dreamer, nothing more. And so, leaving Jesus there, he went out again to the Jews, and pronounced his first emphatic and unhesitating acquittal: 'I FIND IN HIM NO FAULT AT ALL.'

"But this public decided acquittal only kindled the fury of His enemies into yet fiercer flame. After all that they had hazarded, after all that they had inflicted, after the sleepless night of their plots, adjurations, insults, was their purpose to be foiled after all by the intervention of the very Gentiles on whom they had relied for its bitter consummation? Should this victim, whom they had thus clutched in their deadly grasp, be rescued from High Priests and rulers by the contempt or the pity of an insolent heathen? It was too intolerable! Their voices rose in wilder tumult."

Unable to raise the cry of blasphemy, and their charges of sedition and treason having failed, they now burst forth in a panic of pathetic charges. Mark says "the chief priests accused him of many things." But Jesus "answered nothing." Having been "brought as a lamb to the slaughter, and as a sheep before her shearers is dumb, so he openeth not his mouth." (Isa. 53:7.) So fierce were the charges, so vile the things named against him, that, to Pilate, it was unbelievable that Jesus would not respond. "Answerest thou nothing?" he said, "behold how many things they witness against thee." And even to the procurator's words, Jesus remained silent, "so that Pilate marvelled."

Then, amid the babble and tumult, a loud voice acclaimed: "He stirreth up the people, teaching throughout all Jewry, beginning from Galilee to this place." Pilate heard these words; he knew that Galilee had been the scene of most of Jesus' works, and instantaneously a plan was formulated in his mind. "Eager for a chance of dismissing a business of which he was best pleased to be free, he proposed, by a master-stroke of astute policy, to get rid of an embarrassing prisoner, to save himself from a disagreeable decision, and to do an unexpected complaisance to the unfriendly Galilean tetrarch, who, as usual, had come to Jerusalem—nominally to keep the Passover, really to please his subjects, and to enjoy the sensations and festivities offered at that season by the densely-crowded capital. Accordingly Pilate, secretly glad to wash his hands of a detestable responsibility, sent Jesus to Herod Antipas, who was probably occupying the old Asmonean palace, which had been the royal residence at Jerusalem until it had been surpassed by the more splendid one which the prodigal tyrant, his father, had built. And so, through the thronged and narrow streets, amid the jeering, raging, multitudes, the weary Sufferer was dragged once more."

Jesus before Herod
(Luke 23:6-12)

"Herod will kill thee." (Luke 13:31-33.) Such were the

words of warning spoken to Jesus in an earlier day with
reference to the designs and intentions of Herod Antipas;
and now, with Jesus before him in bonds, and with the chief
priests and the people all crying for his blood, what an
opportunity to decree a judicial murder! This same Antipas, the tetrarch of Galilee and Perea, is the one who
ordered the head of John the Baptist brought in before his
reveling courtiers on a charger. He is the one who flaunted
both incest and adultery before the nation and to whom one
or many murders meant no more than did the slaughter of
the Innocents in Bethlehem to his evil father, Herod the
Great. And yet even he, after a mocking and deriding trial,
found in Jesus "nothing worthy of death" (Luke 23:14-15),
and acquitted him publicly for the second time.

Words almost fail us in setting forth the dire and despicable and degenerate state of Herod Antipas, whom the
people in fawning flattery called king, though Rome had
conferred no such title upon him. "If ever there was a man
who richly deserved contempt, it was the paltry, perjured
princeling—false to his religion, false to his nation, false to
his friends, false to his brethren, false to his wife—to whom
Jesus gave the name of 'this fox.' The inhuman vices which
the Caesars displayed on the vast theatre of their
absolutism—the lust, the cruelty, the autocratic insolence,
the ruinous extravagance—all these were seen in pale
reflex in these little Neros and Caligulas of the provinces—these local tyrants, half Idumean, half Samaritan,
who aped the worst degradations of the Imperialism to
which they owed their very existence. Judea might well
groan under the odious and petty despotism of these hybrid
Herodians—jackals who fawned about the feet of the
Caesarean lions. Respect for 'the powers that be' can
hardly, as has well been said, involve respect for all the
impotences and imbecilities." (Farrar, pp. 449–50.)

"We have caught glimpses of this Herod Antipas before, and I do not know that all History, in its gallery of
portraits, contains a much more despicable figure than this

wretched, dissolute Idumean Sadducee—this petty princeling drowned in debauchery and blood.''

At one time Herod had feared that Jesus was John the Baptist risen from the dead to plague him. The mental madness that stirred his soul after the Baptist's murder, however, seems to have subsided; now his interest in Jesus is that of a superstitious simpleton who wants to see some great miracle performed in his kingly presence. Thus we find him questioning Jesus "in many words," taunting, deriding, challenging, all to no avail. Jesus remained silent. "As far as we know, Herod is further distinguished as the only being who saw Christ face to face and spoke to Him, yet never heard his voice. For penitent sinners, weeping women, prattling children, for the scribes, the Pharisees, the Sadducees, the rabbis, for the perjured high priest and his obsequious and insolent underling, and for Pilate the pagan, Christ had words—of comfort or instruction, of warning or rebuke, of protest or denunciation—yet for Herod the fox He had but disdainful and kingly silence." (Talmage, p. 636.)

In his trial before Herod, Jesus was vehemently accused by the chief priests and scribes. In this court, before a Jewish king with Roman power, the accusations made would have included both blasphemy and treason, none of which Herod deigned to consider seriously. Then "Herod with his men of war set him at nought, and mocked him, and arrayed him in a gorgeous robe, and sent him again to Pilate.'' Thus Antipas, though finding no fault in Jesus, and though a just judge is morally obligated to release an innocent man from his bonds, yet sent him back to another court, can it be other than with the hope that another judge will find reason to have this friend of the Baptist put to death as the chief priests and scribes so devoutly desire?

NOTES

1. No man of whom I know has written so consistently and so well—in such shining English prose—about the dramatic and miraculous happenings in the life of our Lord as

has Canon Farrar, whose words I have freely quoted from time to time in this work. It is my observation that when either I, or Elder Talmage, or Edersheim, or other authors—and all of us have done it—when any of us put the thoughts of Farrar in our own words, however excellent our expression may be, it loses much of the incisive and pungent appeal found in the language of our British friend from the Church of England. With this realization in mind, and because it seems a shame not to preserve the best literary craftsmanship available, to portray the greatest events in the most wondrous life ever lived, I shall feel free in this and the remaining chapters of this work to draw more heavily than otherwise upon the genius of Farrar. In the instant chapter, unless otherwise indicated by footnotes, all of the quoted material is from pages 661 to 672 of his work. By way of addendum may I express the hope—nay, offer the prayer—that both Farrar and Edersheim, and others who had faith and believed in the Messiah, according to the best light and knowledge they had, now that they are in the world of spirits where Elder Talmage continues his apostolic ministry, may have received added light and knowledge and will have pursued that strait and narrow course that will make them inheritors of the fulness of our Father's kingdom. Truly they were Eliases of a greater day and harbingers of a greater light.

2. Pilate's reaction was like that of Gallio when the Jews haled Paul before him with the charge: "This fellow persuadeth men to worship God contrary to the law." Gallio responded: "If it were a matter of wrong or wicked lewdness, O ye Jews, reason would that I should bear with you: but if it be a question of words and names, and of your law, look ye to it; for I will be no judge of such matters." (Acts 18:12-16.)

3. "And truth is knowledge of things as they are, and as they were, and as they are to come." (D&C 93:24.)

181

Chapter 106

THE FINAL ROMAN TRIAL

The Jews . . . shall crucify him, . . .
and there is none other nation on earth
that would crucify their God.
For should the mighty miracles be wrought
among other nations they would repent,
and know that he be their God.
But because of priestcrafts and iniquities,
they at Jerusalem will stiffen their necks
against him, that he be crucified.
(2 Ne. 10:3-5.)

Jesus Again before Pilate
(Matthew 27:15-23; JST, Matthew 27:20; Mark 15:6-14;
JST, Mark 15:8-10, 13, 15; Luke 23:13-23; John 18:39-40)

Bound, mocked, derided, smitten, spat upon, wearing
the gorgeous white robe in which he had been scornfully
draped by Herod's men of war, the Judge of all the earth is
now back in the Hall of Judgment to be judged and condemned by wicked men. Pilate has "called together the
chief priests and the rulers and the people," those by
whose mouths the charges of sedition and treason had been
hurled with such vile venom and hatred. Assembling with
them are great hosts from all parts of Jerusalem. Word of

Jesus' arrest has swept like a tidal wave through the streets and into the homes of the people; and, also, this is the day when the idle and the curious come to see the Governor make the Passover release of an infamous prisoner. Will it be this foul felon Bar-Abbas who, under the shallow cover of political aspirations, led an insurrection and committed murder, but for whose revolutionary zeal there was great public sympathy?

Pilate speaks: "Ye have brought this man unto me, as one that perverteth the people," and who forbids the paying of tribute to Caesar, and who claims that he himself is a king, "and, behold, I, having examined him before you, have found no fault in this man touching those things whereof ye accuse him"—'He is innocent; as I said unto you before, I find in him no fault at all'—"No, nor yet Herod: for I sent you to him; and, lo, *nothing worthy of death is done unto Him.*" So spoke Pilate the Procurator; so spoke Herod the king. There was, then, only one just thing to do: Release the Innocent Man; and further, if need be, protect him from the anger and hatred of the wailing mobs.

Thus "came the golden opportunity for him to vindicate the grandeur of his country's imperial justice, and, as he had pronounced Him absolutely innocent, to set Him absolutely free. But exactly at that point he wavered and temporised. The dread of another insurrection haunted him like a nightmare. He was willing to go half-way to please these dangerous sectaries. To justify them, as it were, in their accusation, he would chastise Jesus—scourge Him publicly, as though to render His pretensions ridiculous—disgrace and ruin Him—'make Him seem vile in their eyes'—and *then* set Him free."[1] These were Pilate's words: "I will therefore chastise him, and release him."

This attempt at compromise and appeasement failed; the hunger-maddened pack of ravening wolves would be satisfied with nothing but the blood of the Lamb; their cry was for blood, and blood it must be. Knowing and sensing their refusal—perhaps also it was spoken to him—Pilate felt unable to temporize. But there was another possibility. Because "it was common at the feast, for Pilate to release unto them one prisoner, whomsoever they desired," the Procurator then said: "Ye have a custom, that I should release unto you one at the passover: will ye therefore that I release unto you the King of the Jews?" That is: 'Though he is innocent, I will find him guilty and then release him as a convicted criminal.' He offered, therefore, to make the release of Jesus, not an act of "imperious justice, but of artificial grace."

There were those in the multitude who wanted Jesus freed. He had healed their sick, raised their dead, and spoken sweet words of comfort to their sorrowing souls. "And the multitude, crying aloud," Mark tells us, "began to desire him to deliver Jesus unto them." Heartened by this vocal sentiment, Pilate asked: "Will ye that I release unto you the King of the Jews?" Others, however, cried out for the release of Bar-Abbas, and Pilate yet asked: "Whom will ye that I release unto you? Barabbas, or Jesus which is called Christ?" Though the people might be divided on the issue, the chief priests were not, and, as Pilate knew, they "had delivered him for envy."

The issue was thus squarely put; the choice lay with the people; it was theirs, not Pilate's; such was their custom; and if any prisoner was to be freed, it must be by their voice. Nor could two more divergent extremes than Jesus and Bar-Abbas have been offered to them. One was guilty, the other innocent; one was a murderer, the other brought life where there had been death; one led an insurrection, the other had proclaimed peace; one was guilty of sedition and treason, the other had commanded the people to render unto Caesar the things that were his; one was named Jesus Bar-Abbas, which means Jesus the Son of the Father, the other was the Son of the living God. Do we state it too strongly when we say one was Christ, the other antichrist? The Jewish choice that day was to be made between their

Messiah and a murderer; rejecting their King, they would be denied entrance into his kingdom, and accepting Bar-Abbas (an antichrist), they would themselves be murdered and cursed for generations yet to come.

But before the choice was made, and while "the chief priests and elders" moved among the mob and "persuaded the multitude that they should ask Barabbas, and destroy Jesus," the trial was interrupted. Claudia Procula, the wife of Pilate, who either then or later may have been a prose-lyte to the true faith, sent a dire warning to her husband. "Have thou nothing to do with that just man," she said, "for I have suffered many things this day in a vision because of him."

There are times—not a few in the course of a life—when men would do well to give heed to the wise counsel of their wives. If ever there was such a time in the life of Pilate, this was it. The Lord in his goodness to her—and also, for his own purposes, that another witness might be borne of his Son—had revealed to this woman that Jesus was Lord of all and that calamity and sorrow awaited those who opposed him. Nor was Pilate unsympathetic to her message; in reality it but confirmed his own feelings and desires.

"Gladly, most gladly, would Pilate have yielded to his own presentiments—have gratified his pity and his justice—have obeyed the prohibition conveyed by this mysterious omen. Gladly even would he have yielded to the worse and baser instinct of asserting his power, and thwarting these envious and hated fanatics, whom he knew to be ravening for innocent blood. That they—to many of whom sedition was as the breath of life—should be sincere in charging Jesus with sedition was, as he well knew, absurd. Their utterly transparent hypocrisy in this matter only added to his undisguised contempt. If he could have dared to show his real feelings, he would have driven them from his tribunal with all the haughty insouciance of a Gallio. But Pilate was guilty, and guilt is cowardice, and cowardice is weakness. His own past cruelties, recoiling in kind on his own head, forced him to crush the impulse of pity, and to add to his many cruelties another more heinous still.

"He knew that serious complaints hung over him. Those Samaritans whom he had insulted and attacked— those Jews whom he had stabbed promiscuously in the crowd by the hand of his disguised and secret emissaries— those Galileans whose blood he had mingled with their sacrifices—was not their blood crying for vengeance? Was not an embassy of complaint against him imminent even now? Would it not be dangerously precipitated if, in so dubious a matter as a charge of claiming a kingdom, he raised a tumult among a people in whose case it was the best interest of the Romans that they should hug their chains? Dare he stand the chance of stirring up a new and apparently terrible rebellion rather than condescend to a simple concession, which was rapidly assuming the aspect of a politic, and even necessary compromise? His tortuous policy sprang back upon himself, and rendered impossible his own wishes. The Nemesis of his past wrong-doing was that he could no longer do right."

"Willing to release Jesus," Pilate asked: "Whether of the twain will ye that I release unto you?" The chief priests and elders had done their work well; sentiment among the people had crystallized. "Not this man, but Barabbas," they said. "What shall I do then with Jesus which is called Christ?" To this the cry came back—from them all—"Let him be crucified." Pilate said: "Why, what evil hath he done? *I have found no cause of death in Him:* I will therefore chastise him, and let him go." But they cried out the more, "Deliver him unto us to be crucified. Away with him. Crucify him." "And the voices of them and of the chief priests prevailed."

"Hounded on by the Priests and Sanhedrists, the people impetuously claimed the Paschal boon of which he had reminded them; but in doing so they unmasked still more decidedly the sinister nature of their hatred against their Redeemer. For while they were professing to rage against the asserted seditiousness of One who was wholly obedient and peaceful, they shouted for the liberation of a man whose notorious revolt had been also stained by brigandage and murder. Loathing the innocent, they loved the guilty, and claimed the Procurator's grace on behalf, not of Jesus of Nazareth, but of a man who, in the fearful irony of circumstance, was also called Jesus—Jesus Bar-Abbas—who not only *was* what they falsely said of Christ, a leader of sedition, but also a robber and an assassin. It was fitting that *they,* who had preferred an abject Sadducee to their True Priest, and an incestuous Idumean to their Lord and King, should deliberately prefer a murderer to their Messiah.

"It may be that Bar-Abbas had been brought forth, and that thus Jesus the scowling murderer and Jesus the innocent Redeemer stood together on that high tribunal side by side. The people, persuaded by their priests, clamoured for the liberation of the rebel and the robber. To him every hand was pointed; for him every voice was raised. For the Holy, the Harmless, the Undefiled—for Him whom a thousand Hosannas had greeted but five days before—no word of pity or of pleading found an utterance. 'He was despised and rejected of men.' "

Jesus Is Scourged and Prepared
for the Crucifiers
(Matthew 27:24-30; JST, Matthew 27:26-27; Mark 15:15-19; John 19:1-3)

Pilate next did that which has made all the more terrible the guilt of these blathering, frustrated fiends whose cries, "Crucify him, crucify him," pierced his ears and scourged his soul. He performed in their presence the two symbolical acts which certified to the innocence of the accused—one a Gentile witness, the other a Jewish. First, having declared the innocence of Jesus in plain words, he rose from the judgment seat, signifying he would impose no sentence; that there would be no judicial murder and no shedding of innocent blood; that he would free himself from the blood of the Innocent One. Having in mind the judicial tendency among all peoples, to preserve the rights of the accused, such an act—a Gentile symbol of innocence, if you will—should have freed Jesus without more. But it was not to be so. The legal court was Gentile; the real court was Jewish. The Roman sentence had already been imposed in the Jewish mind, and nothing must hinder the onrolling momentum of that evil cause which was taking their Christ to his cross.

Knowing and sensing all this, Pilate, with a keen and intuitive insight into the Jewish mind, performed before them their own rite, the Jewish rite that symbolized innocence and freed the soul from innocent blood. According to their law, for instance, if an unsolved murder had been committed, the elders of the city were required to slay a heifer, "wash their hands over the heifer," and say: "Our hands have not shed this blood, neither have our eyes seen it. Be merciful, O Lord, unto thy people Israel, whom thou hast redeemed, and lay not innocent blood unto thy people." Thus they were "forgiven," and thus they "put away the guilt of innocent blood" from among them, provided they did that which was "right in the sight of the Lord." (Deut. 21:1-9; Ps. 26:6; 73:13.)

Accordingly, on this dread morning, "When Pilate saw that he could prevail nothing, but that rather a tumult was made, he took water, and washed his hands before the multitude, saying, I am innocent of the blood of this just person; see that ye do nothing unto him." No longer is he saying, "Take ye him, and judge him according to your law," as it was at the first; now Pilate has stood in the Divine Presence; now he knows Jesus is innocent of both Jewish and Roman offenses; in justice the prisoner must be freed; neither the Jew nor the Gentile must do anything to him.

No one will contend that by these acts Pilate freed himself from the awful guilt of sending a God to the cross. Every man is accountable for his own sins, and those of Pilate were deep and red and evil. But we must credit the Procurator with trying to free his prisoner; his instinctive allegiance to justice was right; the spirit was willing but the flesh was weak. Further, this symbolic washing came *before* the decree to scourge and to crucify, and was, in fact, an attempt to free the man so that both Pilate and the Jews might "put away the guilt of innocent blood" because they did the thing—in releasing Jesus—which was "right in the sight of the Lord."

But whatever his intent and whatever his purpose—no matter whether his course was right or wrong—he was no longer an agent unto himself. The truth had not made him free; he was in bondage to the sins of his past. Whatever his purpose, it "was instantly drowned in a yell, the most awful, the most hideous, the most memorable that History records." *"His blood come upon us" and —God help us!—upon "our children."*

"And now mark, for one moment, the revenges of History.[2] Has not His blood been on them, and on their children?[3] Has it not fallen most of all on those most nearly concerned in that deep tragedy? Before the dread sacrifice was consummated, Judas died in the horrors of a loathsome suicide. Caiaphas was deposed the year following. Herod died in infamy and exile. Stripped of his Procuratorship very shortly afterwards, on the very charges he had tried by a wicked concession to avoid, Pilate, wearied out with misfortunes, died in suicide and banishment, leaving behind him an execrated name.[4] The house of Annas was destroyed a generation later by an infuriated mob, and his son was dragged through the streets, and scourged and beaten to his place of murder. Some of those who shared in and witnessed the scenes of that day—and thousands of their children—also shared in and witnessed the long horrors of that siege of Jerusalem which stands unparalleled in history for its unutterable fearfulness. 'It seems,' says Renan, 'as though the whole race had appointed a rendezvous for extermination.'

"They had shouted, 'We have no king but Caesar!' and they *had* no king but Caesar; and leaving only for a time the fantastic shadow of a local and contemptible royalty, Caesar after Caesar outraged, and tyrannised, and pillaged, and oppressed them, till at last they rose in wild revolt against the Caesar whom they had claimed, and a Caesar slaked in the blood of its best defenders the red ashes of their burnt and desecrated Temple. They had forced the Romans to crucify their Christ, and though they regarded this punishment with especial horror, they and their children were themselves crucified in myriads by the Romans outside their own walls, till room was wanting and wood failed, and the soldiers had to ransack a fertile inventiveness of cruelty for fresh methods of inflicting this insulting form of death.[5]

"They had given thirty pieces of silver for their Saviour's blood, and they were themselves sold in thousands for yet smaller sums. They had chosen Bar-Abbas in preference to their Messiah, and for them there has been no Messiah more, while a murderer's dagger swayed the last counsels of their dying nationality. They had accepted the guilt of blood, and the last pages of their history were glued together with the rivers of their blood, and that blood continued to be shed in wanton cruelties from age to age.

"They who will, may see in incidents like these the mere unmeaning *chances* of History; but there is in History nothing unmeaning to one who regards it as the Voice of God speaking among the destinies of men; and whether a man sees any significance or not in events like these, he must be blind indeed who does not see that when the murder of Christ was consummated, the axe was laid at the root of the barren tree of Jewish nationality. Since that day Jerusalem and its environs, with their 'ever-extending miles of grave-stones and ever-lengthening pavement of tombs and sepulchres,' have become little more than one vast cemetery—an Aceldama, a field of blood, a potter's field to bury strangers in. Like the mark of Cain, which clung to the murderer, the guilt of that blood seemed to cling to them—as it ever must until that same blood effaceth it. For, by God's mercy, that blood was shed for them also who made it flow; the voice which they strove to quench in death was uplifted in its last prayer for pity on His murderers. May that blood be efficacious! may that prayer be heard!''[6]

Pilate, having thus announced Jesus' innocence; having risen from the judgment seat; having washed his hands—for himself and for all Israel, that all might remain free from innocent blood—yet, in weakness, unable to withstand the pressures of the Jewish mob, freed Bar-Abbas and had Jesus scourged. ''This scourging was the ordinary preliminary to crucifixion and other forms of capital punishment. It was a punishment so truly fearful, that the mind revolts at it; and it has long been abolished by that compassion of mankind which has been so greatly intensified, and in some degree even created, by the gradual comprehension of Christian truth. The unhappy sufferer was publicly stripped, was tied by the hands in a bent position to a pillar, and then, on the tense quivering nerves of the naked back, the blows were inflicted with leathern thongs, weighted with jagged edges of bone and lead; sometimes even the blows fell by accident—sometimes, with terrible barbarity, were purposely struck—on the face and eyes. It was a punishment so hideous that, under its lacerating agony, the victim generally fainted, often died; still more frequently a man was sent away to perish under the mortification and nervous exhaustion which ensued.''

After the scourging came the derision. After he had borne so great a burden—in Gethsemane, before Pilate and Herod, by means of the lead and leather of the flagellum—Pilate placed him in the hands of those coarse and brutal warriors whose mission it was to wound and kill, and whose chief delight was to gloat over the agonies and pains of their foes. These men of war took the Man of Peace; these scarred and war-trained veterans of many a tumultuous fray took the Prince of Heaven; these cursing, jeering foes of all that is decent in the world took the Son of God—they took him, in bonds, with the approval of Pilate, to do with him according to their evil desires. "The low vile soldiery of the Praetorium—not Romans, who might have had more sense of the inborn dignity of the silent sufferer, but mostly the mere mercenary scum and dregs of the provinces—led Him into their barrack-room, and there mocked, in their savage hatred, the King whom they had tortured. It added keenness to their enjoyment to have in their power One who was of Jewish birth, of innocent life, of majestic bearing. The opportunity broke so agreeably the coarse monotony of their life, that they summoned all of the cohort who were disengaged to witness their brutal sport. In sight of those hardened ruffians"—and Pilate himself may well have been among the observers—"they went through the whole ceremony of mock coronation, a mock investiture, a mock homage. Around the brows of Jesus, in wanton mimicry of the Emperor's laurel, they twisted a green wreath of thorny leaves; in His tied and trembling hands they placed a reed for a sceptre; from His torn and bleeding shoulders they stripped the white robe with which Herod had mocked Him—which must now have been all soaked with blood—and flung on Him an old scarlot paludament—some cast-off war cloak, with its purple laticlave, from the Praetorian wardrobe. This, with feigned solemnity, they buckled over His right shoulder, with its glittering fibula; and then—each with his derisive homage of bended knee—each with his infamous spitting—each with the blow over the head from the reed-sceptre, which His bound hands could not hold—they kept passing before Him with their mock salutation of 'Hail, King of the Jews!' "

Pilate Sends Jesus to the Cross
(John 19:4-16; Luke 23:24-25)

After the great derision, Pilate went forth from the Praetorium where the soldiers had made sport of the King of kings and said to the Jewish multitude: "Behold, I bring him forth to you, that ye may know that I FIND NO FAULT IN HIM." "Even now, even yet, Pilate wished, hoped, even strove to save Him. He might represent this frightful scourging, not as the preliminary to crucifixion, but as an inquiry by torture, which had failed to elicit any further confession. And as Jesus came forth—as He stood beside him, with that martyr-form on the beautiful mosaic of the tribunal—the spots of blood upon His green wreath of torture, the mark of blows and spitting on His countenance, the weariness of His deathful agony upon the sleepless eyes, the *sagum* of faded scarlet, darkened by the weals of His lacerated back, and dropping, it may be, its stains of crimson upon the tessellated floor—even then, even so, in that hour of His extremest humiliation—yet, as He stood in the grandeur of His holy calm on that lofty tribunal above the yelling crowd, there shone all over Him so Godlike a pre-eminence, so divine a nobleness, that Pilate broke forth with that involuntary exclamation which has thrilled with emotion so many million hearts—

" 'BEHOLD THE MAN!'

"But his appeal only woke a fierce outbreak of the scream, 'Crucify! crucify!' The mere sight of Him, even in this His unspeakable shame and sorrow, seemed to add fresh fuel to their hate. In vain the heathen soldier appeals for humanity to the Jewish priest; no heart throbbed with responsive pity; no voice of compassion broke that monotonous yell of 'Crucify!'—the howling refrain of their wild 'liturgy of death.' The Roman who had shed blood like water, on the field of battle, in open massacre, in secret assassination, might well be supposed to have an icy and a stony heart; but yet icier and stonier was the heart of those scrupulous hypocrites and worldly priests.''

With roll on roll of thunderous hate the storm of Saddu-cean evil has reached its peak; priestcraft is in control; Pilate can no longer delay the dread sentence: "Take ye him, and crucify him: FOR I FIND NO FAULT IN HIM." 'Let him die; let it be by your hand; he has committed no crime worthy of death; there is no sedition or treason here; Rome faces no peril; he is innocent; but if this wild tumult, this insensate hate, this vile outpouring of vengeance, if all this cannot be stayed in any other way, I will bend to your will. Let him be crucified!' Roman law bows to Jewish priestcraft, and the Jewish Jesus is sent to his death by Roman hands.

Has the issue now at last been decided? Not so; far from it. "What the Jews want—what the Jews *will have*—is *not* tacit connivance, but absolute sanction. They see their power. They see that this blood-stained Governor dares not hold out against them; they know that the Roman statecraft is tolerant of concessions to local superstition. Boldly, therefore, they fling to the winds all question of a political offense, and with all their hypocritical pretenses calcined by the heat of their passion, they shout, *'We have a law, and by our law He ought to die, because He made Himself a Son of God.'* "

Was there any question in their minds as to the teach-ings of this Galilean? He said he was the Son of God! Was there any doubt as to the charge they hurled against him, as to the reason they thirsted for his blood? It was his claim to Messianic divinity! They had kept it from Pilate until death by crucifixion was approved; now let the world know; let them and their children be in opposition to Christ forever. They have succeeded in their conspiracy; he is to die; and how little they know that his death and resurrection will prove forever his divine Sonship. His death will be but the seed from which his message will sprout; and that seed, growing into his glorious resurrection, will soon become a great vine which covers the whole earth. Yes, let him die, but through death he shall live again; and because he lives, all men shall rise again in mortality.

At this new declaration, Pilate was startled, fearful. Heathen and pagan superstition surpasses that of any other people. The Son of God! What there was about this man that pulled at his heart strings, he did not know. Were his long felt presentiments bringing him a message that he had not yet understood? And the vision and warning of his wife—what of them? Pilate, accordingly, went again into the Judgment Hall and asked Jesus: "Whence art thou?"

Jesus did not deign to answer. Pilate, in anger, demanded: "Speakest thou not unto me? knowest thou not that I have power to crucify thee, and have power to release thee?" To kill or to let live? To scourge and to crucify? Can Pilate save a soul, speak peace to an aching heart, or raise a worthy man in immortal glory? Eternal power rests with the Man of Sorrows, and even such profane power as a worldly despot may exercise is only by the grace of Him in whom all things center. And Pilate—does he dare affront Annas or offend Tiberius by freeing this innocent man? "And Jesus pitied the hopeless bewilderment of this man, whom guilt had changed from a ruler into a slave." Then he who could not look upon any sin with the least degree of allowance spoke first of the sins of Pilate and then of those of Judas and Annas and Caiaphas and the Sanhedrin and the Jewish nation. "Thou couldest have no power at all against me, except it were given thee from above"—'My Father is permitting all this that I may now be lifted up upon the cross, as the Messianic word requires'—"therefore he that delivered me unto thee hath the greater sin."

"In the very depths of his inmost soul Pilate felt the truth of the words—silently acknowledged the superiority of his bound and lacerated victim. . . . All of his soul that was not eaten away by pride and cruelty thrilled back an unwonted echo to these few calm words of the Son of God.

Jesus had condemned his sin, and so far from being offended, the judgment only deepened his awe of this mysterious Being, whose utter impotence seemed grander and more awful than the loftiest power. From that time Pilate was even yet more anxious to save him." But his attempts were futile. Back from the satanic mob came the cry: "If thou let this man go, thou art not Caesar's friend: whosoever maketh himself a king speaketh against Caesar."

Then Pilate, the sin-bound ruler of Judea, led Jesus, the thong-bound ruler of the earth, forth into "a place that is called the Pavement, but in the Hebrew, Gabbatha." Pilate "sat down in the judgment seat." It was Friday, April 7, A.D. 30. The Roman trials had begun about 6 A.M. and it was now some three hours later. To the Jews Pilate said: "BEHOLD YOUR KING!"

Their cries increased; their shrieking wails pierced the Judean air; their faces were as flint, their hearts as stone. There was no mercy here—only hate and envy and a lust for vengeance. Lucifer was their Lord. "Away with him, away with him," they screamed, "crucify him." To this Pilate said: "SHALL I CRUCIFY YOUR KING?" Their answer: "We have no king but Caesar."[7] "At that dark terrible name of Caesar, Pilate trembled. It was a name to conjure with. It mastered him. He thought of that terrible implement of tyranny, the accusation of *laesa majestas,* into which all other charges merged, which had made confiscation and torture so common, and had caused blood to flow like water in the streets of Rome. He thought of Tiberius, the aged gloomy Emperor, then hiding at Caprea his ulcerous features, his poisonous suspicions, his sick infamies, his desperate revenge. At this very time he had been maddened into a yet more sanguinary and misanthropic ferocity by the detected falsity and treason of his only friend and minister, Sejanus, and it was to Sejanus himself that Pilate is said to have owed his position. There might be secret delators in that very mob. Panic-stricken, the unjust judge, in obedience to his own terrors, consciously betrayed the innocent victim to the anguish of death. He who had so often prostituted justice, was now unable to achieve the one act of justice which he desired. He who had so often murdered pity, was now forbidden to taste the sweetness of a pity for which he longed. He who had so often abused authority, was now rendered impotent to exercise it, for once, on the side of right. Truly for him, sin had become its own Erinnys, and his pleasant vices had been converted into the instrument of his punishment!''

"And Pilate gave sentence that it should be as they required."

"He delivered Jesus to their will."

"Then delivered he him therefore unto them to be crucified."

Judas Iscariot Commits Suicide
(Matthew 27:3-10; JST, Matthew 27:5-6, 10; Acts 1:15-21)

As an addendum to this night's evil deeds, we inscribe in our record the death of a devil—not a demon from hell, for such never die; they are doomed to Gnolom, to dwell in hell worlds without end—but a mortal devil, one into whom Satan had entered; one who conspired to put his Lord to death; one who sold his soul for thirty pieces of silver; one who led a cohort of armed men into the seclusion of Gethsemane; one who betrayed the Son of Man with an effusive outpouring of seeming love and respect that was, in fact, jealousy and hate. He was Judas of Kerioth—Judas Iscariot—the only Judean among the Twelve.

We do not know when Judas took his own life—only that he seems to have preceded his Lord in death. As the full impact of his traitorous deed began to dawn upon his sin-sick soul, it ignited within him the fires of Gehenna; a near madness possessed his being. "Terribly soon did the Nemesis fall on the main actor in the lower stages of this [night's] iniquity. Doubtless through all those hours Judas had been a secure spectator of all that had occurred, and when the morning dawned upon that chilly night, and he knew the decision of the Priests and of the Sanhedrin, and saw that Jesus was now given over for crucifixion to the Roman Governor, then he began fully to realize all that he had done. There is in a great crime an awfully illuminating power. It lights up the theatre of the conscience with an unnatural glare, and, expelling the twilight glamour of self-interest, shows the actions and motives in their full and true aspect. In Judas, as in so many thousands before and since, this opening of the eyes which follows the consummation of an awful sin to which many other sins have led, drove him from remorse to despair, from despair to madness, from madness to suicide." (Farrar, p. 659.)

Matthew says that when Judas saw that Jesus "was condemned"—probably by Pilate to be crucified—he "repented himself, and brought again the thirty pieces of silver to the chief priests and elders." Repented? Only in the sense that he had remorse of conscience and wished that he had not lifted up his heel against his own familar Friend, whose bread he ate—not repentance in the true Godly sense. True repentance is a gift of God that grows out of faith in Christ and carries with it a firm determination to love and serve the Lord. Judas regretted what he had done, but he was still a thief at heart, still a traitor, and still destined to suffer the wrath of God in Sheol until death and hell deliver up the dead which are in them. And yet he had the good grace to say: "I have betrayed the innocent blood."

That much at least he knew. The sorrows of the damned were already welling up within him. "The road, the streets, the people's faces—all seemed now to bear witness against him and for Jesus. He read it everywhere; he felt it always; he imagined it, till his whole being was on flame. What had been; what was; what would be! Heaven and earth receded from him; there were voices in the air, and pangs in the

soul—and no escape, help, counsel, or hope anywhere."
(Edersheim 2:574.) And yet this much he knew: "I have
betrayed the innocent blood." 'This Man is innocent; he
ought to go free.'

Their reply, like a dagger thrust into the heart of a
fleeing man, both stunned and cursed him: "What is that to
us?" they said. "See thou to it; thy sins be upon thee."
And thus it ever is: conspirators and traitors forsake each
other, and the devil sustaineth not his own. Judas "must
get rid of these thirty pieces of silver, which, like thirty
serpents, coiled round his soul with [the] terrible hissing of
death." (Edersheim 2:574.) His infamy was his own. "He
felt that he was of no importance any longer; that in guilt
there is no possibility of mutual respect, no basis for any
feeling but mutual abhorrence. His paltry thirty pieces of
silver were all that he would get. For these he had sold his
soul; and these he should no more enjoy than Achan enjoyed the gold he buried, or Ahab the garden he had seized.
Flinging them wildly down upon the pavement into the holy
place where the priests sat, and into which he might not
enter, he hurried out into the despairing solitude from
which he was not destined to emerge alive." (Farrar, p.
659.)

Judas is about to die by his own hand and become not
only the father of traitors but the father of suicides from
henceforth. But he is going to die in a particular manner, at
an appointed place, to fulfill the divine word—a word uttered more than a thousand years before by David, more
than six hundred years before by Jeremiah, and nearly six
hundred years before by Zechariah. It was David who, as
Peter expressed it, said of Judas: "Let his habitation be
desolate, and let no man dwell therein: and his bishoprick
let another take."[8] It was Jeremiah who was commanded
to take a potter's vessel out into the potter's field—into the
Valley of Hinnom; the Valley of Slaughter; the place called
Tophet; the place called Gehenna in Jesus' day; the place
where apostate Israel had burned their children to Baal; the

place which was filled with the blood of innocents. There, in that vile and evil setting, while the leaders of the people listened, Jeremiah was commanded to break the potter's vessel and to prophesy that even so would it be with Judah and Jerusalem. "Thus saith the Lord of hosts; Even so will I break this people and this city, as one breaketh a potter's vessel, that cannot be made whole again: and they shall bury them in Tophet, till there be no place to bury." (Jer. 19.) And then it was Zechariah who prophesied that the chief priests and rulers would weigh, for the price of the Lord, thirty pieces of silver and that they would then be cast "to the potter in the house of the Lord." (Zech. 11:12-13.)

And so, now, in fulfillment of all this, Judas is to do his evil deed. "And he cast down the pieces of silver in the temple," Matthew says, "and departed, and went, and hanged himself on a tree. And straightway he fell down, and his bowels gushed out, and he died." "Out he rushed from the Temple, out of Jerusalem, into solitude. Whither shall it be? Down into the horrible solitude of the Valley of Hinnom, the 'Tophet' of old, with its ghastly memories, the Gehenna of the future, with its ghostly associations. But it was not solitude, for it seemed now peopled with figures, faces, sounds. Across the Valley, and up the steep sides of the mountain! We are now on 'the potter's field' of Jeremiah—somewhat to the west above where the Kidron and Hinnom valleys merge. It is cold, soft clayey soil, where the footsteps slip, or are held in clammy bonds. Here jagged rocks rise perpendicularly: perhaps there was some gnarled, bent, stunted tree. Up there he climbed to the top of that rock. Now slowly and deliberately he unwound the long girdle that held his garment. It was the girdle in which he had carried those thirty pieces of silver. He was now quite calm and collected. With that girdle he will hang himself on that tree close by, and when he has fastened it, he will throw himself off from that jagged rock.

"It is done; but as, unconscious, not yet dead perhaps,

he swung heavily on that branch, under the unwonted burden the girdle gave way, or perhaps the knot, which his trembling hands had made, unloosed, and he fell heavily forward among the jagged rock beneath, and perished in the manner of which St. Peter reminded his fellow disciples in the days before Pentecost." (Edersheim 2:575.)

Then "the chief priests took the silver pieces" and said: "It is not lawful for to put them into the treasury, because it is the price of blood." After counseling together, they—the chief priests!—"bought with them the potter's field, to bury strangers in." Peter says that Judas "purchased a field with the reward of iniquity," and that it was called "Aceldama, . . . The field of blood." Of this whole episode, Edersheim says: "It was not lawful to take into the Temple-treasury, for the purchase of sacred things, money that had been unlawfully gained. In such cases the Jewish Law provided that the money was to be restored to the donor, and, if he insisted on giving it, that he should be induced to spend it for something for the public weal. This explains the apparent discrepancy between the accounts in the Book of Acts and by St. Matthew. By a fiction of law the money was still considered to be Judas', and to have been applied by him in the purchase of the well-known 'potter's field,' for the charitable purpose of burying in it strangers.

"But from henceforth the old name of 'potter's field' became popularly changed into that of 'field of blood.' And yet it was the act of Israel through its leaders: 'they took the thirty pieces of silver—the price of him that was valued, whom they of the children of Israel did value, and gave them for the potter's field!' It was all theirs, though they would have fain made it all Judas': the valuing, the selling, and the purchasing. And the 'potter's field'—the very spot on which Jeremiah had been Divinely directed to prophesy against Jerusalem and against Israel: how was it now all fulfilled in the light of the completed sin and apostasy of the people, as prophetically described by Zechariah! This Tophet of Jeremiah, now that they had valued and sold at thirty shekel Israel's Messiah-Shepherd—truly a Tophet, and become a field of blood! Surely, not an accidental coincidence this, that it should be the place of Jeremy's announcement of judgment: not accidental, but veritably a fulfilment of his prophecy! And so St. Matthew, targuming this prophecy in form as in its spirit, and in true Jewish manner stringing to it the prophetic description furnished by Zechariah, sets the event before us as the fulfilment of Jeremy's prophecy.'' (Edersheim 2:575-76.)

Judas, guilty, thus paid the first installment on the punishment decreed; Judas, guilty, yet added to his guilt by taking that which only God can give; Judas, guilty, thus carried his guilt to hell, where it will remain until he, having paid the uttermost farthing and been beaten with many stripes, bows the knee to Him whom he betrayed, truly repents, and comes forth to receive his place in the realms of Him who is merciful and gracious to all men.

NOTES

1. As explained in note 1 of the previous chapter, we are continuing our practice of quoting Farrar; the quotations in this chapter are from pages 673–87.

2. These same "revenges of history" are summarized by Edersheim in these words: "Some thirty years later, and on that very spot, was judgment pronounced against some of the best in Jerusalem; and among the 3,600 victims of the Governor's fury, of whom not a few were scourged and crucified right over against the Praetorium, were many of the noblest of the citizens of Jerusalem. A few years more, and hundreds of crosses bore Jewish mangled bodies within sight of Jerusalem. And still have these wanderers seemed to bear, from century to century, and from land to land, that burden of blood; and still does it seem to weigh 'on us and our children.' " (Edersheim 2:578.)

3. The student of history will be reminded of the persecutions and slaughter of the Jews, since the day of Farrar, as these have been seen in Russia, Germany, and other nations, particularly those decreed by the evil hand of Hitler during World War II, to say nothing of the Islamic ill will toward their fellow descendants of Abraham. That these national and racial hatreds will yet play a great part in the wars and turmoil leading up to the Second Coming of the Son of Man is known to all students of the scriptures.

4. In this connection, Jeremy Taylor, in his *Life of Christ,* as quoted in a footnote by Farrar, says: "Upon all murderers God hath not thrown a thunderbolt, nor broken all sacrilegious persons upon the wheel of an inconstant and ebbing estate, nor spoken to every oppressor from heaven in a voice of thunder, nor cut off all rebels in the first attempts of insurrection; but because He hath done so to some, we are to look upon those judgments as divine accents and voices of God, threatening all the same crimes with the like events, and with the ruins of eternity.'' And we may add: In the providences of Him whose judgments are just, all men, be they Jew or Gentile, will be accountable for their own sins when they stand before the bar of the Great Jehovah. Others who have

scourged and crucified and persecuted lesser persons—those who are the least of these his brethren—shall be rewarded along with Judas and Annas and Caiaphas and the Jews of that day for the evil deeds that are theirs.

5. Farrar at this point, in a footnote, quotes these apt words of Jeremy Taylor: "The blood of Jesus shed for the salvation of the world became to them a curse. . . . So manna turns to worms, and the wine of angels to vinegar and lees, when it is received into impure vessels or tasted by wanton palates, and the sun himself produces rats and serpents when it reflects upon the slime of Nilus."

6. Lest the words in the text be deemed harsh or intemperate or unfair, Farrar, in a footnote at this point, says: "It is in the deepest sincerity that I add these last words. Any one who traces a spirit of vindictiveness in the last paragraph wholly misjudges the spirit in which it is written. This book may perhaps fall into the hands of Jewish readers. They, of all others, if true to the deepest lessons of the faith in which they have been trained, will acknowledge the hand of God in History. And the events spoken of here are not imaginative; they are indisputable facts. The Jew at least will believe that in external consequences God visits the sins of the fathers upon the children. Often and often in History have the crimes of the guilty *seemed* to be visited even on their *innocent* posterity. The apparent injustice of this is but on the surface. There is a fire that purifies, no less than a fire that scathes; and who shall say that the very afflictions of Israel— afflictions, alas! so largely caused by the sins of Christendom—may not have been meant for a refining of the pure gold? God's judgments—it may be the very sternest and most irremediable of them—come, many a time, in the guise, not of affliction, but of immense earthly prosperity and ease."

We would be remiss if we did not append to these recitations, and to those in the text, all of which are true and must be said, at least this reminder of the more glorious day that lies ahead for the Jewish people: In the wisdom and providences of Him who knoweth all things and who doeth all things well, there shall yet be a day of rejoicing and restoration for the Jewish nation. We do not speak of the political gathering of a remnant of their number back to Palestine, but of that glorious future day when they accept their true King and return to their true Messiah. The full blessings of peace in this life and eternal life in the world to come are received by all men—Jew and Gentile alike—only when they accept Christ as their King and worship the Father in his holy name.

7. *"We have no king but Caesar."* "With this cry Judaism was, in the person of its representatives, guilty of denial of God, of blasphemy, of apostasy. It committed suicide; and, ever since, has its dead body been carried in show from land to land, and from century to century: to be dead, and to remain dead, till He come a second time, Who is the Resurrection and the Life!" (Edersheim 2:581.)

8. Psalms 69 and 109, which are the source of Peter's declaration, abound in Messianic phrases that speak both of Jesus and of Judas.

Chapter 107

THE CRUCIFIXION

He was lifted up upon the cross
and slain for the sins of the world.
(1 Ne. 11:33.)
They shall consider him a man, . . .
and shall crucify him. (Mosiah 3:9.)

From Gabbatha to Golgotha
(Matthew 27:31-33; JST, Matthew 27:35; Mark 15:20-22;
JST, Mark 15:25; Luke 23:26-32; JST, Luke 23:31-32; John 19:16-17;
JST, John 19:17)

As we come now to that awful hour when a Roman
mallet drives rough nails into sinless hands—the hour when
a God dies—we are faced with the awesome task of setting
forth how he died and by whom he was crucified. True it is
that a Roman hammer drove the sharp ferrous spikes into
his quivering and aching hands; true, that a Roman arm
hurled the steel-headed spear into his suffering side; true,
that a Roman Procurator profaned the Holy One by turning
the Sanhedrist shriek, "Crucify him," into a Roman decree. But how can the life of a God be taken? How can the
Great Jehovah, who made heaven and earth and the sea
and the fountains of waters—and all things that in them
are—how can the Lord Omnipotent, the Creator of all

things from the beginning, how can he die? And at whose door is the demonish deed laid?

The Messianic word identifies his murderers as "the Jews"—as a people and as a "nation"—and ascribes their heinous course to "priestcrafts and iniquities." (2 Ne. 10:3-5.) And around his cross, mingling with the gaping crowds who gained vicarious pleasure from his agonies, we find the Sanhedrists and chief priests inciting the people to mock and revile and defy the one who had been lifted up and whose blood then watered the dusty soil of Calvary. As to the dire deeds of this dread day, they happened on this wise:

While seated on the Roman judgment seat in Gabbatha, the sinful and proud Procurator asked if he, Pilate, should crucify their Jewish King Jesus. Cursing themselves with their own words, and dooming their own race out of their own mouths, the chief priests and Sanhedrists said they had no king but Caesar. Then Pilate delivered Jesus to them, the Jews, to be crucified. So it is written by John. Matthew and Mark tell us that before the death procession started for Golgotha, Jesus was taken by the soldiers into the Praetorium where—clothed in purple, pained with a crown of thorns, mocked and smitten by the rude soldiery—he was hailed as the demeaned king of a damned race. After these degrading acts of demonish sport, the men of war and of the world took off the purple robe, reclothed him in his own raiment, and led him away to crucify him. Caesar, their adopted king, would that day do for the Jews what they could not do for themselves—crucify their true King. Among the seed of Jacob the death penalty could only be imposed by strangulation, beheading, burning, or stoning. So it is written in the Mishnah. But Jesus, according to the eternal providences, must suffer the opprobium of a non-Jewish crucifixion. The Romans must do the deed for the Jews. And this is the day; the appointed hour is upon them.

Now it was the custom among them for a condemned man to carry his cross. We do not know the kind and type of cross upon which Jesus was lifted up. Three types were in common usage, one shaped like an "X," another like a "T," and the third in the traditional Latin form. Probably this latter was used as it would have provided a place for the superscription. It consisted of two parts, an eight- or nine-foot pole and a movable crosspiece or patibulum. Ordinarily the patibulum consisted of two parallel beams fastened together between which, as he carried his heavy burden, the neck of the criminal was placed. "The cross was not, and could not have been, the massive and lofty structure with which such hundreds of pictures have made us familiar. Crucifixion was among the Romans a very common punishment, and it is clear that they would not waste any trouble in constructing the instrument of shame and torture. It would undoubtedly be made of the very commonest wood that came to hand, perhaps olive or sycamore, and knocked together in the very rudest fashion."[1]

And so Jesus, bearing his cross, was led along the dolorous way to a place of burial, of skulls, of death. Four Roman soldiers went beside him. It was the purpose and intent to attract attention, to demean the criminal, and to frighten others so they would not themselves come to a like end. A sign, either hanging around his neck or carried by one of the soldiers, announced the crimes of the crucifee. Two condemned criminals, each bearing his cross and each attended by four soldiers, followed Jesus to the place of agony and death.

"To support the body of a man, a cross would require to be of a certain size and weight; and to one enfeebled by the horrible severity of the previous scourging, the carrying of such a burden would be an additional misery. But Jesus was enfeebled not only by this cruelty, but by previous days of violent struggle and agitation, by an evening of deep and overwhelming emotion, by a night of sleepless anxiety and suffering, by the mental agony of the garden"—and this suffering in Gethsemane, when great drops of blood oozed from every pore, bore in more heavily upon him than all else combined—"by three trials and three sentences of death before the Jews, by the long and exhausting scenes in the Praetorium, by the examination before Herod, and by the brutal and painful derisions which He had undergone, first at the hands of the Sanhedrin and their servants, then from Herod's body-guard, and lastly from the Roman cohort. All these, superadded to the sickening lacerations of the scourging, had utterly broken down His bodily powers. His tottering footsteps, if not His actual falls under that fearful load, made it evident that He lacked the physical strength to carry it from the Praetorium to Golgotha."

Shortly after the parade of death began, certainly by the time the melancholy marchers reached the gates of the city, Jesus was no longer able to bear the burden of the cross. Thereupon the soldiers laid hold upon Simon of Cyrene, who chanced—or was it an instance of an intervening providence—to be coming in from the country; him they compelled to bear the cross of Jesus. Mark identifies him as "the father of Alexander and Rufus," showing that at a later date at least the members of his family were disciples of renown whose names were familiar to the saints. It is pleasant to suppose that even as Jesus kept the Feast of the Passover in the home of a devout disciple, so a Divine Providence provided for him at this hour another believing soul who would rejoice in days to come that he had been privileged to lift some of the fatiguing burden from him whose burdens were greater than mortal man can bear.

It is clear that the Roman-Jewish design to herald the crucifixion of Jesus from the housetops surpassed their wildest dreams. Such crowds as had listened to him in the temple were present. A marvelous moving multitude marched with the death party. These were the ten thousands of Judea and the thousands of Galilee, both men and women. As far as the record recites, none of the men in that mighty mass came to his defense, but with the women it was otherwise. "From the *men* in that moving crowd He does not appear to have received one word of pity or of sympathy. *Some* there must surely have been who had seen His miracles, who had heard His words; some of those who had been almost, if not utterly, convinced of His Messiahship, as they hung upon His lips while He uttered His great discourses in the Temple; some of the eager crowd who had accompanied Him from Bethany five days before with shouted hosannas and waving palms. Yet if so, a faithless timidity or a deep misgiving—perhaps even a boundless sorrow—kept them dumb. But these women, more quick to pity, less susceptible to controlling influences, could not and would not conceal the grief and amazement with which this spectacle filled them. They beat upon their breasts and rent the air with their lamentations, till Jesus Himself hushed their shrill cries with words of solemn warning. Turning to them—which He could not have done had He still been staggering under the burden of His cross—He said to them":

Daughters of Jerusalem, weep not for me, but weep for yourselves, and for your children.

For, behold, the days are coming, in the which they shall say, Blessed are the barren, and the wombs that never bare, and the paps which never gave suck. . . .

For if they do these things in a green tree, what shall be done in the dry?[2]

To this expression relative to the green tree and the dry tree, Luke says: "This he spake, signifying the scattering of Israel, and the desolation of the heathen, or in other words, the Gentiles," meaning the Israelitish scattering that took place at the destruction of Jerusalem, and meaning the desolations that would fall upon all men in the latter days, the days of wickedness and vengeance that should precede his Second Coming.

"Many of them, and the majority of their children,

would live to see such rivers of bloodshed, such complications of agony, as the world had never known before—days which would seem to overpass the capacities of human suffering, and would make men seek to hide themselves, if it might be, under the very roots of the hill on which their city stood. The fig-tree of their nation's life was still green: if such deeds of darkness were possible *now,* what should be done when that tree was withered and blasted, and ready for the burning?—if in the days of hope and decency they could execrate their blameless Deliverer, what would happen in the days of blasphemy and madness and despair? If, under the full light of day, Priests and Scribes could crucify the Innocent, what would be done in the midnight orgies and blood-stained bacchanalia of Zealots and Murderers? This was a day of crime; that would be a day when Crime had become her own avenging fury.

"The solemn warning, the last sermon of Christ on earth"—unless he made some unrecorded statements from the cross—"was meant primarily for those who heard it; but, like all the words of Christ, it has deeper and wider meaning for all mankind. These words warn every child of man that the day of careless pleasure and blasphemous disbelief will be followed by the crack of doom; they warn each human being who lives in pleasure on the earth, and eats, and drinks, and is drunken, that though the patience of God waits, and His silence is unbroken, yet the days shall come when He shall speak in thunder, and His wrath shall burn like fire."

They Crucify Their King
(Matthew 27:34-38; JST, Matthew 27:39-42; Mark 15:23-28; JST, Mark 15:26, 28-31; Luke 23:33-34, 38; JST, Luke 23:35; John 19:18-24)

At about 9 A.M. the dread procession arrived at Golgotha, which is Calvary—"a place of burial." There the final preparations for crucifixion were performed. So horrible was death on the cross that custom permitted an act that lessened the pain and agony. "Utterly brutal and revolting as was the punishment of crucifixion, which has now for fifteen hundred years been abolished by the common pity and abhorrence of mankind, there was one custom in Judea, and [also] one occasionally practised by the Romans, which reveal some touch of passing humanity. The latter consisted in giving to the sufferer a blow under the arm-pit, which, without causing death, yet hastened its approach. Of this I need not speak, because, for whatever reason, it was not practised on this occasion." We cannot believe other than that a Divine Providence—which guided in the minutest detail all that this day transpired—so controlled events as to prevent its happening, and that for the very reasons involved in the other proffered act of mercy that Jesus himself voluntarily prevented.

"The former [act of mercy], which seems to have been due to the milder nature of Judaism, and which was derived from a happy piece of Rabbinic exegesis on Proverbs 31:6, consisted in giving to the condemned, immediately before his execution, a draught of wine medicated with some powerful opiate.[3] It had been the custom of wealthy ladies in Jerusalem to provide this stupefying potion at their own expense, and they did so quite irrespectively of their sympathy for any individual criminal. It was probably taken freely by the two malefactors, but when they offered it to Jesus He would not drink it. The refusal was an act of sublimest heroism. The effect of the draught was to dull the nerves, to cloud the intellect, to provide an anesthetic against some part, at least, of the lingering agonies of that dreadful death. But He, whom some modern skeptics have been base enough to accuse of feminine feebleness and cowardly despair, preferred rather 'to look Death in the face'—to meet the king of terrors without striving to deaden the force of one agonising anticipation, or to still the throbbing of one lacerated nerve."

This, then, is the awful hour. They crucify him. The

scene probably was acted out somewhat along this line: "The three crosses were laid on the ground—that of Jesus, which was doubtless taller than the other two, being placed in bitter scorn in the midst. Perhaps the cross-beam was now nailed to the upright, and certainly the title, which had either been borne by Jesus fastened round His neck, or carried by one of the soldiers in front of Him, was now nailed to the summit of His cross. Then He was stripped of His clothes, and then followed the most awful moment of all. He was laid down upon the implement of torture. His arms were stretched along the cross-beams; and at the centre of the open palms, the point of a huge iron nail was placed, which, by the blow of a mallet, was driven home into the wood. Then through either foot separately, or possibly through both together as they were placed. one over the other, another huge nail tore its way through the quivering flesh. Whether the sufferer was *also* bound to the cross we do not know; but, to prevent the hands and feet being torn away by the weight of the body, which could not 'rest upon nothing but four great wounds,' there was, about the centre of the cross, a wooden projection strong enough to support, at least in part, a human body which soon became a mass of agony."[4]

We are wont to speak of seven words or utterances made by Jesus from the cross. It was probably at this point that he made the first of these: "Father, forgive them; for they know not what they do." The reference, of course, is to "the soldiers who crucified him," not to Judas or Annas or Caiaphas or the chief priests or the Sanhedrin or Pilate or Herod or Lucifer or any who have rebelled against him and chosen to walk in darkness at noonday. All these are left in the hands of Divine Justice, and mercy cannot rob justice, else God would cease to be God.[5]

Jesus is speaking, rather, of the Roman soldiers who have no choice but to do the will of Pilate and those whose minions they are. And he is not asking the Father to forgive them of their sins and to prepare them, thus, to dwell with clean and pure persons in celestial rest. He is simply asking that the deed of crucifixion be not laid at their door; let the responsibility rest with the Jews and with the Procurator of Rome, not with these who are doing—albeit in a gross and cruel manner—no more than they have been commanded to do. Had his concern been the remission of their sins, he could have acted on his own, for, as his ministry amply attests, the Son of Man had power to forgive sins on earth. And, further, if these Roman robots are to receive forgiveness of sins and the salvation that flows therefrom, it must be on the same basis as with all others who cleanse themselves from sin. The course is one of faith, repentance, baptism, and the receipt of that baptism of fire which burns dross and evil out of a human soul as though by fire. Yet the mercy and majesty and might of Him who conquered all is manifest in his petition. As pains beyond compare wrack his tortured body, his concern and interest centers in the spiritual well-being of these ruffians of the baser sort who are the creators of much of the agony.

But back now to the modus operandi of the crucifixion. As the cross lay on the ground, Jesus was nailed thereto. "And then the accursed tree—with its living human burden hanging upon it in helpless torment, and suffering fresh tortures as every movement irritated the fresh rents in hands and feet—was slowly heaved up by strong arms, and the end of it fixed firmly in a hole dug deep in the ground for that purpose. The feet were but a little raised above the earth. The victim was in full reach of every hand that might choose to strike, in close proximity to every gesture of rage and hatred. He might hang for hours to be abused, insulted, even struck, by the ever-moving multitude who, with that desire to see what is horrible which always characterises the coarsest hearts, had thronged to gaze upon a sight which should rather have made them weep tears of blood.

"And there, in tortures which grew ever more insupportable, ever more maddening as time flowed on, the unhappy victims might linger in pain so cruelly intolerable, that often they were driven to entreat and implore the spectators, or the executioners, for dear pity's sake, to put an end to anguish too awful for man to bear—conscious to the last, and often, with tears of abject misery, beseeching from their enemies the priceless boon of death.[6]

"For indeed a death by crucifixion seems to include all that pain and death *can* have of [the] horrible and [the] ghastly—dizziness, cramp, thirst, starvation, sleeplessness, traumatic fever, tetanus, publicity of shame, long continuance of torment, horror of anticipation, mortification of untended wounds—all intensified just up to the point at which they can be endured at all, but all stopping just short of the point which would give to the sufferer the relief of unconsciousness. The unnatural position made every movement painful; the lacerated veins and crushed tendons throbbed with incessant anguish; the wounds, inflamed by exposure, gradually gangrened; the arteries—especially of the head—became swollen and oppressed with surcharged blood; and while each variety of misery went on gradually increasing, there was added to them the intolerable pang of a burning and raging thirst; and all these physical complications caused an internal excitement and anxiety, which made the prospect of death itself—of death, the awful unknown enemy, at whose approach man usually shudders most—bear the aspect of a delicious and exquisite release."

Lest there be any question in any mind as to the identity of the one on the chief of the three crosses—for Jerusalem was full of Passover pilgrims, assembled from all Palestine and from Jewish settlements in distant lands—Pilate wrote "a title," "a superscription," "his accusation," and put it upon the cross. The words were recorded in the official Latin, in the current Greek, and in the vernacular Aramaic. The message read: "JESUS OF NAZARETH, THE KING OF THE JEWS."

"When the cross was uplifted, the leading Jews, for the first time, prominently noticed the deadly insult in which

Pilate had vented his indignation. Before, in their blind rage, they had imagined that the manner of His crucifixion was an insult aimed at *Jesus;* but now that they saw Him hanging between the two robbers, on a cross yet loftier, it suddenly flashed upon them that it was a public scorn inflicted upon *them.* . . . With the passionate ill-humour of the Roman governor there probably blended a vein of seriousness. While he was delighted to revenge himself on his detested subjects by an act of public insolence, he probably meant, or half meant, to imply that this *was,* in one sense, the King of the Jews—the greatest, the noblest, the truest of His race, whom therefore His race had crucified. The King was not unworthy of His kingdom, but the kingdom of the King. There was something loftier even than royalty in the glazing eyes which never ceased to look with sorrow on the City of Righteousness, which had now become a city of murderers. The Jews felt the intensity of the scorn with which Pilate had treated them. It so completely poisoned their hour of triumph, that they sent their chief priests in deputation, begging the Governor to alter the obnoxious title.''

"It should be written and set up over his head," they said to Pilate, "his [own] accusation, This is he that said he was Jesus, the King of the Jews." To their importuning plea, Pilate answered curtly: "What I have written, I have written; let it alone." And the superscription remained to testify to them and to all men that here indeed was he of whom Moses and the prophets spake—the one who came to deliver, to redeem, and to save: their Messiah, their King, their Lord and their God.

Strange as it may seem to the carnal mind, the hidden hand of Him who governs in the affairs of men did not let so much as a jot or a tittle of the Messianic word fall. Mark testifies that with him were crucified two thieves, "the one on his right hand, and the other on his left," that Isaiah's word might be fulfilled, "And he was numbered with the transgressors." (Isa. 53:12.) And when he was crucified, the four soldiers ordered to guard the cross—lest a half-dead person be taken down by his friends and revived—both divided and cast lots for his garments. His headgear, the outer cloaklike garment, the girdle, and the sandals, differing little in value, were easily divided among them. But for the seamless woven inner garment, an article of appreciable worth, they cast lots, "that the scripture might be fulfilled, which saith, They parted my raiment among them, and for my vesture they did cast lots." (Ps. 22:18.)

NOTES

1. Quotations in this chapter that are not otherwise footnoted are from pages 688–99 of Farrar.

2. "If Israel's oppressors could do what was then in process to the 'Green Tree,' who bore the leafage of freedom and truth and offered the priceless fruit of life eternal, what would the powers of evil not do to the withered branches and dried trunk of apostate Judaism?" (Talmage, p. 654.) Farrar gives the traditional interpretation of Jesus' statement thus: "If, in the fulfillment of God's purposes, I the Holy and the Innocent must suffer thus—if the green tree be thus blasted—how shall the dry tree of a wicked life, with its abominable branches, be consumed to the uttermost burning?" With reference to the martyrdom of the Prophet and the Patriarch of this dispensation, the inspired account contains this expression: "If the fire can scathe a green tree for the glory of God, how easy it will burn up the dry trees to purify the vineyard of corruption." (D&C 135:6.)

3. "Give strong drink unto him that is ready to perish, and wine unto those that be of heavy hearts." (Prov. 31:6.)

4. The spiritually enlightened will envision, in this connection, the fulfillment of Isaiah's Messianic word concerning "the nail that is fastened in the sure place." (Isa. 22:21-25.)

5. Near the close of a long sermon on mercy and justice, Alma says: "Justice exerciseth all his demands, and also mercy claimeth all which is her own; and thus, none but the truly penitent are saved. What, do ye suppose that mercy can rob justice? I say unto you, Nay; not one whit. If so, God would cease to be God." (Alma 42:24-25.) Alma's reasoning, thus, is that unless God conformed to his eternal laws he would not be God, for it is his total and complete conformity to law that makes him God. Jesus, thus, could not abandon the whole system of law and forgive and save the thieves who were far from being penitent and obedient as of the time they hung with him on their crosses.

6. Edersheim suggests a somewhat different modus operandi with reference to the crucifixion of Jesus. "Avowedly, the punishment was invented to make death as painful and as lingering as the power of human endurance. First, the upright wood was planted in the ground. It was not high, and probably the Feet of the Sufferer were not above one or two feet from the ground. Thus could the communication described in the Gospels take place between Him and others; thus, also, might His Sacred Lips be moistened with the sponge attached to a short stalk of hyssop. Next, the transverse wood was placed on the ground, and the Sufferer laid on it, when His Arms were extended, drawn up, and bound to it. Then (this not in Egypt, but in Carthage and Rome) a strong, sharp nail was driven, first into the Right, then into the Left Hand. Next, the Sufferer was drawn up by means of ropes, perhaps ladders; the transverse either bound or nailed to the upright, and a rest or support for the Body fastened on it. Lastly, the Feet were extended, and either one nail hammered into each, or a larger piece of iron through the two. We have already expressed our belief that the indignity of exposure was not offered at such a Jewish execution. And so might the crucified hang for hours, even days, in the unutterable anguish of suffering, till consciousness at last failed." (Edersheim 2:589.)

215

Chapter 108

ON THE CROSS OF CALVARY

My Father sent me
that I might be lifted up upon the cross;
and after that I had been lifted up
upon the cross, that I might draw
all men unto me,
that as I have been lifted up
by men even so should men be lifted up
by the Father, to stand before me,
to be judged of their works,
whether they be good
or whether they be evil—
And for this cause have I been lifted up;
therefore, according to the power
of the Father I will draw
all men unto me, that they may be judged
according to their works.
(3 Ne. 27:14-15.)

The Sanhedrists Incite Mockery and Derision against Him
(Matthew 27:39-43; JST, Matthew 27:46; Mark 15:29-32; Luke 23:35-37)

With Jesus nailed to the cross, with the nails driven in a sure place, with an agonizing death assured, the floodgates

216

of derision and hatred and venom are opened upon him. All of the vile passions and evil powers that framed the cry, "Crucify him, for we have no king but Caesar," are now hurled at him in the base challenge to prove his claimed divinity by saving himself and ascending an earthly throne.

The Roman soldiers have done their cruel deed and done it well. While Jesus hangs in agony they have naught to do but keep the peace and protect the cross, lest any of his friends steal the body of the Suffering One. They seat themselves before the instrument of death which they have raised; they begin to eat and drink and make merry. They quaff the cheap wine of the countryside and drink pledges to the Jewish King, and even offer him some of their vinegar-like liquor so that he can toast them. Theirs, we should note, is no special hatred toward him as a person; to them he is just another Jew, another member of a hated and despised race, another religious fanatic whose zeal has brought him to a deserved death. Their derision comes forth against him in his representative capacity, against him as a symbol of the benighted people who are so repulsive to them, against him as a supposed king. "If thou be the king of the Jews, save thyself," they say.

But it was not of a quarterion of coarse and brutal Gentile warriors that the Messianic word spake. The Jewish Messiah, whose hands and feet had been pierced, whose garments had been parted among them, and for whose vesture they had cast lots, said of himself, by the mouth of David: "All they that see me laugh me to scorn: . . . They gaped upon me with their mouths, as a ravening and a roaring lion." (Ps. 22:7, 13.) It was a nation and a people and their priestly rulers who crucified their King, not simply a few alien men of war; and it was a nation and a people and their priestly rulers who mocked and scoffed before his cross. We have seen how incensed the chief priests were over the mocking superscription nailed to the summit of the cross; this wound was deepened by the raillery of the soldiers that ascribed Jewish kingship to their mortal enemy. To turn these Roman taunts away from the Jews and to this Jesus of Galilee, we see the rulers and the chief priests and the scribes and the elders both mocking him and inciting the people to go and do likewise. The same satanic souls who had orchestrated the calls for crucifixion now led the same chorus of voices in chanting a derisive hymn of hate and vengeance against the one who had been crucified.

Their taunting cries assailed the whole ministry and work of Jesus among them. If they had planned and labored for long hours in their secret chambers to formulate their derisive charges, they could not have done better than they did in reciting those which Lucifer put into their minds almost without forethought. Their jeers cast contempt upon him in these respects:

He had announced that the Mosaic law was no longer binding upon them; that their temple-centered sacrificial system of salvation was now to cease; that they would be saved through the temple of his body; and that the destruction of that bodily temple and its resurrection in three days would be the only sign given them of his divine Sonship. Now, as they passed by and reviled and wagged their heads, they taunted him with the cry: "Ah, thou that destroyest the temple, and buildest it in three days, Save thyself, and come down from the cross." 'If salvation centers in thee, and not in Moses' law, come down now from thy cross and save thyself first and us later.'

He had testified that God was his Father; that he and the Father were one; that no man came unto the Father but by the Son; and that he was the Son of God. Now they taunt: "If thou be the Son of God, come down from the cross." What are these words but an echo, by the mouths of the Jews, of those spoken in the wilderness by the devil: "If thou be the Son of God, command that these stones be made bread," or 'Cast thyself down from the pinnacle of the Temple' (Matt. 4:1-11), to prove it. Whether by his own

218

voice or by the voice of his servants, Lucifer's word is the same!

Jesus had saved others from all manner of disease and perils; he had calmed storms and fed multitudes; he had even raised rotting corpses from stench-filled tombs—all in similitude of the spiritual healings and salvation found in his words. Miracles were a way of life with him. Now they challenge him to save himself. "He saved others; himself he cannot save." "He saved others; let him save himself, if he be Christ, the chosen of God." Such were their words.

He had proclaimed himself as their King, their Deliverer, their Messiah. He came to reign in the hearts of the righteous. His kingdom, though not of this world, was as real as any realm ever inhabited by any people. Now they tempted him with these words: "If he be the King of Israel, let him now come down from the cross, and we will believe him." "Let Christ the King of Israel descend now from the cross, that we may see and believe." Believe? Yes, as they did when he opened the eyes of one who was blind from birth, or when he cast evil spirits from a Gadarene demoniac, or when he raised a man from Bethany from death!

As though to put an eternal seal on Him whom they derided, the Sanhedrists said—quoting, wittingly or otherwise, the Messianic word: "He trusted on the Lord that he would deliver him: let him deliver him, seeing he delighted in him" (Ps. 22:8)—the Sanhedrists said: "He trusted in God; let him deliver him now; if he will save him, let him save him; for he said, I am the Son of God." Thus bore they testimony against themselves. He trusted in God! They knew he had lived a righteous life!

Jesus Ministers from His Cross
(Matthew 27:44; JST, Matthew 27:47-48; Mark 15:32;
JST, Mark 15:37; Luke 23:39-43; JST, Luke 23:40; John 19:25-27)

Our Lord's earthly mission to the wicked and ungodly among men ceased when he implored his Father to forgive the Roman soldiers who drove the sharp nails into his quivering flesh. Thereafter, through all the taunts and insults, as the heads of the wicked wagged and the jeering of the ungodly bespoke its satanic source, he maintained a kingly silence. The blasphemous bleatings of the black sheep of Israel no longer concerned him. He had delivered his Father's word to them in days past; he had raised the warning voice with power and conviction; now their sins were upon their own heads; his garments were clean. But to those who sought him, and those who yet relied on the strength of his eternal arm, he still had words of comfort and counsel. One of these was the so-called penitent thief; another was his mother, the Blessed Virgin.

One of the malefactors who was crucified with him joined the general chorus of hate and satanism; he cast into Jesus' teeth the same blasphemous cries as did those beneath the cross. "If thou art the Christ, save thyself and us," he taunted, *knowing* within himself that Jesus was *not* the Christ and that there was no hope of salvation. But the other one rebuked his fellow criminal. "Dost not thou fear God, seeing thou art in the same condemnation? And we indeed justly; for we receive the due reward of our deeds: but this man hath done nothing amiss." It is pleasant to suppose that this partially penitent prisoner-on-his-cross may have had some prior contact with the Chief Prisoner on the Cross of Calvary. Perhaps it was on a mountain in Galilee when Jesus said, "Blessed are they that mourn: for they shall be comforted" (Matt. 5:4), or near Bethany when the brother of the beloved sisters came forth from his tomb, still enwrapped in the clothes of death—but no matter, there was in any event some spark of spirituality in his darkened soul. "As a flame sometimes leaps up among dying embers, so amid the white ashes of a sinful life which lay so thick upon his heart, the flame of love towards his God and his Saviour was not quite quenched." He was not yet prepared to join such voices as still felt to sing songs of redeeming love to Him who had been lifted up, but at least he would not curse and defame the Innocent One.

"Under the hellish outcries which had broken loose around the cross of Jesus, there had lain a deep misgiving. Half of them seemed to have been instigated by doubt and fear. Even in the self-congratulations of the priests we catch an undertone of dread. Suppose that even now some imposing miracle should be wrought? Suppose that even now that martyr-form should burst indeed into Messianic splendour, and the King, who seemed to be in the slow misery of death, should suddenly with a great choice summon His legions of angels, and springing from His cross upon the rolling clouds of heaven, come in flaming fire to take vengeance upon His enemies? And the air seemed to be full of signs. There was a gloom of gathering darkness in the sky, a thrill and tremor in the solid earth, a haunting presence as of ghostly visitants who chilled the heart and hovered in awful witness above that scene." (Farrar, p. 702.)

Whatever the feelings of the more wicked of the malefactors, the other's heart was touched with remorse and pity—remorse that he had led a life of sin, pity for the suffering of one who had done no sin. "This man is just, and hath not sinned," he said. Then, "he cried unto the Lord that he would save him." "Lord, remember me when thou comest into thy kingdom," he pleaded. If this plea came from a Jewish heart, which envisioned only that temporal Messianic kingdom for which they all so fervently prayed, the penitent thief must have thought that Jesus was the Messiah—in spite of the cross—and that he would yet reign in the promised kingdom. But we would rather hope that the one in whose heart the fires of remorse and repentance were beginning to burn knew something of another kingdom, a kingdom that is not of this world, a kingdom into which the righteous will go, and where they will serve their Eternal King forever. Pleased that here was one, even

221

in death, who would seek him and desire blessings, Jesus uttered the marvelous, though hidden and enigmatic statement, "THIS DAY THOU SHALT BE WITH ME IN PARADISE." This is the second utterance from the cross.

Paradise—the abode of righteous spirits, as they await the day of their resurrection; paradise—a place of peace and rest where the sorrows and trials of his life have been shuffled off, and where the saints continue to prepare for a celestial heaven; paradise—not the Lord's eternal kingdom, but a way station along the course leading to eternal life, a place where the final preparation is made for that fulness of joy which comes only when body and spirit are inseparably connected in immortal glory! Thither Jesus this day is going. And in that general realm—the realm of departed spirits—so also will the so-called penitent thief find himself. He will not this day sit down on a throne on the right side of the Lord; even James and John were denied an assurance of such a reward. He will not stand in the congregation of the righteous when Jesus meets with Adam and Noah and Abraham and all the righteous dead; but he will be in the realm of the departed where he can learn from the Lord's legal administrators all that he must do to work out his salvation. If we had the most accurate possible translation, one that conveyed Jesus' real intent, his words to his fellow crucifee would convey this thought: 'This day shalt thou be with me in the world of spirits. There you can learn of me and my gospel; there you can begin to work out your salvation with fear and trembling before me.'

The issue is not deathbed repentance, as it were, under which a dying soul by simply saying, "I believe," or, "I repent," is immediately, without more, ready for the same eternal reward reserved for Peter and Paul, who fought good fights and laid their all upon the altar of service and sacrifice. The issue is that there is a possibility of repentance and conversion and progress after death and in the realm of the departed. There Jesus went when he left his life; there he met the righteous of all ages who had preceded him in death; there he taught the gospel; there he organized his work so that penitent thieves and repentant sinners—those who would have believed and obeyed had the fulness of truth been offered to them in this life—may yet become heirs of eternal salvation.[1] Thus it is written: "For this cause was the gospel preached also to them that are dead, that they might be judged according to men in the flesh, but live according to God in the spirit." (1 Pet. 4:6.)

And in all this the Messianic word is fulfilled. Isaiah foretold: "When thou shalt make his soul an offering for sin, he shall see his seed." (Isa. 53:10.) And in his death our Lord visited his seed in the spirit world. He visited those who had taken upon themselves his name; those who had been adopted into his family; those who had become his sons and his daughters by faith. (D&C 138.)

Jesus' attention is now turned to a scene of sorrow and despair. By the cross stands his mother, the Virgin of Galilee, the one chosen of God to bear his Son, the one who had suckled and cradled and reared Israel's Messiah. With her are three other faithful women—her sister, Salome, the wife of Zebedee and the mother of James and John (who thus were cousins of Jesus); Mary the wife of Cleophas; and Mary Magdalene. On the resurrection morn Jesus will pay to Mary Magdalene one of the greatest compliments ever given a mortal being: he will appear to her first, even ahead of Peter and the Twelve. But now his concern is his mother. A sword is piercing her soul as the saintly Simeon had prophesied that day in the temple. How the mother must have suffered to see her Son bear the infinite burden placed upon him!

With these four sisters was the Beloved John, the one who leaned on Jesus' breast and for whom the Master had greater love than for any other. It is clear that Joseph, the husband of Mary, had passed on; it appears also that Mary's other sons had not yet joined the household of faith and accepted Jesus, their brother, as the Son of God; and we are led to believe that the apostle John had a home in Jerusalem. Clearly, Mary's future lot must be cast with the Twelve and the Church and the apostolic witnesses whom Jesus will soon command to carry his message to all the world. Thus to his mother he says: "Woman, behold thy son!" And to John the word is given: "Behold thy mother!" These words comprise the third utterance from the cross. "And from that hour that disciple took her unto his own home."

Atonement Completed on the Cross
(Matthew 27:45-51; JST, Matthew 27:54; Mark 15:33-38; JST, Mark 15:41; Luke 23:44-46; John 19:28-30; JST, John 19:29; 3 Ne. 8:5-25)

That which began in Gethsemane was finished on the cross and crowned in the resurrection. Jesus took upon himself the sins of all men when he suffered and sweat great drops of blood from every pore in Gethsemane. It was then that his suffering caused himself, even God, to suffer both body and spirit in a way which is totally beyond mortal comprehension. Then again on the cross—in addition to all the physical pain of that horrifying ordeal—he felt the spiritual agonies of the sins of others, as we shall see. How the resurrection ties in to the atonement, we do not know and cannot tell, only that the scriptures testify that the effects of the resurrection of Christ passed upon all men so that, because he rose from death, all are raised in immortality. In some way, incomprehensible to us, Gethsemane, the cross, and the empty tomb join into one grand and eternal drama, in the course of which Jesus abolishes death, and out of which comes immortality for all and eternal life for the righteous.

Jesus has now been hanging in agony on the accursed tree for about three hours, from somewhere near 9 A.M. to noon. He will continue to suffer the curses of crucifixion for another three hours, until around 3 P.M. when he voluntarily gives up the ghost. Of these coming hours, Matthew and Mark say only that it was a period when there was darkness over all the land; Luke extends this turning of day into night to cover a greater area. "There was a darkness over all the earth," he says, "and the sun was darkened." The fact of the darkness, for which there is no known scientific explanation, is known to us, but its purpose and what happened during those three seemingly endless hours remain outside the bounds of our understanding. Could it be that this was the period of his greatest trial, or that during it the agonies of Gethsemane recurred and even intensified?

That this darkness did cover the whole earth we surmise from the Book of Mormon account. The Nephite prophets had spoken, Messianically, of three days of darkness that would be a sign unto them of the crucifixion of Christ. At that time the rocks would rend and there would be such upheavals in nature that those on the isles of the sea would say, "The God of nature suffers." (1 Ne. 19:10-12; Hel. 14:20-24.) The Nephite record tells of the fulfillment of these prophecies; of the darkness and storms and destructions that then occurred; of cities sinking into the seas; of mountains and valleys being created; of the rocks rending and the whole face of the earth being deformed. It is of more than passing import that the storms and tempests and earthquakes lasted "for about the space of three hours," and then "there was darkness upon the face of the land." It was a "thick darkness," and the people could "feel the vapor of darkness. And there could be no light, because of the darkness, neither candles, neither torches; neither could there be fire kindled with their fine and exceedingly dry wood, so that there could not be any light at all; And there was not any light seen, neither fire, nor glimmer, neither the sun, nor the moon, nor the stars, for so great were the mists of darkness which were upon the face of the land."

Among the Nephites, where the darkness was accompanied with destructions, "there was great mourning and howling and weeping among all the people." If the darkness in the Old World was like that in the Americas, we can suppose that the hearts of those around the cross were filled with deep misgivings. Emotions of dread and horror must have filled the hearts of the guilty and the innocent. "Of the incidents of those last three hours we are told nothing, and that awful obscuration of the noonday sun may well have overawed every heart into an inaction respecting which there was nothing to relate. What Jesus suffered *then* for us men and our salvation we cannot know, for during those hours He hung upon His cross in silence and darkness; or, if He spoke, there were none there to record His words. But towards the close of that time His anguish culminated, and—emptied to the very uttermost of that glory which He had since the world began—drinking to the very deepest dregs the cup of humiliation and bitterness—enduring, not only to have taken upon Him the form of a servant, but also to suffer the last infamy which human hatred could impose on perfect helplessness—He uttered that mysterious cry, of which the full significance will never be fathomed by man."[2]

"Eli, Eli, lama sabachthani?" That is: *"My God, My God, why hast thou forsaken me?"*

Spoken with a loud voice, these words, quoted from David's Messianic prophecies, are the fourth utterance from the cross. "What mind of man can fathom the significance of that awful cry? It seems, that in addition to the fearful suffering incident to crucifixion, the agony of Gethsemane had recurred, intensified beyond human power to endure. In that bitterest hour the dying Christ was alone, alone in most terrible reality. That the supreme sacrifice of the Son might be consummated in all its fulness, the Father seems to have withdrawn the support of His immediate Presence, leaving to the Savior of men the glory of complete victory over the forces of sin and death." (Talmage, p. 661.)

Some of those who stood by said, "Behold, he calleth

for Elias," whose name was associated in their legends with the coming and work and ministry of the Messiah. "The readiness with which they seized this false impression is another proof of the wild state of excitement and terror—the involuntary dread of something great, and unforeseen, and terrible—to which they had been reduced from their former savage insolence. For Elijah, the great prophet of the Old Covenant, was inextricably mingled with all the Jewish expectations of a Messiah, and these expectations were full of wrath. The coming of Elijah would be the coming of a day of fire, in which the sun should be turned into blackness and the moon into blood, and the powers of heaven should be shaken. Already the noonday sun was shrouded in unnatural eclipse: might not some awful form at any moment rend the heavens and come down, touch the mountains and they should smoke? The vague anticipation of conscious guilt was unfulfilled." (Farrar, p. 705.)

The infinite and eternal atonement has now been wrought. Jesus has gained the victory; he has done all that his Father sent him to do; now he faces only the physical agonies of the cross, and he can think of his own bodily needs. He calls out, "I thirst," and these are the fifth words from the cross. "It is probable that a few hours before, the cry would have only provoked a roar of frantic mockery; but now the lookers-on were reduced by awe to a readier humanity. Near the cross there lay on the ground the large earthen vessel containing the *posca,* which was the ordinary drink of the Roman soldiers. The mouth of it was filled with a piece of sponge, which served as a cork. Instantly some one—we know not whether he was friend or enemy, or merely one who was there out of idle curiosity—took out the sponge and dipped it in the *posca* to give it to Jesus. But low as was the elevation of the cross, the head of the Sufferer, as it rested on the horizontal beam of the accursed tree, was just beyond the man's reach: and therefore he put the sponge at the end of a stalk of hyssop—about a foot

227

long—and held it up to the parched and dying lips." (Farrar, pp. 706–7.) Jesus drank what was offered, thus fulfilling the Messianic prophecy: "They gave me also gall for my meat; and in my thirst they gave me vinegar to drink." (Ps. 69:21.)

As he drank, the heartless among them called out: "Let him alone; let us see whether Elias will come to take him down." At Jesus' behest Elijah and twelve legions of angels would have attended the cross at any time; at his word heaven and earth would pass away; by his voice nothing was impossible—and yet there was no divine intervention. Our Pattern, our Prototype, our Exemplar marked the path for all men. He endured to the end.[3] Would God that it may be so for all of us!

Thereupon Jesus made his final earthly report to the one who had sent him. 'Father, it is finished, thy will is done,' he said; and this is the sixth utterance from the cross. How, then, does a God die? It is a voluntary act; no man taketh his life from him; he lays it down of himself; he has power to lay it down and power to take it again. Jesus makes his seventh utterance from the cross. He says simply: "Father, into thy hands I commend my spirit," quoting thus, as was his wont, the Messianic word concerning himself. (Ps. 31:5.) "And having said thus, he gave up the ghost." He did not taste of death, for it was sweet unto him. As he, with the Eleven, had sung in the Hallel the night before: "Precious in the sight of the Lord is the death of his saints." (Ps. 116:15.)

As Jesus passed through the door from mortality to the spirit world; as his eternal spirit divested itself of its tenement of clay; as he left his mortal remains to be cared for by the loving persons whose friend he was—two portentous events marked his glorious victory. For one, "the earth did quake, and the rocks rent"; and, for another, "the veil of the temple was rent in twain from the top to the bottom."

As to the earthquake, it came in fulfillment of Enoch's word. He, among others of the ancients, had seen "the Son of Man lifted up on the cross, after the manner of men; And he heard a loud voice; and the heavens were veiled; and all the creations of God mourned; and the earth groaned; and the rocks were rent." (Moses 7:55-56.) Had the earthquake among the Jews been as it was among the Nephites, Jerusalem itself would have scarcely survived.

As to the rending of the veil of the temple, it was the one thing that would symbolize, in power, the end of the old Jewish dispensation and the beginning of the new Christian day. The veil itself—shielding the Holy of Holies from the gaze of any but the high priest, and from him except once a year, on the day of atonement, when he entered the sacred portal to atone for the sins of the people—the veil is said to have been sixty feet long, thirty feet wide, "of the thickness of the palm of the hand, and wrought in 72 squares, which were joined together." It was so heavy that it took hundreds of priests to manipulate it. "If the Veil was at all such as is described in the Talmud, it could not have been rent in twain by a mere earthquake or the fall of the lintel, although its composition in squares fastened together might explain, how the rent might be as described in the Gospel.

"Indeed, everything seems to indicate that, although the earthquake might furnish the physical basis, the rent of the Temple-Veil was—with reverence be it said—really made by the Hand of God. As we compute, it may just have been the time when, at the Evening-Sacrifice, the officiating Priesthood entered the Holy Place, either to burn the incense or to do other sacred service there. To see before them, not as the aged Zacharias at the beginning of this history the Angel Gabriel, but the Veil of the Holy Place rent from top to bottom—that beyond it they could scarcely have seen—and hanging in two parts from its fastenings above and at the side, was, indeed, a terrible portent, which would soon become generally known, and must, in some form or other, have been preserved in tradition. And they all must have understood, that it meant that God's Own Hand had rent the Veil, and for ever deserted

229

and thrown open that Most Holy Place where He had so long dwelt in the mysterious gloom, only lit up once a year by the glow of the censer of him, who made atonement for the sins of the people.'' (Edersheim 2:611-12.)

Thus did Jesus, the Atoning One, through whose blood all men may freely pass through the veil into the presence of the Lord, thus did he, by the rending of the veil of the old temple, signify that its ordinances of atonement and forgiveness were done away in him. Thus did he, making his own body a new temple, as it were, signify that his atonement, and the forgiveness of sins made possible thereby, shall admit all true believers into his eternal Holy of Holies. ''For Christ is not entered into the holy places made with hands, which are the figures of the true; but into heaven itself, now to appear in the presence of God for us.'' (Heb. 9:24.)

And as every true believer ponders upon the wonder and glory of it all—as he contemplates the atonement wrought in the garden and on the cross; as he meditates about the immortality and eternal life that come through Christ—he marvels at what God has done for him. ''He sees in the cross of Christ''—and the cross is used in the prophetic word as a symbol for the atonement—''He sees in the cross of Christ something which far transcends its historical significance. He sees in it the fulfillment of all prophecy as well as the consummation of all history; he sees in it the explanation of the mystery of birth, and the conquest over the mystery of the grave. In that life he finds a perfect example; in that death an infinite redemption. As he contemplates the Incarnation and the Crucifixion, he no longer feels that God is far away, and that this earth is but a disregarded speck in the infinite azure, and he himself but an insignificant atom chance-thrown amid the thousand million living souls of an innumerable race, but he exclaims in faith and hope and love, 'Behold, the tabernacle of God is with men; yea, He will be their God, and they shall be His people.' 'Ye are the temple of the living God; as God

230

hath said, I will dwell in them, and walk in them.' " (Farrar, p. 711; Ezek. 37:27; 2 Cor. 6:16.)

NOTES

1. The common sectarian heresy that Jesus went to Hades while his body lay in the tomb has at least a grain of truth in it. He did go to a world of departed spirits, where he "preached unto the spirits in prison" (1 Pet. 3:18-20), to those who considered the long separation of their bodies from their spirits as a prison. (D&C 138.)

2. Farrar, p. 704.

3. Our friend Farrar gives us his summary of the sufferings of the Lord Jesus in these words:

"It is difficult adequately to realise the multitude and variety of the forms of spiritual distress and mental anguish, of scorn, and torture, to which the sinless Son of Man was continuously subjected from the time that He left the mount of Olives to enter Jerusalem for the Last Supper.

"1. At the Last Supper He had the heavy sorrow of reading the heart of the traitor, and of uttering His last farewells—mingled with prophecies of persecution as the path to final triumph—to those whom He loved best on earth.

"2. Then came the agony in the garden, which filled Him with speechless amazement and shuddering, until He had to fling Himself with His face to the earth in the tense absorption of prayer, and His sweat was like great gouts of blood streaming to the ground."

This was the hour of his greatest agony. It was here that he took upon himself, in a way incomprehensible to us, the sins of all men on conditions of repentance. It was here that he suffered in body and in spirit more than it is possible for other mortals to suffer. Those hours in the Garden of Gethsemane have no parallel among mortals in any age. Only a God could suffer or endure the lot that then and there was his.

"3. Then the horror of Judas's over-acted traitor-kiss, the seizure, the binding, the leading away, the desertion of Him by all His disciples in His hour of need.

"4. Then the long trials which, only broken by insult, lasted the whole night through; the sense of utter injustice; the proof that all those hierophants who should have been the very first to welcome Him with humble yet triumphant gladness, were fiercely bent on destroying Him by any means, however foul.

"5. Then the insolent blow in the face from one of the servants.

"6. Then the hearing His chief Apostle deny Him with oaths and curses.

"7. Then the night trial before Caiaphas and his most confidential adherents, with all its agitating incidents, its tumult of sneering voices, its dreadful adjuration, and the sentence on Him as 'a Man of Death' by the 'spiritual' court.

"8. Then the accumulations of brutal insult as the crowd of vile underlings mocked Him, and slapped and beat Him, and spat into His face, and, bandaging His eyes, bade Him name the wretches who had smitten Him.

"9. Then the early morning trial before the whole Sanhedrin, with its continuance of agitating appeals, and the final proof that 'He had come unto His own possessions, and His people received Him not.'

"10. Then, if we read the record rightly, another derision by the Priests and Sanhedrists.

"11. Then the long and thrilling scenes of the trial before Pilate, as He stood in the centre of a crowd thirsting for His blood, yelling for His crucifixion; heaping lies and insults upon Him; preferring to Him the robber and the murderer; defeating, by their ferocious pertinacity, the obvious desire of the Roman Governor to set Him free.

"12. Then the leading through the city to Herod, and the vain attempt of that despicable prince to wring some answer or some sign from Him.

"13. Then the coarse derision of Herod's myrmidons as, in mock homage, they stripped Him of His own garments and arrayed Him in a shining robe, with every accumulation of disdainful insolence and cruelty.

"14. Then the final sentence of crucifixion, pronounced by Pilate after vain appeals and efforts to overcome the furious animosity of His accusers.

"15. Then the brutal mockery by the whole band of Roman soldiers as He stood helpless among them. These coarse legionaries were only too much rejoiced to pour on Him the contempt and detestation which they felt for all Jews, and seized the opportunity to vent their callous savagery on One who, as they were taught to believe, had claimed to be a King. This King should have the insignia of royalty—a cast-off military *sagum* of scarlet; a crown—only twisted of torturing thorns; a sceptre—a reed which they could every now and then snatch out of His tied hands, and beat Him with it as well as with rods; the mock homage of bended knees varied by execrable spitting, and blows on the head, and slaps on the face with the open palm, and words of uttermost contempt.

"16. Then He was mangled and lacerated almost to death by the horrible and excruciating *flagellum,* inflicted by executioners who had no sense of pity,with scourges loaded with balls of lead and sharp-pointed bones.

"17. Then came the stripping bare of the robes, and the bending under the load of the cross—or, rather, of its *patibulum*—the transverse beam of the cross, which He was too much exhausted to carry, while the herald went before Him proclaiming the supposed crime for which He was condemned.

"18. Then the sight of the weeping and wailing daughters of Jerusalem.

"19. Then the driving of the lacerating, crushing nails through His feet, and through either hand, and the uplifting on the cross. . . .

"20. Then the sight of all the world's worst vileness flowing beneath His eyes in its noisy stream, as the Elders, in their heartlessness, wagged their heads at Him, and jeered, and blasphemed; and the soldiers mocked, and the crowd howled their insults, and the two wretched robbers who shared with Him that hour of shame—though *they* were guilty and He was innocent—joined in the continuous pitiless reviling.

"21. Then the sight of His mother in her unspeakable desolation.

"22. Then the darkening by anguish of His human soul, which wrung from Him the cry, 'My God, My God, why hast Thou forsaken Me?'

"Yet, amid all these accumulations of anguish, only one word of physical pain was wrung from Him—the cry, *'I thirst'*:—and so deep was the impression caused by His majestic patience, as well as by the portents which followed, that the whole crowd was overawed and hushed, and returned to Jerusalem beating their breasts, and saying, 'Truly, this was a righteous man;' and the penitent robber implored Him to receive him into His Kingdom; and even the Pagan Roman centurion spoke of Him as 'a Son of God.'

"The uttermost depth of superhuman woe seems to be revealed by His cry, 'My God, My God, why hast Thou forsaken Me?' " (F. W. Farrar, *The Life of Lives,* pp. 506–11.)

To this we add, if we interpret the holy word aright, that all of the anguish, all of the sorrow, and all of the suffering of Gethsemane recurred during the final three hours on the cross, the hours when darkness covered the land. Truly there was no sorrow like unto his sorrow, and no anguish and pain like unto that which bore in with such intensity upon him.

Chapter 109

IN THE ARIMATHEAN'S TOMB

Verily, verily, I say unto you,
The hour is coming, and now is,
when the dead shall hear the voice
of the Son of God:
and they that hear shall live. . . .
Marvel not at this:
for the hour is coming,
in the which all that are in the graves
shall hear his voice.
(John 5:25-29.)

The Roman Spear Pierces His Side
*(John 19:31-37; Matthew 27:54-56; JST, Matthew 27:59;
Mark 15:39-41; JST, Mark 15:45; Luke 23:47-49)*

Never was there such a crucifixion as this one. Scourging was always or often a prelude to the cross. Nails had been pounded into hands and feet by the thousands. To insult and demean dying sufferers was the common sport of the coarse ruffians who gaped on the mangled bodies. Perhaps others had been crowned with plaited thorns. But whenever did the rocks rend, and the earth shake, and a dire and deep darkness envelop the whole land for three long hours? And when else did the dying one, yet having strength and vigor in his whipped and beaten body, shout with a loud voice and seem to end his mortality of his own will and in full control of his faculties?

To all this the centurion and his soldiers were witnesses, and when they saw it all, they greatly feared and said: "Truly this was the Son of God." And the centurion himself glorified God—perhaps in praise and prayer—and said: "Certainly this was a righteous man."[1]

Nor were the centurion and his soldiers alone in their fearful and awe-filled feelings. A congregation of the friends and acquaintances and disciples of Jesus had now gathered at the cross, many of them being Galileans. They "smote their breasts," and were sorrowful. Particular mention is made of "the women that followed from Galilee." They had come to minister unto him "for his burial," and among them were Mary Magdalene, Mary the mother of James the younger and Joses, and Salome the wife of Zebedee and the mother of James and John. The Blessed Virgin is not mentioned, leaving us to suppose that John has by now taken her to his home so she will no longer be a personal witness of the agonies of her Son. Since Jesus' friends were there, we take the liberty of assuming this included the Eleven; surely all of them, scattered at Gethsemane, would have long since rallied again round his side.

But now, "the sun was westering as the darkness rolled away from the completed sacrifice. They who had not thought it a pollution to inaugurate their feast by the murder of their Messiah, were seriously alarmed lest the sanctity of the following day—which began at sunset—should be compromised by the hanging of the corpses on the cross. And, horrible to relate, the crucified often lived for many hours—nay, even for two or three days—in their torture." (Farrar, pp. 711-12.) According to their law the body of an executed criminal could not be left hanging overnight lest the land be defiled. (Deut. 21:22-23.) And, further, in this instance the coming day was doubly sacred; it was both a Sabbath and the second Paschal day, the one on which the wavesheaf was offered to the Lord. Hence the Jews besought Pilate to have the legs of the three crucified persons broken. "Sometimes there was added to the punishment of crucifixion that of breaking the bones (*crurifragium*) by means of a club or hammer. This would not itself bring death, but the breaking of the bones was always followed by a *coup de grace,* by sword, lance, or stroke, which immediately put an end to what remained of life. Thus the 'breaking of the bones' was a sort of increase of punishment, by way of compensation for its shortening by the final stroke that followed." (Edersheim 2:613.)

Pilate acceded to their pleas; the soldiers broke the legs and then killed the two malefactors with the sword. Finding Jesus already dead, "they brake not his legs," that it might be fulfilled which was written concerning him as the Paschal Lamb ("Neither shall ye break a bone thereof"), and concerning him as the Suffering Servant ("He keepeth all his bones: not one of them is broken"). (Ex. 12:46; Num. 9:12; Ps. 34:20.) However, one of the soldiers, perhaps to make sure that Jesus was dead, hurled his spear into his side, in the region of the heart, this, again, happening that the prophetic word might come to pass. Zechariah, speaking of the millennial day when "the spirit of grace and of supplication" shall be poured out upon the Jews "and upon the inhabitants of Jerusalem," foretold that their Messiah would then say: "They shall look upon me whom they have pierced." This, our inspired New Testament author tells us, shall come to pass because of the wound then gashed into Jesus' side. And we might add, as Zechariah promises, that in that future day the Jews will say to Jesus: "What are these wounds in thine hands?" and he will answer: "Those with which I was wounded in the house of my friends." (Zech. 12:10; 13:6.) Or, more perfectly, as the account is found in latter-day revelation: "What are these wounds in thine hands and in thy feet?" Of this question the Wounded One says: "Then shall they know that I am the Lord; for I will say unto them: These wounds are the wounds with which I was wounded in the house of my friends. I am he who was lifted up. I am Jesus that was crucified. I am the Son of God. And then shall they weep because of their iniquities; then shall they lament because they persecuted their king." (D&C 45:51-53.)

But there is more. From the spear wound—and it was of major proportion, as witness Jesus' statement to the Nephites, "Thrust your hands into my side" (3 Ne. 11:14)—from the spear wound, "forthwith came there out blood and water." Of this unusual occurrence, John testifies: "And he that saw it bare record, and his record is true: and he knoweth that he saith true, that ye might believe."

"Why does John, as though he were recording some great miracle, tell us that both blood and water flowed from Christ's pierced side, and then add his solemn certification that he spoke the truth in so stating? It appears that the Beloved Disciple was showing how one of the great doctrines of revealed religion, that of being born again, rests upon and is efficacious because of the atonement. As the inspired record recites, men are 'born into the world by water, and blood, and the spirit' thereby becoming mortal souls. To gain salvation they must thereafter 'be born again into the kingdom of heaven, of water, and of the Spirit, and be cleansed by blood,' meaning the blood of Christ. Thus when men see birth into this world, they are reminded of what is required for birth into the kingdom of heaven.

"Since this spiritual rebirth and consequent salvation in the kingdom of heaven are available because of the atonement, how fitting it is that the elements present in that infinite sacrifice are also water, blood, and spirit. Accordingly, when men think of the crucifixion of Christ, they are reminded of what they must do to be born again and gain that full salvation which comes because of his atonement.

"John, who was eye witness to the water and blood gushing from Jesus' side after his spirit had left his body, later wrote of being 'born of God' through the atonement in these words: 'Whatsoever is born of God overcometh the world. . . . Who is he that overcometh the world, but he that believeth that Jesus is the Son of God? This is he that came by water and blood, even Jesus Christ; not by water only, but by water and blood. And it is the Spirit that beareth witness, because the Spirit is truth. . . . And there are three that bear witness in earth, the spirit, and the water, and the blood.' (1 John 5:1-8.)" (*Commentary* 1:834-35.)

Jesus' Body Is Claimed, Buried, Guarded
(Matthew 27:57-66; JST, Matthew 27:65;
Mark 15:42-47; JST, Mark 15:47-48;
Luke 23:50-56; JST, Luke 23:51-52; John 19:38-42)

Those three corpses, hanging on their accursed crosses, must be disposed of before the setting sun ushers in the Sabbath. "The Jews had taken every precaution to prevent the ceremonial pollution of a day so sacred, and were anxious that immediately after the death of the victims had been secured, their bodies should be taken from the cross. About the sepulture they did not trouble themselves, leaving it to the chance good offices of friends and relatives to huddle the malefactors into their nameless graves. The dead body of Jesus was left hanging till the last, because a person who could not easily be slighted had gone to obtain leave from Pilate to dispose of it as he wished." (Farrar, p. 716.) Without this aid—shall we not say there was a divine hand in it?—and as far as the chief priests were concerned, the body of Jesus might have been dumped with the refuse in the Valley of Hinnom, there to rot and decay and be burned by the everlasting fires of Gehenna. Perhaps this is what happened to the bodies of the two thieves.

All four of the Gospel authors speak in laudatory tones of Joseph of Arimathea. They identify him as a rich man, an honorable counselor, one who waited for the kingdom of God, a good man and a just one, and a disciple (although John says he kept his discipleship secret, "for fear of the

Jews"). So they speak of the man in whose new tomb the body of the Lord Jesus was to lie for a few brief hours. "This was Joseph of Arimathea, a rich man, of high character and blameless life, and a distinguished member of the Sanhedrin. Although timidity of disposition, or weakness of faith, had hitherto prevented him from openly declaring his belief in Jesus, yet he had abstained from sharing in the vote of the Sanhedrin, or countenancing their crime. And now sorrow and indignation inspired him with courage. Since it was too late to declare his sympathy for Jesus as a living Prophet, he would at least give a sign of his devotion to Him as the martyred victim of a wicked conspiracy. Flinging secrecy and caution to the winds, he no sooner saw that the cross on Golgotha now bore a lifeless burden, than he went to Pilate on the very evening of the crucifixion, and begged that the dead body might be given him. Although the Romans left their crucified slaves to be devoured by dogs and ravens, Pilate had no difficulty in sanctioning the more humane and reverent custom of the Jews, which required, even in extreme cases, the burial of the dead." (Farrar, pp. 716–17.)

Pilate marveled at the report of such an early death, apparently not yet knowing that in the case of the two thieves death had been hastened by the *crurifragium*. First, Pilate asked the Arimathean if Jesus "were already dead," and then, "calling the centurion, he asked him, If he had been any while dead." Receiving the sure witness of his own military commander—and with what severity and finality divine providence is *proving* His death, as a prelude to *proving* his resurrection—receiving this assurance, Pilate gave the body to Joseph.

Then the cross was lowered and laid upon the ground; from the mangled hands and bloody feet the Roman nails were drawn out; and the body was washed and cleaned and taken to a new tomb, hewn but recently from the rock. "At the entrance to the tomb—and within the rock—there was a court, nine feet square, where ordinarily the bier was deposited, and its bearers gathered to do the last offices for the Dead. Thither we suppose Joseph to have carried the Sacred Body.'' (Edersheim 2:617.) At some time, probably when the cross was lowered or else in the court of the tomb, Joseph was joined by Nicodemus, who had come to Jesus by night three years before at the First Passover. "If, as seems extremely probable, he be identical with the Nakdimon Ben Gorion of the Talmud, he was a man of enormous wealth; and however much he had held back during the life of Jesus, now, on the evening of His death, his heart was filled with a gush of compassion and remorse, and he hurried to His cross and burial with an offering of truly royal munificence. The faith which had once required the curtain of darkness can now venture at least into the light of sunset, and [be] brightened finally into noonday confidence. Thanks to this glow of kindling sorrow and compassion in the hearts of these two noble and wealthy disciples, He who died as a malefactor was buried as a king. 'He made His grave with the wicked, and with the rich in His death.' The fine linen which Joseph had purchased was richly spread with the hundred *litras* of myrrh and perfumed aloe-wood which Nicodemus had brought, and the lacerated body—whose divinely-human spirit was now in the calm of its Sabbath rest in the Paradise of God—was thus carried to its loved and peaceful grave. . . .

"The preparations had to be hurried, because when the sun had set the Sabbath would have begun. All that they could do, therefore, was to wash the corpse, to lay it amid the spices, to wrap the head in a white napkin, to roll the fine linen round and round the wounded limbs, and to lay the body reverently in the rocky niche. Then they rolled a *golal,* or great stone, to the horizontal aperture; and scarcely had they accomplished this when, as the sun sank behind the hills of Jerusalem, the new Sabbath dawned.

"Mary of Magdala, and Mary the mother of James and Joses, had seated themselves in the garden to mark well the place of sepulture, and other Galilean women had also noticed the spot, and hurried home to prepare fresh spices and ointments before the Sabbath began, that they might hasten back early on the morning of Sunday, and complete that embalming of the body which Joseph and Nicodemus had only hastily begun. They spent in quiet that miserable Sabbath, which, for the broken hearts of all who loved Jesus, was a Sabbath of anguish and despair.

"But the enemies of Christ were not so inactive. The awful misgiving of guilty consciences was not removed even by His death upon the cross. They recalled, with dreadful reminiscence, the rumored prophecies of His resurrection—the sign of the prophet Jonah, which He had said would alone be given them—the great utterance about the destroyed Temple, which He would in three days raise up; and these intimations, which were but dim to a crushed and wavering faith, were read, like fiery letters upon the wall, by the illuminating glare of an uneasy guilt. Pretending, therefore, to be afraid lest His body should be stolen by His disciples for the purposes of imposture, they begged that, until the third day, the tomb might be securely guarded. Pilate gave them a brief and haughty permission to do anything they liked; for—apparently in the evening, when the great Paschal Sabbath was over—they sent their guard to seal the *golal,* and to watch the sepulchre." (Farrar, pp. 717–19.)

In the Realm of Disembodied Spirits
(D&C 138)

"And he bowed his head, and gave up the ghost." (John 19:30.) Between life and death there is only the twinkling of an eye, only a breath of air in the lungs of a man, only an eternal spirit in its tenement of clay. The spirit steps out of the body, to live in another realm, and we call it death. Jesus died—voluntarily, for he had the power of immortality, and no man could take his life from him—he died of his own will and choice; his spirit laid down its temporal body

240

of flesh and blood and chose to live in an unembodied state in the realm of the departed. Jesus gave up the ghost and entered the paradise of God. He was as other men in that his spirit went to live in a spirit world to await the day of his resurrection, the day when the eternal spirit would be reunited with its body, thereafter to live eternally in immortal glory, having a body of flesh and bones.

When Jesus died—that very moment—his mortal ministry ended and his ministry among the spirits in prison began. Then it was, according to the Messianic word, that he began to "proclaim liberty to the captives, and the opening of the prison to them that are bound" (Isa. 61:1); then the work commenced "to bring out the prisoners from the prison, and them that sit in darkness out of the prison house" (Isa. 42:7); then it was that he who had now suffered for our sins, the Just for the unjust, having been put to death in the flesh but continuing to live in the spirit, "went and preached unto the spirits in prison" (1 Pet. 3:18-20).

How marvelous are the dealings of God with man! How infinite is his mercy, how glorious his grace! He provideth a way whereby all his children—either in mortality or in the spirit world, awaiting their resurrection—may hear the gospel of salvation. All shall stand before his eternal bar to be judged according to their works. All "shall give account to him that is ready to judge the quick and the dead." And "for this cause"—that the living and the dead shall all be judged by the same gospel standard—is "the gospel preached also to them that are dead, that they might be judged according to men in the flesh, but live according to God in the spirit." (1 Pet. 4:5-6.)

From Adam to Christ, through four thousand years of births and deaths, unnumbered millions died without a knowledge of Christ and the salvation which is in him. And yet his is the only name given under heaven—now or ever, in time or in eternity—whereby men can be saved. His gospel is the one plan of salvation; it charts the one course to celestial rest; no man cometh unto the Father but by him and his law. From righteous Abel to Zacharias the son of Barachias who was slain for the testimony of the truth, all the righteous dead had gone to the paradise of peace and beauty, there to await the day of their coming forth in the resurrection of the just. Even they considered the long separation of their bodies and spirits as a prison. During the same long millenniums of rebellion and war and disease and death, millions died without a knowledge of the truth and went to hell, an abode of darkness and suffering and sorrow, there to await the resurrection of the unjust. In their benighted state they were without hope, not even knowing whether there would be a resurrection and an eventual reward for them in one of the kingdoms of their Father. Truly, if ever spirits were in prison, these were they. And so the Messianic word proclaims: "And they shall be gathered together, as prisoners are gathered in the pit, and shall be shut up in the prison, and after many days shall they be visited." (Isa. 24:22.)

With the death of Jesus, the day of their visitation is at hand. He goes to the spirit world to preach the gospel, which is the plan of salvation; if they believe its laws and desire to obey its ordinances, they may be heirs of salvation. For them, the living will perform the vicarious ordinances needed for their salvation. And when the day comes for "death and hell" to deliver up the dead which are in them, then all shall be judged by gospel standards. (Rev. 20:12-15.) Even David's soul will not always be left "in hell." (Ps. 16:10.) Those who lived in the days of Noah shall again hear the truth, for they, too, are among "the spirits of men kept in prison, whom the Son visited, and preached the gospel unto them, that they might be judged according to men in the flesh; Who received not the testimony of Jesus in the flesh, but afterwards received it." (D&C 76:71-80.) Theirs, however, shall be a terrestrial inheritance, and not a celestial, because they rejected the gospel in this life and then received it in the spirit world.

As the body of Jesus lies in its borrowed grave, what,

then, do we see in the spirit world? We see a great host assembled to greet the Son of God. We see Joseph the husband of Mary; we see some of the shepherds who heard the angelic choir sing glory to God in the highest and peace and goodwill to men on earth; we see the saintly Simeon and the blessed Anna, who testified of Him in the temple; we see Zacharias and Elisabeth and John the Baptist; we see the faithful of all the ages—all assembled to hear the voice of Him in whom they trusted.

And there were gathered together in one place an innumerable company of the spirits of the just, who had been faithful in the testimony of Jesus while they lived in mortality; And who had offered sacrifice in the similitude of the great sacrifice of the Son of God, and had suffered tribulation in their Redeemer's name. . . .

I beheld that they were filled with joy and gladness, and were rejoicing together because the day of their deliverance was at hand. They were assembled awaiting the advent of the Son of God into the spirit world, to declare their redemption from the bands of death. . . .

While this vast multitude waited and conversed, rejoicing in the hour of their deliverance from the chains of death, the Son of God appeared, declaring liberty to the captives who had been faithful; And there he preached to them the everlasting gospel, the doctrine of the resurrection and the redemption of mankind from the fall, and from individual sins on conditions of repentance. . . .

And the saints rejoiced in their redemption, and bowed the knee and acknowledged the Son of God as their Redeemer and Deliverer from death and the chains of hell. Their countenances shone, and the radiance from the presence of the Lord rested upon them, and they sang praises unto his holy name.

Then, as he ministered in the world of spirits, Jesus

"organized his forces and appointed messengers, clothed with power and authority, and commissioned them to go forth and carry the light of the gospel to them that were in darkness, even to all the spirits of men; and thus was the gospel preached to the dead." And what a glorious day it was! Adam, Seth, and Enos; Abel, Noah, and Shem; Abraham, Isaac, and Jacob; Isaiah, Ezekiel, and Daniel; Nephi, Alma, and Abinadi; Helaman, Mormon, and Moroni—all the prophets! all the saints! all the righteous! of all past ages!—all assembled to bow the knee, and hear the voice, and cry hosanna.

In his mortal ministry, Jesus the King, as a mortal, had spoken such words as never before man spake; yet they were addressed to weak and faltering and oftentimes rebellious mortals, none of whose hearts had yet begun to burn with the fires of the Spirit. Now in the paradise of God, among the righteous, who already knew the doctrines of salvation; who already had a hope of eternal life; and, above all, whose souls were already afire with the Holy Spirit of God—what wonders of divine truth he must have spoken as he prepared them for their not-distant resurrection! We assume he ministered and spoke almost continuously from the hour of his death to the hour of his resurrection, for, among them, there was no need to rest; none would grow weary or become inattentive. The weaknesses of the flesh were no longer theirs. Perhaps, also, he opened their minds and quickened their understandings so that they saw in vision the wonders of eternity. That we have not yet learned by revelation what was said and done there simply means that our weak and fragile spiritual stature does not as yet qualify us to know and understand what others more worthy and more qualified have received.

These righteous dead "had looked upon the long absence of their spirits from their bodies as a bondage." And all "these the Lord taught"—there in the quiet peace and perfect serenity of a paradisiacal Eden—"and gave them power to come forth, after his resurrection from the dead, to enter into his Father's kingdom, there to be crowned with immortality and eternal life, And continue thenceforth their labor as had been promised by the Lord, and be partakers of all blessings which were held in reserve for them that love him."

Jesus, As a Spirit, Speaks to the Nephites
(3 Nephi 9:1-22; 10:1-8)

After the great destructions in the Americas that took place during the three hours of darkness, and while Jesus' body lay in the Arimathean's tomb, his voice was raised among the Nephites. He did not then appear and his face was not seen among them. But "there was a voice heard among all the inhabitants of the earth, upon all the face of this land." The first spoken words were:

Wo, wo, wo unto this people; wo unto the inhabitants of the whole earth except they shall repent; for the devil laugheth, and his angels rejoice, because of the slain of the fair sons and daughters of my people.

A day of destruction and desolation shall surely come upon all the wicked and rebellious. When their cup of iniquity is full, they are always swept from the face of the earth. Fire and brimstone consumed those in Sodom and Gomorrah and the cities of the plains; the floods swept those in Noah's day to a watery grave; the Jaredite and Nephite nations fell by the sword; Titus turned Jerusalem into a dung heap; and at the Second Coming the wicked and ungodly shall be as stubble. During the three hours of darkness, sixteen cities in the Americas, together with their inhabitants, were utterly destroyed. All this the voice announced, saying repetitiously that it was done "to hide their wickedness and abominations from before my face, that the blood of the prophets and the saints should not come up any more unto me against them." Those who had been spared were identified as the more righteous and were called upon to repent and be converted that Jesus might heal them.

Yea, verily I say unto you, if ye will come unto me ye shall have eternal life. Behold, mine arm of mercy is extended towards you, and whosoever will come, him will I receive; and blessed are those who come unto me.

Behold, I am Jesus Christ the Son of God. I created the heavens and the earth, and all things that in them are. I was with the Father from the beginning. I am in the Father, and the Father in me; and in me hath the Father glorified his name.

I came unto my own, and my own received me not. And the scriptures concerning my coming are fulfilled.

And as many as have received me, to them have I given to become the sons of God; and even so will I to as many as shall believe on my name, for behold, by me redemption cometh, and in me is the law of Moses fulfilled.

I am the light and the life of the world. I am Alpha and Omega, the beginning and the end.

And ye shall offer up unto me no more the shedding of blood; yea, your sacrifices and your burnt offerings shall be done away, for I will accept none of your sacrifices and your burnt offerings.

And ye shall offer for a sacrifice unto me a broken heart and a contrite spirit. And whoso cometh unto me with a broken heart and a contrite spirit, him will I baptize with fire and with the Holy Ghost. . . .

Behold, I have come unto the world to bring redemption unto the world, to save the world from sin.

Therefore, whoso repenteth and cometh unto me as a little child, him will I receive, for of such is the kingdom of God. Behold, for such I have laid down

*my life, and have taken it up again; therefore repent,
and come unto me ye ends of the earth, and be
saved.*

So the voice spoke to the Nephites; and nowhere in the
whole New Testament account, where the same doctrines
are taught, is there such a plain and sweet and simple
summary of the glorious mission of Jesus the Messiah as
these words contain. They stand by themselves, scarcely
needing further exposition, though in fact the shining truths
they set forth have been explained in this work in their
various New Testament contexts. For clarity's sake we
need only add that the climax of this sermon, which speaks
of Jesus having laid down his life and having taken it up
again, is merely reciting what is to be as though it were
already accomplished; just so surely would his almost-then
resurrection come to pass.

The voice ceased, and "there was silence in the land for
the space of many hours." And the people "did cease
lamenting and howling for the loss of their kindred which
had been slain." Then the voice came again, uttering words
applicable to them, and to the Jews in Jerusalem, and to all
the house of Israel, no matter when or where they lived.

*O ye people of these great cities which have
fallen, who are descendants of Jacob, yea, who are
of the house of Israel, how oft have I gathered you
as a hen gathereth her chickens under her wings,
and have nourished you.*

*And again, how oft would I have gathered you as
a hen gathereth her chickens under her wings, yea,
O ye people of the house of Israel, who have fallen;
yea, O ye people of the house of Israel, ye that dwell
at Jerusalem, as ye that have fallen; yea, how oft
would I have gathered you as a hen gathereth her
chickens, and ye would not.*

O ye house of Israel whom I have spared, how oft

will I gather you as a hen gathereth her chickens under her wings, if ye will repent and return unto me with full purpose of heart.

But if not, O house of Israel, the places of your dwellings shall become desolate until the time of the fulfilling of the covenant to your fathers.

With these words our knowledge of the disembodied ministry of Jesus ends. The next time we hear the voice it will be housed in its celestial body, and the words will let us know that the redemption has been brought to pass and that though a man dies, yet shall he live again.

NOTE

1. Edersheim indulges in the interesting speculation that the centurion may thereafter have been converted to Christianity and been the source of some of the details of the crucifixion which Luke alone records. (Edersheim 2:612.)

SECTION XIII

HE RISETH;
HE MINISTERETH;
HE ASCENDETH

HE RISETH; HE MINISTERETH; HE ASCENDETH

I know that ye seek Jesus,
which was crucified. He is not here:
for he is risen, as he said.
(Matt. 28:5-6.)
Ye seek Jesus of Nazareth,
which was crucified: he is risen;
he is not here.
(Mark 16:6.)
Why seek ye the living among the dead?
He is not here, but is risen.
(Luke 24:5-6.)
Behold my hands and my feet,
that it is I myself:
handle me, and see;
for a spirit hath not flesh and bones,
as ye see me have.
(Luke 24:39.)

Death is swallowed up in victory; Jesus comes forth from the tomb; he is the firstfruits of them that slept. Though a man dies, yet shall he live again.

He appears to Mary Magdalene, of eternal fame and renown, and she is the first mortal to see a resurrected soul. She is restrained from embracing him.

He appears to the other women, who hold him by the feet.

Next, as we suppose, he appears to Simon Peter, and then to Cleopas and Luke on the Emmaus road, to whom he expounds the Messianic prophecies.

Then in the upper room, to a group of disciples, including ten of the Twelve, he appears, invites them to feel the prints of the nails in his hands and in his feet, and before them he eats a piece of broiled fish and of an honeycomb.

One week later he appears to Thomas and the others of the Twelve, again in the upper room, and invites his doubting friend to reach forth his finger and feel the prints of the nails and to thrust his hand into the spear wound.

Next he appears at the Sea of Tiberias to seven of the Twelve, who had fished all night and caught nothing. He fills their net with fish and they eat fish and bread which he has prepared. Peter is commanded, thrice, to feed the flock of God.

Then on a mountain in Galilee to more than five hundred brethren at once (and, as we suppose, to women and children also) he comes, ministers, and sends his messengers forth to proclaim his gospel in all the world.

At some unspecified time he appears to his own blood brother James, and then upon the Mount of Olives he ascends up to his Father with the promise that he shall come again to reign personally upon the earth.

Thereafter came the Nephite ministry during which thousands upon thousands (we suppose tens and scores of thousands) heard his voice, felt the nail marks in his hands and feet, thrust their hands into his side, and (many of them) wet his feet with their tears.

Among the Nephites he preached the gospel, wrought miracles, called Twelve Disciples, perfected his work among the seed of Joseph, and left a witness of his holy name that exceeds that which is preserved in the Bible itself.

He also visited the Lost Tribes of the house of Israel and did for them, as we suppose, what he had done for others.

Among the Nephites his doctrine, his miracles, and the outpouring of the Holy Ghost exceeded anything manifest among the Jews. Among them he expounded all the scriptures from the beginning and taught that the coming forth of the Book of Mormon would be the sign whereby all men might know that the work of the Father had commenced in the latter days unto the fulfilling of the covenant made with the house of Israel.

Chapter 110

CHRIST IS RISEN

He will swallow up death in victory;
and the Lord God will wipe away tears
from off all faces; . . .
And it shall be said in that day,
Lo, this is our God.
(Isa. 25:8-9.)
Trust ye in the Lord for ever:
for in the Lord Jehovah is everlasting strength. . . .
Thy dead men shall live,
together with my dead body shall they arise.
Awake and sing, ye that dwell in dust:
for thy dew is as the dew of herbs,
and the earth shall cast out the dead. . . .
The earth also shall disclose her blood,
and shall no more cover her slain.
(Isa. 26:4, 19, 21.)
There is no saviour beside me. . . .
I will be thy king. . . .
I will ransom them from the power of the grave;
I will redeem them from death:
O death, I will be thy plagues;
O grave, I will be thy destruction.
(Hosea 13:4, 10, 14.)

"Death Is Swallowed Up in Victory"

And now the dawn!

After the midnight of starlit darkness comes the rising of the morning sun. After the sorrow and scourging of mortality come the joy and peace of immortality. After the darkness of death comes the light of a new day of life. After the pain and blood and burden of Gethsemane and Golgotha come the joy and peace and glory of the resurrection.

Once there was mangled flesh and spilt blood; now there is glorious immortality in a state where sorrow and pain fade away into nothingness. Once the creature was earth-bound, limited, an inhabitant of a few dusty feet of earth-soil; now the Creature comes forth with power to traverse the sidereal heavens and to receive, inherit, and possess worlds without number.

There is a death and there is a resurrection; there is an earth-bound body and a heaven-healed body; there is flesh and blood and there is flesh and bones; there is a temporary tenement for the spirit man, and there is an eternal and perfected palace in which the Son of the Father shall dwell everlastingly. "It is sown in corruption; it is raised in incorruption: It is sown in dishonour; it is raised in glory; it is sown in weakness; it is raised in power: It is sown a natural body; it is raised a spiritual body."

And, be it known, "The first man Adam"—Adam in the generic sense, Adam as the name for all mankind—"The first man Adam was made a living soul." We are all mortal; we all live in an earthy sphere; we are all living souls, mortal souls. But, "the last Adam was made a quickening spirit. . . . The first man is of the earth, earthy: the second man is the Lord from heaven. As is the earthy, such are they also that are earthy: and as is the heavenly, such are they also that are heavenly. And as we have borne the image of the earthy, we shall also bear the image of the heavenly. Now this I say, brethren, that flesh and blood cannot inherit the kingdom of God; neither doth corruption inherit incorruption."

But glory be to God who is the Father, and praise be to God who is the Son, the earthy shall become heavenly, and the mortal shall live again in immortality. "And the dead shall be raised incorruptible, . . . For this corruptible must put on incorruption, and this mortal must put on immortality. So when this corruptible shall have put on incorruption, and this mortal shall have put on immortality, then shall be brought to pass the saying that is written, Death is swallowed up in victory. O death, where is thy sting? O grave, where is thy victory?" (1 Cor. 15:42-55.)

And so the dawn. This is resurrection morn. Christ the firstfruits rises from the tomb; his is the first immortal flesh; his body is now like that of his Father's. "The Father has a body of flesh and bones as tangible as man's; the Son also." (D&C 130:22.) And as Jesus rose from the dead, as he burst the bands of death, as he came forth in immortal glory, so shall it be with all men; all shall come forth from the prison of the grave; all shall live again; all shall become immortal. Death and hell shall deliver up the dead which are in them, "For as in Adam all die, even so in Christ shall all be made alive." (1 Cor. 15:22.) We know not how it is done any more than we know how creation commenced or how Gods began to be. Suffice it to say, man is; and suffice it to say, he shall live again. "For as death hath passed upon all men, to fulfill the merciful plan of the great Creator, there must needs be a power of resurrection." (2 Ne. 9:6.) And Christ is the resurrection and the life; immortality and eternal life come by him. He "hath abolished death, and hath brought life and immortality to light through the gospel." (2 Tim. 1:10.)

We speak thus as a prelude to proclaiming the rising from the grave of the Son of God; as a prelude to hearing the testimonies of those who saw and felt and handled his immortal body; as a prelude to gaining a renewed witness from the Holy Spirit of God that the Risen Lord is our Lord, our God, and our King. For, be it known, the resurrection proves the divine Sonship. If Jesus rose from the dead, he is God's Son; if he is divine, his gospel and his alone can save men. Thus Paul speaks of "the gospel of God, (Which he had promised afore by his prophets in the holy scriptures,) Concerning his Son Jesus Christ our Lord, which was made of the seed of David according to the flesh." And how shall we know that Jesus is the Son of God? Paul gives answer: He is "declared to be the Son of God with power, according to the spirit of holiness, *by the resurrection from the dead.*" (Rom. 1:1-4. Italics added.) The resurrection proves the divine Sonship.

Thus also, Peter, in meeting with Cornelius and his friends, told them "how God anointed Jesus of Nazareth with the Holy Ghost and with power," and how this same Jesus "went about doing good, and healing all that were oppressed of the devil; for God was with him." Then came this mighty testimony—the testimony which contains the sure knowledge of the divinity of the Son and, therefore, of the saving power of his gospel. "And we are witnesses of all things which he did," Peter says, "both in the land of the Jews, and in Jerusalem; whom they slew and hanged on a tree: Him God raised up the third day, and shewed him openly; Not to all the people, but unto witnesses chosen before of God, even to us, who did eat and drink with him after he rose from the dead. And he commanded us to preach unto the people, and to testify that it is he which was ordained of God to be the Judge of quick and dead. To him give all the prophets witness, that through his name whosoever believeth in him shall receive remission of sins." (Acts 10:34-43.)

We repeat: The resurrection proves the divinity of the gospel cause. And so, with Paul, we say: "If there be no resurrection of the dead, then is Christ not risen: And if Christ be not risen, then is our preaching vain, and your faith is also vain. Yea, and we are found false witnesses of God; because we have testified of God that he raised up Christ: whom he raised not up, if so be that the dead rise not. For if the dead rise not, then is not Christ raised: And if Christ be not raised, your faith is vain; ye are yet in your sins. Then they also which are fallen asleep in Christ are perished. If in this life only we have hope in Christ, we are of all men most miserable. But now is Christ risen from the dead, and become the firstfruits of them that slept." (1 Cor. 15:13-20.)

"At the moment when Christ died, nothing could have seemed more abjectly weak, more pitifully hopeless, more absolutely doomed to scorn, and extinction, and despair, than the Church which He had founded. It numbered but a handful of weak followers, of whom the boldest had denied his Lord with blasphemy, and the most devoted had forsaken Him and fled. They were poor, they were ignorant, they were helpless. They could not claim a single synagogue or a single sword. If they spoke their own language, it bewrayed them by its mongrel dialect; if they spoke the current Greek, it was despised as a miserable *patois.* So feeble were they and insignificant, that it would have looked like foolish partiality to prophesy for them the limited existence of a Galilean sect. How was it that these dull and ignorant men, with their cross of wood, triumphed over the deadly fascinations of sensual mythologies, conquered kings and their armies, and overcame the world? What was it that thus caused strength to be made perfect out of abject weakness? There is one, and one only *possible* answer—the resurrection from the dead. All this vast revolution was due to the power of Christ's resurrection." (Farrar, pp. 715–16.)

Jesus Appears to Mary Magdalene
(John 20:1-18; JST, John 20:1, 17; Matthew 28:2-4;
JST, Matthew 28:2-3; Mark 16:9-11;
Luke 24:12; JST, Luke 24:11; 3 Ne. 10:9-17)

Jesus appeared first to Mary Magdalene and then to certain other women, speaking peace to their troubled souls. Then he came to the Brethren, at various times and places, giving them counsel and direction concerning their

259

own salvation and the administration of the affairs of his earthly kingdom. The sequence of events, insofar as they can be determined, and the transcendent wonders attending these appearances of the First Immortal One to various of his friends and loved ones, we shall attempt, reverentially, to recount. There is a certain awe and an infinite spiritual depth where visitations from the unseen world are concerned that few can plumb. Let us, then, rely on such accounts as have been preserved for us; let us ponder them in our hearts; and let us seek the Spirit as we strive to know and to feel what is here involved. Perhaps our hearts, too, shall burn with living fire as did the hearts of those of old who saw and felt and knew and testified.

It is now the first Easter day. In the Americas the darkness has dispersed from off the face of the land, the rocks have ceased to rend, and the earth is cleaving together again. The mourning and lamentations of the people have ended, and they are now united in songs of praise and hymns of thanksgiving "unto the Lord Jesus Christ, their Redeemer. . . . And it was the more righteous part of the people who were saved, and it was they who received the prophets and stoned them not; and it was they who had not shed the blood of the saints, who were spared"—spared from all the natural desolations that swept from one end of the land to the other. They, in their isolated land, are coming to know that he who is their Messiah also has worked out the infinite and eternal atonement. Later in the year he will minister personally among them, and their joy will be full. Then they will see him and feel the nail marks in his hands and in his feet; then they will thrust their hands into the great gaping wound in his side; and then will they become personal witnesses of his resurrection.

But the setting of our present story is laid in Palestine. There the body of Jesus, anointed and wrapped in choice linen, but only partially cared for—for he was buried in haste—lies in Joseph's tomb; his Spirit is nearby in Paradise where he has now finished his ministrations among the just. How and in what way it was done we know not, but at the appointed moment, the infinitely great Spirit Being entered again into the body which was his—the body conceived in the womb of Mary; the body which was begotten of the Father; the body from which that Spirit had departed when his mortal work was finished—and that Spirit, now housed in its eternal home, now inseparably connected with its body in immortal glory, that Spirit, together with the reanimated dust of the earth, became the first immortal soul. Christ is risen; immortality is assured; the victory has been won; death is abolished.

Thereupon, or at least in immediate connection therewith, perhaps after the resurrection itself, "two angels of the Lord descended from heaven, and came and rolled back the stone from the door, and sat upon it." Their heaven-created power caused "a great earthquake, . . . And their countenance was like lightning, and their raiment white as snow; and for fear of them the keepers did shake, and became as though they were dead." So much for the guards set by the chief priests, lest, as they pretended to suppose, Jesus' disciples might steal the dead body and fabricate a story that he has risen on the third day as he said. But now, as the angelic visitants stood by, the open tomb itself testified of the Risen Lord; its solid rocks wept for joy, and all eternity joined the great Hallelujah chorus: He is risen; he is risen; Christ the Lord is risen today!

It is now Sunday, April 9, A.D. 30—the 17th of Nisan—the day of the resurrection. It is the first day of the week—"according to Jewish reckoning the third day from His Death." According to Jewish tradition, "the soul hovered round the body till the third day, when it finally parted from its earthly tabernacle," and it was on that day that "corruption was supposed to begin." Up to that time relatives and friends were in the habit of "going to the grave, . . . so as to make sure that those laid there were really dead." (Edersheim 2:630-31.) These Rabbinical concepts grew out of Hosea's statement, "in the third day he will raise us up, and we shall live in his sight." (Hosea 6:2.)

We cannot suppose that Mary Magdalene had any of this in mind when very early—"when it was yet dark," John says—she went to the sepulchre. Hers was a mission of pure love and proper honor to Him who had healed her and with whom, along with the Twelve, she had traveled on many missionary journeys. Indeed, no female name plays a more prominent part in the gospel accounts than that of the convert from Magdala, save only the Blessed Virgin herself. Arriving at the garden tomb, the Magdalene found "the stone taken away from the sepulchre, and two angels sitting thereon." Without question she looked in and found an empty tomb. Immediately she ran to Peter and to John—the inference is that they abode at separate places—and announced to them: "They have taken away the Lord out of the sepulchre, and we know not where they have laid him."

"What a picture John has left us of this unique moment in history. Fear fills the hearts of Peter and John; wicked men must have stolen the body of their Lord. They race to the tomb. John, younger and more fleet, arrives first, stoops down, looks in, but does not enter, hesitating as it were to desecrate the sacred spot even by his presence. But Peter, impetuous, bold, a dynamic leader, an apostle who wielded the sword against Malchus and stood as mouthpiece for them all in bearing testimony, rushes in. John follows. Together they view the grave-clothes-linen strips that have not been unwrapped, but through which a resurrected body has passed. And then, upon John, reflective and mystic by nature, the reality dawns first. It is true! They had not known before; now they do. It is the third day! Christ is risen! 'Death is swallowed up in victory.' " (*Commentary* 1:841-42.)

Then the two apostles went again to their homes. But Mary Magdalene, having returned, "stood without at the sepulchre weeping." She stooped down and looked in and saw "two angels in white sitting, the one at the head, and the other at the feet, where the body of Jesus had lain." Presumably they are the same two whom she had already seen sitting on the stone that had blocked the door. If they were present when Peter and John entered the tomb—and certainly they would have been—the spiritual eyes of these apostles were not opened so as to see them.

"Woman, why weepest thou?" the angelic visitants asked. "Because they have taken away my Lord," she replied, "and I know not where they have laid him." As much as she knew about the doctrine of the resurrection; as frequently as she had heard Jesus tell that he would be crucified and rise again the third day; as great as was her faith in him and in his word—yet in the dawning light of this Easter day, the full import of the open tomb had not yet dawned within her soul.

It was then that she turned away from the tomb and "saw Jesus standing, and knew not that it was Jesus." He asked: "Woman, why weepest thou? whom seekest thou?" In her anxiety, concerned only with her own sorrow, having neither interest in nor concern about others at that moment, she supposed the speaker was the gardener. The garden tomb was empty; who but the gardener would have carried away the body of her Lord? "Sir, if thou have borne him hence," she pleaded, "tell me where thou hast laid him, and I will take him away." Though none others were available to help, yet she would do all that a mortal can to reverence a departed loved one.

Jesus said simply: "Mary." Mary, his beloved; he spoke her name, nothing more. It was as when the still small voice sank into the soul of Elijah; it was as though the heavens had been rent and the very throne of God set forth before men; it was as though angelic choirs had sung her name—MARY! The recognition was instantaneous. Her river of tears became a sea of joy. It is He; he has risen; he lives; I love him as of old. With soul-filled exuberance she cried, "Rabboni"—'Oh, my Master!'—and would have embraced him as she had done so many times before in earlier days. His gentle word:

> Hold me not; for I am not yet ascended to my Father; but go to my brethren, and say unto them, I ascend unto my Father, and your Father; and to my God, and your God.

We cannot believe that the caution which withheld from Jesus the embrace of Mary was anything more than the building of a proper wall of reserve between intimates who are now on two sides of the veil. If a resurrected brother appeared to a mortal brother, or if a resurrected husband appeared to a mortal wife, would they be free to embrace each other on the same terms of intimacy as had prevailed when both were mortals? But perhaps there was more in Jesus' statement than Mary related or than John recorded, for in a very short time we shall see a group of faithful women hold Jesus by his feet as they worship him.[1] The seeming refusal of Jesus to permit Mary to touch him, followed almost immediately by the appearance in which the other women were permitted to hold his feet, has always been the source of some interpretative concern. The King James Version quotes Jesus as saying "Touch me not." The Joseph Smith Translation reads "Hold me not." Various translations from the Greek render the passage as "Do not cling to me" or "Do not hold me." Some give the meaning as "Do not cling to me any longer," or "Do not hold me any longer." Some speak of ceasing to hold him or cling to him, leaving the inference that Mary was already holding him. There is valid reason for supposing that the thought conveyed to Mary by the Risen Lord was to this effect: "You cannot hold me here, for I am going to ascend to my Father." But the great message that was preserved for us is Jesus' eternal relationship to his Father. "My" Father and "your" Father—Elohim is the Father of all men in the spirit, and of the Lord Jesus in an added and special sense. He is the Father of both Jesus' spirit and his body. "My" God and "your" God—and again Elohim is the God of all men, but in Jesus' case, though he himself is a God and has all power, though he is a member of the very Godhead itself, yet is he everlastingly in subjection to the same God who is our Father.

After these things Mary Magdalene, as he had directed, went to the Twelve, told them all that happened, and bore to them this testimony: 'I have seen the Lord!'

Jesus Appears to the Other Women
(Matthew 28:1, 5-10; JST, Matthew 28:1, 4; Mark 16:1-8; JST, Mark 16:3-6; Luke 24:1-11; JST, Luke 24:1-4)

For reasons of his own, the Risen Lord singled out Mary Magdalene to be the first witness, in point of time, of his resurrection. She was the first mortal of all mortals ever to see a resurrected person. She saw his face and heard his voice, and she was commanded to tell the Twelve of the appearance and of the coming ascension when he would report to Him whose he was.[2] Then, still in his own infinite wisdom, Jesus chose to appear to and be handled by a group of other women—all before he came even to Peter and the rest of the Twelve, all before his appearances to the hundreds of brethren who were privileged to see him before that day on the Mount of Olives when he ascended to reign on the right hand of Everlasting Power forever.

These other women included Mary the mother of Joses; Joanna, evidently the wife of Chuza, Herod's steward (Luke 8:3); and Salome, the mother of James and John. Among them were women who had been with Jesus in Galilee. Certainly the beloved sisters from Bethany were there; and, in general, the group would have been made up of the same ones who had hovered in sorrow around the cross. Their total number may well have been in the dozens or scores. We know that women in general are more spiritual than men, and certainly their instincts and desires to render compassionate service exceed those of their male counterparts. And these sisters came "bringing the spices

265

which they had prepared" to anoint the body of their Lord.

It was very early, just as the Sunday dawn began to pierce the darkness of the night. They said among themselves: "Who shall roll us away the stone from the door of the sepulchre?" But when they came to the sepulchre, they found the stone already rolled away, though it was very great, "and two angels sitting thereon, clothed in long white garments; and they were affrighted." When they entered the tomb, they "found not the body of the Lord Jesus," and "they were much perplexed." At this point the angels delivered their message, but the accounts vary as to what was said, quite possibly because more than one group of devout sisters was involved, or because they could only crowd into or around the sepulchre in small groups. It seems evident that each account, though partial, is true and accurate as far as it goes. As recorded by Matthew the angels said:

Fear not ye; for we know that ye seek Jesus who was crucified.

He is not here: for he is risen, as he said. Come, see the place where the Lord lay.

And go quickly, and tell his disciples that he is risen from the dead; and, behold, he goeth before you into Galilee; there shall ye see him: lo, I [or, rather, we] *have told you.*

The message is one of peace for themselves; of crucifixion; of resurrection; of linen death-cloths lying unwound with the head-napkin by itself; of the sisters announcing the glorious message to the brethren; and of Jesus preceding them into Galilee, where the Twelve and the other brethren shall see him. The women "departed quickly from the sepulchre with fear and great joy; and did run to bring his disciples word."

Jesus met them with a cry of "All hail." The recognition was immediate; they knew their Lord; in awe and reverence "they came and held him by the feet, and worshipped him." What tears of joy they must have shed as they kissed his feet, felt the nail marks therein, and bathed them with their tears. We do not know what words of comfort and assurance he spoke to the group, or to individuals among them; the inspired authors pass over the holy words and holy feelings of the holy occasion in reverent silence. This only of what he said has come down to us:

Be not afraid: go tell my brethren that they go into Galilee, and there shall they see me.

He thus confirms the angelic word and sends the women to give the word to the Brethren. Certainly among those faithful sisters there were some or all of the wives of the apostles; perhaps also there were sisters or even daughters. But whoever they were, Jesus is using them and the fact of his resurrection to show the unity and oneness and equality of the man and the woman. "Neither is the man without the woman, neither the woman without the man, in the Lord." (1 Cor. 11:11.) Together they form an eternal family unit; together they serve in the earthly kingdom; together they gain the spiritual stature to see visions and converse with those who abide beyond the veil. To such of the women as heard what Mark records, the angelic word was:

Be not affrighted: Ye seek Jesus of Nazareth, which was crucified: he is risen; he is not here: behold the place where they laid him.

But go your way, tell his disciples and Peter that he goeth before you into Galilee: there shall ye see him, as he said unto you.

Again there is the calm counsel to banish fear; the reminder of the crucifixion; the divine pronouncement that he has risen; and the invitation to see where he had lain and how the burial clothes were placed. But this time the instruction is to tell both Peter and the disciples that He goeth before them into Galilee where they shall see him. This use of Peter's name leaves an added witness that he was called to preside over the Twelve and the church and was expected to lead out in governing the affairs of the earthly kingdom; it also leaves us to assume that some woman with a special relationship to Peter was in the group hearing these particular angelic words. And this time the meeting in Galilee is described as one of which the Brethren already know; on the night of his betrayal and arrest, he had said unto them: "After I am risen again, I will go before you into Galilee." (Matt. 26:32.) The meeting itself took place when Jesus manifested himself to more than five hundred brethren at once on a mountain in Galilee and there gave his great and eternal commission to the Twelve.

To his account Mark adds that the women, "entering into the sepulchre, saw the place where they laid Jesus," thus becoming eye witnesses that his body was gone and that the burial clothes were left in such a way as to show that his resurrected body had passed through their folds and strands without the need of unwinding the strips or untying the napkin. Then the account says "they went out quickly, and fled from the sepulchre; for they trembled and were amazed: neither said they any thing to any man; for they were afraid"—this latter meaning that they did not, at that time, speak to any except those to whom they had been sent.

And now as to Luke's account, it gives us yet another view and some added understanding of the glorious drama that was then unfolding. He tells us how the women, arriving very early with their spices, "found the stone rolled away from the sepulchre, and two angels standing by it in shining garments. And they entered into the sepulchre, and not finding the body of the Lord Jesus, they were much perplexed thereabout; And were affrighted, and bowed down their faces to the earth. But behold the angels said unto them":

Why seek ye the living among the dead? He is not here, but is risen: remember how he spake unto you when he was yet in Galilee, Saying, The Son of man must be delivered into the hands of sinful men, and be crucified, and the third day rise again.

268

These are women who were with Jesus in Galilee. There they heard him say: "The Son of man shall be betrayed into the hands of men: And they shall kill him, and the third day he shall be raised again." (Matt. 17:22-23; Mark 9:30-32; Luke 9:44-45.) Matthew tells us that from the time of Peter's confession in the coasts of Caesarea Philippi, Jesus had begun to reveal these things to his disciples; and it seems clear that he must have done so *in extenso*. (Matt. 16:21.) Now the angelic voices bring these teachings to their remembrance, lest they think the death-dealing deeds of Annas and the Jews, and of Pilate and his soldiers, had thwarted the designs and purposes of Divine Providence. Again, it is worthy of note that among those who heard the word in Galilee were these very women who now in faith and sorrow sought their Lord in a sepulchre. It is just as important to preach the gospel to a woman as to a man, for the souls of all are equally precious in the sight of Him whose we all are.

Then these women returned from the sepulchre, told what they had seen and heard to the apostles and all the rest, "and their words seemed to them as idle tales, and they believed them not." But soon they shall believe, for they too shall hear and see and feel and know. The Risen Lord has manifest himself to the faithful women of his kingdom, for their spiritual insight warranted such precedence; soon the same witness shall be given to the Brethren.

NOTES

1. "One may wonder why Jesus had forbidden Mary Magdalene to touch Him, and then, so soon after, had permitted other women to hold Him by the feet as they bowed in reverence. We may assume that Mary's emotional approach had been prompted more by a feeling of personal yet holy affection than by an impulse of devotional worship such as the other women evinced. Though the resurrected Christ manifested the same friendly and intimate regard as He had shown in the mortal state toward those with whom He had been closely associated, He was no longer one of them in the literal sense. There was about Him a divine dignity that forbade close personal familiarity. To Mary Magdalene Christ had said: 'Touch me not; for I am not yet ascended to my Father.' If the second clause was spoken in explanation of the first, we have to infer that no human hand was to be permitted to touch the Lord's resurrected and immortalized body until after He had

presented Himself to the Father. It appears reasonable and probable that between Mary's impulsive attempt to touch the Lord, and the action of the other women who held Him by the feet as they bowed in worshipful reverence, Christ did ascend to the Father, and that later He returned to earth to continue His ministry in the resurrected state." (Talmage, p. 682.)

2. Of her Edersheim says: "Mary Magdalene—as prominent among the pious women as Peter was among the Apostles." (Edersheim 2:631.)

Chapter 111

JESUS' RESURRECTED MINISTRY

Jesus began both to do and teach,
Until the day in which he was taken up,
after that he through the Holy Ghost
had given commandments unto the apostles
whom he had chosen:
To whom also he shewed himself alive
after his passion by many infallible proofs,
being seen of them forty days,
and speaking of the things
pertaining to the kingdom of God.
(Acts 1:1-3.)

Peter and Others Learn of His Resurrection
(Matthew 27:52-53; 28:11-15; JST, Matthew 27:56; Luke 24:34)

He is risen; he has gained the victory over the grave; he hath abolished death; life and immortality are available to all; these glad tidings of great joy have commenced to go forth; already faithful women are bearing witness that he lives again; and he now has begun his resurrected ministry among mortals. Let God be praised for the wonder of it all!

Now his work must be organized, and his apostles must be sent forth to bear witness of his holy name and to build up and regulate all the affairs of his kingdom in all the

271

world, first unto the Jews and then unto the Gentiles. What then is his next step? It must needs be that he appear to Peter—to Peter the rock; to Peter the seer; to Peter the chief apostle; to Peter to whom he has already given the keys of his earthly kingdom. Peter must now step forward and preside and govern during the absence of his Lord. He is the senior apostle of God on earth. As long as he lives—and he too, according to Jesus' word, will suffer death upon the cross—he will teach and preach and govern, and the gospel net will begin to gather in fish of all kinds.

That Jesus did appear to Peter we know; that this appearance came after that to Mary Magdala, and after that to the other women, we also know—thus making it, as we suppose, his third appearance. But we do not know where or under what circumstances he came, or what words of comfort and counsel and direction he gave. In the upper room, with Peter present, the apostolic witness was borne: "The Lord is risen indeed, and hath appeared to Simon"; and Paul says, "he was seen of Cephas, then of the twelve." (1 Cor. 15:5.)

No longer are the words of the women "as idle tales"; the chief apostle has himself seen and heard and, we suppose, felt the nail marks in the mangled hands and in the bruised feet. Neither Peter nor any of the inspired authors, except Luke and Paul, make mention of this appearance, but we feel free to suppose it was one in which the tears of Peter's denial in the court of Caiaphas were dried; one in which he was assured that though Satan desired to sift him as wheat, yet because Jesus had prayed for him, the noble Peter would yet come off triumphant; one in which a blessed bond of unity, of love, and of peace was established between the Master and his servant. As we have indicated with so many other things, there will surely be a day—when we are worthy to receive the enlightenment involved—when we, by revelation, shall learn in full of that holy appearance of the Lord to his chief apostle on the very day he came forth from the grave.

In this connection, and in this time frame, some events transpired involving great numbers of people, all of which stand as an everlasting witness of the raising of Jesus from death. Be it remembered that when Jesus ministered in the spirit world, he preached to "an innumerable company of the spirits of the just." With reference to all of these the holy word says: "Their sleeping dust was to be restored unto its perfect frame, bone to his bone, and the sinews and the flesh upon them, the spirit and the body to be united never again to be divided, that they might receive a fulness of joy." And also: "These the Lord taught, and gave them power to come forth, after his resurrection from the dead, to enter into his Father's kingdom, there to be crowned with immortality and eternal life." (D&C 138:12, 17, 51.)

Matthew tells us that these righteous spirits exercised the power given them. "And the graves were opened," he says, "and the bodies of the saints which slept, arose, who were many, And came out of the graves after his resurrection, and went into the holy city, and appeared unto many." Similar manifestations were poured out among the Nephites in the New World at this same time. Samuel the Lamanite had prophesied that in the day when the Father glorified his own name by raising his Son Jesus from the grave, then "there were many saints who should arise from the dead, and should appear unto many, and should minister unto them"—all of which came to pass. (3 Ne. 23:9-13.) And all of this—on both continents—bore record that Jesus had risen from the dead, thereby making possible the resurrection of all men, each in his own order.

And we cannot doubt that the chief witness borne by each resurrected saint, as he ministered to a mortal friend or relative, would be to testify that the Son of God had himself come forth from the grave, and that the effects of his resurrection were now passing upon others. Our knowledge of the resurrection is such that we can envision these righteous dead coming forth, each in his own order, each at the appointed moment, each prepared to enter into that eternal glory which is prepared for those who love and serve their Lord. Indeed, it was to be with them as it was with their Lord. They were to sit down with Abraham, Isaac, and Jacob, and all the prophets, in the kingdom of God, to go no more out.

Thus did the proclamation of the resurrection go forth among the righteous, to be carried by them to all men. But among the wicked and ungodly it was an entirely different thing. The chief priests learned of it from the guards whose mission it had been to keep the tomb sealed. "It was useless for the guards to stay beside an empty grave. With fear for the consequences, and horror at all that they had seen, they fled to the members of the Sanhedrin who had given them their secret commission. To these hardened hearts belief and investigation were alike out of the question. Their only refuge seemed to be in lies. They instantly tried to hush up the whole matter. They suggested to the soldiers that they must have slept, and that while they did so the disciples had stolen the body of Jesus. But such a tale was too infamous for credence, and too ridiculous for publicity. If it became known, nothing could have saved these soldiers, supposing them to have been Romans, from disgrace and execution. The Sadducees therefore bribed the men to consult their common interests by burying the whole matter in secrecy and silence. It was only gradually and later, and to the initiated, that the base calumny was uttered. Within six weeks of the resurrection, that great event was the unshaken faith of every Christian; within a few years of the event the palpable historic proofs of it and the numerous testimonies of its reality—strengthened by a memorable vision vouchsafed to himself—had won assent from the acute and noble intellect of a young Pharisaic zealot and persecutor whose name was Saul. But it was only in posthumous and subterranean whispers that the dark falsehood was disseminated which was intended to counteract this overwhelming evidence. St. Matthew says that when he wrote his Gospel it was still commonly

274

bruited among the Jews. It continued to be received among them for centuries, and is one of the blaspheming follies repeated and amplified twelve centuries afterwards in the *Toldoth Jeshu*.'' (Farrar, pp. 722–23.)

Jesus Appears on the Emmaus Road
(Luke 24:13-32; Mark 16:12-13)

Jesus now chooses to appear, first, on the Emmaus road, and then in the upper room, under circumstances that prove he has risen from the grave and that also teach the literal and corporeal nature of a resurrected body. During all his mortal ministry he had chosen the perfect teaching moments and brought forth the ideal illustrations to teach his doctrines and present his message in a way none other had ever done. Nor will he depart from that practice now. None but he could have done what he is now commencing. The two appearances, which are part of the same sermon in stone, as it were, comprise the only way in which both the fact and the nature of the resurrection could be taught in perfection.

It is the afternoon of the day of his resurrection. Two disciples not of the Twelve, one called Cleopas, the other undoubtedly Luke,[1] who recorded the events, are walking the some eight miles from Jerusalem to Emmaus. They can think and ponder and speak of only one thing—the Lord Jesus and his death and the reports relative to his resurrection. There is a sense of anxiety and perplexity and wonder in their words as they commune and reason together. There has never been such a Passover as this one, never such a trial and crucifixion as Jesus suffered, never such a day of wonder and rumor as this day, no, not from the beginning of time until now. Their minds are not at rest, and their spirits are stirred and anxious within them.

A stranger, Jesus himself, seemingly but another Passover pilgrim, draws nigh and walks with them. They feel some irritation, perhaps are a little peevish, that this unknown one should intrude himself on a conversation that is both personal and sacred. It suits his purpose not to be recognized, and so their eyes are covered with a veil, as it were, and the stranger is an unknown one. He asks: "What manner of communications are these that ye have one to another, as ye walk, and are sad?"

There is surprise and skepticism in the voice of Cleopas as he turns to speak to the uninvited intruder. How could anyone have been in Jerusalem this week and been unaware of the tumult and trials and crucifixion of the most renowned person in all Palestine? He asks: "Art thou only a stranger in Jerusalem, and hast not known the things which are come to pass there in these days?" Jesus said: "What things?"

Both of the disciples responded with a fluent outpouring of words that stir the soul. Luke digests their response: "Concerning Jesus of Nazareth," they said, "which was a prophet mighty in deed and word before God and all the people." There is no doubt here, no equivocation; they knew the wonder of his words, the depth of his deeds, the might of his ministry. "And how the chief priests and our rulers delivered him to be condemned to death," they continued, "and have crucified him." Herein lay their sorrow; their Friend had suffered, died, and was buried. All his promises and teachings seemed vague and uncertain in their minds.

"But we trusted that it had been he which should have redeemed Israel: and beside all this, to day is the third day since these things were done." The third day! Had he not promised to rise again the third day? But where was he? Had their Redeemer's work failed? "Yea, and certain women also of our company made us astonished, which were early at the sepulchre," they continued, "And when they found not his body, they came, saying, that they had also seen a vision of angels, which said that he was alive." This we cannot understand, they say, "And certain of them which were with us went to the sepulchre, and found it even so as the women had said: but him they saw not."

Peter and John had checked the "idle tales" of the women, but Jesus was not to be found. (Apparently Cleopas and Luke had not yet heard the clear witness of Mary Magdalene and of the other women that they had seen the Lord.) Having let them lay the foundation for his words, Jesus then said:

O fools, and slow of heart to believe all that the prophets have spoken:

Ought not Christ to have suffered these things, and to enter into his glory?

Having so spoken, Jesus quoted from Moses and all the prophets and expounded to them from all of the scriptures "the things concerning himself." How marvelous it would be if we knew what he said. They may have walked together for as long a time as two hours. And all the while to have the Son of God interpret for them the Messianic word! Are there meanings in the Messianic words of Moses and David and Isaiah, and "all the prophets," that so far have escaped us? Perhaps some day the conversations of this Emmaus walk will be revealed. But our Lord had a purpose over and above that of interpreting the Messianic word— he could leave that to Peter and Paul and the others, as they were enlightened by the power of the Holy Spirit; his mission was to show them what a resurrected person is like, and so far he has seemed so much like any mortal that his identity has remained hidden.

Nearing Emmaus, Jesus acted as though he would travel on. They constrained him to stay with them. "Abide with us: for it is toward evening, and the day is far spent," they said. Having heard his scriptural explanations, all feelings of anxiety and resentment vanished; now they sought his continuing company. He consented. And as they sat at meat, "he took bread, and blessed it, and brake, and gave to them." It was as though he removed the veil from their eyes; the sweet words of blessing, the passing of the bread, the loving demeanor of their Lord—it was all familiar to them. He was doing what he had done before, a rite that identified him in their minds. The covering—first imposed, but now removed, all by divine power—was no more. "They knew him; and he was taken up out of their sight."

Then they said—and the feelings thus described are the conclusive witness of the divine Sonship—they said: "Did not our heart burn within us, while he talked with us by the way, and while he opened to us the scriptures?" Cleopas and Luke now knew for themselves that He had risen. They must tell the others, and so they returned immediately to Jerusalem.

Jesus Appears in the Upper Room
(Luke 24:33-49; JST, Luke 24:34, 40; Mark 16:14; John 20:19-23)

As "it becometh every man who hath been warned to warn his neighbor" (D&C 88:81); as every person who has received the gospel is duty-bound to carry the same glad tidings to our Father's other children; as living witnesses of the truth and divinity of the Lord's work have become such, among other reasons, so they can bear their witness to their fellowmen—so Cleopas and Luke hastened to Jerusalem to testify to their fellow disciples that they had seen the Lord. They knew the trysting place and went directly there. We believe it was an upper room—perhaps the same room, in the home of John Mark, where Jesus and the Twelve celebrated the Feast of the Passover. A large group of disciples was present, including all of the eleven except Thomas. Certainly it was not a meeting for men only. Many faithful women were there and possibly even children. The whole group was eating an evening meal and, in effect, holding a testimony meeting as they ate. What each had seen and heard and knew of that day's happenings was recited and particularly the account of the appearance of the Lord to Peter. No doubt the Chief Apostle told them freely all that had transpired on that holy occasion.

Into this dinner meeting—this assemblage where both temporal and spiritual food was being freely dispensed—

came the two who had walked and conversed with Jesus on the Emmaus road. They heard the account of Jesus' appearance to Peter—"The Lord is risen indeed, and hath appeared to Simon," someone said—and as one testimony builds upon another, they were thus encouraged to testify on their own. "And they told what things they saw and heard in the way, and how he was known to them, in breaking of bread." How the believing souls there assembled must have rejoiced in the description of the stranger; in the Messianic interpretations he gave of the words of Moses and David and all the prophets; in the reminder they heard of his known practice of blessing and breaking bread; in the hearing about the flaming fires of testimonial surety that burned in the hearts of Cleopas and Luke as the Master Teacher had interpreted for them the scriptures!

Just at this moment, as the ones from Emmaus concluded their testimony, as though materializing from the midst of eternity, "Jesus himself stood in the midst of them." The doors were closed and locked; there was no window through which a man could enter; these friends of Jesus were guarding themselves "for fear of the Jews." His first words were the familiar "Peace be unto you." Mark tells us he "upbraided them with their unbelief and hardness of heart, because they believed not them"—Mary Magdalene and the other women—"which had seen him after he was risen." The inference is that they have believed the witness of Peter, but that they felt that the sisters had seen not a resurrected person, but some ghostly spectre, some spirit, some ethereal impression of wispy nothingness from another sphere. And even now, Luke records, "they were terrified and affrighted, and supposed that they had seen a spirit." How else, they thought, could this seeming man have entered the room? Jesus spoke:

Why are ye troubled? and why do thoughts arise in your hearts? Behold my hands and my feet, that it is I myself: handle me, and see; for a spirit hath not flesh and bones, as ye see me have.

He stood there as a man; a spirit is a man; this they knew. He had been a spirit before his birth. "This body, which ye now behold, is the body of my spirit; . . . and even as I appear unto thee to be in the spirit will I appear unto my people in the flesh" (Ether 3:16), he had said to the brother of Jared in days gone by. He had been a spirit when he preached to the other spirits in paradise. But now he had a body—not of flesh and blood as do mortals, but of flesh and bones as do those whose bodies and spirits are inseparably joined in immortality. Flesh and bones is tangible; it can be felt and handled. He is continuing his "living sermon"; he is teaching them the reality and corporeity of the resurrection; though he had come through the enclosed room, yet he was a tangible being.

Then "he shewed them his hands and his feet." They felt the nail marks therein. What a marvel it is for mortal flesh to handle immortal flesh. "And while they yet wondered and believed not for joy, he said unto them, Have ye here any meat?" Their meal included broiled fish and honeycomb. These were handed to Jesus, and—marvel of marvels—he took them and ate them. A resurrected person eats and digests food; the body, though immortal, is tangible and real. If ever there was a "living sermon," such is being seen and believed and understood by the favored faithful in the upper room this night! Then he said:

These are the words which I spake unto you, while I was yet with you, that all things must be fulfilled, which were written in the law of Moses, and in the prophets, and in the psalms, concerning me.

The Messianic prophecies! Every jot, every tittle have been fulfilled; not one word in the Psalms, not a single prophetic utterance, not one sacrificial similitude has been overlooked—all things have been fulfilled in Christ. He gave the word, he fulfilled the word, and the work is now accomplished. "Then opened he their understanding, that they might understand the scriptures." The miraculous nature of this gift should not be overlooked. They had not yet received the companionship of the Holy Ghost, but, nonetheless, their understandings are being quickened, though the total fulfillment of this will not be theirs until after Pentecost. Jesus continued:

Thus it is written, and thus it behoved Christ to suffer, and to rise from the dead the third day:

And that repentance and remission of sins should be preached in his name among all nations, beginning at Jerusalem.

And ye are witnesses of these things.

Christ came; he was crucified, died, and rose again the third day; he worked out the infinite and eternal atonement, all with but one end in view: to bring to pass the immortality and eternal life of man, to enable men to repent and be baptized and gain eternal life. That message is now to go to "all nations," not to the Jews only, but to every nation and kindred and tongue and people. And it is to be carried by testimony. The disciples are to teach the gospel and seal their teachings with the witness that God has revealed to them that Jesus rose from the dead, that as a consequence his gospel is true, and that to gain salvation men must believe and obey.

And, behold, I send the promise of my Father upon you: but tarry ye in the city of Jerusalem, until ye be endued with power from on high.

Herein we see a dual promise: one, that the disciples shall receive that sacred endowment which is given in holy places,[2] and the other, that they shall receive the gift of the Holy Ghost, which is itself an endowment from on high. They are already under instructions to go to Galilee and there meet the Lord on a mountain. This they will do shortly, and they will then return to Jerusalem, where they will tarry until Pentecost, when they will receive the Holy Ghost. We suppose they tarried in Jerusalem for the other sacred endowment and received it before they went to Galilee; otherwise Jesus' instruction loses its plain meaning.

*Peace be unto you: as my Father hath sent me,
even so send I you.*

Those to whom Jesus thus spoke had been called, ordained, given priesthood and keys and authority, and promised the companionship of the Holy Ghost, and now they are being sent forth to do among men as they have seen their Master do. They are to preach, ordain, and work miracles. They are legal administrators who represent the Lord Jesus, saying and doing what he wants said and done, even as he acted in a like capacity for his Father.

Then, as John expressed it, Jesus "breathed on them"—which in the very nature of things must be taken as a figure of speech—and said:

Receive ye the Holy Ghost:

Whose soever sins ye remit, they are remitted unto them; and whose soever sins ye retain, they are retained.

As to the receipt of the Holy Ghost, we know from many revelations exactly what is involved. The Holy Ghost is a personage of spirit, a spirit man, a member of the Godhead. Because he is a spirit person he has power to reveal truth to our spirits, to sanctify our souls, and to dwell in us in a figurative sense. We do not know how the eternal laws involved operate, only that they do. The gift of the Holy Ghost is the right to the constant companionship of this member of the Godhead based on faithfulness. This gift is given by the laying on of hands after baptism. It is reserved for members of the Church. These members may or may not actually receive the companionship of the Spirit; those who are clean and pure and worthy do; others do not. Jesus here tells his disciples to receive the Holy Ghost, meaning the gift of the Holy Ghost. In the very nature of things this means that he either conferred the gift upon them by the laying on of hands, or he confirmed verbally that he had theretofore given them that gift by the laying on of hands. The gift itself came on the day of Pentecost.

As to remitting and retaining sins, this is something that is implicit in the gospel system. The gospel is the plan of salvation; by obedience to its laws and ordinances men have power to free themselves from sin; their sins are washed away in the waters of baptism; and sin and evil are burned out of their souls as though by fire when they are baptized by the Holy Spirit. Thus the legal administrators who preach the gospel have power to remit the sins of men in the waters of baptism, and they have power to retain the sins of those who do not repent and are not baptized for the remission of sins.

And further: Those to whom power is given to bind on earth and seal in heaven have power to remit the sins of the saints on conditions of repentance or to retain them if they do not repent. In the ultimate sense, God alone forgives sins; but he can and does use his servants to speak for him in this as in many things, and whether by his own voice or by the voice of his servants, the result is the same. Needless to say, this, the Lord's system of forgiveness, operates only in the Church and kingdom of God on earth; only legal administrators who have been endowed with power from on high can either remit or retain sins; and they must be guided by the power of the Holy Ghost in all that they do, or their acts will not be binding on earth and sealed everlastingly in the heavens.[3]

Jesus Appears to Thomas and the Disciples
(John 20:24-29)

Once again it is Sunday,[4] the first weekly anniversary of the first resurrection. The disciples, beginning the practice of worshipping on Sunday rather than on the Jewish Sabbath, and coming together to commemorate the rising of Jesus from death, are again in the upper room. The doors are shut, probably guarded. No mention is made of food, but the worshipful group may have been eating, and certainly they were conversing about the resurrection and

283

reciting the accounts of His appearances. So far there have been five of which we know—to Mary Magdalene, to the other women, to Peter, to Cleopas and Luke on the Emmaus road, and to a small congregation of saints in the upper room.

During the week the disciples had said to Thomas, "We have seen the Lord," and, 'We felt the nail marks in his hands and in his feet: we gave him a piece of a broiled fish and of a honeycomb, both of which he ate before us. And he told us such and such things about himself and about our commission to testify of him in all nations.' Thomas had believed in the resurrection, but not in the literal corporeity of His body, not in the fact that Jesus now ate food, not in the fact that the nail marks remained in his flesh and bones. He had said: "Except I shall see in his hands the print of the nails, and put my finger into the print of the nails, and thrust my hand into his side, I will not believe."

Thomas is now present with the others, and of a sudden, as on the week afore, Jesus "stood in the midst." Again he utters the familiar greeting: "Peace be unto you." Then to Thomas came the command:

Reach hither thy finger, and behold my hands;
and reach hither thy hand, and thrust it into my side:
and be not faithless, but believing.

Thomas complied; he would not have dared to do otherwise. He now felt and handled as the others had done; he was a living, personal witness of the corporeity of the body of the Lord Jesus. Whether Jesus called for food and ate again is not recorded. Such would not have been necessary, because Thomas, feeling the nail prints and the spear wound, could not do other than believe the account about the broiled fish and the honeycomb. From the lips of the now believing apostle, we suppose as he knelt to touch the marks in Jesus' feet, came the worshipful cry: "My Lord and my God." Thereupon Jesus said:

Thomas, because thou hast seen me, thou hast

*believed: blessed are they that have not seen, and
yet have believed.*

Thomas, who once offered to go with Jesus to Bethany,
there to die with him, saw and believed—believed in the
literal nature of the resurrection and that Jesus after death
lived again as a man. Ever since he has been called, somewhat unkindly, Doubting Thomas. Whatever they may
have been, his doubts were of a passing and transitory
nature. He became and remained a believer in the full
sense. Rather than point the finger of scorn at his supposed
disbelief, would it not be better to be fearful of the fate of
the ten thousand times ten thousand, plus unnumbered
more, of the Doubting Thomases in a doubting Christendom where none believe that the Lord Jesus now reigns
with his Father in eternal glory—both of them glorying in
their exalted bodies of flesh and bones?

Thus we know that resurrected beings, containing their
glory within themselves, can walk as mortals do on earth;
that they can converse and reason and teach as they once
did in mortality; that they can both withhold and manifest
their true identities; that they can pass with corporeal
bodies through solid walls; that they have bodies of flesh
and bones that can be felt and handled; that, if need be, and
at special times, they can retain the scars and wounds of
the flesh; that they can eat and digest food; that they can
vanish from mortal eyes and transport themselves by
means unknown to us.

How glorious it has been to hear the living sermon
preached by the greatest Preacher of all time as he ministered on the Emmaus road and in the upper room!

NOTES

1. If, as is generally believed, the unnamed disciple was our Gospel author Luke,
then, interestingly, "each of the Gospels would, like a picture, bear in some dim corner
the indication of its author: the first, that of the publican; that by St. Mark, that of the
young man, who, in the night of the Betrayal, had fled from his captors; that of St. Luke
in the companion of Cleopas; and that of St. John, in the disciple whom Jesus loved."
(Edersheim 2:638.)

2. "I gave unto you a commandment that you should build a house," the Lord said to his Latter-day Saints, "in the which house I design to endow those whom I have chosen with power from on high; For this is the promise of the Father unto you; therefore I command you to tarry, even as mine apostles at Jerusalem." (D&C 95:8-9; 105:11-12, 18, 33.)

3. "I have conferred upon you the keys and power of the priesthood," the Lord said to Joseph Smith, "and whosesoever sins you remit on earth shall be remitted eternally in the heavens; and whosesoever sins you retain on earth shall be retained in heaven." (D&C 132:45-46.)

4. John, speaking after the Jewish pattern, says "after eight days," meaning, to us, seven days later. Their measurement of Jesus' tenure in the tomb is also counted this same way.

Chapter 112

THE GALILEAN APPEARANCES

Arise and come forth unto me,
that ye may thrust your hands into my side,
and also that ye may feel
the prints of the nails
in my hands and in my feet,
that ye may know that I am the God of Israel,
and the God of the whole earth,
and have been slain
for the sins of the world.
And it came to pass that the multitude went forth,
and thrust their hands into his side,
and did feel the prints of the nails
in his hands and in his feet;
and this they did do,
going forth one by one
until they had all gone forth,
and did see with their eyes
and did feel with their hands,
and did know of a surety and did bear record,
that it was he, of whom it was written
by the prophets, that should come.
And when they had all gone forth

and had witnessed for themselves,
they did cry out with one accord, saying:
Hosanna! Blessed be the name
of the Most High God!
And they did fall down at the feet of Jesus,
and did worship him.
(3 Ne. 11:14-17.)

Jesus Appears at the Sea of Tiberias
(John 21:1-24)

After Jesus rose from the dead, our apostolic friends received two commands—one, to go to Galilee and meet Jesus on a mountain according to a prior appointment; the other, to tarry in Jerusalem until he sent the promise of the Father upon them and they were endowed with power from on high. Apparently they have been endowed in the initial sense of the word—though an additional heavenly endowment of divine power will come, in Jerusalem, on the day of Pentecost—for they have now left the Holy City and traveled to their native Galilee. It will be remembered that all of the Twelve, save Judas, were Galileans, and that most of their apostolic training, as well as their ministerial service, had been in their beloved homeland. Their appointment to meet the Lord was a definite one to which more than five hundred brethren had been invited. As they awaited the day, and having need to supply their families with this world's goods, Peter said: "I go a fishing." Six of the eleven were with him—James, John, Thomas, Nathanael, and two who are not named but probably were Andrew and Philip, since those two had been engaged with Peter and the others in like ventures in earlier days. This group said to Peter: "We also go with thee."

They all went forth into a ship and spent the whole night fishing in the Sea of Galilee, also known as the Sea of Tiberias and as the Lake of Gennesaret. They caught nothing. In the morning Jesus stood on the shore, "but the disciples knew not that it was Jesus." Apparently he withheld his identity as he had done to the two who walked with him on the Emmaus road. He called out: "Children, have ye any meat?" They answered, "No." He said, "Cast the net on the right side of the ship, and ye shall find." They did so, and immediately the net was so full "they were not able to draw it for the multitude of fishes." Perhaps the three—Peter, James, and John—remembered that other occasion when they had toiled all night on the same lake, had caught nothing, and then, casting again at His word, had filled their net until it brake. In any event, John, who seems to have been more spiritually sensitive than the rest, said to Peter: "It is the Lord." Peter, who was naked, "girt his fisher's coat unto him," jumped from the ship, and swam to shore to meet the Master. The others changed into a small ship and dragged the net and the fish about a hundred yards to the shore.

When they came to shore they found a fire of coals with fish broiling and a supply of bread. Jesus said: "Bring of the fish which ye have now caught." Peter waded into the shallow water, pulled the net to shore, and the fish were counted—a hundred and fifty-three in all, so many that the record marvels that the net was not broken. Jesus said: "Come and dine." John says none of the disciples dared ask him, "Who art thou?" because they knew "it was the Lord." Jesus then gave them bread and fish to eat, and although the account does not so state, he himself must also have eaten, for, as in the upper room, such would have been one of the main purposes of providing the food. John says this was "the third time that Jesus shewed himself to his disciples"—meaning to them as a group—"after that he was risen from the dead."

"So when they"—meaning, as we suppose, both Jesus and the apostles—"had dined," Jesus said to Simon Peter: "Simon, son of Jonas, lovest thou me more than these?" More than these fish, more than the things of this world, more than all else, even life itself! 'Lovest thou me above all? If so, Keep my commandments.' To Peter—who but a short while before had said, "Lord, I am ready to go with thee, both into prison, and to death," and who, as Jesus foretold, had then thrice denied that he even knew Christ, and that before the cock crew twice (Luke 22:32-34)—to Peter, the Chief Apostle, Jesus was asking for a new and unshakable avowal of allegiance. Peter said: "Yea, Lord; thou knowest that I love thee." Jesus said: "Feed my lambs." Once near this spot Jesus had said to Peter and Andrew, "Follow me, and I will make you fishers of men." (Matt. 4:18-22.) That call was still in force, but to it now was added the commission to feed the flock of God.

Jesus asked a second time: "Simon, son of Jonas, lovest thou me?" Again came the answer: "Yea, Lord; thou knowest that I love thee." To this Jesus said: "Feed my sheep." Then again, for the third time, came the question: "Simon, son of Jonas, lovest thou me?" Peter, grieved at the repetition, responded: "Lord, thou knowest all things; thou knowest that I love thee." Again came the test of love and of true discipleship: "Feed my sheep." He who had thrice denied, now thrice affirmed; he who with an oath had said, "I know not this man of whom ye speak" (Mark 14:66-72), now pledged, in the presence of his brethren, to love his Lord with all his heart; he who had said he would die for Christ, now is committed to live for him.

Lovest thou me! Jesus had asked and Peter had answered; thrice was the question put and thrice the answer came. Lovest thou me! Ah, Peter, truly hast thou testified of thy love for thy Lord. And how shall that love be measured? In service to thy fellowmen ("Feed my sheep") and in obedience to the holy law ("If ye love me, keep my commandments" [John 14:15])—in these two ways while thou livest. But there is more. Thy love for me shall be perfected and sanctified by thy death. ("Greater love hath no man than this, that a man lay down his life for his friends." [John 15:13.]) And so Jesus, still singling out the leader among the apostolic witnesses, said to his servant: "When thou wast young, thou girdedst thyself, and walkedst whither thou wouldest: but when thou shalt be old, thou shalt stretch forth thy hands, and another shall gird thee, and carry thee whither thou wouldest not." Of this John said: "This spake he, signifying by what death he should glorify God," meaning that Peter would lay down his life for his Chief Friend, lay it down upon a cruel cross, lay it down even as that Friend had laid down his life for his friends. "I will lay down my life for thy sake," Peter had said. "Thou shalt follow me" in death, was Jesus' assurance to him. (John 13:36-38.) "How literally the Master then spoke, and how fully Peter is to do as he offered, he now learns. He is to be crucified, a thing which John in this passage assumes to be known to his readers. Peter's arms are to be stretched forth upon the cross, the executioner shall gird him with the loin-cloth which criminals wear when crucified, and he shall be carried where he would not, that is to his execution." (*Commentary* 1:863-64.)

Having so spoken, Jesus said to Peter, "Follow me"— follow me apart from the others; follow me in ministerial service; follow me in faith and obedience and righteousness; follow me in all things. And as they walked, Peter, "turning about," saw John, his closest colleague and most intimate mortal friend, and asked Jesus: "Lord, and what shall this man do?" Shall he also have his arms stretched forth upon the cross? Will he too be girded and bound upon the inhuman instrument of torture? Shall it be with him, as thou hast said of me? Jesus said: "If I will that he tarry till I come, what is that to thee? follow thou me."

Perhaps it was at this time that John, joining Jesus and Peter as they walked, was asked by the Lord: "John, my beloved, what desirest thou? For if you shall ask what you will, it shall be granted unto you." In John's reply we see the measure of the man; the apostolic witness he desired to bear; the works he desired to do; the souls he desired to save: "Lord, give unto me power over death," he asked, "that I may live and bring souls unto thee." Such a request, aside from the perfect faith that knows that such a plea can be granted, is a manifestation of missionary zeal scarce known among men. To preach the gospel and save souls until the Son of Man comes in his glory—what a wondrous work! And Jesus replied:

Verily, verily I say unto thee, because thou desirest this thou shalt tarry until I come in my glory, and shalt prophesy before nations, kindreds, tongues and people.

In writing of this promise John gives a more amplified account of the conversation there on the shores of Gennesaret. Not only did Jesus say to Peter, "If I will that he tarry till I come, what is that to thee?" but also: "He desired of me that he might bring souls unto me, but thou desiredst that thou mightest speedily come unto me in my kingdom. I say unto thee, Peter, this was a good desire; but my beloved has desired that he might do more, or a greater work yet among men than what he has before done. Yea, he has undertaken a greater work; therefore I will make him as a flaming fire and a ministering angel; he shall minister for those who shall be heirs of salvation who dwell on the earth. And I will make thee to minister for him and for thy brother James; and unto you three I will give this power and the keys of this ministry until I come. Verily I say unto you, ye shall both have according to your desires, for ye both joy in that which ye have desired." (D&C 7:1-8.)

And thus endeth such knowledge as we have of the words of him who is Lord of all as he spoke them this wondrous morning in the calm setting of a Galilean lake where he and his hearers had spent so many pleasant hours together. Without doubt he then told them many other things. Oh, how little we know of all that he said! How little we have seen of all that he did! And how seldom do we get in tune with the Infinite so that we can both know and feel even that which has been preserved for us! We suppose, however, that he confirmed with them the time and the place of their coming meeting on a Galilean mountain; for it is there we shall see them next.

Jesus Appears on a Mountain in Galilee
(Matthew 28:16-20; Mark 16:15-18; 3 Nephi 11)

We come now to the greatest of all the appearances of the Risen Lord to and among his disciples in Palestine—to his appearance on a mountain in Galilee. What happened at this appearance is not even mentioned by John or Luke; and Matthew uses only five verses to recount its wonders, and Mark only four. But in all of this there was a divine purpose; in it all there was a reason of surpassing import why more was not preserved in the New Testament—which purpose and reason we shall hereafter set forth.

First, however, we must give to this Galilean appearance such a setting and such a New Testament background as the sacred record does provide. Jesus himself was a Galilean; he lived as a child in Nazareth, and his boyish feet trod the Galilean hills. The eleven were all Galileans; most of his ministry and most of theirs had been in the cities and villages of that rustic, rugged, rural part of Palestine. There was more believing blood and less priestcraft, more pure worship and less rebellion, more of the love of the Lord and less of the worship of worldliness, in Galilee than in Judea. The spies that dogged his footsteps came from Jerusalem; the scribes and Rabbinical schools were centered in the Holy City. The proud Sadducees and the haughty Sanhedrists made the temple their headquarters. Pharisaic sophistry and priestly ritualism centered in Judea, not in Galilee. What would have been more natural than that the thoughts and hearts of the apostles would have turned to their beloved homeland in the trials of these days? And how compassionate and tender was their Friend in choosing to take them back to their own land to manifest himself to them and to renew with them in glory the experiences they had once had with him there in the days of their trials? Would their thoughts have been as the words of our hymn?

Each cooing dove and sighing bough
That makes the eve so blest to me
Has something far diviner now
It bears me back to Galilee.

Each flow'ry glen and mossy dell
Where happy birds in song agree
Thro' sunny morn the praises tell
Of sights and sounds in Galilee.

And when I read the thrilling lore
Of Him who walked upon the sea
I long, oh, how I long once more
To follow Him in Galilee.

O Galilee! sweet Galilee!
Where Jesus loved so much to be;
O Galilee! blue Galilee!
Come, sing thy song again to me.
—*Hymns,* no. 38

And so that night in the upper room, at the Paschal feast, having quoted the Messianic word that the Shepherd will be smitten and the sheep scattered, Jesus said: "But after I am risen again, I will go before you into Galilee." (Matt. 26:32.) And so, lest they forget, at the open tomb the angelic ministrants told the faithful women: "Go your way, tell his disciples and Peter that he goeth before you into Galilee: there shall ye see him, as he said unto you." (Mark 16:7.) And even the Risen Lord himself said to these same women: "Go tell my brethren that they go into Galilee, and there shall they see me." (Matt. 28:10.) The import, glory, and grandeur of this Galilean meeting could not have been impressed more strongly upon them. Nor can we doubt that the word went out—repetitiously—to all who were invited and that elaborate preparations were made. This was to be no small and insignificant thing; many of them had already seen the Risen Lord, but all that had gone before was but a shadow and a foretaste of what was to be.

Paul recounted some of the resurrected appearances. He reminded the Corinthians that he had preached to them the gospel by which salvation comes. "For I delivered unto you first of all," he said, "that which I also received, how that Christ died for our sins according to the scriptures; And that he was buried, and that he rose again the third day according to the scriptures"—and these things are what comprise the gospel—"And that he was seen of Cephas." Peter saw him, as was announced that night in the upper room. Then he was seen "of the twelve," meaning in the upper room when Cleopas and Luke made their report, and again a week later in that same place by the same group with Thomas also being present. "After that, he was seen of above five hundred brethren at once; of whom the greater part remain unto this present, but some are fallen asleep." This is the appearance on the Galilean mountain of which we are about to speak. "After that, he was seen of James." This is understood to be an appearance to James the brother of the Lord, who became one of the Twelve and a mighty pillar of strength and righteousness in due course. Of it the scriptures say nothing except the words here quoted from Paul.[1] Then he was seen, Paul continues, "of all the apostles," having reference to the time of his ascension on the Mount of Olivet. "And last of all he was seen of me also, as of one born out of due time," our apostolic friend records, identifying himself as one abortively added to the apostolic family. (1 Cor. 15:1-8.)

Paul's recitation is not intended in any sense to be complete. He says nothing about the appearance—the first of all others—to Mary Magdalene; nor to the other women; nor to the two disciples on the Emmaus road; nor to seven of the Twelve on the shore of the sea of Tiberias; nor does he mention, as Luke does, that when Jesus first came to the upper room there were others present in addition to the apostles. Indeed, all of the inspired authors record only fragments and slivers of the full story. Matthew mentions the "eleven disciples" only as being present on the mountain in Galilee, and Mark strings together the appearance in the upper room and the commission, given in Galilee, to go into all the world, as though they both occurred at the same time and place. Providentially we can take a sliver from here and a sliver from there and construct a large board. And having thus learned how the accounts must be interpreted, we can reach reasonable conclusions as to what happened. Thus when Paul speaks of more than five hundred brethren being present on one occasion, we have every reason to believe there may have been five hundred or a thousand women in the same congregation and perhaps an unnumbered host of children. We know how and under what circumstances the Lord ministered among the Nephites and have every reason to believe that he followed the same pattern in Palestine. The Nephites were a select group of saints because the wicked among them had been destroyed during the period of darkness at the crucifixion, and the group that assembled on the mountain in Galilee was one called from the midst of the wicked in the land so that they might receive on a mountain sanctuary the mysteries of the kingdom.

We must not leave this part of our discussion without recording that, without question, there were many unmentioned appearances. We know He was with them, from time to time, for forty days; and it is unthinkable to assume that he did not appear to the Blessed Virgin whose Son he was, to Lazarus whom he called forth from four days of death, to Mary and Martha whom he loved, and to hosts of others whose names were written in the Lamb's Book of Life, never to be blotted out. It is true that various of these may have been with the "other women" at the tomb, with the apostles in the upper room, or with the great congregation on the Galilean mountain. But it is not the time or the place that matters; rather, it is the reality of the appearances and the fact that it was clearly his purpose to manifest himself to all who had prepared themselves to stand in the Divine Presence. It is written of Jared's brother that "because of the knowledge of this man, . . . he could not be kept from within the veil; therefore he saw Jesus; and he did minister unto him." (Ether 3:19-20.) And so it was with the faithful among whom Jesus had ministered before his death. They too had a perfect knowledge that he was the Son of God; they knew he had fulfilled his promise and risen from the dead; they knew he had appeared to Peter and to others; and they knew he would appear to them also if they sought him with all their hearts. Further: He desired to appear to them, to give comfort and consolation in their sorrow, and to wipe away all tears from their crying eyes; he wanted them to grow in faith and to bear witness to the world of his resurrection and of the resurrection of all men; and, we may rest assured, by obedience to the laws involved the veil was rent and they saw and felt and handled and worshipped.

But now, as to the appearance on the mountain Galilee, it is pleasant to suppose it happened at the same site on which he preached the Sermon on the Mount, for that was the ordination sermon of the Twelve, and he now designs to give those same apostolic witnesses their great commission to carry the gospel into all the world. What would be more fitting than to have the great commission to take the gospel to all the world come forth at the same sacred spot whence they received their first apostolic commission, from the mountain which had become to them a holy temple? It is also pleasant to suppose that after the invited disciples were all assembled, awaiting his appearance in reverential awe, perhaps seated, at the direction of Peter and the Twelve, on the greening slopes in prayer and meditation, at such a moment he appeared, and that his first words to them paralleled those to be spoken later to his Nephite disciples:

> Behold, I am Jesus Christ, whom the prophets testified shall come into the world.
>
> And behold, I am the light and the life of the world; and I have drunk out of that bitter cup which

the Father hath given me, and have glorified the Father in taking upon me the sins of the world, in the which I have suffered the will of the Father in all things from the beginning.

When Jesus spoke these words among the Nephites, "the whole multitude," in a spontaneous act of reverential worship, "fell to the earth," even as Thomas had done when he was invited to feel the nail prints and thrust his hand into the side of the Risen One. Then Jesus invited these New World Hebrews—these Nephite Jews whose fathers had come forth from Jerusalem—to themselves come forth and thrust their hands into his side and feel the prints of the nails in his hands and in his feet, and learn for themselves that he was the God of Israel, and the God of the whole earth, and that he had been slain for the sins of the world. This they did, worshipping Jesus and rending the air with cries of Hosanna. And we do not suppose that the divine scene was much different on the Galilean mountain. Of it Matthew says, "when they saw him, they worshipped him," adding, sadly we suppose, "but some doubted," meaning that among the multitude there were those who had not yet come to know—as all of the apostles then knew—of the tangible nature of his body of flesh and bones. That this doubt, as with Thomas, blossomed into glorious faith we cannot doubt as soon as they—as it had been with Thomas and all of the Twelve—had felt and handled the once mangled and now glorified body of their Lord. How marvelous it is that Jesus welcomes those of all lands and nations, and that, from his standpoint, there cannot be too many who are worthy to see and touch and handle and know for themselves that he is the Redeemer of the world and the Savior of all who come unto him with full purpose of heart.

In this setting of worship and adoration, Jesus bore to his Galilean friends this testimony of himself: "ALL POWER IS GIVEN UNTO ME IN HEAVEN AND IN EARTH." Even for a

God, this is a new day of power and might and dominion! A resurrected body adds eternal blessings that cannot be gained in any other way. Even a God must be resurrected to inherit, possess, and receive all things. Thus saith Jehovah: "My dead body shall . . . arise." (Isa. 26:19.) Jesus, who is Jehovah, was God before the world was. Speaking to good king Benjamin, the angelic ministrant called him "the Lord Omnipotent who reigneth, who was, and is from all eternity to all eternity." (Mosiah 3:5.) To Isaiah he was "The mighty God, The everlasting Father" (Isa. 9:6), and to Abinadi he was "God himself" who should "come down among the children of men" and "redeem his people" (Mosiah 15:1). He was the Lord God Almighty before he was ever born, because he was "like unto God" (Abr. 3:24), and he was, under the Father, the Creator of worlds without number. There are no words to describe, no language to convey, no tongue which can tell, his greatness and glory as it was even before the foundations of the world were laid. And yet, even he came to earth to be "added upon" (Abr. 3:26), to undergo the trials and tests of mortality, and to come forth in the resurrection with a body of flesh and bones like that of his Father. The Spirit Jehovah, thus clothed in immortal glory, became an inheritor of eternal life in the full and unlimited sense. In the resurrection "he received a fulness of the glory of the Father; And he received all power, both in heaven and on earth, and the glory of the Father was with him, for he dwelt in him." (D&C 93:16-17.)

Jesus has thus finished his mortal labors; now he is eternal; from henceforth he shall reign on the right hand of the Majesty on High; others, who are yet mortal, must carry forward the work of salvation among men on earth. And so he says to his apostles:

Go ye therefore, and teach all nations, baptizing them in the name of the Father, and of the Son, and of the Holy Ghost:

Teaching them to observe all things whatsoever I have commanded you: and, lo, I am with you alway, even unto the end of the world.

Thus the Twelve are commissioned anew. Apostolic power came to them on the Mount of Beatitudes when they were ordained to the holy apostleship; they received the keys of the kingdom of God on earth after Jesus was transfigured on the heights of Holy Hermon; they were recalled to ministerial service when he appeared to them in the upper room and again at the sea of Tiberias; now they are to go to all nations and take the message of salvation to all men. Once they were sent only to the lost sheep of the house of Israel; now all our Father's children, of all nations and kindreds, are to hear the divine word. The gospel must be taught; baptism is for all; salvation is available to all on conditions of obedience. All that Jesus has taught them is to be taught to all men as rapidly as they are able to bear it, and he will be with the faithful in all nations always.

Go ye into all the world, and preach the gospel to every creature. He that believeth and is baptized shall be saved; but he that believeth not shall be damned.

Thus saith thy God. The gospel is for all; baptism is for all; salvation is for all—for all who will believe and obey. The residue of men, and they are many, shall be damned. Men must first be baptized, then they must "observe all things"—meaning, keep the commandments—and thus, having endured to the end, they shall be saved with an everlasting salvation.

Nor were these eternal truths taught in Galilee any different from those presented among the Nephites. After that branch of the house of Israel had gained their witness of the divine Sonship of Jesus and had felt and handled the flesh and bones he then possessed, he called Nephi the Disciple to come forth. Nephi "bowed himself before the Lord and did kiss his feet," and Jesus said to him: "I give

unto you power that ye shall baptize this people when I am
again ascended into heaven." Others were called forth and
given like power. That these disciples were already performing authoritative baptisms we know; but it was now to
be with them as with their Old World counterparts. They
were receiving a new commission as part of a new dispensation. What we have come to call—somewhat inaccu-
rately—the Christian era was beginning among them. Their
commission, however, was to administer salvation to the
Nephites in the Americas as contrasted with that of the Old
World Twelve who were sent to all nations. To his Nephite
disciples Jesus then said, as in all likelihood he did to his
Galilean followers:

*On this wise shall ye baptize; and there shall be no
disputations among you. Verily I say unto you, that
whoso repenteth of his sins through your words and
desireth to be baptized in my name, on this wise
shall ye baptize them—Behold, ye shall go down
and stand in the water, and in my name shall ye
baptize them.*

*And now behold, these are the words which ye
shall say, calling them by name, saying: Having
authority given me of Jesus Christ, I baptize you in
the name of the Father, and of the Son, and of the
Holy Ghost. Amen.*

*And then shall ye immerse them in the water, and
come forth again out of the water. And after this
manner shall ye baptize in my name; for behold,
verily I say unto you, that the Father, and the Son,
and the Holy Ghost are one; and I am in the Father,
and the Father in me, and the Father and I are one.*

That all of this had been taught to and was in operation
among the Twelve of Jerusalem is not open to question; but
so also was it the case among the Nephites. They too had
been taught true principles and were practicing true ordinances. And yet Jesus now renews and clarifies these poli-

301

cies and procedures among them, as we suppose he did also in Galilee. There must be no divergence of belief or practice on matters of such eternal import.

And according as I have commanded you thus shall ye baptize. And there shall be no disputations among you, as there have hitherto been; neither shall there be disputations among you concerning the points of my doctrine, as there have hitherto been.

For verily, verily I say unto you, he that hath the spirit of contention is not of me, but is of the devil, who is the father of contention, and he stirreth up the hearts of men to contend with anger, one with another.

Behold, this is not my doctrine, to stir up the hearts of men with anger, one against another; but this is my doctrine, that such things should be done away.

O that the blaspheming self-exulters of Christendom, who contend from their pulpits and before the microphones of their so-called radio ministries, O that they knew what the Lord thinks of contention!

O that those who say, Lo here is Christ and lo there, who say, Believe this or believe that in order to be saved, O that they knew he reveals himself, not in the midst of debate, but in the sanctuary of peace!

O that those in the Church who are more concerned with defending their prejudices and upholding their private interpretations than they are in seeking the truth, O that they would shun contention and seek for unity with the Lord's earthly standard bearers and with those whom he hath appointed to interpret and define his doctrines for the children of men!

Behold, verily, verily, I say unto you, I will declare unto you my doctrine. And this is my doctrine, and it is the doctrine which the Father hath given unto me; and I bear record of the Father, and the Father

302

beareth record of me, and the Holy Ghost beareth record of the Father and me; and I bear record that the Father commandeth all men, everywhere, to repent and believe in me.

Even Jesus has no doctrine of his own; even he receives his doctrine from the Father; and it is the doctrine of the Father, and of the Son, and of the Holy Ghost, that all men must believe in Christ, repent of their sins, and live his laws to be saved. Men choose what they believe and what they do at the peril of their own salvation. Ought we not to learn and know what Deity thinks about a doctrine, rather than what seems, for one reason or another, to be desirable to us?

And whoso believeth in me, and is baptized, the same shall be saved; and they are they who shall inherit the kingdom of God.

And whoso believeth not in me, and is not baptized, shall be damned.

Verily, verily, I say unto you, that this is my doctrine, and I bear record of it from the Father; and whoso believeth in me believeth in the Father also; and unto him will the Father bear record of me, for he will visit him with fire and with the Holy Ghost.

And thus will the Father bear record of me, and the Holy Ghost will bear record unto him of the Father and me; for the Father, and I, and the Holy Ghost are one.

Jesus' words, thus spoken, are so plain, so easy, so simple, that none need err with reference to them. The course is clearly marked. And if any, reading what he here says, do not have their bosoms burn as did those of Cleopas and Luke on the Emmaus road, they may know thereby that they are not the Lord's sheep, and that they need to repent and get in tune with the Holy Spirit so they can believe and understand the witness of the Father and of the Son and of the Holy Ghost, which is one God everlastingly.

And again I say unto you, ye must repent, and

become as a little child, and be baptized in my name, or ye can in nowise receive these things.

And again I say unto you, ye must repent, and be baptized in my name, and become as a little child, or ye can in nowise inherit the kingdom of God.

Verily, verily, I say unto you, that this is my doctrine, and whoso buildeth upon this buildeth upon my rock, and the gates of hell shall not prevail against them.

And whoso shall declare more or less than this, and establish it for my doctrine, the same cometh of evil, and is not built upon my rock; but he buildeth upon a sandy foundation, and the gates of hell stand open to receive such when the floods come and the winds beat upon them.

Therefore, go forth unto this people, and declare the words which I have spoken, unto the ends of the earth.

None who are enlightened by the power of the Spirit need further commentary on these glorious words—words that testify of the goodness and grace of Jesus and of the divine mission of the Prophet Joseph Smith, because they have come forth in our day through his instrumentality. Let us, rather, turn to the remainder of the New Testament account of the greatest of all the appearances of the Risen Lord:

And these signs shall follow them that believe; In my name shall they cast out devils; they shall speak with new tongues; They shall take up serpents; and if they drink any deadly thing, it shall not hurt them; they shall lay hands on the sick, and they shall recover.

These words were spoken almost verbatim by Jesus to the Nephite disciples, and to them he then added: "And whosoever shall believe in my name, doubting nothing, unto him will I confirm all my words, even unto the ends of the earth." (Morm. 9:22-25.) And thus it is in all ages and at all times and among all people: signs and miracles abound where faith is found. As gravity pulls down the raindrops from the sky, so faith brings forth signs and miracles; as law operates in the natural field, so it does in the spiritual; and so when faith is exercised, miracles are wrought. As God is our witness, we testify that whenever and wherever there is faith, there the gifts of the Spirit will be manifest. Signs always have, do now, and always will follow those who believe. If there are none of the gifts, there is no faith, men have not believed the true gospel, and they do not have a hope of salvation. Faith is power; and if a people do not have power to open blind eyes, and unstop deaf ears, and loose dumb tongues, and raise dead corpses, how can they have power to save a soul? So it has always been, so it is now, and so it will ever be. Signs follow those who believe.

NOTE

1. "Respecting this appearance to James we know nothing further, unless there be any basis of true tradition in the story preserved to us in the Gospel of the Hebrews. We are there told that James, the first Bishop of Jerusalem, and the Lord's brother, had, after the Last Supper, taken a solemn vow that he would neither eat nor drink until he had seen Jesus risen from the dead. Early, therefore, after His resurrection, Jesus, when He had given the *sindon* to the servant of the priest, had a table with bread brought out, blessed the bread, and gave it to James, with the words, 'Eat thy bread now, my brother, since the Son of Man has risen from the dead.' " (Farrar, p. 731.)

Chapter 113

THE NEPHITE MINISTRY

I lay down my life for the sheep.
And other sheep I have, which are not
of this fold: them also I must bring,
and they shall hear my voice;
and there shall be one fold, and one shepherd.
(John 10:15-16.)
Ye are they of whom I said:
Other sheep I have which are not of this fold;
them also I must bring,
and they shall hear my voice;
and there shall be one fold, and one shepherd.
(3 Ne. 15:21.)
There is one God and one Shepherd
over all the earth.
(1 Ne. 13:41.)

Appearances to the Other Sheep
(3 Nephi 11–15; 16:1-3)

The Nephites adjusted their calendar so as to begin a new dating era with the birth of Jesus; and according to their chronology, the storms and the darkness and the crucifixion came to pass on the fourth day of the first month of the thirty-fourth year. (3 Ne. 8.) Then "in the ending" of that year (3 Ne. 10:18-19), several months after the Ascension on Olivet, Jesus ministered personally among the Nephites for many hours on many days. He came as "a Man descending out of heaven"; introduced himself as the God of Israel; permitted the multitude to feel the prints of the nails in his hands and feet and to thrust their hands into his side; called a quorum of twelve; gave them keys and powers and authorities; healed the Nephite sick and introduced the sacramental ordinance in the Western Hemisphere; taught the people in plainness and with an excellence surpassing much that was done in his Palestinian ministry; gave them the gift of the Holy Ghost; and ascended to his Father.

Third Nephi is often called the fifth Gospel because it preserves for us so much that was said and so much that was done among the Nephites that parallels what he said and did among the Jews. Many of these teachings and ministerial acts we have considered in their "Jewish-Nephite" contexts. There remain, however, some matters of transcendent glory and wonder to which we must now refer for these reasons:

1. The words he spoke and the deeds he did among the Nephites are a crowning capstone to his earthly ministry. Many of the passages far excel anything in the biblical accounts; they reveal his grandeur and greatness in a way not otherwise known, and they round out our knowledge of the nature and kind of life that he lived among men.

2. The literary excellence and the doctrinal clarity of his teachings in the Americas is so great as to place the Book of Mormon as the equal or superior of the Bible. Shakespeare could not have coined better phrases than Jesus used among the Nephites, and Peter and Paul could not have propounded such glorious doctrines.

3. These Book of Mormon recitations, coming as they did through the instrumentality of Joseph Smith, prove to

the honest in heart everywhere that this seer of latter days was called of God; that he translated the Nephite record by the gift and power of God; and that he was and is the Lord's prophet, revealer, and witness for this generation.

4. And, finally, the glorious restoration of latter days; the promised marvelous work and a wonder that was destined to come forth in our day; the restitution of all things which God hath spoken by the mouth of all his holy prophets since the world began; the setting up anew of the Church and kingdom of God on earth; the gathering of scattered Israel from the ends of the earth into the fold of their True Shepherd; the position of The Church of Jesus Christ of Latter-day Saints as the only true and living Church upon the face of the whole earth—all these things are established, proved if you will, because the Book of Mormon and the ministry of the Risen Lord, as therein recorded, are eternal verities.

And so, as the account attests, after Jesus came and was known to the Nephites; after he preached the sermon on baptism, which we have equated with his similar teachings in Galilee; and after he had called the Nephite Twelve, then he delivered the Sermon on the Mount, as it were. And, may we say, it is found in a more excellent form in Third Nephi, chapters 12, 13, and 14, than it is in Matthew, chapters 5, 6, and 7. We have already considered in their contexts the many teachings of this sermon. Having respoken its wondrous truths for his Nephite sheep, Jesus said:

Behold, ye have heard the things which I taught before I ascended to my Father; therefore, whoso remembereth these sayings of mine and doeth them, him will I raise up at the last day.

Salvation comes by living the doctrines proclaimed in the Sermon on the Mount! That sermon—properly understood—is far more than a recitation of ethical principles; rather, it summarizes the Christian way of life, and it charts the course true saints must pursue to become even as He is.

In the Nephite version of the Sermon on the Mount, as he had done among the Jews, Jesus made the contrasts between the law of Moses and the gospel standard, saying that various things which Moses had approved were done away and that now men should live by a higher law. These included the commandments about murder, adultery, divorce, the taking of oaths, the requirement of an eye for an eye and a tooth for a tooth, and the like. But having so spoken to the Nephites, he added these words, which could not, properly, have been said to the Jews at the *beginning* of his ministry:

Therefore those things which were of old time, which were under the law, in me are all fulfilled. Old things are done away, and all things have become new.

When he spoke on the Mount of Beatitudes, the law was not yet fulfilled; now that he had eaten the Last Supper and introduced the sacrament; now that he had suffered in the garden and on the cross; now that he had come forth in immortality—the law was fulfilled. It would appear, however, that many among the Nephites, during these transitional months, had not fully envisioned that the lesser law of Moses had been supplanted by the higher law of Christ. And so now Jesus "perceived that there were some among them who marveled, and wondered what he would concerning the law of Moses; for they understood not the saying that old things had passed away, and that all things had become new." He said:

Marvel not that I said unto you that old things had passed away, and that all things had become new. Behold, I say unto you that the law is fulfilled that was given unto Moses.

Behold, I am he that gave the law, and I am he who covenanted with my people Israel; therefore, the law in me is fulfilled, for I have come to fulfil the law; therefore it hath an end.

'I am the Lord Jehovah. Moses spake my word; at my

command he gave the law. And the whole purpose of the law was to prepare men for my coming; its ordinances and performances prefigured my atoning sacrifice. Now I have come; the atonement hath been wrought; that which the sacrifices of your fathers prefigured has been accomplished; and the law in me is fulfilled.'

Behold, I do not destroy the prophets, for as many as have not been fulfilled in me, verily I say unto you, shall all be fulfilled.

And because I said unto you that old things have passed away, I do not destroy that which hath been spoken concerning things which are to come.

For behold, the covenant which I have made with my people is not all fulfilled; but the law which was given unto Moses hath an end in me.

O if only all the saints among the Jews had known and understood these things! As Paul said, "The law was our schoolmaster to bring us unto Christ, that we might be justified by faith. But after that faith is come, we are no longer under a schoolmaster." (Gal. 3:24-25.) The law was fulfilled, but the prophetic promises pertaining to the future remained! Also: The covenant Jehovah made with Abraham and all the righteous saints in all dispensations remained! The gospel promises and the gospel covenants—which were before the law—were still in force, and all the prophetic recounting of what was yet to be would surely come to pass.

Behold, I am the law, and the light. Look unto me, and endure to the end, and ye shall live; for unto him that endureth to the end will I give eternal life.

Behold, I have given unto you the commandments; therefore keep my commandments. And this is the law and the prophets, for they truly testified of me.

'Look no more to Moses, except insofar as he testified of me. I am the light; salvation comes by my law; turn ye to

my everlasting gospel; I am the law. Believe in me; keep
my commandments; endure to the end; and I will give you
eternal life, for I am God and the atonement comes by me.
In this way you shall honor Moses, for he was my witness.
If ye keep my commandments ye thereby fulfill both the
law and the prophets, for they testify of me.'

Then to the Nephite Twelve Jesus spake these words,
which affirmed the place and status of the Nephites in the
house of Israel:

*Ye are my disciples; and ye are a light unto this
people, who are a remnant of the house of Joseph.
And behold, this is the land of your inheritance; and
the Father hath given it unto you.*

As Jesus is the Light of the world, so his ministers,
reflecting his light, are lights to those to whom they are
sent. The Americas are the land of Joseph—the land of
Ephraim and Manasseh, the land of the Nephites, the land
of the Ephraimites who are gathering in the latter days.

*And not at any time hath the Father given me
commandment that I should tell it unto your brethren at Jerusalem. Neither at any time hath the Father given me commandment that I should tell unto
them concerning the other tribes of the house of
Israel, whom the Father hath led away out of the
land.*

*This much did the Father command me, that I
should tell unto them: That other sheep I have which
are not of this fold; them also I must bring, and they
shall hear my voice; and there shall be one fold, and
one shepherd.*

*And now, because of stiff-neckedness and unbe-
lief they understood not my word; therefore I was
commanded to say no more of the Father concerning this thing unto them.*

*But, verily, I say unto you that the Father hath
commanded me, and I tell it unto you, that ye were*

separated from among them because of their iniquity; therefore it is because of their iniquity that they know not of you.

And verily, I say unto you again that the other tribes hath the Father separated from them; and it is because of their iniquity that they know not of them.

And where, we might even now ask, are the lost tribes of Israel? And why is it that we do not know about them? Is it because of our stiffneckedness and unbelief? And how many other things might we know if we were faithful and true in all things?

And verily I say unto you, that ye are they of whom I said: Other sheep I have which are not of this fold; them also I must bring, and they shall hear my voice; and there shall be one fold, and one shepherd.

And they understood me not, for they supposed it had been the Gentiles; for they understood not that the Gentiles should be converted through their preaching.

And they understood me not that I said they shall hear my voice; and they understood me not that the Gentiles should not at any time hear my voice—that I should not manifest myself unto them save it were by the Holy Ghost.

But behold, ye have both heard my voice, and seen me; and ye are my sheep, and ye are numbered among those whom the Father hath given me.

Is not the soul of a Jew in the Americas as precious in the sight of the Lord as the soul of a Jew in Jerusalem? Or the soul of any of the lost tribes of the house of Israel? Will not the Lord Jehovah treat all Israel on the same basis, if their erring members repent and come unto him? And if one branch of the house of Jacob is entitled to hear his voice and see his face, does not every other branch have the same right? Let the message go by the power of the Holy Ghost to the Gentiles; but Israel—the Israel of God—they are the chosen seed; and Jesus will fulfill in them the covenants made with Abraham, Isaac, and Jacob, that in them and in their seed—the literal seed of the body—should all the nations of the earth be blessed.

And verily, verily, I say unto you that I have other sheep which are not of this land, neither of the land of Jerusalem, neither in any parts of that land round about whither I have been to minister.

For they of whom I speak are they who have not as yet heard my voice; neither have I at any time manifested myself unto them.

But I have received a commandment of the Father that I shall go unto them, and that they shall hear my voice, and shall be numbered among my sheep, that there may be one fold and one shepherd; therefore I go to show myself unto them.

Jesus Promises the Gospel to the Gentiles
(3 Nephi 16:4-20)

Even as on the mountain in Galilee, when Jesus commanded his Jewish apostles to go into all the world and preach the gospel to every creature—to go beyond the borders of Israel, out among the Gentiles—so now among the Nephites he teaches the same doctrine, the doctrine of a Gentile harvest of souls. And the Book of Mormon—a volume of holy scripture, a new witness for Christ, an inspired account containing the fulness of the everlasting gospel—the Book of Mormon will be the means of gathering in the remnants of scattered Israel and of proclaiming the gospel of salvation among the Gentiles in the last days. After announcing that he would visit the lost tribes of Israel, even as he was then visiting the "other sheep" who were Nephites, he said:

And I command you that ye shall write these sayings after I am gone, that if it so be that my people at Jerusalem, they who have seen me and

313

been with me in my ministry, do not ask the Father in my name, that they may receive a knowledge of you by the Holy Ghost, and also of the other tribes whom they know not of, that these sayings which ye shall write shall be kept and shall be manifested unto the Gentiles, that through the fulness of the Gentiles, the remnant of their seed, who shall be scattered forth upon the face of the earth because of their unbelief, may be brought in, or may be brought to a knowledge of me, their Redeemer.

This matter of identifying the Jews, Gentiles, and those who are of Israel is an extremely complex and difficult problem, primarily because the words are used in varying and even contradictory senses. They are used by the prophets and in holy writ to mean one thing in one age and another at a different time. To the Nephites, the Jews were the nationals of the kingdom of Judah whence they came, and all other peoples and nations were aliens or Gentiles, including those among them who were remnants of the various tribes of Israel. Gentiles were aliens, citizens of other nations, nations who served other gods than the Lord Jehovah.

To the Nephites, the Jews were the Jewish nationals in Jerusalem and elsewhere who rejected their Deliverer and crucified their King when he ministered among them as the Mortal Messiah. Tribal descent was not the issue; among them were those of Judah and Gad and Benjamin and other tribes, but all these were Jews and Jewish and all others were Gentiles, including the members of the lost tribes who were scattered among them. To the Nephites, they themselves were Jews because they came out from the nation of the Jews, brought with them the worship of the Jewish Jehovah, and kept the law of Moses as had their fathers. (2 Ne. 33:8.)

Thus the fulness of the gospel as restored to and through Joseph Smith was given by the Lord "unto the Gentiles." (1 Ne. 15:13.) Joseph Smith and his associates were considered by the Nephites to be Gentiles—for they were not Jewish nationals—even though they were of the pure blood of Israel. Thus the Book of Mormon came forth by way of the Gentiles though it is the Stick of Joseph in the hands of Ephraim. Thus the United States is a nation of the Gentiles; and thus all the nations of the earth are Gentile nations, even though the people in them who accept the gospel are blood descendants of Father Jacob.

Having this perspective, then, we can envision what Jesus here said to the Nephites. His words have been fulfilled in that (1) the Jews at Jerusalem did not ask the Father in his name for a knowledge of their Nephite kinsmen; (2) nor did they learn of the lost tribes of Israel; (3) hence, the sayings of Jesus, recorded and preserved in the Book of Mormon, were manifest to the Gentiles (meaning to us); (4) and, when the fulness of the Gentiles comes in (meaning the appointed period or times when the gospel goes preferentially to us Gentiles), (5) then it will go to the remnant of the seed of the Jews who lived at Jerusalem, which remnant will then be scattered "upon all the face of the earth because of their unbelief"; (6) and then shall the Jews (as here defined and as now generally known in the world) "be brought to a knowledge of me, their Redeemer."

And then will I gather them in from the four quarters of the earth; and then will I fulfill the covenant which the Father hath made unto all the people of the house of Israel.

Two things are here promised: (1) When the fulness of the Gentiles is come in, then the remnant of the Jews will be gathered in from the ends of the earth—gathered into the true fold and be numbered with their Shepherd's sheep, gathered to the land of their fathers; and (2) the covenant to save all the tribes of Israel, though they be lost and unknown and scattered, will be fulfilled.

And blessed are the Gentiles, because of their belief in me, in and of the Holy Ghost, which wit-

nesses unto them of me and of the Father.

Those of us Israelites who are here deemed to be Gentiles shall in the last days be blessed because we believe in Christ, as he is manifest by the power of the Holy Ghost, in contrast to his personal appearances among the Jews of Jerusalem and the Jews in the Americas.

Behold, because of their belief in me, saith the Father, and because of the unbelief of you, O house of Israel, in the latter day shall the truth come unto the Gentiles, that the fulness of these things shall be made known unto them.

Israel of old forsook the Lord Jehovah, and their nation and kingdom went into oblivion. Because they rejected Christ they were scattered and persecuted. But—O glorious promise!—in the latter days those among the Gentiles who believe shall receive the fulness of the gospel and the fulness of the blessings that flow therefrom.

But wo, saith the Father, unto the unbelieving of the Gentiles—for notwithstanding they have come forth upon the face of this land, and have scattered my people who are of the house of Israel; and my people who are of the house of Israel have been cast out from among them, and have been trodden under feet by them;

And because of the mercies of the Father unto the Gentiles, and also the judgments of the Father upon my people who are of the house of Israel, verily, verily, I say unto you, that after all this, and I have caused my people who are of the house of Israel to be smitten, and to be afflicted, and to be slain, and to be cast out from among them, and to become hated by them, and to become a hiss and a byword among them—

And thus commandeth the Father that I should say unto you: At that day when the Gentiles shall sin against my gospel, and shall be lifted up in the pride of their hearts above all nations, and above all the people of the whole earth, and shall be filled with all manner of lyings, and of deceits, and of mischiefs, and all manner of hypocrisy, and murders, and priestcrafts, and whoredoms, and of secret abominations; and if they shall do all those things, and shall reject the fulness of my gospel, behold, saith the Father, I will bring the fulness of my gospel from among them.

How plainly Jesus foretells what is to be in the day of restoration: (1) The unbelieving among the Gentiles who are assembled in the Americas shall scatter the house of Israel; (2) Lehi's seed, in both North and South America, shall be cast out and trodden under foot by the Gentiles; (3) these things shall come to pass because of the mercies of the Father upon the Gentiles and because of his judgments upon his Israelitish people; (4) but then, the Gentiles in the New World—meaning the generality of them—shall reject the gospel and pursue an evil and ungodly course; (5) so that the gospel will be taken from among them.

And then will I remember my covenant which I have made unto my people, O house of Israel, and I will bring my gospel unto them.

And I will show unto thee, O house of Israel, that the Gentiles shall not have power over you; but I will remember my covenant unto you, O house of Israel, and ye shall come unto the knowledge of the fulness of my gospel.

Jehovah's covenant with his people is that through Abraham and his seed shall all the nations of the earth be blessed; it is that the seed of Abraham, Isaac, and Jacob shall have a right to the gospel and the priesthood; it is that they shall bear his priesthood and be his ministers to take his gospel to all people; it is that the house of Israel shall be saved with an everlasting salvation in the kingdom of the Father. (Abr. 2:8-11.) And after the gospel has been restored in a Gentile nation, those of scattered Israel in all nations shall begin to believe, and they shall come into the latter-day kingdom and be blessed according to the promises.

But if the Gentiles will repent and return unto me, saith the Father, behold they shall be numbered among my people, O house of Israel.

This shall come to pass according to the promise made by Jehovah to his friend Abraham: "As many as receive this Gospel shall be called after thy name, and shall be accounted thy seed, and shall rise up and bless thee, as their father." (Abr. 2:10.) For, as Nephi said: "All are alike unto God, both Jew and Gentile." (2 Ne. 26:33.)

And I will not suffer my people, who are of the house of Israel, to go through among them, and tread them down, saith the Father.

But if they will not turn unto me, and hearken unto my voice, I will suffer them, yea, I will suffer my people, O house of Israel, that they shall go through among them, and shall tread them down, and they shall be as salt that hath lost its savor, which is thenceforth good for nothing but to be cast out, and to be trodden under foot of my people, O house of Israel.

These things lie ahead; they are pre-millennial; as the great destructions and wars unfold that shall usher in that reign of peace, then we shall learn how and in what manner they shall be fulfilled. Our feelings are that the Gentiles will not repent and that there will be a day when Israel shall triumph over her ancient enemies according to the promises.

Verily, verily, I say unto you, thus hath the Father commanded me—that I should give unto this people this land for their inheritance.

And then the words of the prophet Isaiah shall be fulfilled, which say: Thy watchmen shall lift up the voice; with the voice together shall they sing, for

*they shall see eye to eye when the Lord shall bring
again Zion.*

*Break forth into joy, sing together, ye waste
places of Jerusalem; for the Lord hath comforted his
people, he hath redeemed Jerusalem.*

*The Lord hath made bare his holy arm in the eye
of all the nations; and all the ends of the earth shall
see the salvation of God.*

These words are millennial. They exult in the final glory
and triumph of Israel—after her warfare with the Gentiles,
after the days of her sorrows and suffering, after she has
been a hiss and a byword among all people. Israel—Jacob's
seed!—shall come off triumphant, and those Gentiles who
join with her shall be as she is, and be accounted the seed of
him who fathered Israel in the flesh, and Him also whose
house it is.

Chapter 114

STILL AMONG
THE AMERICAN JEWS

We are made alive in Christ because
of our faith. . . . :
And we talk of Christ, we rejoice in Christ,
we preach of Christ, we prophesy of Christ,
and we write according to our prophecies,
that our chidren may know
to what source they may look
for a remission of their sins. . . .
The right way is to believe in Christ
and deny him not; for by denying him
ye also deny the prophets and the law. . . .
Christ is the Holy One of Israel;
wherefore ye must bow down before him,
and worship him with all your might, mind,
and strength, and your whole soul;
and if ye do this ye shall in nowise
be cast out.
(2 Ne. 25:25-29.)

A Ministry of Miracles
and Angelic Ministrations
(3 Nephi 17:1-25)

What a blessed day this is, a day when the Blessed One—resurrected and glorified—ministers among his people!

They have now heard the announcement of the atonement; felt the prints of the nails in his hands and in his feet; been instructed as to baptism and the witness that both the Father and the Holy Ghost bear of him; heard the calling of his American apostolic witnesses; rejoiced in the wondrous words of the Sermon on the Mount; learned of the fulfillment of the law of Moses; been identified as the Lord's "other sheep"; and heard the glad tidings of the restoration of the gospel, of its proclamation among the Gentiles, of the latter-day gathering of Israel and the final triumph of the chosen seed. Hours have elapsed. How can any congregation absorb more of the Lord's word at one time than this? And so we hear him say:

Behold, my time is at hand. I perceive that ye are weak, that ye cannot understand all my words which I am commanded of the Father to speak unto you at this time.

Therefore, go ye unto your homes, and ponder upon the things which I have said, and ask of the Father, in my name, that ye may understand, and prepare your minds for the morrow, and I come unto you again.

But now I go unto the Father, and also to show myself unto the lost tribes of Israel, for they are not lost unto the Father, for he knoweth whither he hath taken them.

Such is the perfect pattern for hearing the word of the Lord. Let the speaker speak by the power of the Holy Ghost; let the hearers hear by that same power; then let the hearers ponder and pray and seek to know—by

321

revelation—the full meaning of the spoken word; and then let them join again in the assembly of the saints to hear more of the eternal saving word. But in this instance the multitude is in tears; the unspoken pleas of their heart are that Jesus will tarry longer and teach more, and their faith prevails.

Behold, my bowels are filled with compassion towards you. Have ye any that are sick among you? Bring them hither. Have ye any that are lame, or blind, or halt, or maimed, or leprous, or that are withered, or that are deaf, or that are afflicted in any manner? Bring them hither and I will heal them, for I have compassion upon you; my bowels are filled with mercy.

For I perceive that ye desire that I should show unto you what I have done unto your brethren at Jerusalem, for I see that your faith is sufficient that I should heal you.

All those who were sick—their lame, their blind, and their dumb, and those with any manner of affliction—all were brought, and one by one he healed them. Then they who were whole and they who were healed bowed down at his feet and worshipped him, and "they did bathe his feet with their tears." Jesus then asked them to bring their little children, which they did, and "he commanded the multitude that they should kneel down upon the ground." Then Jesus, standing in the midst of them, said: "Father, I am troubled because of the wickedness of the people of the house of Israel." At this point "he himself also knelt upon the earth; and behold he prayed unto the Father, and the things which he prayed cannot be written."

There are things that it is "not lawful for man to utter; Neither is man capable to make them known, for they are only to be seen and understood by the power of the Holy Spirit, which God bestows on those who love him, and purify themselves before him." (D&C 76:115-116.) Such was it on this occasion. As to what Jesus said in his prayer we know not, only that the multitude testified: "The eye hath never seen, neither hath the ear heard, before, so great and marvelous things as we saw and heard Jesus speak unto the Father; And no tongue can speak, neither can there be written by any man, neither can the hearts of men conceive so great and marvelous things as we both saw and heard Jesus speak; and no one can conceive of the joy which filled our souls at the time we heard him pray for us unto the Father." Indeed, "so great was the joy of the multitude that they were overcome," and they could not arise until Jesus bade them to do so. "Blessed are ye because of your faith," he said unto them. "And now behold, my joy is full."

Then he wept, and "took their little children, one by one, and blessed them, and prayed unto the Father for them." Then he wept again and said: "Behold your little ones." Then came the miracle that testifies of the purity and perfection of innocent children, children who have but recently left the presence of the Father, children whose lives are not yet tainted with sin, children who, should they die in their innocence, shall return in purity to the Father and there inherit eternal life. And so, as the multitude "looked to behold they cast their eyes towards heaven, and they saw the heavens open, and they saw angels descending out of heaven as it were in the midst of fire; and they came down and encircled those little ones about, and they were encircled about with fire; and the angels did minister unto them." And of this the multitude—all twenty-five hundred of them—did bear record.

The Nephites Receive
the Gift of the Holy Ghost
(3 Nephi 18:1-39; 19:1-36; 20:8-9)

Our Blessed Lord then had bread and wine brought, which he gave to them to eat and drink in remembrance of his broken flesh and spilt blood. Of these Nephite ministrations we have written in connection with the same ordinance as administered among those in Jerusalem. As the sacramental ordinance was concluded Jesus said to the Twelve:

> *Blessed are ye if ye shall keep my commandments, which the Father hath commanded me that I should give unto you.*
>
> *Verily, verily, I say unto you, ye must watch and pray always, lest ye be tempted by the devil, and ye be led away captive by him.*
>
> *And as I have prayed among you even so shall ye pray in my church, among my people who do repent and are baptized in my name. Behold I am the light; I have set an example for you.*

Above all others Satan seeks to ensnare the shepherds of the Lord's flock, thereby preparing the way for the scattering of the sheep. Church officers are to live and pray as Jesus lived and prayed, that they may be lights to the saints. Then to the multitude Jesus said:

> *Behold, verily, verily, I say unto you, ye must watch and pray always lest ye enter into temptation; for Satan desireth to have you, that he may sift you as wheat.*
>
> *Therefore ye must always pray unto the Father in my name; And whatsoever ye shall ask the Father in my name, which is right, believing that ye shall receive, behold it shall be given unto you.*
>
> *Pray in your families unto the Father, always in my name, that your wives and your children may be blessed.*

Never has it been stated better. Unless the saints watch their conduct and keep it in harmony with the divine will, and unless they pray to the Father in the name of Christ, with all the energy of their souls, Satan—not the Lord—will harvest their souls. The grim reaper of death and destruction will cut them down, and they will be stored with the wicked in the granaries of despair. But—O glorious

324

promise!—all of the righteous desires of the faithful saints shall be granted. Anything they ask for that is right shall be given them! And for whom shall they pray with more fervor and faith than for themselves and their wives and their children? God be praised for the power of prayer!

And behold, ye shall meet together oft; and ye shall not forbid any man from coming unto you when ye shall meet together, but suffer them that they may come unto you and forbid them not;

But ye shall pray for them, and shall not cast them out; and if it so be that they come unto you oft ye shall pray for them unto the Father, in my name.

As the body needs bread, so also must the soul be fed. Man does not live by bread alone; unless the soul is fed, man dies spiritually. There must be frequent gospel banquets; the soul of man must be offered every word that proceedeth forth from the mouth of God. And we must pray for those who come to our meetings desiring to feast upon the good word of God, but whose souls as yet can only digest the milk and not the meat of the word.

Therefore, hold up your light that it may shine unto the world. Behold I am the light which ye shall hold up—that which ye have seen me do. Behold ye see that I have prayed unto the Father, and ye all have witnessed.

And ye see that I have commanded that none of you should go away, but rather have commanded that ye should come unto me, that ye might feel and see; even so shall ye do unto the world; and whosoever breaketh this commandment suffereth himself to be led into temptation.

Jesus is the light; his example is perfect; all who do as he did shall be as he is; and such places them on the course leading to eternal life. And having so taught them, Jesus said to the Twelve: "Behold verily, verily, I say unto you, I give unto you another commandment, and then I must go unto my Father that I may fulfil other commandments which he hath given me." The other commandment was that they, as his administrators and representatives on earth, should not suffer anyone knowingly to partake of his flesh and blood in unworthiness. All such, he said, would eat and drink damnation to their own souls. All this we have considered in its Jewish context in the Jerusalem account. To it Jesus appended the commandment that they should not cast such persons out of their synagogues, but should pray for them, plead with them to repent, offer them the blessings of baptism, and guide them in all things toward that salvation which the gospel promises. If they pursued such a course they would not be condemned by the Father. This counsel was given to them, he said, because of prior disputations among them. "And blessed are ye if ye have no disputations among you," he said. Then he announced he must go to the Father, and he touched each of the Twelve and "gave them power to give the Holy Ghost," after which a cloud overshadowed the multitude so they could not see Jesus, but the Twelve saw and bore record that "he ascended again into heaven."

For the rest of that day, and for all the night long, messengers carried forth the word of Jesus' ministry among them and of his promise to return on the morrow; and "an exceeding great number, did labor exceedingly all that night" so as to be at the appointed place on the next day. Their number was so great—surely there must have been scores of thousands—that the Twelve divided them into twelve bodies so as to teach them. They all—the disciples and the multitude—knelt and prayed to the Father in the name of Jesus. Then the Twelve—and the pattern thus set is perfect—"ministered those same words which Jesus had spoken—nothing varying from the words which Jesus had spoken." All the multitude thus received a verbatim account of all that was said and done by the Lord of Life to the smaller congregation of twenty-five hundred on the previous day. Then the disciples knelt and prayed again. "And they did pray for that which they most desired; and they desired that the Holy Ghost should be given unto them.''

Then they went down to the water's edge; Nephi and the rest of the Twelve were baptized, and ''the Holy Ghost did fall upon them, and they were filled with the Holy Ghost and with fire.'' It was the New World Pentecost! Cloven tongues of fire, and more, rested upon them! ''And behold, they were encircled about as if it were by fire; and it came down from heaven, and the multitude did witness it, and did bear record; and angels did come down out of heaven and did minister unto them.''

While the heavens were thus open; while angels ministered and holy fire cleansed their souls from sin; while righteousness was falling as the gentle dew from heaven— ''Jesus came and stood in the midst and ministered unto them.'' He commanded them all, both the disciples and the multitude, to kneel and pray, ''and they did pray unto Jesus, calling him their Lord and their God.'' Jesus separated himself from the group, bowed himself to the earth, and prayed:

Father, I thank thee that thou hast given the Holy Ghost unto these whom I have chosen; and it is because of their belief in me that I have chosen them out of the world.

Father, I pray thee that thou wilt give the Holy Ghost unto all them that shall believe in their words.

Father, thou hast given them the Holy Ghost because they believe in me; and thou seest that they believe in me because thou hearest them, and they pray unto me; and they pray unto me because I am with them.

And now Father, I pray unto thee for them, and also for all those who shall believe on their words, that they may believe in me, that I may be in them as thou, Father, art in me, that we may be one.

By the power of the Holy Ghost the saints are one— they in Christ, and he in them; the Father in them, and they in him; and all the saints in each other—for they are one. This we have already seen in our consideration of the Intercessory Prayer. Having so spoken, Jesus came to the disciples who continued to pray, "and they did not multiply many words, for it was given unto them what they should pray, and they were filled with desire." Thereupon, "Jesus blessed them as they did pray unto him; and his countenance did smile upon them, and the light of his countenance did shine upon them, and behold they were as white as the countenance and also the garments of Jesus; and behold the whiteness thereof did exceed all the whiteness, yea, even there could be nothing upon earth so white as the whiteness thereof." Jesus told them to continue to pray, and he went a little way off, bowed himself to the earth, and prayed again:

Father, I thank thee that thou hast purified those whom I have chosen, because of their faith, and I pray for them, and also for them who shall believe on their words, that they may be purified in me, through faith on their words, even as they are purified in me.

Father, I pray not for the world, but for those whom thou hast given me out of the world, because of their faith, that they may be purified in me, that I may be in them as thou, Father, art in me, that we may be one, that I may be glorified in them.

These concepts, though not expressed as well as in this Book of Mormon account, we heard in the Intercessory Prayer. Having here spoken them, Jesus returned to the Twelve, smiled upon them as they continued to pray— "and behold they were white, even as Jesus"—and then "went again a little way off and prayed unto the Father." Of what then transpired the inspired record recites: "And tongue cannot speak the words which he prayed, neither can be written by man the words which he prayed." But the multitude heard and bore record, "and their hearts were open and they did understand in their hearts the words which he prayed. Nevertheless, so great and marvelous were the words which he prayed that they cannot be written, neither can they be uttered by man." After his prayer, Jesus said:

> *So great faith have I never seen among all the Jews; wherefore I could not show unto them so great miracles, because of their unbelief.*
>
> *Verily I say unto you, there are none of them that have seen so great things as ye have seen; neither have they heard so great things as ye have heard.*

In our view, these marvelous happenings—when the Holy Ghost fell mightily upon the people; when the sanctifying power of the Holy Spirit of God cleansed their souls; when mortal men were quickened by the Spirit until their countenances shone (as did that of Moses after he was with the Lord for forty days in the holy mount); when Jesus spoke words that could not be written and could only be understood by the power of the Spirit—these marvelous events were the high point of Jesus' ministry among his "other sheep." Seldom, if ever, has there been such a scene on planet earth. Perhaps in the Zion of Enoch, when the Lord came and dwelt with his people; perhaps at Adam-ondi-Ahman, in the assembly of high priests, when the Lord appeared and ministered comfort unto Adam, and the Ancient of Days predicted whatsoever should befall his posterity unto the latest generation; perhaps on the Mount of Transfiguration, when only Peter, James, and John were present—perhaps there have been other like outpourings of God's goodness and grace, of which we have no knowledge, but nowhere do our scriptures preserve in such detail such wondrous events as are here recorded. Truly they are a sample and an illustration of what shall be in that great millennial day when He whose we are reigns personally among those who remain on earth after the wicked and ungodly have been burned as stubble.

After the events of this hour had been savored to the full, Jesus commanded the multitude to cease their vocal prayers but to continue to pray in their hearts. Then as a seal on the spiritual experience they had enjoyed, he provided bread and wine miraculously, blessed the sacred emblems, and distributed them to the Twelve. At his direction they in turn brake bread and passed it and the wine to the multitude. Then Jesus said, as we have heretofore quoted in connection with the Old World sacramental performances, what is probably the greatest one sentence pronouncement on the sacrament of the Lord's Supper which is found in all holy writ:

He that eateth this bread eateth of my body to his soul; and he that drinketh of this wine drinketh of my blood to his soul; and his soul shall never hunger nor thirst, but shall be filled.

And as a perfect account of the blessings which are poured out upon those who partake worthily of the emblems representing the broken flesh and spilt blood, the Nephite scripture says: "Now, when the multitude had all eaten and drunk, behold, they were filled with the Spirit; and they did cry out with one voice, and gave glory to Jesus, whom they both saw and heard."

And thus are these glorious things recorded in that holy book, the Book of Mormon, which causes us to marvel greatly and wonder why it is that all who call themselves Christians do not accept and believe this volume of American scripture as readily as they suppose they believe the scriptural accounts originating in the Old World. Surely a tree is known by its fruits.

Chapter 115

THE RESTORATION OF THE KINGDOM TO ISRAEL

For a small moment have I forsaken thee,
but with great mercies will I gather thee.
In a little wrath I hid my face
from thee for a moment,
but with everlasting kindness
will I have mercy on thee,
saith the Lord thy Redeemer. . . .
For the mountains shall depart
and the hills be removed,
but my kindness shall not depart from thee,
neither shall the covenant of my people
be removed, saith the Lord
that hath mercy on thee. . . .
And all thy children shall be taught
of the Lord; and great shall be the peace
of thy children. In righteousness
shalt thou be established;
thou shalt be far from oppression
for thou shalt not fear, and from terror
for it shall not come near thee.
(3 Ne. 22:7-8, 10, 13-14.)

Israel Shall Be Gathered
(3 Nephi 20:10-24)

Soon we shall hear the Twelve in Jerusalem ask the Resurrected One: "Lord, wilt thou at this time restore again the kingdom to Israel?" and we will observe with great interest the answer he gives them. But before we turn back to that scene on Olivet, just before he ascends to his Father, it is our privilege to learn about the restoration of the kingdom to Israel, as he expounded the glorious truths involved to his Nephite-Jews in the Americas.

Israel the chosen seed; Israel the Lord's people; Israel the only nation since Abraham that had worshipped Jehovah; Israel the children of the prophets; Israel who had been cursed and scattered for her sins; Israel in whose veins believing blood flows—the Israel of God shall be gathered, and fed, and nurtured, and saved, in the last days! Let there be no misunderstanding about this; salvation is of the Jews, and if there are believing Gentiles, they will be adopted into the believing family and inherit with the chosen seed. "And so all Israel shall be saved: as it is written, There shall come out of Sion the Deliverer, and shall turn away ungodliness from Jacob: For this is my covenant unto them, when I shall take away their sins." (Rom. 11:26-27.) But sadly: "They are not all Israel, which are of Israel" (Rom. 9:6), and only those who turn to their God and accept him as the Promised Messiah shall inherit with the chosen seed either in time or in eternity.

While his Nephite sheep were filled with the Spirit, and were singing praises to his holy name—and blessed be that glorious name forever!—Jesus said: "Behold now I finish the commandment which the Father hath commanded me concerning this people, who are a remnant of the house of Israel." He then began to preach unto them the doctrine that his Father—the Father of us all—desired them (and us!) to hear:

> *Ye remember that I spake unto you, and said that when the words of Isaiah should be fulfilled—behold*

they are written, ye have them before you, therefore search them—

And verily, verily, I say unto you, that when they shall be fulfilled then is the fulfilling of the covenant which the Father hath made unto his people, O house of Israel.

Be it recalled also that when we recorded what Jesus quoted from Isaiah—how the watchmen should see eye to eye when the Lord brought again Zion; how the Lord would comfort his people and redeem Jerusalem; how he would make bare his arm in the eyes of *all* nations, so that *all* the ends of the earth should see the salvation of God—when we recorded these words, we identified them as being millennial. That is, they shall come to pass when the Son of Man comes to dwell and reign on earth. To this we now add that certain initial fulfillment will commence before that dread yet glorious day of his coming. As we shall now see, when the gospel is restored, preparatory to the establishment of the Zion and the Jerusalem of old, men shall begin to see eye to eye, and the message of salvation shall begin to go forth to the nations of the earth. The gathering of Israel must needs begin before Zion is fully established so there will be a people to build the city and man the walls and serve in the watchtowers.

And then shall the remnants, which shall be scattered abroad upon the face of the earth, be gathered in from the east and from the west, and from the south and from the north; and they shall be brought to the knowledge of the Lord their God, who hath redeemed them.

The gathering of Israel is twofold: it is both spiritual and temporal. It is (1) into the Church and kingdom of God on earth; into the true fold where the true faith is found; into The Church of Jesus Christ of Latter-day Saints, which is the kingdom of God on earth, and which administers the gospel, which is the plan of salvation; and (2) unto those portions of the earth's surface which are appointed by revelation as places of gathering, so there may be congregations that can worship together, whose members can strengthen each other, and where all the blessings of the house of the Lord may be gained. In our day the gathering of Israel is in all the nations of the earth; in all the places where stakes of Zion are being established; in the lands where houses of the Lord are being built; in "all the nations," so that "all the ends of the earth shall see the salvation of God." To these Nephites, however, Jesus said:

And the Father hath commanded me that I should give unto you this land, for your inheritance.

America is the land of Joseph. The Nephites are of the house of Joseph; and they, along with us, who also have that tribal ancestry, are destined to inherit these lands which are choice above all other lands.

And I say unto you, that if the Gentiles do not repent after the blessing which they shall receive, after they have scattered my people—

Then shall ye, who are a remnant of the house of Jacob, go forth among them; and ye shall be in the midst of them who shall be many; and ye shall be among them as a lion among the beasts of the forest, and as a young lion among the flocks of sheep, who, if he goeth through both treadeth down and teareth in pieces, and none can deliver.

Thy hand shall be lifted up upon thine adversaries, and all thine enemies shall be cut off.

This is millennial; it refers to the Second Coming of Christ. It is not a war that a few Lamanites or any remnant of Israel shall wage against Gentile oppressors; the Lord does not operate in that manner. When he comes the wicked shall be destroyed and the righteous preserved; those who have not hearkened to the prophets shall be cut off from among the people; thus, the "enemies" of Israel "shall be cut off." And it shall be with power, as though a young lion went forth rending and tearing in pieces a helpless flock of sheep. And so, if the Gentiles do not repent and believe in Christ after the gospel is restored among them, then, when the Lord comes, they will be destroyed and the triumph of Israel—because they kept the commandments and did receive the gospel—that triumph will be complete.

And I will gather my people together as a man gathereth his sheaves into the floor.

In all this Jesus is but quoting and paraphrasing what the Lord revealed to Micah concerning the *whole* house of Israel. After that ancient prophet foretold the establishment of the house of the Lord in the tops of the mountains in the last days, and spoke of all nations flowing unto it; after he prophesied about the Second Coming and the day when men would beat their swords into plowshares and their spears into pruning hooks; after he spoke of the whole earth being at peace and of the Lord reigning in Mount Zion forever, then he told about the destruction of the Gentile nations in that day. "Now also many nations are gathered against thee"—meaning against Israel—"that say, Let her be defiled, and let our eye look upon Zion." To this there is an answer; it comes from the Lord; he says: "But they know not the thoughts of the Lord, neither understand they his counsel: for he shall gather them as the sheaves into the floor." Israel shall be gathered out of the Babylonish nations; she shall return to the true fold. "Arise and thresh, O daughter of Zion: for I will make thine horn iron, and I will make thy hoofs brass: and thou shalt beat in pieces many people: and I will consecrate their gain unto the Lord, and their substance unto the Lord of the whole earth." (Micah 4:1-13.) Or, as Jesus now says it to the Nephites:

For I will make my people with whom the Father hath covenanted, yea, I will make thy horn iron, and I will make thy hoofs brass. And thou shalt beat in pieces many people; and I will consecrate their gain unto the Lord, and their substance unto the Lord of the whole earth. And behold, I am he who doeth it.

335

And it shall come to pass, saith the Father, that the sword of my justice shall hang over them at that day; and except they repent it shall fall upon them, saith the Father, yea, even upon all the nations of the Gentiles.

Again the message is the triumph of his people in the day of his coming. It is the destruction of all the wicked in all nations among all the Gentiles in that great and dreadful day. Here the reference is broader than to the Nephite remnants of Israel; it is to all those of Israel with whom the covenant has been made; it is to all the house of Israel. It is speaking of the sword of justice falling "upon all the nations of the Gentiles," not alone on those Gentile nations which scattered and persecuted the seed of Lehi.

And it shall come to pass that I will establish my people, O house of Israel.

The Lord's people—Israel—scattered in all the nations of the earth shall, wherever they are, be gathered into the true fold of Christ in their nations; then the Lord will come and destroy the wicked, who are their enemies, and then they will triumph to the full. But as to the Nephites, Jesus continued:

And behold, this people will I establish in this land, unto the fulfilling of the covenant which I made with your father Jacob; and it shall be a New Jerusalem. And the powers of heaven shall be in the midst of this people; yea, even I will be in the midst of you.

As to the house of Joseph, their inheritance is in the Americas, even as Father Jacob promised in the blessing given to Joseph, that he should be "a fruitful bough, even a fruitful bough by a well; whose branches run over the wall," and that the blessings of Joseph should prevail above those of all the other tribes and extend "unto the utmost bound of the everlasting hills." (Gen. 49:22, 26.) All this shall find total fulfillment only in that day when the Lord reigns in the midst of men. Then, still having in mind the destruction of the Gentile nations who have opposed his people, and who are their enemies and his enemies, Jesus reminded the Nephites of the words of Moses concerning their Messiah:

Behold, I am he of whom Moses spake, saying: A prophet shall the Lord your God raise up unto you of your brethren, like unto me; him shall ye hear in all things whatsoever he shall say unto you. And it shall come to pass that every soul who will not hear that prophet shall be cut off from among the people.

Verily I say unto you, yea, and all the prophets from Samuel and those that follow after, as many as have spoken, have testified of me.

Those who will not hear the voice of the Lord, as proclaimed by his servants the prophets, shall be cut off from among the people when he comes again, comes, as Paul expresses it, "in flaming fire taking vengeance on them that know not God, and that obey not the gospel of our Lord Jesus Christ." (2 Thes. 1:8.) This is the promise that "all thine enemies shall be cut off." There ought not be any confusion or misunderstanding on these points.

"Ye Are the Children of the Covenant"
(3 Nephi 20:25-46)

Why is the Lord gathering Israel in these last days? It is to fulfill the covenant made with Abraham and renewed with Isaac and Jacob and others. What is that covenant? It is not the gathering of Israel *per se,* but something far more important than the mere assembling of a people in Jerusalem or on Mount Zion or at any designated place. It is not the allocation of Palestine for the seed of Abraham, or the designation of the Americas as the inheritance of Joseph, though each of these arrangements has a bearing on the fulfillment of the covenant. The gathering of Israel, at whatever place Deity specifies, is a necessary condition precedent, something that makes possible the fulfilling of

337

the ancient covenant. What, then, is the covenant itself?

Jehovah promised—covenanted with—his friend Abraham that in him and in his seed, meaning the literal seed of his body, should "all the families of the earth be blessed, even with the blessings of the Gospel, which are the blessings of salvation, even of life eternal." (Abr. 2:8-11.)

Jehovah promised—covenanted with—his friend Abraham that his seed after him, again meaning the literal seed of his body, should have the right to the priesthood and the gospel, and should be the Lord's ministers to carry these blessings to all nations and kindreds.

Jehovah promised—covenanted with—his friend Abraham that he and his seed after him should have the ordinance of celestial marriage, which opens the door to a continuation of the family unit in eternity, which is what constitutes eternal life in our Father's kingdom.

Jehovah promised—covenanted with—his friend Abraham that his seed, the fruit of his loins, should continue eternally, "both in the world and out of the world should they continue as innumerable as the stars; or, if ye were to count the sand upon the seashore ye could not number them." (D&C 132:29-32.)

These same promises were made to Isaac and to Jacob and to their posterity after him. They are "the promises made to the fathers," which, by the hand of Elijah the prophet, have been planted in "the hearts of the children." (D&C 2:1-3.) These are the promises that make us "the children of the covenant," the covenant made with our fathers, the covenant into which we are privileged to enter, the covenant of eternal life, of eternal lives, of a continuation of the seeds forever and ever. And in order to fulfill this covenant, Jehovah promised to gather Israel; he promised to bring them into the fold of Christ, so they could strengthen each other in the holy faith; he promised to prepare them for the ordinances of his holy house, through which the blessings of eternal life come. And so now Jesus says to the remnant of Jacob that he has gathered around him in the land of the Nephites in the meridian of time:

And behold, ye are the children of the prophets; and ye are of the house of Israel; and ye are of the covenant which the Father made with your fathers, saying unto Abraham: And in thy seed shall all the kindreds of the earth be blessed.

The Father having raised me up unto you first, and sent me to bless you in turning away every one of you from his iniquities; and this because ye are the children of the covenant.

These American Israelites were natural heirs according to the flesh of all the blessings of Abraham, Isaac, and Jacob. It was their right to receive, inherit, and possess the fulness of the Father's kingdom through the continuation of the family unit in eternity. It was their privilege to have a continuation of the seeds forever and ever, to have posterity in eternity as numerous as the stars in the heavens or as the sand upon the seashore. And all of this shall have efficacy, virtue, and force because Jesus atoned for the sins of the world, because he took upon himself the sins of all men on conditions of repentance, because he turned away every obedient man "from his iniquities."

And after that ye were blessed then fulfilleth the Father the covenant which he made with Abraham, saying: In thy seed shall all the kindreds of the earth be blessed—unto the pouring out of the Holy Ghost through me upon the Gentiles, which blessing upon the Gentiles shall make them mighty above all, unto the scattering of my people, O house of Israel.

Not only shall the seed of Abraham be blessed through the covenant made with their father, but all the kindreds of the earth, even the Gentile nations, may be blessed in like manner, if they will believe in Christ and receive the Holy Ghost and keep the commandments, for, as Jehovah said to Abraham, "as many as receive this Gospel shall be called after thy name, and shall be accounted thy seed, and shall rise up and bless thee, as their father." (Abr. 2:10.) Then, speaking of the American Gentiles and their dealings with the seed of Lehi, Jesus said:

And they shall be a scourge unto the people of this land. Nevertheless, when they shall have received the fulness of my gospel, then if they shall harden their hearts against me I will return their iniquities upon their own heads, saith the Father.

Neither Jew nor Gentile shall be cleansed from sin through the gospel, by the Holy Ghost, except on conditions of repentance and obedience. The iniquities of the rebellious shall return upon their own heads. Having thus spoken of the American-Israelites and the American-Gentiles, Jesus turns to his ancient covenant people, the Jews, who are scattered in all nations.

And I will remember the covenant which I have made with my people; and I have covenanted with them that I would gather them together in mine own due time, that I would give unto them again the land of their fathers for their inheritance, which is the land of Jerusalem, which is the promised land unto them forever, saith the Father.

The covenants are for all the house of Israel; all are entitled to the blessings of the priesthood and the gospel and that eternal life which consists of the continuation of the family unit in the celestial kingdom. But all shall not gather to the same lands; all shall not be taught in the same synagogues; all shall not receive their blessings in the same temples. The Jews of Palestine shall return to the land of Jerusalem, there to be blessed from on high.

And it shall come to pass that the time cometh, when the fulness of my gospel shall be preached unto them; And they shall believe in me, that I am Jesus Christ, the Son of God, and shall pray unto the Father in my name.

When the times of the Gentiles are fulfilled, the times of the Jews will commence. The gospel will then go to the

Jewish seed of Abraham, and they shall believe; and, except for a limited few, the great day of Jewish conversion will be in the millennial day, after they have seen him whom they crucified and have heard him attest that the wounds in his hands and in his feet are those with which he was wounded in the house of his friends. Of that millennial day, Jesus continues:

Then shall their watchmen lift up their voice, and with the voice together shall they sing; for they shall see eye to eye. Then will the Father gather them together again, and give unto them Jerusalem for the land of their inheritance.

Then shall they break forth into joy—Sing together, ye waste places of Jerusalem; for the Father hath comforted his people, he hath redeemed Jerusalem.

The Father hath made bare his holy arm in the eyes of all the nations; and all the ends of the earth shall see the salvation of the Father; and the Father and I are one.

Such is Jesus' interpreting paraphrase of the words of Isaiah—a Nephite targum, if you will—that he had before quoted to them. It is the setting forth of the millennial glory of the Jews, the glory that will be theirs when they accept their Messiah and become heirs of all the promises made to Abraham their father. "And then," Jesus continues— meaning in the day when the kingdom has been restored in all its fulness to Israel; in the day when Zion has been redeemed; in the day when He rules whose right it is— "then shall be brought to pass that which is written" (and what he quotes is an improved version of Isaiah):

Awake, awake again, and put on thy strength, O Zion; put on thy beautiful garments, O Jerusalem, the holy city, for henceforth there shall no more come into thee the uncircumcised and the unclean.

Shake thyself from the dust; arise, sit down, O Jerusalem; loose thyself from the bands of thy neck,

O captive daughter of Zion. For thus saith the Lord: Ye have sold yourselves for naught, and ye shall be redeemed without money.

Verily, verily, I say unto you, that my people shall know my name; yea, in that day they shall know that I am he that doth speak.[1]

Jerusalem—Jerusalem of the Jews—David's ancient city shall become holy; no more shall Gentile dogs defile its holy streets with their uncircumcised hearts. No longer will the Jews boast that salvation is theirs simply because of the Abrahamic token cut in their flesh, for then it will come to pass, as the apostle has written: "He is not a Jew, which is one outwardly; neither is that circumcision, which is outward in the flesh: But he is a Jew, which is one inwardly; and circumcision is that of the heart, in the spirit, and not in the letter; whose praise is not of men, but of God." (Rom. 2:25-29.) In that blessed day, those who walk the streets of the Holy City shall be clean, clean because they have "come forth out of the waters of Judah, or out of the waters of baptism." (1 Ne. 20:1.)

Jerusalem—Jerusalem of the Jews—she who sold herself for naught and went into captivity for her sins, she shall arise from the dust and sit down with the mighty. Her captive daughters will loose the bands of darkness with which they have been bound and return unto the Lord who will reveal himself to them. In that day they shall know their King, their Messiah, their Lord. And he is Christ. He it is that shall then speak to them.

And then shall they say: How beautiful upon the mountains are the feet of him that bringeth good tidings unto them, that publisheth peace; that bringeth good tidings unto them of good, that publisheth salvation; that saith unto Zion: Thy God reigneth![2]

Surely in this day, as never before, shall the hearts of the Jews—for the Lord will give them a new heart and a new spirit—surely in this day shall the Jews, having a new

342

heart, acclaim the beauty of the feet of those who brought them the gospel. How glorious are the messengers who bring us the gospel of peace! Who has expressed it better than Abinadi? "And these are they who have published peace," he said, "who have brought good tidings of good, who have published salvation; and said unto Zion: Thy God reigneth! And O how beautiful upon the mountains were their feet! And again, how beautiful upon the mountains are the feet of those that are still publishing peace! And again, how beautiful upon the mountains are the feet of those who shall hereafter publish peace, yea, from this time henceforth and forever! And behold, I say unto you, this is not all. For O how beautiful upon the mountains are the feet of him that bringeth good tidings, that is the founder of peace, yea, even the Lord, who has redeemed his people; yea, him who has granted salvation unto his people; For were it not for the redemption which he hath made for his people, which was prepared from the foundation of the world, I say unto you, were it not for this, all mankind must have perished." (Mosiah 15:14-19.)

It is here that Isaiah, in his discourse, speaks of the watchmen who shall see eye to eye when the Lord brings again Zion, of Jerusalem being redeemed, and of all the ends of the earth seeing the salvation of God. As Jesus has twice already quoted these words to the Nephites, he now passes them by and picks up Isaiah's account by saying: "And then shall a cry go forth":

Depart ye, depart ye, go ye out from thence, touch not that which is unclean; go ye out of the midst of her; be ye clean that bear the vessels of the Lord.

For you shall not go out with haste nor go by flight; for the Lord will go before you, and the God of Israel shall be your rearward. [3]

When the kingdom is restored to Israel and the redemption of Zion begins, then the Jews who are scattered in all nations must flee from their Babylonish habitats and return unto their God. That this should now commence is our witness, for already the ecclesiastical kingdom has been set up; already the pure in heart—who are Zion—are beginning to build up again the Zion of God, and the millennial day is not far off. Then the political kingdom will be restored to Israel and Jerusalem will become a world capital whence the word of the Lord shall go to all nations.

At this point the subject seems to change, and what Jesus continues to quote is Messianic. The words are Isaiah's introduction to his great prophecy about the Suffering Servant:

> *Behold, my servant shall deal prudently; he shall be exalted and extolled and be very high.*
>
> *As many were astonished at thee—his visage was so marred, more than any man, and his form more than the sons of men—*
>
> *So shall he sprinkle many nations; the kings shall shut their mouths at him, for that which had not been told them shall they see; and that which they had not heard shall they consider.*

In these words we see a triumphant millennial Christ—one whose visage was marred and whose form was mangled when he dwelt among men—we see him in glory and dominion, in whose presence kings remain silent and before whom their mouths are shut. We see his cleansing blood sprinkle all nations, with devout men everywhere turning to the saving truths that they have not before heard and to the words of truth that they have not theretofore considered. And having finished, for the moment, his quotations, Jesus said:

> *Verily, verily, I say unto you, all these things shall surely come, even as the Father hath commanded me. Then shall this covenant which the Father hath covenanted with his people be fulfilled; and then shall Jerusalem be inhabited again with my people, and it shall be the land of their inheritance.*

Then shall the children of the covenant inherit, receive,

and possess—equally and fully—with their fathers of old! Then shall the Lamanites flourish in the Americas; then shall the Jews prosper in Jerusalem; then shall Ephraim—the Lord's firstborn!—confer on all the tribes their eternal blessings; and then shall all the promises relative to Israel and Zion be fulfilled.

The Lord be praised for what lies ahead for his people!

NOTES

1. Compare Isaiah 52:1-3, 6. In this connection, and by way of question and answer, the inspired word says: "What is meant by the command in Isaiah, 52d chapter, 1st verse, which saith: Put on thy strength, O Zion—and what people had Isaiah reference to? He had reference to those whom God should call in the last days, who should hold the power of priesthood to bring again Zion, and the redemption of Israel; and to put on her strength is to put on the authority of the priesthood, which she, Zion, has a right to by lineage; also to return to that power which she had lost. What are we to understand by Zion loosing herself from the bands of her neck; 2d verse? We are to understand that the scattered remnants are exhorted to return to the Lord from whence they have fallen; which if they do, the promise of the Lord is that he will speak to them, or give them revelation. See the 6th, 7th, and 8th verses. The bands of her neck are the curses of God upon her, or the remnants of Israel in their scattered condition among the Gentiles." (D&C 113:7-10.)

2. Compare Isaiah 52:7.

3. These words and those that follow have their root in Isa. 52:11-15, though as the astute student will observe, Jesus here gives them in a more perfect form.

Chapter 116

THE BUILDING UP
OF ZION

The Lord loveth the gates of Zion
more than all the dwellings of Jacob.
Glorious things are spoken of thee,
O city of God. . . .
And of Zion it shall be said,
This and that man was born in her:
and the highest himself shall
establish her.
(Ps. 87:2-5.)
Thou shalt arise, and have mercy upon Zion:
for the time to favour her,
yea, the set time, is come.
For thy servants take pleasure in her stones,
and favour the dust thereof.
So the heathen shall fear the name of the Lord,
and all the kings of the earth thy glory.
When the Lord shall build up Zion,
he shall appear in his glory.
He will regard the prayer of the destitute,
and not despise their prayer.
This shall be written for the generation to come:
and the people which shall be created
shall praise the Lord.
(Ps. 102:13-18.)

Reading the Signs of the Times
(3 Nephi 21:1-13)

When, O when, will all these things come to pass? When will the Lord restore again the kingdom to Israel? When will Jerusalem become holy and Zion be redeemed? The promises are so wondrous, the glories so grand, the triumph so splendid, that every believing heart cries out— When, O Lord, will it be? And every prayerful voice pleads that it may be in his day. In a great chorus of worship and desire, the prayers of the saints ascend to the Great God: "Thy kingdom come. Thy will be done in earth, as it is in heaven," they say. (Matt. 6:10.) 'Even so come Lord Jesus that we, the children of the covenant, may receive that which was promised to Abraham and his seed; that in us and in our seed all generations may be blessed; that we may have a continuation of the seeds forever and ever; that our posterity also may be as numerous as the sands upon the seashore or the stars in the broad expanse of heaven. Let the gospel be restored; let Israel be gathered; let Jerusalem be redeemed; let Zion be established; let the Lord Jesus reign in peace and glory on earth for a thousand years.'

That the times and the seasons might be known; that his ancient covenant people might know when and under what circumstances the glorious promises would be fulfilled; but, more particularly, that his covenant people in the last days might know and believe and prepare for the wonders that are to be, Jesus said to his Nephite saints:

And verily I say unto you, I give unto you a sign, that ye may know the time when these things shall be about to take place—that I shall gather in, from their long dispersion, my people, O house of Israel, and shall establish again among them my Zion.

The restoration of the gospel, the gathering of Israel, and the establishment of Zion are one and the same thing; or, at least, they are so inseparably intertwined as one that they cannot be separated—for it is the Lord who gives the gospel, and it is the gospel that gathers Israel, and it is

347

Israel that builds Zion. Now it is not the Lord's plan to hide his purposes from those who seek him. True, the day and the hour of his Second Coming is between him and his Father. It is wisdom in them to let the saints in successive ages look forward with expectancy, in the spirit of watchfulness and prayer, for that great day. But the times and the seasons in which the great events associated with that coming are to transpire—wherein the gospel is to be restored, Israel gathered, and Zion established—these are to be known, so that men in those days will be more watchful and more prayerful as they await the wonders that are to be.

And behold, this is the thing which I will give unto you for a sign—for verily I say unto you that when these things which I declare unto you, and which I shall declare unto you hereafter of myself, and by the power of the Holy Ghost which shall be given unto you of the Father, shall be made known unto the Gentiles that they may know concerning this people who are a remnant of the house of Jacob, and concerning this my people who shall be scattered by them.

(For clarity's sake we must interject our commentary into Jesus' sermon, even before he finishes his thoughts, for his presentation is so complex and his expressions are so broad that we might otherwise fail to envision their full meaning.) Thus, the promised sign is to include (1) the things Jesus now speaks, (2) those he shall thereafter speak to them, and (3) those he shall later reveal by the power of the Holy Ghost—when all these things shall be made known to the Gentiles in the latter days (through the coming forth of the Book of Mormon), so that the Gentiles learn of the ancient Nephites, and also of the latter-day Lamanites whom they have scattered.

Verily, verily, I say unto you, when these things shall be made known unto them of the Father, and

348

shall come forth of the Father, from them unto you;

That is, when all the doctrine and all the witness of truth found in the Book of Mormon shall come forth by the power of God, and shall go from the Gentiles to the seed of Lehi.

For it is wisdom in the Father that they should be established in this land, and be set up as a free people by the power of the Father, that these things might come forth from them unto a remnant of your seed, that the covenant of the Father may be fulfilled which he hath covenanted with his people, O house of Israel;

That is, in the eternal providences of Him who governs in the affairs of men; who raises up nations and casts down thrones; who gives one nation, and then another, a rulership for a season—according to his eternal purposes a great nation (the United States of America) shall be set up, with constitutional guarantees of freedom, by the power of God, so that the gospel may be restored, the Book of Mormon come forth, its message go to the American remnant of Jacob, all to the end that the eternal covenants of the Lord with his people might be fulfilled.

Therefore, when these works and the works which shall be wrought among you hereafter shall come forth from the Gentiles, unto your seed which shall dwindle in unbelief because of iniquity;

That is, when all that was then done and that should thereafter be done among the Nephites, should come forth in the Book of Mormon and go from the Gentiles unto Father Lehi's children, who by then would have dwindled in unbelief because of their sins.

For thus it behooveth the Father that it should come forth from the Gentiles, that he may show forth his power unto the Gentiles, for this cause that the Gentiles, if they will not harden their hearts, that they may repent and come unto me and be baptized in my name and know of the true points of my doctrine, that they may be numbered among my people, O house of Israel;

That is: It is the Father's good pleasure that the Book of Mormon shall come forth by way of the Gentiles, that they too may know his power, receive revelation, and learn the wonders of eternity, all to the end that the Gentiles, if they will, may repent and come unto Christ, and be baptized, and learn the doctrines of salvation, and be numbered with the house of Israel.

And when these things come to pass that thy seed shall begin to know these things—it shall be a sign unto them, that they may know that the work of the Father hath already commenced unto the fulfilling of the covenant which he hath made unto the people who are of the house of Israel.

What wonders the Lord has in store for his people! How glorious is his plan; how marvelous are his purposes; what great things he has reserved for the latter days! Israel—his chosen ones—shall be gathered in from their long dispersion; though they have been scattered in all the nations of the earth, yet they shall come out of darkness into the marvelous light of Christ when the Lord raises an ensign to the nations. "Ye shall be gathered one by one, O ye children of Israel . . . and shall worship the Lord in the holy mount at Jerusalem." (Isa. 27:12-13.)

Zion—the Holy City, the pure in heart, the people of the Most High—Zion shall be established "on the mountains of Adam-ondi-Ahman, and on the plains of Olaha Shinehah, or the land where Adam dwelt." (D&C 117:8.) A New Jerusalem shall arise in the tops of the mountains and in the land of Missouri; Jerusalem of old shall shine forth in the waste places long trodden down of the Gentiles; and the Lord's people shall be redeemed in all the nations of the earth. The Lord Jehovah "shall cause them that come of Jacob to take root: Israel shall blossom and bud, and fill the face of the world with fruit." (Isa. 27:6.)

350

The longings and desires, the prayers and the pleadings of all the prophets have been that Israel would come off triumphant; that she would tread on the necks of her foes; that a remnant would be among the Gentiles as a young lion among the flocks of sheep; that the Lord would make the horn of his people iron and their hoofs brass; that they would shine forth as a nation, "fair as the moon, clear as the sun, and terrible as an army with banners" (Song. 6:10); and, in fine, that all Israel would be saved. All the prophets looked forward to the day when the ancient covenant would be renewed with the seed of Abraham; when the Lord would make anew the old covenant; when men again would know that in them and in their seed all generations should be blessed; when they would rejoice again in the prophetic promise that their seed—"out of the world"— would be as the stars and the sands. Or in other words: All of the prophets and all of the saints of olden times looked forward to the restitution of all things, to the restoration of the fulness of the everlasting gospel. All of them looked forward to the day when those who did not give heed to the words of the apostles and prophets then sent among them would, as Moses said, be cut off from among the people.

The great issue was not *what* the Lord designed to do in the latter days, but *when* it should come to pass. What was the sign and when should it be given? And now Jesus has given the answer, an answer that is plain and clear to us. The promised sign is the Book of Mormon. When that volume of holy scripture comes forth, then all men may know that the Lord has already commenced his work.

It is the Book of Mormon that gathers Israel. When the Stick of Judah and the Stick of Joseph, in the hands of Ephraim, become one in the hands of his people, then the Lord God will gather them; then will they come forth from among the heathen and receive the gospel; then shall they come into their own land according to the covenant. And "Thus saith the Lord God: . . . Neither shall they defile themselves any more with their idols, nor with their detestable things, nor with any of their transgressions: but I will save them out of all their dwellingplaces, wherein they have sinned, and will cleanse them: so shall they be my people, and I will be their God." (Ezek. 37:20-23.)

We cannot state it too plainly; we cannot affirm it too positively; we cannot proclaim it with too great a fervor—the Book of Mormon is the sign given of God to herald the fulfillment of the covenants made of old. And now that holy volume is going forth to Lehi's seed and to all men, that all may know that the work of the Lord has commenced anew and that all that was promised will soon come to pass. That holy book has come forth, "Proving to the world that the holy scriptures are true, and that God does inspire men and call them to his holy work in this age and generation, as well as in generations of old; Thereby showing that he is the same God yesterday, today, and forever." (D&C 20:11-12.) It has come forth "to the convincing of the Jew and Gentile that Jesus is the Christ, the Eternal God, manifesting himself unto all nations." (Title Page, Book of Mormon.) It has come forth as a new witness of Christ; as a witness that the everlasting gospel has been restored; as a witness that Joseph Smith and his successors wear the prophetic mantle; as a witness that The Church of Jesus Christ of Latter-day Saints is the only true and living church upon the face of the whole earth; as a witness that the Lord has raised his latter-day ensign to the nations; as a witness that the covenant made with Abraham of old is now being fulfilled.

And when that day shall come, it shall come to pass that kings shall shut their mouths; for that which had not been told them shall they see; and that which they had not heard shall they consider.

Jesus now begins to speak of the things that shall come to pass after the coming forth of the Book of Mormon, after the restoration of the gospel. What he says is not a chronological listing of successive events, but simply an announcement of and a commentary on various things that are to be. We are left—as wisdom dictates should be the

352

case—to interpret and apply his inspired utterances, the first being that the great and mighty shall be so amazed at the Lord's latter-day work that they shall not know what to say and shall feel impelled to consider the wondrous work which rolls before their eyes. So far there has been a small amount of this; what the future holds is limitless.

For in that day, for my sake shall the Father work a work, which shall be a great and a marvelous work among them; and there shall be among them those who will not believe it, although a man shall declare it unto them.

The restoration of the gospel, including all that appertains to it, is a marvelous work and a wonder. How men ought to marvel at the wonders that have already come in these the latter days! What can compare with the appearance of the Father and the Son to a young lad in his fifteenth year; or to the coming forth of the Book of Mormon, which contains a record of God's dealings with a people who had the fulness of the everlasting gospel; or to the ministry of Moroni, and John the Baptist, and Peter and James and other resurrected beings again on earth; or to the setting up of the true church and kingdom of God again on earth; or to the gathering of millions of our Father's children out of Babylon into the True Fold? And all of this is but the beginning; the marvels and wonders that lie ahead are beyond the capacities of us mortals to comprehend or conceive.

"I will proceed to do a marvellous work among this people," the Lord said by the mouth of Isaiah, "even a marvellous work and a wonder: for the wisdom of their wise men shall perish, and the understanding of their prudent men shall be hid." (Isa. 29:14.) Then, as our dispensation dawned, the Lord repeatedly said such things as: "A great and marvelous work is about to come forth unto the children of men," and that "the field is white already to harvest; therefore, whoso desireth to reap, let him thrust in his sickle with his might, and reap while the day lasts, that he may treasure up for his soul everlasting salvation in the kingdom of God.'' (D&C 6:1-4.) And also: "By your hands I will work a marvelous work among the children of men, unto the convincing of many of their sins, that they may come unto repentance, and that they may come unto the kingdom of my Father.'' (D&C 18:44.)

Implicit in all this, as Jesus has just stated to the Nephites, is the fact that many will not believe the latter-day message of salvation, though it be declared unto them by the man whom God hath sent to reveal his word. It shall be among us as it was when He whose gospel it is ministered personally on earth, of which ministry the Messianic word asks: "Who hath believed our report? and to whom is the arm of the Lord revealed?'' (Isa. 53:1.)

But behold, the life of my servant shall be in my hand; therefore they shall not hurt him, although he shall be marred because of them. Yet I will heal him, for I will show unto them that my wisdom is greater than the cunning of the devil.

Isaiah's prophecy about the marred servant is clearly Messianic and applies to Jesus who was crucified and rose from the dead to sprinkle the saving power of his blood in all nations. It is of him that kings shall shut their mouths as they ponder the marvel of his resurrection and all that he did. (Isa. 52:13-15.) But in this whole discourse Jesus is applying the prophetic word to the latter days, meaning that, as with many prophecies, the divine word has a dual fulfillment. In this setting we may properly say that Joseph Smith—whose voice declared the word for this dispensation—was marred, as his Lord had been, and yet should be healed, in the eternal sense, as was his Lord. And it may yet well be that there will be other latter-day servants to whom also it will apply. All of the Lord's servants who are marred or hurt or persecuted in this life—and who remain faithful—shall have all their sorrows made up to them in manifold measure in the resurrection.

Therefore it shall come to pass that whosoever will not believe in my words, who am Jesus Christ, which the Father shall cause him to bring forth unto the Gentiles, and shall give unto him power that he shall bring them forth unto the Gentiles, (it shall be done even as Moses said) they shall be cut off from among my people who are of the covenant.

Those who do not believe the restored gospel; who reject the messengers of salvation who are sent to them; and who continue to live after the manner of the world—they shall be cut off from among the people who are of the covenant. This we have already noted. It refers to the return of the Son of Man; to the day when every corruptible thing shall be destroyed; to the day when the wicked shall be burned as stubble; to the day when the vineyard shall be burned and none shall remain except those who are able to abide the day. It is then, and in this way, that the Lord's people will triumph over their enemies.

And my people who are a remnant of Jacob shall be among the Gentiles, yea, in the midst of them as a lion among the beasts of the forest, as a young lion among the flocks of sheep, who, if he go through both treadeth down and teareth in pieces, and none can deliver.

Their hand shall be lifted up upon their adversaries, and all their enemies shall be cut off.

Building the New Jerusalem
(3 Nephi 21:14-29)

Having spoken of the coming forth of the Book of Mormon; having announced the restoration of the gospel in the latter days; having promised that Israel would be gathered again into the fold of the True Shepherd; having assured his people that the Great Jehovah would renew with their seed the covenant made with their fathers—Jesus now turns to building a New Jerusalem. Zion, as a place and as a city, is to be established, so that Zion, as a people and as the pure in heart, may have a capital whence the law may go forth. The building of the New Jerusalem grows out of these other things that he has taught them, and we must take care to study his words in the setting he gave them.

Jesus has made repeated references—both quoting and paraphrasing, as best suited his purposes—to the words of Micah. That ancient prophet said: "And the remnant of Jacob shall be in the midst of many people as a dew from the Lord, as the showers upon the grass, that tarrieth not for man, nor waiteth for the sons of men." That is, the Lord's people will be everywhere, scattered in all nations, and their presence will seem as natural as the settling of the dew and the falling of the rains; their influence will be to give life and strength to the nations, even as the moisture from heaven gives life and growth to the crops of the earth.

"And the remnant of Jacob shall be among the Gentiles in the midst of many people as a lion among the beasts of the forest, as a young lion among the flocks of sheep: who, if he go through, both treadeth down, and teareth in pieces, and none can deliver. Thine hand shall be lifted up upon thine adversaries, and all thine enemies shall be cut off." These concepts, including most of the very words themselves, Jesus has quoted, and he has explained that their fulfillment will be in the day when the wicked are cut off as Moses promised. After Micah gave them, he said: "And it shall come to pass in that day, saith the Lord, that I will" do such and such, referring to certain conditions that will prevail during the Millennium and after the destruction of the wicked at the Second Coming of the Son of Man. (Micah 5:7-15.) After Jesus said the same things, he also, using most of the very words of Micah, spoke of these millennial events:

Yea, wo be unto the Gentiles except they repent;
for it shall come to pass in that day, saith the Father,

*that I will cut off thy horses out of the midst of thee,
and I will destroy thy chariots; And I will cut off the
cities of thy land, and throw down all thy strong-
holds.*

When the Lord comes and Israel triumphs, the armies
of the Gentile nations will be destroyed, their fortifications
thrown down, and their cities cease to be. Every corruptible thing—including the wicked Jew and the evil
Gentile—shall be destroyed.

*And I will cut off witchcrafts out of thy land, and
thou shalt have no more soothsayers; Thy graven
images I will also cut off, and thy standing images
out of the midst of thee, and thou shalt no more
worship the works of thy hands; And I will pluck up
thy groves out of the midst of thee; so will I destroy
thy cities.*

False doctrine, false ordinances, false worship, false
religion—all shall cease. The images and idols, in their
churches and in their hearts, shall be as when God over-
threw Sodom and Gomorrah. The groves where Baal of old
was worshipped, and the cathedrals where Baal of the
latter days was adored, shall be as when the walls and
buildings of Jericho fell.

*And it shall come to pass that all lyings, and
deceivings, and envyings, and strifes, and priestcrafts, and whoredoms, shall be done away.*

*For it shall come to pass, saith the Father, that at
that day whosoever will not repent and come unto
my Beloved Son, them will I cut off from among my
people, O house of Israel.*

These words are not in Micah's account; Jesus here
inserts them to give depth and understanding to the Old
Testament account from which he is quoting. They tell of
that day when wickedness, as we know it, ceases, the day
when men have beaten their swords into plowshares and
their spears into pruning hooks, the day when peace pre-

vails and the Prince of Peace is Lord over all the earth. And in that day wo unto those who do not repent and believe in the Beloved Son. Of them the divine word is:

And I will execute vengeance and fury upon them, even as upon the heathen, such as they have not heard.

With these words the quotations from Micah cease, at least as far as our Bible preserves his words for us. The meaning is, of course, self-evident and accords with Zechariah's word that those families and nations—after the Second Coming—who go not up to Jerusalem to keep the Feast of Tabernacles, upon them no rain shall fall and they shall be smitten with a plague. (Zech. 14:16-19.)

But if they will repent and hearken unto my words, and harden not their hearts, I will establish my church among them, and they shall come in unto the covenant and be numbered among this the remnant of Jacob, unto whom I have given this land for their inheritance;

And they shall assist my people, the remnant of Jacob, and also as many of the house of Israel as shall come, that they may build a city, which shall be called the New Jerusalem.

Both Jew and Gentile shall build the New Jerusalem. The remnant of Jacob in the Americas (meaning the Lamanites), and the gathered remnants of the whole house of Israel—indeed, all people from all nations who are righteous and pure and believing, all who keep the commandments—all shall join in building the Holy City. And the Jews (other than the Lamanite Jews) who believe and repent and purify themselves shall build up anew the Jerusalem of old. All this is set forth by Moroni, as he wrote of Ether, in these words: "Behold, Ether saw the days of Christ, and he spake concerning a New Jerusalem upon this land. And he spake also concerning the house of Israel, and the Jerusalem from whence Lehi should come—after it should be destroyed it should be built up

358

again, a holy city unto the Lord; wherefore, it could not be a new Jerusalem for it had been in a time of old; but it should be built up again, and become a holy city of the Lord; and it should be built unto the house of Israel. And that a New Jerusalem should be built upon this land, unto the remnant of the seed of Joseph, for which things there has been a type. For as Joseph brought his father down into the land of Egypt, even so he died there; wherefore, the Lord brought a remnant of the seed of Joseph out of the land of Jerusalem, that he might be merciful unto the seed of Joseph that they should perish not, even as he was merciful unto the father of Joseph that he should perish not. Wherefore, the remnant of the house of Joseph shall be built upon this land; and it shall be a land of their inheritance; and they shall build up a holy city unto the Lord, like unto the Jerusalem of old; and they shall no more be confounded, until the end come when the earth shall pass away.

"And there shall be a new heaven and a new earth; and they shall be like unto the old save the old have passed away, and all things have become new. And then cometh the New Jerusalem; and blessed are they who dwell therein, for it is they whose garments are white through the blood of the Lamb; and they are they who are numbered among the remnant of the seed of Joseph, who were of the house of Israel. And then also cometh the Jerusalem of old; and the inhabitants thereof, blessed are they, for they have been washed in the blood of the Lamb; and they are they who were scattered and gathered in from the four quarters of the earth, and from the north countries, and are partakers of the fulfilling of the covenant which God made with their father, Abraham." (Ether 13:4-11.) And of this day when Zion, the New Jerusalem, is established on the American continent, Jesus said:

And then shall they assist my people that they
may be gathered in, who are scattered upon all the
face of the land, in unto the New Jerusalem. And

then shall the power of heaven come down among them; and I also will be in the midst.

The prophecies relative to the gathering of Israel will be fulfilled both before and after the Second Coming. The remnants shall first assemble, set up the ecclesiastical kingdom, and build up Zion. Then the Lord will come and the final glorious gathering and triumph of Israel will come to pass. It will be in the day when the Lord is in the midst of men. Having so taught, Jesus returns to general commentary about the sign whereby men may know that his strange and wondrous work—the marvelous work and a wonder of latter days—has commenced again on earth.

And then shall the work of the Father commence at that day, even when this gospel shall be preached among the remnant of this people. Verily I say unto you, at that day shall the work of the Father commence among all the dispersed of my people, yea, even the tribes which have been lost, which the Father hath led away out of Jerusalem.

Yea, the work shall commence among all the dispersed of my people, with the Father, to prepare the way whereby they may come unto me, that they may call on the Father in my name.

Yea, and then shall the work commence, with the Father, among all nations, in preparing the way whereby his people may be gathered home to the land of their inheritance.

And they shall go out from all nations; and they shall not go out in haste, nor go by flight, for I will go before them, saith the Father, and I will be their rearward.

In this summary we are reminded: (1) that when the gospel goes to the Lamanites, it will be a sign that the great latter-day work has begun; (2) that in that day the gospel will go to all the dispersed of Israel, including the lost tribes; (3) that its purpose will be to bring Israel unto Christ so they can call upon the Father in his name; (4) that the work will go forward in all nations so that the chosen seed may be gathered to the lands of their inheritances; and (5) that they shall go out, not as escapees from oppression or for political reasons, but in glory and beauty and truth—the Lord himself going before and preparing the way and being also their rearward.

Let God be praised for the wonders that now are and for the even greater wonders that are to be!

Chapter 117

EXPOUNDING
THE SCRIPTURES

Search the scriptures;
for . . . they are they which testify of me.
(John 5:39.)
The holy scriptures . . . are able
to make thee wise unto salvation
through faith which is in Christ Jesus.
And all scripture given by inspiration of God,
is profitable for doctrine,
for reproof, for correction,
for instruction in righteousness;
That the man of God may be perfect,
thoroughly furnished unto all good works.
(JST, 2 Tim. 3:15-17.)
And whoso treasureth up my word,
shall not be deceived. (JS-M 1:37.)

Searching the Scriptures
(3 Nephi 22:1-17; 23:1-5)

Jesus' teachings among the Nephite Jews rose to far
greater heights than did his teachings among the Palestinian
Jews. At least the biblical accounts do not compare in
doctrinal beauty and scriptural exposition with those in the

Book of Mormon. Jesus gave no parables to the Nephites, for he had no occasion to hide his doctrines or conceal his concepts as far as they were concerned. He spent no time contending with them about their traditions and false beliefs, and he was not at any time faced with a spirit of disbelief or rebellion among them. Such things as the Sermon on the Mount, the Intercessory Prayer, and the doctrine relative to the sacrament were given in plainness on both continents. But many doctrinal concepts were given to the Nephites of which there is no New Testament account. It is true, of course, that on the mountain in Galilee or in other private gatherings Jesus gave the Jews more than is recorded in the New Testament. But in the very nature of things—the wicked and ungodly among the Nephites having been destroyed—there is a higher tone and a more pleasing feel to what he told the Nephites than to what he gave the people in the Old World. And one of the things he did among his New World saints was to quote extensively from the prophets, and to do it in such a way as to endorse and to show the true meaning and intent of the prophetic word.

And so, having presented his doctrine relative to the restoration of the gospel, the gathering of Israel, and the establishment of Zion—all in the latter days—Jesus said: "And then shall that which is written come to pass," at which point he quoted, with minor improvements, the whole fifty-fourth chapter of Isaiah. In poetic language, using figures of speech common in his day, Isaiah proclaimed that Israel—scattered, barren, without seed born under the covenant—would again break forth into singing; that Zion would enlarge her borders, strengthen her stakes, break forth on the right hand and on the left, and build up the ancient and desolate cities; and that the saints of latter days would no longer be ashamed, nor remember the reproach of their scattered days nor the sorrows of their widowhood.

He announced that Jehovah was their Bridegroom, their

363

Husband, their Maker, their Redeemer, and that he was the God of Israel and of the whole earth. He told how Israel had been forsaken for a small moment but would be gathered with great mercies; and how in a little wrath the Lord had hidden his face from her, but with everlasting kindness would shower mercy upon her children. He gave the Lord's promise (1) that as the flood of Noah was assuaged, never to return, so Jehovah's wrath against Israel would cease, and (2) that though the mountains and hills should depart, yet the Lord would not break his covenant to show mercy upon Israel. Her children—"afflicted, tossed with tempest, and not comforted"—would be gathered in peace into Zion.

The Holy City would be built with riches and jewels, and all her children would be taught of the Lord who reigned among them. The saints would then dwell in peace, and righteousness would prevail; oppression would cease, terror flee away, and all who opposed them would fall. No weapon formed against the Lord's people should prosper, and every tongue that spoke against them should be condemned. Such, said Isaiah, "is the heritage of the servants of the Lord," for their righteousness is of him. And when Jesus had quoted all these words, he said:

And now, behold, I say unto you, that ye ought to search these things. Yea, a commandment I give unto you that ye search these things diligently; for great are the words of Isaiah.

For surely he spake as touching all things concerning my people which are of the house of Israel; therefore it must needs be that he must speak also to the Gentiles.

Scripturalists are wont to refer to Isaiah as the Messianic prophet because of his many prophecies about the birth and ministry and death and resurrection of the Lord Jehovah. And truly he was; no Old Testament seer has left us a greater wealth of words about the Eternal Word than this son of Amoz, who prophesied in the days of Uzziah,

Jotham, Ahaz, and Hezekiah, all kings of Judah, and who, according to tradition, was sawn asunder for the counsel he gave and the testimony of Jesus he bore. But what is of equal or even greater import is that Isaiah's Messianic word shines forth far beyond time's meridian; he is the great prophet of the restoration. It is his voice that speaks of the restoration of the gospel in the last days, of the coming forth of the Book of Mormon, of the raising of an ensign to the nations, of the gathering of Israel, of the building of the house of the Lord in the tops of the mountains, of the conversion of many Gentiles, of the building of Zion, of the Second Coming of the Son of Man, and of the millennial era of peace and righteousness. Truly, "great are the words of Isaiah."

And all things that he spake have been and shall be, even according to the words which he spake.

Therefore give heed to my words; write the things which I have told you; and according to the time and the will of the Father they shall go forth unto the Gentiles.

And whosoever will hearken unto my words and repenteth and is baptized, the same shall be saved. Search the prophets, for many there be that testify of these things.

When the words of Isaiah go forth unto the Gentiles— and are understood by them—they will believe in Christ, repent of their sins, be baptized by the legal administrators sent of God in this day, and become members of The Church of Jesus Christ of Latter-day Saints. And with this all the prophetic word accords.

Adding to the Scriptures
(3 Nephi 23:6-14; 24:1-18; 25:1-6; 26:1-2)

Jesus now did something among the Nephites that he had never done, as far as we know, among the Jews. He "expounded all the scriptures unto them which they had received." What a wondrous thing this must have been! On the Emmaus road he expounded to Cleopas and Luke "in all the scriptures the things concerning himself." (Luke 24:27.) But here to thousands upon thousands of saints who had received the gift of the Holy Ghost and were prepared to receive the mysteries of the kingdom, he expounded all that was written in their holy books. They had the brass plates, which contain the five books of Moses, and the prophecies of the prophets down to the reign of Zedekiah, king of Judah, including many prophecies and covenants of the Lord that have been lost from our Old Testament. They had the plates of Nephi and other records telling what the Lord had revealed to their fathers during the 634 years since Lehi left Jerusalem. And, above all, they had the Jaredite scriptures, those inspired accounts which are in the sealed portion of the Book of Mormon. When we think that all these things were expounded unto them by Him who gave the holy word and whose scriptures they were, it makes us feel somewhat insignificant spiritually. When we compare the small stream of revelation we have received with the mighty rivers of revealed truth that flowed to those of old, we long for the day when the Lord will come and reveal all things to us so that we will know what our counterparts of old knew in their days.

Then Jesus said to the people, "Behold, other scriptures I would that ye should write, that ye have not." To Nephi he commanded: "Bring forth the record which ye have kept," which they did. Finding it did not contain the prophecy of Samuel the Lamanite, that many saints would come forth from their graves after the resurrection of Christ, he said: "How be it that ye have not written this thing, that many saints did arise and appear unto many and did minister unto them?" Samuel's prophetic words were then duly recorded, and Jesus "expounded all the scriptures in one," and "commanded them that they should teach the things which he had expounded unto them."

After the Jews returned from Babylon, and after the days of Ezra and Nehemiah and the building of the walls of

Jerusalem, the Lord sent the great prophet Malachi to give his word to the chosen seed. That the seed of those who had escaped from the Holy City before Nebuchadnezzar took their fathers into captivity, that the seed of Joseph that had been separated from their brethren might rejoice in the words of so great a one as Malachi, whose words close our Old Testament, Jesus first gave many of them to his American saints, and then expounded to them their deep and wondrous meanings. All we know of what then happened is that he gave them chapters 3 and 4 in almost the verbatim language of our Bible.

Malachi's prophetic words here involved speak of the messenger who should prepare the way before the face of the Lord, in a sense for his mortal ministry, but primarily in that great millennial day when the wicked will be destroyed and the sons of Levi serve again in their priestly roles. They tell us that Judah and Jerusalem shall be restored to their ancient glory, and that their Lord—who is Jehovah—coming to reign on earth will destroy the wicked: the sorcerers, adulterers, false swearers, those who oppress their fellowmen and who do not fear the Lord.

They speak of robbing God and being cursed therefor, through failure to pay tithes and offerings, and of the temporal and spiritual blessings reserved for tithe payers. Those who walk mournfully before the Lord are promised great reward in due time, though the proud and the wicked seem to enjoy greater rewards in this life. Those who serve the Lord shall be his when he comes to make up his jewels; he will spare them in that day, and then shall all discern between the righteous and the wicked.

Malachi foretells the day of the Second Coming when the proud and the wicked shall be burned as stubble; when the Son of Righteousness shall arise with healing in his wings; when Israel shall grow up as calves in the stall with all their needs cared for; and when they shall tread down the wicked—their enemies—as ashes under the soles of their feet. And then, as a fitting climax, Malachi speaks of the return of Elijah the prophet to reveal the priesthood before the great and dreadful day of the Lord and to plant in the hearts of the children the promises made to the fathers, lest the whole earth be utterly wasted in that day. Then Jesus said:

These scriptures, which ye had not with you, the Father commanded that I should give unto you; for it was wisdom in him that they should be given unto future generations.

They are primarily for our benefit. We live in the day of which they speak; we are the children in whose hearts the promises have been planted; we are the ones who are striving so to live that we will abide the day of His coming. And it is in our day that Elijah has come, according to the promises, bringing again the sealing power so that legal administrators may bind on earth and have it sealed eternally in the heavens—for all of which the Lord be praised.

Seeking More Scriptures
(3 Nephi 26:3-21; Ether 4:1-19)

Who has seen such marvelous things as Jesus did among the Nephites? And who has heard such wondrous words of divine wisdom as fell from his lips on the American continent? To our shame we know only the hundredth part. Our friend Mormon—the prophet-historian who has given us such as we do have—at this point in his inspired writing said of the teachings of the Blessed One, which he so freely gave to the spiritually attuned ears in the New World: Jesus "did expound all things, even from the beginning until the time that he should come in his glory—yea, even all things which should come upon the face of the earth, even until the elements should melt with fervent heat, and the earth should be wrapt together as a scroll, and the heavens and the earth should pass away; And even unto the great and last day, when all people, and all kindreds, and all nations and tongues shall stand before God, to be judged of their works, whether they be good or whether they be evil—If they be good, to the resurrection of ever-lasting life; and if they be evil, to the resurrection of damna-tion; being on a parallel, the one on the one hand and the other on the other hand, according to the mercy, and the justice, and the holiness which is in Christ, who was before the world began."

In the providences of the Lord, we have slivers and fragments of what Jesus gave the Nephites. Sections 29, 45, 63, 76, 77, 88, 93, 101, 107, 132, 133, and 138 in the Doctrine and Covenants, and the books of Moses and Abraham in the Pearl of Great Price, all contain truths of transcendent worth about the doings of Deity from the beginning to the end. But what we have is only the milk of the present, which prepares us for the meat of the future. We do not have what he told the Nephites, and we do not have what he revealed to the brother of Jared, nor will we until the sealed portion of the Book of Mormon comes forth. "There cannot be written in this book even a hundredth part of the things which Jesus did truly teach unto the people," Mor-mon says. The plates of Nephi do contain the more part of his teachings, but with reference to the lesser part that has come to us, Mormon says: "I have written them to the intent that they may be brought again unto this people, from the Gentiles, according to the words which Jesus hath spoken." Then Mormon gives us this concept of infinite worth:

And when they shall have received this, which is expedient that they should have first, to try their faith, and if it shall so be that they shall believe these things then shall the greater things be made manifest unto them.

And if it so be that they will not believe these things, then shall the greater things be withheld from them, unto their condemnation.

Behold, I was about to write them, all which were engraven upon the plates of Nephi, but the Lord forbade it, saying: I will try the faith of my people.

Along with the teachings given by Jesus in that day, the Nephites had also the inspired writings of the brother of Jared. These accounts had been sealed up for some two millenniums, so they would not "come unto the children of men until after" Jesus had been "lifted up upon the cross." During the golden era of Nephite worship they were opened before all the people. But when these Israelites, after some two centuries of true worship, again dwindled in unbelief, these sacred words were again sealed up and their glories withheld from men. They are now found in the sealed portion of the Book of Mormon, and of them Moroni said: "There never were greater things made manifest than those which were made manifest unto the brother of Jared." And with respect to them, the Lord said:

> *They shall not go forth unto the Gentiles until the day that they shall repent of their iniquity, and become clean before the Lord.*

> *And in that day that they shall exercise faith in me, saith the Lord, even as the brother of Jared did, that they may become sanctified in me, then will I manifest unto them the things which the brother of Jared saw, even to the unfolding unto them all my revelations, saith Jesus Christ, the Son of God, the Father of the heavens and of the earth, and all things that in them are.*

It is with the writings of Jareditish Moriancumer even as it is with most of the Nephite teachings of Jesus. They are reserved for the faithful, they can be understood only by the power of the Spirit, and they have not been revealed as yet to us. Though the milk of the word, as found in the translated portion of the Book of Mormon, has been given to prepare us for the meat of the word, as found in the sealed portion of that holy book, it is clear that our faith is not yet great enough to enable us to receive the hidden mysteries of the kingdom.

And he that will contend against the word of the Lord, let him be accursed; and he that shall deny these things, let him be accursed; for unto them will I show no greater things, saith Jesus Christ; for I am he who speaketh.

And at my command the heavens are opened and are shut; and at my word the earth shall shake; and at my command the inhabitants thereof shall pass away, even so as by fire.

How can those who do not believe and obey the law already given ever expect to receive more revelation from on high? If men will not believe the Book of Mormon, they shut out of their lives the other revelations that have come in this dispensation. And if they do not believe all that God has now revealed, what justification would there be for him to reveal other great and important things pertaining to his earthly affairs and his heavenly kingdom?

And he that believeth not my words believeth not my disciples; and if it so be that I do not speak, judge ye; for ye shall know that it is I that speaketh, at the last day.

But he that believeth these things which I have spoken, him will I visit with the manifestations of my Spirit, and he shall know and bear record. For because of my Spirit he shall know that these things are true; for it persuadeth men to do good.

And whatsoever thing persuadeth men to do good is of me; for good cometh of none save it be of me. I am the same that leadeth men to all good; he that will not believe my words will not believe me—that I am; and he that will not believe me will not believe the Father who sent me. For behold, I am the Father, I am the light, and the life, and the truth of the world.

How wondrous are the words of Christ! Their plainness, the reasoning and logic they set forth, the self-evident witness they bear of their divine origin—where else in all that is written are there words like these? Truly he that does not believe these words and others like them does not believe in Christ, and he that does believe shall receive the manifestations of the Holy Spirit and shall prepare himelf for ever greater revelations. And so the cry goes forth among us:

Come unto me, O ye Gentiles, and I will show unto you the greater things, the knowledge which is hid up because of unbelief.

Come unto me, O ye house of Israel, and it shall be made manifest unto you how great things the Father hath laid up for you, from the foundation of the world; and it hath not come unto you, because of unbelief.

The call is unto us; the call is unto the Jews; the call is unto the Gentiles; the call is unto all men: Come, believe, obey, and prepare for the greater revelation that is promised!

Behold, when ye shall rend that veil of unbelief which doth cause you to remain in your awful state of wickedness, and hardness of heart, and blindness of mind, then shall the great and marvelous things which have been hid up from the foundation of the world from you—yea, when ye shall call upon the Father in my name, with a broken heart and a contrite spirit, then shall ye know that the Father hath remembered the covenant which he made unto your fathers, O house of Israel.

O that we might rend the heavens and know all that the ancients knew! O that we might pierce the veil and see all that our forebears saw! O that we might see and know and feel what the elect among the Jaredites and among the Nephites saw and heard and felt! He who is no respecter of persons calls us with his own voice; if we will but attune our ears we shall hear his words!

372

And then shall my revelations which I have caused to be written by my servant John be unfolded in the eyes of all the people. Remember, when ye see these things, ye shall know that the time is at hand that they shall be made manifest in very deed.

Therefore, when ye shall receive this record ye may know that the work of the Father has commenced upon all the face of the land.

Soon the apocalypse of John shall appear before men in plainness, for the same truths are found on the sealed plates. And we know that the work of the Father has already commenced among men.

Therefore, repent all ye ends of the earth, and come unto me, and believe in my gospel, and be baptized in my name; for he that believeth and is baptized shall be saved; but he that believeth not shall be damned; and signs shall follow them that believe in my name.

And blessed is he that is found faithful unto my name at the last day, for he shall be lifted up to dwell in the kingdom prepared for him from the foundation of the world. And behold it is I that hath spoken it. Amen.

As we recount these Nephite teachings, and as we learn thereby why Jesus has withheld from the generality of men those great and wondrous things given to an elect few in days gone by, we know exactly why our New Testament friends did not record more of what happened on the mountain in Galilee. What there transpired was for those then present. Such truths as found their way into the biblical accounts were to prepare the way for the greater truths yet to come. The Lord is testing our faith. When we believe the Bible and the Book of Mormon and the other things he has revealed in our day, then will the greater things be manifest unto us.

For the moment, however, we can at least rejoice that

Jesus did minister so gloriously among our Nephite brethren. As Mormon sets forth, the Lord taught the people for three days and thereafter showed himself to them often, "and did break bread oft, and bless it, and give it unto them." We know that he performed healings of every sort among them and that he raised a man from the dead. We know that he taught their children and loosed their tongues so that "they did speak unto their fathers great and marvelous things, even greater than he had revealed unto the people," and that "even babes did open their mouths and utter marvelous things; and the things which they did utter were forbidden that there should not any man write them."

We know also that the disciples went forth preaching, baptizing, and conferring the Holy Ghost. "And many of them saw and heard unspeakable things, which are not lawful to be written." In that day "they had all things common among them, every man dealing justly, one with another." They were saints of God indeed and were worthy of their membership in Christ's Church.

Chapter 118

THE HOLY GOSPEL

The gospel of God, . . .
Concerning his Son Jesus Christ our Lord,
which was made of the seed of David
according to the flesh;
And declared to be the Son of God with power,
according to the spirit of holiness,
by the resurrection from the dead:
By whom we have received grace
and apostleship. . . .
For it is the power of God unto salvation
to every one that believeth;
. . . For therein is the righteousness
of God revealed.
(Rom. 1:1-5, 16-17.)

What Is the Name of the True Church?
(3 Nephi 27:1-12)

Jesus, name of wondrous glory!

Jesus, blessed name, holy name, the name above all names!

Salvation is in Christ—how often have we said it! His is the only name given under heaven whereby man may be saved!

375

He "made himself of no reputation, and took upon him the form of a servant, and was made in the likeness of men: And being found in fashion as a man, he humbled himself, and became obedient unto death, even the death of the cross. Wherefore God also hath highly exalted him, and given him a name which is above every name: That at the name of Jesus every knee should bow, of things in heaven, and things in earth, and things under the earth; And that every tongue should confess that Jesus Christ is Lord, to the glory of God the Father." (Philip. 2:7-11.)

We are commanded to repent and call upon God in the name of the Son forevermore.

We take upon ourselves his name in the waters of baptism and again when we partake of the emblems of his suffering and death.

Whatsoever we ask the Father, in his name, that is right and good, in faith believing that we shall receive, it is granted.

In his name the lame walk, the blind see, the deaf hear. His name raises the dead, parts the Red Sea, quenches the violence of fire, closes the mouths of lions. His name rends the heavens, sends angels to earth, pours out revelation upon the faithful, sends visions to the seers.

In his name death is abolished and life and immortality reign. Through him the Father brings to pass the immortality and eternal life of man.

The gospel of God is also his gospel—his everlasting gospel—the plan of salvation revealed in all dispensations to all the holy prophets.

He is our King, our Lawgiver, our Lord, and our God.

How then and in what name shall his Church be called? Is there any name, other than his, that can identify the saving truths administered by the Church and kingdom of God on earth?

From our vantage point it is difficult to understand why there should have been any question about this either among the Nephites, among the early Christians in the Old

376

World, or among the early Latter-day Saints in this dispensation. It is *his* Church; all things are done in *his* name; and therefore the Church should bear *his* name. True, his names are many and his manners of manifesting himself to men are numerous; one name emphasizes one aspect of his mission and work, and another name singles out some other aspect of these. He is the Creator because he created, the Redeemer because he redeemed, the Savior because he saves, the Son of God because God is his Father. A knowledge of his many names helps us to envision the majesty and extent of his doings.

There might be a legitimate question as to which names to select, or as to what combination of them to use, but there can be no question as to whose name the Church should bear. There is no record that this question was resolved in perfection in the Old World—though we must assume it was; indeed, it could not have been otherwise—but the Nephite record does preserve both the reasoning and the inspiration underlying the name by which the Lord's people should be called.

Mormon's account tells us that "they who were baptized in the name of Jesus were called the church of Christ." (3 Ne. 26:21.) Then he recounts how their knowledge on this point came to them. The Twelve were out in their ministry, journeying, preaching, and baptizing in the name of Jesus. And as they "were gathered together and were united in mighty prayer and fasting," Jesus again appeared. "What will ye that I shall give unto you?" he asked. They said: "Lord, we will that thou wouldst tell us the name whereby we shall call this church; for there are disputations among the people concerning this matter." Jesus replied:

> *Verily, verily, I say unto you, why is it that the people should murmur and dispute because of this thing?*
>
> *Have they not read the scriptures, which say ye must take upon you the name of Christ, which is my*

name? For by this name shall ye be called at the last day; And whoso taketh upon him my name, and endureth to the end, the same shall be saved at the last day.

Men cannot be saved unless they take upon themselves the name of Christ. The saints are adopted into his family; they become his sons and his daughters; they are born again; they have a new Father; and they bear the name of their Father, who is Christ. "Take upon you the name of Christ," King Benjamin said to his people, "And it shall come to pass that whosoever doeth this shall be found at the right hand of God, for he shall know the name by which he is called; for he shall be called by the name of Christ."[1] And those who honor their new name and retain membership in their new family shall dwell with their Father in the heavenly home he has prepared for all those who bear his name. They shall be called by the name of Christ here and now and shall continue to bear that sacred name in eternity. And if all individuals who are baptized into his Church, and are thus born again, if they all bear the name of Christ, then the Church is the family of Christ, or in other words it is the Church of Christ.

Therefore, whatsoever ye shall do, ye shall do it in my name; therefore ye shall call the church in my name; and ye shall call upon the Father in my name that he will bless the church for my sake.

In every age from Adam to the present, and from this hour until time is no more, the family of Christ is the Church of Christ. We today—as with our fellow believers in days of old—are members of "the Church of Christ." (D&C 20:1.) And wherever the true Church is found, there also is revelation; and so the Lord reveals to his people the specific and formal words by which his Church shall be known at any given time. We were known as "the Church of Christ" from April 6, 1830, to April 26, 1838, when the Lord announced the formal title, "The Church of Jesus Christ of Latter-day Saints." (D&C 115:3-4.)

378

*And how be it my church save it be called in my
name? For if a church be called in Moses' name
then it be Moses' church; or if it be called in the
name of a man then it be the church of a man; but if
it be called in my name then it is my church, if it so
be that they are built upon my gospel.*

If a church is Moses' church, it can offer any rewards
Moses is able to give; and salvation does not come by the
law of Moses, but through the atonement of Him who was
Moses' Lord. If a church is that of a man, it can offer any
rewards that a man has power to create; and no man can
resurrect himself or create a celestial realm where saved
beings may dwell, for salvation is in Christ and in him only.
If a church is the church of the devil, it can offer such
rewards as Lucifer has prepared for those who walk in
carnal paths and worship him, and his great reward is a
place in the kingdom of the devil. And if a church pretends
to be the Church of Christ and to bear that name, but is not
so in reality and in fact, the name alone adds nothing. Thus
it is written of those who shall go to a telestial kingdom:
"For these are they who are of Paul, and of Apollos, and of
Cephas. These are they who say they are some of one and
some of another—some of Christ and some of John, and
some of Moses, and some of Elias, and some of Esaias, and
some of Isaiah, and some of Enoch; But [they] received not
the gospel, neither the testimony of Jesus, neither the
prophets, neither the everlasting covenant." (D&C 76:99-
101.)

*Verily I say unto you, that ye are built upon my
gospel; therefore ye shall call whatsoever things ye
do call, in my name; therefore if ye call upon the
Father, for the church, if it be in my name the Father
will hear you;*

*And if it so be that the church is built upon my
gospel then will the Father show forth his own works
in it.*

The ultimate test of the truth and divinity of any church

is its fruits. Do men gather grapes of thorns or figs of thistles? Signs shall follow them that believe. Those who belong to the true Church—which is built upon the true gospel—increase in righteousness; they acquire the attributes of godliness; virtue and integrity and morality shine in their faces; they heal the sick and raise the dead, for they are the Lord's people.

But if it be not built upon my gospel, and is built upon the works of men, or upon the works of the devil, verily I say unto you they have joy in their works for a season, and by and by the end cometh, and they are hewn down and cast into the fire, from whence there is no return.

For their works do follow them, for it is because of their works that they are hewn down; therefore remember the things that I have told you.

Those portions of Jesus' words that Mormon was permitted to record, in the account destined to come forth in our day, contain the directions and counsel needed in today's world. Let the world, learning these things, take heed, lest those who are in the world cleave unto those churches which allow men to perform works of unrighteousness, which works lead not to heaven, but to hell.

What Is the Gospel of Salvation?
(3 Nephi 27:13-22)

How glorious is the gospel; how wondrous is the word; how marvelous are its messengers; how blessed is the Lord!

The gospel is the plan of salvation—the eternal plan of the Eternal Father. It is the laws and truths and powers by conformity to which the spirit children of the Father (Christ included) can advance and progress and become like him. It includes the creation and peopling of the earth, the testing processes of mortality, and death, the resurrection, and eternal judgment. It is founded and grounded upon the atoning sacrifice of Christ and is operative because he laid down his life for all men.

Behold I have given unto you my gospel, and this is the gospel which I have given unto you—that I came into the world to do the will of my Father, because my Father sent me.

It is the gospel of God; the plan originated with the Father; it is his gospel. It concerns Jesus Christ our Lord because he was chosen to come into this world as the Son of God, to work out the infinite and eternal atonement, and to put into full force all of the terms and conditions of the Father's plan. The Son does the will of the Father; the Son did not devise a plan and suggest it to the Father; the Son obeyed and conformed and adopted. He espoused and championed the cause of his Father.

And my Father sent me that I might be lifted up upon the cross; and after that I had been lifted up upon the cross, that I might draw all men unto me, that as I have been lifted up by men even so should men be lifted up by the Father, to stand before me, to be judged of their works, whether they be good or whether they be evil—

And for this cause have I been lifted up; therefore, according to the power of the Father I will draw all men unto me, that they may be judged according to their works.

Jesus came to die—to die upon the cross. He came to ransom men from the temporal and spiritual death brought into the world by the fall of Adam; he came to abolish death, both temporal and spiritual; he came to bring immortality to all men and eternal life to all who believe and obey. Through his atoning sacrifice, begun in Gethsemane and completed on the cross, he has power to draw all men unto him, to bring them from the grave, to arraign them before his bar, to judge them according to their works. Annas engineered his death; Caiaphas issued the decree of the Sanhedrin that he was worthy of death; Pilate sent him to the cross; and the elders and chief priests rejoiced in his death. All these shall stand before his bar. He died for them and for all men; he died for the Jews and for the Gentiles; he is the Redeemer of the world.

> *And it shall come to pass, that whoso repenteth and is baptized in my name shall be filled; and if he endureth to the end, behold, him will I hold guiltless before my Father at that day when I shall stand to judge the world.*
>
> *And he that endureth not unto the end, the same is he that is also hewn down and cast into the fire, from whence they can no more return, because of the justice of the Father.*
>
> *And this is the word which he hath given unto the children of men. And for this cause he fulfilleth the words which he hath given, and he lieth not, but fulfilleth all his words.*

Repent, be baptized, be filled with the Holy Ghost, endure to the end, and be saved. Jesus shall judge the world. Those who have entered in at the gate of repentance and baptism, those who are members of the Church, those who have started out on the strait and narrow path leading to eternal life—all such who do not endure to the end shall be hewn down and cast into the fire. They shall be damned. Such is according to the justice of the Father; it is part of his eternal plan.

> *And no unclean thing can enter into his kingdom; therefore nothing entereth into his rest save it be those who have washed their garments in my blood, because of their faith, and the repentance of all their sins, and their faithfulness unto the end.*

Fallen men are carnal, sensual, and devilish by nature; they are unclean; they are worldly. To be saved they must become clean; God himself is clean and pure, and only those who become as he is can dwell in his presence. None others are saved. Of the saints John said: "If we walk in the light, as he is in the light, we have fellowship one with

382

another, and the blood of Jesus Christ his Son cleanseth us from all sin." (1 Jn. 1:7.) This is the doctrine of blood atonement.

Now this is the commandment: Repent, all ye ends of the earth, and come unto me and be baptized in my name, that ye may be sanctified by the reception of the Holy Ghost, that ye may stand spotless before me at the last day.

How can men become clean and pure? How can they be sanctified? What power can burn dross and evil out of a human soul as though by fire? To be saved men must be born again; they must be sanctified by the Spirit; they must receive the baptism of fire and of the Holy Ghost; they must become clean and spotless by obedience to law. The Holy Ghost is a sanctifier; no man can be saved unless he receives the gift of the Holy Ghost. Men humble themselves and are baptized by legal administrators sent of God so that, following the laying on of hands, they may receive the companionship of the Holy Spirit of God.

Verily, verily, I say unto you, this is my gospel; and ye know the things that ye must do in my church; for the works which ye have seen me do that shall ye also do; for that which ye have seen me do even that shall ye do; Therefore, if ye do these things blessed are ye, for ye shall be lifted up at the last day.

This is my gospel! As Jesus began his ministry so he ended it: "preaching the gospel of the kingdom of God, And saying, The time is fulfilled, and the kingdom of God is at hand: repent ye, and believe the gospel." (Mark 1:14-15.) The gospel, the everlasting gospel, the gospel of God! Jesus calls it "my gospel," and so it is, for he has adopted it; and the Father—that all men might honor the Son even as they honor the Father—has called his own gospel after the name of his Son: *The Gospel of Jesus Christ.* His part in the eternal plan was to work out the infinite and eternal atonement. Man's part is to believe and obey; as far as any act on

383

our part is concerned, the gospel is faith, repentance, baptism, the receipt of the Holy Ghost, and enduring in righteousness all our days. Such is the message Jesus gave to the Nephites; and such—we cannot doubt—is the same message, stated with the same clarity, that he gave to worthy persons in his own Galilee.

By Whom Shall Men Be Judged?
(3 Nephi 27:23-33)

How glorious is the Judge of all the earth! And—if we may paraphrase Isaiah's words about the messengers who preach us the gospel of peace—how beautiful upon the mountains are the feet of them who stand with Him to judge the nations of men. Yea, how glorious are the messengers who, first, preach the gospel, and who, then, sit in judgment at the Eternal Bar. And so Jesus continues:

Write the things which ye have seen and heard, save it be those which are forbidden. Write the works of this people, which shall be, even as hath been written, of that which hath been.

For behold, out of the books which have been written, and which shall be written, shall this people be judged, for by them shall their works be known unto men.

And behold, all things are written by the Father; therefore out of the books which shall be written shall the world be judged.

When the judgment is set and the books are opened, all men will be judged out of that which is written in the books. They will be judged by the recitations there found of their own deeds. The tithing records will name the full tithe payers; the books on Sabbath observance will tell those who went to the house of prayer on the Lord's day to pay their devotions to the Most High. But, beyond this, the books will specify the standards that men should have met and tell the way they should have lived. Christians will be

judged out of the Bible, for that holy book tells them how to
live to please the Lord. People to whom the Book of Mormon comes will be judged out of it and will be accountable
for rejecting the witness it bears of the Lord Jesus and of
the prophet by whose instrumentality this latter-day witness of truth came forth. And, even beyond this, every man
will be judged out of the book of his own life, out of the
record of obedience or disobedience that is written in the
flesh and sinews and soul of his own body. And however
imperfect the records kept on earth may be, all things are
written by the Father, into the very body and spirit of each
person, so that none will be judged amiss or from an imperfect ledger.

*And know ye that ye shall be judges of this people,
according to the judgment which I shall give unto
you, which shall be just. Therefore, what manner of
men ought ye to be? Verily I say unto you, even as
I am.*

Jesus is the Judge of all. The Father judgeth no man but
hath committed all judgment unto the Son. But the Twelve
in Jerusalem shall sit on twelve thrones judging the whole
house of Israel; the Nephite Twelve, having been so
judged, will in turn judge the Nephite nation; and we may
well conclude that the hierarchy of judgment expands out
to other legal administrators in the various dispensations.
Just as the noble and great participated with the Great
Creator in the creation, so those who are chosen and worthy shall participate with the Great Judge in the day of
judgment. That the lesser judges must be as the Great
Judge is self-evident.

*And now I go unto the Father. And verily I say
unto you, whatsoever things ye shall ask the Father
in my name shall be given unto you.*

*Therefore, ask, and ye shall receive; knock, and it
shall be opened unto you; for he that asketh, receiveth; and unto him that knocketh, it shall be
opened.*

How often it must be said: "Ask, and ye shall receive." How many things we might know if we would ask. How many doors might be opened if we would but knock. The Lord wants us to seek light and truth and revelation.

And now, behold, my joy is great, even unto fulness, because of you, and also this generation; yea, and even the Father rejoiceth, and also all the holy angels, because of you and this generation; for none of them are lost.

Behold, I would that ye should understand; for I mean them who are now alive of this generation; and none of them are lost; and in them I have fulness of joy.

When else was it ever thus? In Zion of Enoch, be it answered, for the saints of that day were translated and taken up into heaven; but there has been no other time of which we have knowledge when righteousness has prevailed among so many people to the degree here manifest. And what joy is found in heaven when the righteous so live as to merit eternal life.

But behold, it sorroweth me because of the fourth generation from this generation, for they are led away captive by him even as was the son of perdition; for they will sell me for silver and for gold, and for that which moth doth corrupt and which thieves can break through and steal. And in that day will I visit them, even in turning their works upon their own heads.

When men set their hearts upon the wealth of the world and the good things of the earth in preference to the things of the Spirit, they thereby sell Christ for silver and gold and lose their own souls. Hence Jesus said:

Enter ye in at the strait gate; for strait is the gate, and narrow is the way that leads to life, and few there be that find it; but wide is the gate, and broad the way which leads to death, and many there be that travel therein, until the night cometh, wherein no man can work.

Again the message is primarily for us. Life or death lies before us all; obedience brings life, rebellion, death; and for the rebellious, those who have rejected the gospel in this life, the night of darkness holds no hope of salvation.

NOTE

1. Mosiah 5:7-14. To us in this day the Lord has said: "Take upon you the name of Christ, and speak the truth in soberness. And as many as repent and are baptized in my name, which is Jesus Christ, and endure to the end, the same shall be saved. Behold, Jesus Christ is the name which is given of the Father, and there is none other name given whereby men can be saved; Wherefore, all men must take upon them the name which is given of the Father, for in that name shall they be called at the last day; Wherefore, if they know not the name by which they are called, they cannot have place in the kingdom of my Father." (D&C 18:21-25.)

Chapter 119

THE THREE NEPHITES

If I will that he tarry till I come,
what is that to thee?
(John 21:22.)
Thou shalt tarry until I come in my glory,
and shalt prophesy before nations,
kindreds, tongues and people.
(D&C 7:3.)

They Shall Never Taste of Death
(3 Nephi 28:1-12)

It appearing that the allotted time of his Nephite ministry is over, Jesus prepares to return to his Father. Before
doing so, he asks the Twelve: "What is it that ye desire of
me, after that I am gone to the Father?" Nine of them
reply: "We desire that after we have lived unto the age of
man, that our ministry, wherein thou hast called us, may
have an end, that we may speedily come unto thee in thy
kingdom." We conclude from this that they desired to
remain in paradise for but a short time, after which they
would come forth in immortal glory and sit down with
Abraham, Isaac, and Jacob in the kingdom of God, to go no
more out. Jesus grants their request. "Blessed are ye because ye desired this thing of me," he said, "therefore,

after that ye are seventy and two years old ye shall come unto me in my kingdom; and with me ye shall find rest."

Jesus then turns to the other three. "What will ye that I should do unto you, when I am gone unto the Father?" he asks. Though they are spiritual giants and feel themselves on intimate terms with the Lord, they sorrow in their hearts and dare not give vocal expression to their desires. "Behold, I know your thoughts," Jesus says, "and ye have desired the thing which John, my beloved, who was with me in my ministry, before that I was lifted up by the Jews, desired of me." These three Nephite disciples, because of their desires, had in store for themselves such blessings as we have no way of comprehending, nor has the Lord seen fit to do more than reveal a sliver of what was to be in their future lives.

Therefore, more blessed are ye, for ye shall never taste of death; but ye shall live to behold all the doings of the Father unto the children of men, even until all things shall be fulfilled according to the will of the Father, when I shall come in my glory with the powers of heaven.

Eternal life—no, not that glorious immortality in which resurrected beings become like their God, but to live forever on earth, as mortals, without disease or sorrow, having health and vigor, preaching the gospel and being witnesses to and participants in all that was to be! What a tempting prospect. How many faithful souls would rejoice in such a ministerial assignment. And wonder of wonders, for them it was to be.

And ye shall never endure the pains of death; but when I shall come in my glory ye shall be changed in the twinkling of an eye from mortality to immortality; and then shall ye be blessed in the kingdom of my Father.

Will translated beings ever die? Remember John's enigmatic words relative to his own translation: "Then went this saying abroad among the brethren, that that disciple should not die: yet Jesus said not unto him, He shall not die; but, If I will that he tarry till I come, what is that to thee?'' (John 21:23.) Note the distinction between avoiding death as such and living till the Lord comes. Then note that Jesus promises the Three Nephites, not that they shall not die, but that they "shall never taste of death" and shall not "endure the pains of death." Again it is an enigmatic declaration with a hidden meaning. There is a distinction between death as we know it and tasting of death or enduring the pains of death. As a matter of doctrine, death is universal; every mortal thing, whether plant or animal or man, shall surely die. Jacob said: "Death hath passed upon all men, to fulfil the merciful plan of the great Creator." (2 Ne. 9:6.) There are no exceptions, not even among translated beings. Paul said: "As in Adam all die, even so in Christ shall all be made alive." (1 Cor. 15:22.) Again the dominion of death over all is acclaimed. But the Lord says of *all* his saints, not that they will not die, but that "those that die in me shall not taste of death, for it shall be sweet unto them; And they that die not in me, wo unto them, for their death is bitter." (D&C 42:46-47.) The distinction is between dying as such and tasting of death itself. Again the Lord says: "He that liveth when the Lord shall come, and hath kept the faith, blessed is he; nevertheless, it is appointed to him to die at the age of man. Wherefore, children shall grow up until they become old; old men shall die; but they shall not sleep in the dust, but they shall be changed in the twinkling of an eye." (D&C 63:50-51.) Thus, this change from mortality to immortality, though almost instantaneous, is both a death and a resurrection. Thus, translated beings do not suffer death as we normally define it, meaning the separation of body and spirit; nor do they receive a resurrection as we ordinarily describe it, meaning that the body rises from the dust and the spirit enters again into its fleshly home. But they do pass through death and are changed from mortality to immortality, in the eternal sense, and they thus both die and are resurrected in the eternal sense.

This, we might add, is why Paul wrote: "Behold, I shew you a mystery; We shall not all sleep, but we shall all be changed, In a moment, in the twinkling of an eye, at the last trump: for the trumpet shall sound, and the dead shall be raised incorruptible, and we shall be changed." (1 Cor. 15:51-52.)

And again, ye shall not have pain while ye shall dwell in the flesh, neither sorrow save it be for the sins of the world; and all this will I do because of the thing which ye have desired of me, for ye have desired that ye might bring the souls of men unto me, while the world shall stand.

During the Millennium all men will be translated, as it were; in that day "there shall be no sorrow because there is no death. In that day an infant shall not die until he is old; and his life shall be as the age of a tree; And when he dies he shall not sleep, that is to say in the earth, but shall be changed in the twinkling of an eye, and shall be caught up, and his rest shall be glorious." (D&C 101:29-31.)

And for this cause ye shall have fulness of joy; and ye shall sit down in the kingdom of my Father; yea, your joy shall be full, even as the Father hath given me fulness of joy; and ye shall be even as I am, and I am even as the Father; and the Father and I are one;

And the Holy Ghost beareth record of the Father and me; and the Father giveth the Holy Ghost unto the children of men, because of me.

These words—the last recorded words spoken by Jesus in his Nephite ministry—contain the greatest doctrinal concept ever revealed. They are the Book of Mormon pronouncement that as God now is, man may become; they are the Book of Mormon proclamation that those who gain eternal life inherit, receive, and possess all that the Father hath; they are the Book of Mormon announcement that man—in glorious exaltation—becomes one with the Father, Son, and Holy Ghost.

And as we hear such words as these fall from the lips of the Son of God, there is no better place to insert our witness of the truth and divinity of that volume of holy scripture—the Book of Mormon—which contains the account of Jesus' Nephite ministry. In words of soberness we say: No man having the Spirit of the Lord as his guide can read the Book of Mormon account without knowing in the depths of his soul that it came from God and is verily true. No such man can read it and think that either Joseph Smith or any man wrote the account of himself. It came from God by the power of the Holy Ghost, and it is the mind and will and voice of the Lord to all men. And because it came forth through the instrumentality of Joseph Smith, it follows that the book itself, being true, is a witness, beyond any peradventure of doubt, that Joseph Smith was called of God.

But back to our Nephite setting. After Jesus had spoken the wondrous words which burn with eternal conviction in our heart, he touched the nine apostles, but not the three, with his finger, "and then he departed."

Their Transfiguration and Ministry
(3 Nephi 28:13-40)

Mortal man—shackled as it were in a tabernacle of clay; imprisoned on a single planet that is itself but a speck of dust in an endless universe; bound by time and space, and living for only a few brief moments—mortal man, a spirit son of God, dwells in the depths of ignorance, away from his Father, without a knowledge of eternal things. We are born, we live, we die, and in the process we are privileged—some of us—to receive a few little glimmerings of eternal truth by revelation. And there are few among us, even in sober moments, who ponder the wonders of eternity and seek to know what lies beyond the ken of humankind. What of creation itself, of worlds without number, all inhabited, all crowned with an infinite variety of life? How did Gods begin to be, and whence came the order and system in a universe whose outer limits we shall never see? How little we know of preexistence, both ours and that of all forms of life; or of death and the world of waiting spirits; or of the resurrection which raises sleeping dust to glorious life. What are Abraham, Isaac, and Jacob doing today? How can Moroni hie to Kolob in the twinkling of an eye? Where are Annas and Caiaphas and Pilate, and what kind of a life are they living? How little we know about creation, about redemption, about immortal glory.

And yet there are those—a favored few—who break the time-bound bands, who see beyond the veil, who come to know the things of eternity. Portions of what they learn they are permitted to reveal to the rest of us. Enoch, after his translation, was high and lifted up, even in the bosom of the Father and the Son, where he saw and heard things of infinite wonder and glory, some few of which are recorded in the Book of Moses. Moriancumer saw and beheld and knew and recorded such glorious things that they were withheld from the children of men until after the resurrection of Christ, and even then they were shown only to the Nephites, and that for a brief season. Since then they have been sealed up, and, as we suppose, they shall not be manifest again until after the Second Coming of the Son of Man. John the Revelator saw the wonders of eternity, some few of which he was permitted to record, in figures and types and shadows, in the Book of Revelation. Others of the prophets—and for aught we know their number may be many—have seen and heard and felt and known far more than has come to us in any of our scriptures. Among these are the Three Nephite Disciples.

We do not know the great things revealed to the chosen three, nor could we comprehend them if they were recorded in our holy books. Milk must precede meat, and those who have yet to learn the basics of arithmetic can scarcely comprehend the mysteries of calculus. Hence, as Alma said: "It is given unto many to know the mysteries of God; nevertheless they are laid under a strict command that they shall not impart only according to the portion of his word which he doth grant unto the children of men, according to the heed and diligence which they give unto him." (Alma 12:9.) Of the experience of the Three Nephites, Mormon wrote: "And behold, the heavens were opened, and they were caught up into heaven, and saw and heard unspeakable things. And it was forbidden them that they should utter; neither was it given unto them power that they could utter the things which they saw and heard; And whether they were in the body or out of the body, they could not tell; for it did seem unto them like a transfiguration of them, that they were changed from this body of flesh into an immortal state, that they could behold the things of God."

It was with them as with Paul and Joseph Smith and others of the prophets. There are no words that can convey the spiritual feelings or the truths learned by those who receive these greater manifestations of divine understanding. Speaking of himself, Paul says he was "caught up to the third heaven," which is the celestial kingdom— "whether in the body, or out of the body, I cannot tell: God knoweth," he says—and that he "heard unspeakable words, which it is not lawful for a man to utter." (2 Cor. 12:1-4.) After recording the vision of the degrees of glory, Joseph Smith spoke similarly of other things that he had seen and heard while enwrapped in the heavenly manifestation then vouchsafed to him.[1]

In recording that the Three Disciples were caught up into heaven, Mormon first wrote: "Whether they were mortal or immortal, from the day of their transfiguration, I know not." After pondering and praying about their status, however, he said: "Since I wrote, I have inquired of the Lord, and he hath made it manifest unto me that there must needs be a change wrought upon their bodies, or else it needs be that they must taste of death; Therefore, that they might not taste of death there was a change wrought upon their bodies, that they might not suffer pain nor sorrow save it were for the sins of the world. Now this change was not equal to that which shall take place at the last day; but there was a change wrought upon them, insomuch that Satan could have no power over them, that he could not tempt them; and they were sanctified in the flesh, that they were holy, and that the powers of the earth could not hold them. And in this state they were to remain until the judgment day of Christ; and at that day they were to receive a greater change, and to be received into the kingdom of the Father to go no more out, but to dwell with God eternally in the heavens." These words apply equally to John the Beloved, whose mission and ministry is the same as that of his Nephite brethren.

As to their ministry among those of that generation, they went forth preaching the gospel, baptizing, conferring the Holy Ghost, and building up the Church of Christ, until all of that generation were blessed as Jesus had promised.

As to their later ministry among the Nephites, though they continued to serve with unwearying diligence, opposition arose. They were cast into prisons, which were rent at their word, and they went forth free. They were cast into pits of the earth and freed by the power of God. "And thrice they were cast into a furnace and received no harm. And twice were they cast into a den of wild beasts; and behold they did play with the beasts as a child with a suckling lamb, and received no harm." Finally, in the days of Mormon, in about A.D. 322, the Lord took them from among the people (Morm. 1:13), and in the year A.D. 401, Moroni records that, though their whereabouts was unknown, they had ministered unto him and his father (Morm. 8:10-11).

As to their continuing mortal ministry, we know only that they shall be among the Jews, and among the Gentiles, and among "all the scattered tribes of Israel," and among "all nations, kindreds, tongues and people, and shall bring out of them unto Jesus many souls." And this also applies to John the Beloved. "And they are as the angels of God, and if they shall pray unto the Father in the name of Jesus they can show themselves unto whatsoever man it seemeth them good. Therefore, great and marvelous works shall be wrought by them, before the great and coming day when all people must surely stand before the judgment-seat of Christ; Yea even among the Gentiles shall there be a great and marvelous work wrought by them, before that judgment day."

At this point in his writing, Mormon, as moved upon by the Holy Ghost, gives us this word from the Lord:

And wo be unto him that will not hearken unto the words of Jesus, and also to them whom he hath chosen and sent among them; for whoso receiveth not the words of Jesus and the words of those whom he hath sent receiveth not him; and therefore he will not receive them at the last day;

And it would be better for them if they had not been born. For do ye suppose that ye can get rid of the justice of an offended God, who hath been trampled under feet of men, that thereby salvation might come?

Jesus and his servants are one; to believe in those whom he hath sent is to believe in him, and to reject his messengers is to reject him.

Nephite, Jewish, and Gentile Apostasy
(3 Nephi 29, 30; 4 Nephi; Mormon 1 to 9; Moroni 1 to 10)

We cannot leave our study of the life of him whose gospel is the power that saves without recording what happened to the saving truths he gave to men on both continents. Jesus restored the gospel in the Old World and set up his earthly kingdom among men. In the New World he added to the gospel truths they already had, perfected his kingdom, and shed forth upon them such rays of heavenly light as have seldom pierced the gloom and darkness of earth. In the Old World the true Church was set up in the midst of worldly forces, and after a century or so the world prevailed, the saints became sinners, and the churches of men and of devils replaced the true Church of Christ. Among the Nephites all the people were converted, and for 167 or so years, until A.D. 201, perfect peace and righteousness prevailed. Then apostasy began; false churches sprang up; wickedness prevailed; wars swept the land; and except for a few saints, the true Church was overcome by the world. By A.D. 421 Satan's triumph was complete and the whole Nephite civilization had been destroyed, with Moroni only remaining true to the faith.

We can scarcely imagine the gospel blessings that first prevailed among the Nephites. Contentions and disputations ceased; every man dealt justly with his brother; they had all things common among them; there were no rich nor poor; none were in bondage; all were free and partook of the heavenly gift. "And there were great and marvelous works wrought by the disciples of Jesus, insomuch that they did heal the sick, and raise the dead, and cause the lame to walk, and the blind to receive their sight, and the deaf to hear; and all manner of miracles did they work among the children of men." Of these American saints Mormon said: "There was no contention in the land, because of the love of God which did dwell in the hearts of the people. And there were no envyings, nor strifes, nor tumults, nor whoredoms, nor lyings, nor murders, nor any manner of lasciviousness; and surely there could not be a happier people among all the people who had been created by the hand of God. There were no robbers, nor murderers, neither were there Lamanites, nor any manner of -ites; but they were in one, the children of Christ, and heirs to the kingdom of God. And how blessed were they! For the Lord did bless them in all their doings."

But beginning in the 201st year some were lifted up in pride; they began to wear costly apparel; the people no longer had all things in common; society was divided into classes; and men "began to build up churches unto themselves to get gain, and began to deny the true church of Christ.'' Soon "there were many churches which professed to know the Christ, and yet they did deny the more parts of his gospel, insomuch that they did receive all manner of wickedness, and did administer that which was sacred unto him to whom it had been forbidden because of unworthiness.'' And "there was another church which denied the Christ; and they did persecute the true church of Christ, because of their humility and their belief in Christ; and they did despise them because of the many miracles which were wrought among them.'' These were the days when the Three Disciples were persecuted and imprisoned and cast into fiery furnaces.

By the day of Mormon, miracles and healings had ceased; "there were no gifts from the Lord, and the Holy Ghost did not come upon any, because of their wickedness and unbelief.'' Once again the Gadianton robbers infested the land, and "there were sorceries, and witchcrafts, and magics; and the power of the evil one was wrought upon all the face of the land.'' There was war, and blood, and carnage, and revolution everywhere; women and children were sacrificed to idols, and the judgments of God rested upon the land. "It is impossible for the tongue to describe,'' Mormon said, "or for man to write a perfect description of the horrible scene of the blood and carnage which was among the people, both of the Nephites and of the Lamanites; and every heart was hardened, so that they delighted in the shedding of blood continually. And there never had been so great wickedness among all the children of Lehi, nor even among all the house of Israel, according to the words of the Lord, as was among this people.'' Those whose fathers had been more righteous and who had received greater blessings than any in all Israel had now sunk to greater wickedness and were more severely cursed than any of the chosen seed had ever been.

Our inspired records let us speak thus—with accuracy

398

and verity—of what transpired in the Americas. In principle it was the same among the Jews and Gentiles of the Old World. Grievous wolves attacked the flock; lewd and evil men led them astray; pride welled up in the hearts of many; and shortly after the death of the apostles the apostasy was complete. As in the New World "there were many churches which professed to know the Christ, and yet they did deny the more parts of his gospel." All manner of wickedness prevailed, and sacred ordinances were administered to those who were unworthy. Gifts and miracles ceased, and darkness covered the earth. Wars and anarchy and desolation have been poured out upon all nations ever since, and it will continue so to be until the great and dreadful day of the Lord comes.

In this setting we return to the writings of Mormon. He refers to the coming forth of the Book of Mormon as a sign "that the covenant which the Father hath made with the children of Israel, concerning their restoration to the lands of their inheritance, is already beginning to be fulfilled." Mormon is directing his words to us in this day, to the scattered remnants of Israel, and to the Gentile nations. When the Book of Mormon comes forth, "Ye may know that the words of the Lord, which have been spoken by the holy prophets, shall all be fulfilled," he says, "and ye need not say that the Lord delays his coming unto the children of Israel."

And further: "Ye need not imagine in your hearts that the words which have been spoken are vain, for behold, the Lord will remember his covenant which he hath made unto his people of the house of Israel. And when ye shall see these sayings coming forth among you, then ye need not any longer spurn at the doings of the Lord, for the sword of his justice is in his right hand; and behold, at that day, if he shall spurn at his doings he will cause that it shall soon overtake you." Then come these superlative words of power and inspiration:

Wo unto him that spurneth at the doings of the Lord; yea, wo unto him that shall deny the Christ and his works!

Yea, wo unto him that shall deny the revelations of the Lord, and that shall say the Lord no longer worketh by revelation, or by prophecy, or by gifts, or by tongues, or by healings, or by the power of the Holy Ghost!

Yea, and wo unto him that shall say at that day, to get gain, that there can be no miracle wrought by Jesus Christ; for he that doeth this shall become like unto the son of perdition, for whom there was no mercy, according to the word of Christ!

Next he delivers a message as to what our attitude should be toward the Jews. "Yea, and ye need not any longer hiss, nor spurn, nor make game of the Jews, nor any of the remnant of the house of Israel; for behold, the Lord remembereth his covenant unto them, and he will do unto them according to that which he hath sworn. Therefore ye need not suppose that ye can turn the right hand of the Lord unto the left, that he may not execute judgment unto the fulfilling of the covenant which he hath made unto the house of Israel."

Our great and good friend, in fine, issues a mighty proclamation to the Gentiles: "Hearken, O ye Gentiles," he says, "and hear the words of Jesus Christ, the Son of the living God, which he hath commanded me that I should speak concerning you, for, behold he commandeth me that I should write, saying":

Turn, all ye Gentiles, from your wicked ways; and repent of your evil doings, of your lyings and deceivings, and of your whoredoms, and of your abominations, and your idolatries, and of your murders, and your priestcrafts, and your envyings, and your strifes, and from all your wickedness and abominations, and come unto me, and be baptized in my

*name, that ye may receive a remission of your sins,
and be filled with the Holy Ghost, that ye may be
numbered with my people who are of the house of
Israel.*

NOTE

1. D&C 76:114-119. In beginning the account of the vision of his brother Alvin in the celestial kingdom, the Prophet wrote: "The heavens were opened upon us, and I beheld the celestial kingdom of God, and the glory thereof, whether in the body or out I cannot tell." (D&C 137:1.)

Chapter 120

THE ASCENSION

It is finished. (John 19:30.)
I ascend unto my Father, and your Father;
and to my God, and your God.
(John 20:17.)
For I know that my redeemer liveth,
and that he shall stand at the latter day
upon the earth: And though
after my skin worms destroy this body,
yet in my flesh shall I see God:
Whom I shall see for myself,
and mine eyes shall behold, and not another;
though my reins be consumed within me.
(Job 19:25-27.)

Jesus Returns to His Father
(Acts 1:1-14; Mark 16:19-20; Luke 24:50-53)

The day has arrived; the hour is at hand; the Lord Jesus who descended from the courts of glory is about to return to the presence of the Father forever. He who "made himself of no reputation, and took upon him the form of a servant, and was made in the likeness of men" is about to be exalted above all thrones and principalities and to sit down "on the right hand of the Majesty on high." He who was "found in fashion as a man," who "humbled himself, and became obedient unto death, even the death of the cross," is about to ascend the throne of eternal power and wear a kingly crown. He who, "being in the form of God, thought it not robbery to be equal with God," is about to be given a name above all names. (Philip. 2:5-11; Heb. 1:3.)

"It is finished." His mortal work is done; the atonement hath been wrought; let all men praise his holy name forever. "Worthy is the Lamb that was slain to receive power, and riches, and wisdom, and strength, and honour, and glory, and blessing." (Rev. 5:12.)

"I have finished the work which thou gavest me to do!" He has glorified the name of the Father on earth. His High Priestly Prayer is about to be answered: "And now, O Father, glorify thou me with thine own self with the glory which I had with thee before the world was." (John 17:4-5.)

He is going to his Father; they are one; let both their holy names be in every worshipping heart and on every praising lip forever. "Blessing, and honour, and glory, and power, be unto him that sitteth upon the throne, and unto the Lamb for ever and ever." (Rev. 5:13.)

What work has he done; what wonders hath he wrought; what achievements now are his? By the grace of God—by the condescension, mercy, and love of the Father—he came to earth, because his Father sent him, to die upon the cross for the sins of the world. By his own goodness and grace—by the condescension, mercy, and love of the Son—he stepped down from the throne of eternal power, to be like man almost, to save men from their sins. He came as the Light of the World to lead all men to salvation.

> He marked the path and led the way,
> And every point defines
> To light and life and endless day
> Where God's full presence shines.
> —*Hymns*, no. 68

And by him salvation comes. He paid the price for Adam's fall; he ransomed men from death and hell; he gave his life that man might live.

> For us the blood of Christ was shed,
> For us on Calvary's cross he bled,
> And thus dispelled the awful gloom
> That else were this creation's doom.
>
> The law was broken; Jesus died
> That justice might be satisfied,
> That man might not remain a slave
> Of death, of hell, or of the grave,
>
> But rise triumphant from the tomb,
> And in eternal splendor bloom,
> Freed from the power of death and pain,
> With Christ, the Lord, to rule and reign.
> —*Hymns,* no. 217

And now his work is done. A God has died; a God has risen; a God ascends to his Father.

> The rising Lord forsook the tomb.
> In vain the tomb forbade him rise;
> Cherubic legions guard him home,
> And shout him welcome to the skies.
> —*Hymns,* no. 263

From the Sunday of his rising to the holy day of his ascension was forty days, and from the Friday of his crucifixion to the day of Pentecost was fifty days. Thus he died on a Friday; he rose on a Sunday (which was three days as the Jews counted time); he ministered among his disciples, from time to time, for forty days; he then ascended to his Father; and on the day of Pentecost they received the gift of the Holy Ghost. "They were all with one accord in one place," on the day of Pentecost. "And suddenly there came a sound from heaven as of a rushing mighty wind, and it filled all the house where they were sitting." They could have been in that same memorable upper room where so many of the wonders of eternity had been poured out upon them.[1] "And there appeared unto them cloven tongues like as of fire, and it sat upon each of them." We shall note shortly the names and identities of those who in all probability were present, and who received this divine outpouring of grace from on high. "And they were all filled with the Holy Ghost, and began to speak with other tongues, as the Spirit gave them utterance."

When word of this Pentecostal outpouring of heavenly fire was "noised abroad," a great "multitude came together." Among them were "Jews, devout men, out of every nation under heaven." And they "were confounded, because that every man heard them speak in his own language. And they were all amazed and marvelled, saying one to another, Behold, are not all these which speak Galileans? And how hear we every man in our own tongue, wherein we were born?" Then Peter, the chief disciple, preached a mighty sermon and bore a powerful testimony of Jesus his Lord. "Let all the house of Israel know assuredly," he said by way of climax, "that God hath made that same Jesus, whom ye have crucified, both Lord and Christ."

Having seen the miracle, having heard the sermon, and having felt the power of the Spirit, as Luke tells us, "they were pricked in their heart, and said unto Peter and to the rest of the apostles, Men and brethren, what shall we do?" Faith was beginning to sprout in their hearts. They were believers of the Eternal Word; the Holy Ghost changes the hearts of men. Peter said:

Repent, and be baptized every one of you in the name of Jesus Christ for the remission of sins, and ye shall receive the gift of the Holy Ghost. For the promise is unto you, and to your children, and to all that are afar off, even as many as the Lord our God shall call.

"And with many other words did he testify and exhort, saying, Save yourselves from this untoward generation.

Then they that gladly received his word were baptized: and the same day there were added unto them about three thousand souls. And they continued stedfastly in the apostles' doctrine and fellowship, and in breaking of bread, and in prayers. And fear came upon every soul: and many wonders and signs were done by the apostles. And all that believed were together, and had all things common; And sold their possessions and goods, and parted them to all men, as every man had need. And they, continuing daily with one accord in the temple, and breaking bread from house to house, did eat their meat with gladness and singleness of heart, Praising God, and having favour with all the people. And the Lord added to the church daily such as should be saved." (Acts 2:1-47.) And thus, by the power of the Holy Ghost, the work went forth among the Jews, even as it would among the Nephites in due course.

But let us return to the Ascension. As Luke tells us, the Risen Lord "shewed himself alive after his passion by many infallible proofs, being seen of them forty days, and speaking of the things pertaining to the kingdom of God." We have considered such of these infallible proofs of the resurrection as are found in holy writ. And there is no more infallible proof than the testimony of one who has seen with his eyes and felt with his hands and known by the power of the Spirit that the Risen One now has a body of flesh and bones. How else can the resurrection be proved except by testimony?

Thus Jesus was with them "until the day in which he was taken up, after that he through the Holy Ghost had given commandments unto the apostles whom he had chosen." These commandments included one that they "should not depart from Jerusalem, but wait for the promise of the Father, which, saith he, ye have heard of me. For John truly baptized with water; but ye shall be baptized with the Holy Ghost not many days hence." And so, having kept their appointment on the mountain in Galilee, having been taught all that it was expedient for them to know at that time, and having been commanded and commissioned to go into all the world, to preach the gospel, and to build up the kingdom, they are now back in Jerusalem awaiting the receipt of the gift of the Holy Ghost.

They are assembled together. Jesus leads them out toward Bethany. It is their last walk with him, reminiscent of all the other times they have traversed this same course. They arrive at the Mount of Olives. He is about to ascend, but they are still troubled with one thing. They ask: "Lord, wilt thou at this time restore again the kingdom to Israel?"

What words are these? *Restore again the kingdom to Israel!* Are these the Nephite Twelve who are speaking? Reversing the chronology—that a more cohesive account of the life of our Lord might be given—we have already considered *in extenso* Jesus' discussion about the restoration of the kingdom to his people in the latter days. Surely the kingdom will be restored as of old, for so all the prophets have foretold. Indeed, the ponderings of their hearts, the desires of their souls, and their continuing petitions to the Majesty on High—all sought for the restoration of Israel. And further: All the prophets knew that the children of the prophets—the children of the covenant—should again receive the ancient promise of eternal life and the assurance that in them and in their seed all generations should be blessed. Jehovah's word to Abraham would not return unto him void. And so we have seen that the sign letting all men know when these things shall be is the coming forth of the Book of Mormon. How plainly and how repetitively it was said among the Nephites.

Now the apostles in Jerusalem desire to learn the same thing. But the Old World witnesses—whose lack of faith had kept them from knowing of their Nephite brethren— are not to learn the sign, at least not in its plainness and perfection. It is true that Peter and the others will hereafter speak of the restoration of all things (including the kingdom to Israel); that is, they will talk of a universal apostasy and of the setting up anew of God's kingdom on earth in the latter days—but they shall not, as mortals, learn the account with that fulness which was given to the "other sheep." And so Jesus said:

It is not for you to know the times or the seasons, which the Father hath put in his own power.

But ye shall receive power, after that the Holy Ghost is come upon you: and ye shall be witnesses unto me both in Jerusalem, and in all Judea, and in Samaria, and unto the uttermost part of the earth.

That is, in a day subsequent to New Testament times, the Lord will perform a mighty work with Israel. He will give them their kingdom as of old; they will have revelation and visions and prophets; the heavens will be opened again; the covenants and promises made to the ancients will be fulfilled; Israel will be gathered into all their lands of promise; Zion shall be built up again; a New Jerusalem shall rise; the waste places of the Old Jerusalem shall be reclaimed; the children of the prophets and the children of the covenant will glory in the ancient promises given anew in their times; and the Lord—the God of Israel—will reign gloriously among his saints. But this is not to be the work of the apostles of that day; other apostles must arise to do the work of latter days. Those who were with him then are to be witnesses of his name unto the uttermost parts of the earth. Let them preach to those then living; their successors in interest and in power and in faith shall carry on the work of latter days when the times and the seasons shall arrive.

"And when he had spoken these things, while they beheld"—and while with uplifted hands he blessed them—"he was taken up; and a cloud received him out of their sight. And while they looked stedfastly toward heaven as he went up, behold, two men stood by them in white apparel; Which also said,"

Ye men of Galilee, why stand ye gazing up into heaven? this same Jesus, which is taken up from you

*into heaven, shall so come in like manner as ye have
seen him go into heaven.*

These apostles, all of whom were Galileans (Judas only,
the one traitor among them, was a Judean), were now left
to do the work appointed for them. After Pentecost, with
the Holy Spirit of God as their monitor, how gloriously they
succeeded! But we cannot leave this scene on Olivet without testifying that Jesus' ascension was literal and personal
and real. A Man having a body of flesh and bones—a
Personal Being who walked and talked and ate with his
disciples—ascended bodily into heaven. "The Father has a
body of flesh and bones as tangible as man's; the Son
also." (D&C 130:22.) And Jesus our Lord has just "ascended into heaven, to sit down on the right hand of the
Father, to reign with almighty power according to the will
of the Father." (D&C 20:24.) And as he went up, so is he
now; and as he is now, so will he be when he comes again to
reign on earth a thousand years; and as he will be during the
Millennium, so will he remain to all eternity: a glorified,
perfected, exalted Man—the Son of Man of Holiness, who
is his Father. Praise ye the Lord.

After the Ascension, as Luke writes in his Gospel account, "They worshipped him, and returned to Jerusalem
with great joy: And were continually in the temple, praising
and blessing God." Quite naturally they would go to the
temple, the holiest spot known to them, to continue their
worship. The break with the past would come by degrees.
In his account in Acts, Luke says: "Then returned they
unto Jerusalem from the mount called Olivet, which is from
Jerusalem a sabbath day's journey. And when they were
come in, they went up into an upper room, where abode
both Peter, and James, and John, and Andrew, Philip, and
Thomas, Bartholomew, and Matthew, James the son of
Alpheus, and Simon Zelotes, and Judas the brother of
James. These all continued with one accord in prayer and
supplication, with the women, and Mary the mother of
Jesus, and with his brethren."

We have speculated, in connection with the Last Supper, that the upper room was in the home of the father of John Mark and have given our reasons therefor. All of the Eleven have come together and are living at the same place as they await the Pentecostal outpouring of the Spirit that will soon come upon them. What is more natural than that they should come to this same large and spacious building? We suppose that it was the same upper room where the saints were assembled at meat when Jesus, following the walk on the Emmaus Road, appeared and invited them to handle and feel and learn that he had a body of flesh and bones. Still further, on the day of Pentecost they—and we assume this means the apostles and others—were in a "house" when the Spirit first fell upon them. Again we suggest that this may have been the upper room of note and fame. And when Peter standing in the midst of a hundred and twenty of them arranged for the selection of a successor to Judas, we suppose it was in the same meeting place. We must keep in mind also that there were believers other than the apostles present on all these sacred occasions, including that Pentecostal day when cloven tongues of fire rested upon them. "Mary the mother of Jesus," and her other children, "his brethren," and those called only "the women," meaning Mary Magdalene and the others, are named as being among the saints on these memorable occasions. The new kingdom was starting out, not as a church for apostles only, but as the New Sheepfold for all believers, including the more than three thousand converts who were baptized on the day of Pentecost.

Jesus Is the Son of God
(John 20:30-31; 21:24-25)

Jesus hath ascended into heaven to sit down on the right hand of the Majesty on high. "When he ascended up on high," Paul says, "he led captivity captive," meaning that he broke the bands of death which up to then held all men captive, and he "gave gifts unto men." (Eph. 4:8-16.) Glorious doctrine this! The effects of Jesus' resurrection pass upon all men so that all shall rise from the dead, all shall become immortal, all shall live forever having bodies of flesh and bones. And also, he "gave gifts unto men." What gifts? Paul names apostles, prophets, evangelists, pastors, and teachers (those who teach the gospel). We add elders, seventies, and high priests, deacons, teachers (holders of the ordained office), priests, and bishops, and all the officers of the kingdom of God on earth. Apostles, prophets, and seventies, in particular, and all officers in general, are appointed to be witnesses of the name of Christ, to bear record of his divine Sonship, and to teach his gospel to the world.

Our revelations in naming the gifts of the Spirit list as the first the gift of prophecy, which gift, by definition, is to have the testimony of Jesus, "for the testimony of Jesus is the spirit of prophecy." (Rev. 19:10.) "To some it is given by the Holy Ghost," the revealed word says, "to know that Jesus Christ is the Son of God, and that he was crucified for the sins of the world." Then the inspired word adds: "To others it is given to believe on their words, that they also might have eternal life if they continue faithful." (D&C 46:13-14.)

We have, thus, two gifts named as coming from the Ascended One. The first is to know by personal revelation, given of God by the power of the Holy Ghost, that Jesus is the Lord, the Son of the Highest, whose atoning blood ransoms men from the spiritual and temporal death brought into the world by the fall of Adam. The second gift is to believe the testimony of those officers who are appointed to bear witness of his divine Sonship and of the salvation which he has made available. And those who believe the testimony of His witnesses, and continue faithful, shall have eternal life in his everlasting kingdom.

In this setting, then, we come to the words of the Beloved John, who says of his Gospel account (called by

411

Joseph Smith The Testimony of St. John), "These are written," meaning the things in his Gospel account, "that ye might believe that Jesus is the Christ, the Son of God; and that believing ye might have life through his name."

Thus, the heart and core of our message; the very purpose of all the scriptures ever given; the reason why there are legal administrators, sent of God, to preach the gospel—all that the Lord has given us is to bear testimony and to prove that Jesus, who is called Christ, is in literal reality the Son of the living God and that he was crucified for the sins of the world. And we have written this work—in agony and in ecstasy; in sweat and in tears; in depression and in elation; through seasons of sorrow and in times of unbounded joy—all to the end that men might believe and know that God's Almighty Son ministered as a Man among men, and that believing, perchance, they might be faithful and gain eternal life.

We know that "God is no respecter of persons," and that "in every nation he that feareth him, and worketh righteousness," is acceptable before him. And, with Peter, we testify that salvation is for "the children of Israel," and for the Gentiles, and for those of every nation and kindred and tongue and people; and that the word of God—"preaching peace by Jesus Christ: he is Lord of all"—that word is for all men everywhere. We know that "God anointed Jesus of Nazareth with the Holy Ghost and with power"; that he "went about doing good, and healing all that were oppressed of the devil, for God was with him"; that he was slain "and hanged on a tree"; that "Him God raised up the third day, and shewed him openly, Not to all the people, but unto witnesses chosen before of God"; and that they "did eat and drink with him after he rose from the dead." And we testify that he has commanded us, as he commanded them, "to preach unto the people, and to testify that it is he which was ordained of God to be the Judge of quick and dead." And further: "To him give all the prophets witness, that through his name whosoever believeth in him shall receive remission of sins." (Acts 10:34-43.)

We testify, with Paul, that "God was manifest in the flesh, justified in the Spirit, seen of angels, preached unto the Gentiles, believed on in the world, received up into glory." (1 Tim. 3:16.) We rejoice that "God hath not given us the spirit of fear; but of power, and of love, and of a sound mind"; that we, therefore, are "not . . . ashamed of the testimony of our lord," but account it, rather, a privilege to partake "of the afflictions of the gospel according to the power of God." We glory in the fact that he "hath saved us, and called us with an holy calling, not according to our works, but according to his own purpose and grace, which was given us in Christ Jesus before the world began"; and above all that "our Saviour Jesus Christ . . . hath abolished death, and hath brought life and immortality to light through the gospel." (2 Tim. 1:7-10.)

We say with Peter: "Thou art the Christ, the Son of the living God." (Matt. 16:16.) And with Martha: "I believe that thou art the Christ, the Son of God, which should come into the world." (John 11:27.) And with Mary Magdalene: "Rabboni." (John 20:16.) And with Thomas: "My Lord and my God." (John 20:28.) And with Joseph Smith: "I saw two Personages, whose brightness and glory defy all description, standing above me in the air. One of them spake unto me, calling me by name and said, pointing to the other—*This is My Beloved Son. Hear Him!*" (JS-H 1:17.) And again: "We saw the Lord standing upon the breastwork of the pulpit, before us; and under his feet was a paved work of pure gold, in color like amber. His eyes were as a flame of fire; the hair of his head was white like the pure snow; his countenance shone above the brightness of the sun; and his voice was as the sound of the rushing of great waters, even the voice of Jehovah, saying: I am the first and the last; I am he who liveth, I am he who was slain; I am your advocate with the Father." (D&C 110:2-4.) And yet again: "And now, after the many testimonies which

413

have been given of him, this is the testimony, last of all, which we give of him: That he lives! For we saw him, even on the right hand of God; and we heard the voice bearing record that he is the Only Begotten of the Father—That by him, and through him, and of him, the worlds are and were created, and the inhabitants thereof are begotten sons and daughters unto God." (D&C 76:22-24.) And all of these witnesses are our witness also.

With John we have seen him, as it were, in heaven, upon a white horse, bearing the name "Faithful and True," and judging and making war "in righteousness." "His eyes were as a flame of fire, and on his head were many crowns. . . . He was clothed with a vesture dipped in blood: and his name is called The Word of God. And the armies which were in heaven followed him upon white horses, clothed in fine linen, white and clean. And out of his mouth goeth a sharp sword, that with it he should smite the nations: and he shall rule them with a rod of iron: and he treadeth the winepress of the fierceness and wrath of Almighty God. And he hath on his vesture and on his thigh a name written, KING OF KINGS, AND LORD OF LORDS." (Rev. 19:11-16.)

And, in fine, let Job's words be our words: "I know that my redeemer liveth, and that he shall stand at the latter day upon the earth." (Job 19:25.) We need not multiply witnesses. This work itself is our witness. It testifies that he was God before the worlds were; that he was born of Mary in a stable, God himself being his Father; that he ministered among men, preaching the gospel and working miracles; that he was delivered into the hands of wicked men, and by them hanged upon a tree; that he bore the sins of all who believe and obey; that he is the Resurrection and the Life; that immortality and eternal life come by him; that he hath risen from the dead; and that finally he ascended to his Father, there to reign with almighty power until he shall come again to reign on earth. The fact of the resurrection is the most certain surety in all history; a cloud of witnesses testify thereto, including those in our day who also have

414

seen and felt and handled; and all who will, may receive the same sure witness from the Holy Spirit of God. The resurrection from the dead—above all else—proves he is the Son of God. This is our witness; there is no doubt whatever: Jesus Christ is the Son of the Living God who was crucified for the sins of the world.

NOTE

1. In chapter 9 we reasoned that the disciples were in fact in the temple itself when the Pentecostal fires of the Spirit fell so mightily upon them. This seems more likely than the suggestion here given that they could have been in the upper room.

Chapter 121

"THE BRIDEGROOM COMETH"

And, lo, I am with you alway,
even unto the end of the world.
(Matt. 28:20.)
Let the cry go forth among all people:
Awake and arise and go forth
to meet the Bridegroom;
behold and lo, the Bridegroom cometh;
go ye out to meet him.
Prepare yourselves
for the great day of the Lord.
(D&C 133:10.)

Jesus Is with Us Yet

Lo, he is with us—always!

Though he has returned to his Father, yet where two or three are gathered together in his name, having perfect faith and worshipping the Father in his name, he will be in their midst—by the power of his Spirit.

Some of the faithful and elect, on occasion, see his face and hear his voice. "It is your privilege, and a promise I give unto you," he says to all the faithful elders of his kingdom, "that inasmuch as you strip yourselves from jealousies and fears, and humble yourselves before me, . . .

the veil shall be rent and you shall see me and know that I am—not with the carnal neither natural mind, but with the spiritual." (D&C 67:10.) His command to his ministers is: "Sanctify yourselves that your minds become single to God, and the days will come that you shall see him; for he will unveil his face unto you, and it shall be in his own time, and in his own way, and according to his own will." (D&C 88:68.) And his promise to all is: "It shall come to pass that every soul who forsaketh his sins and cometh unto me, and calleth on my name, and obeyeth my voice, and keepeth my commandments, shall see my face and know that I am." (D&C 93:1.)

Such is his law, and he is no respecter of persons. The reason more people do not pierce the veil and see his face is simply that more do not live the law qualifying them for such a transcendent spiritual experience. "For no man has seen God at any time in the flesh, except quickened by the Spirit of God. Neither can any natural man abide the presence of God, neither after the carnal mind. Ye are not able to abide the presence of God, neither after the carnal mind. Ye are not able to abide the presence of God now"—he is speaking to some of the early elders of this dispensation, and conditions have not materially changed since then—"neither the minstering of angels; wherefore, continue in patience until ye are perfected."[1] For most of us a cloud has received him out of our sight, a cloud that can only be pierced by the eye of faith.

"Between us and His visible presence—between us and that glorified Redeemer who now sitteth at the right hand of God—that cloud still rolls. But the eye of Faith can pierce it; the incense of true prayer can rise above it; through it the dew of blessing can descend. And if He is gone away, yet He has given us in His Holy Spirit a nearer sense of His presence, a closer infolding in the arms of His tenderness, than we could have enjoyed even if we had lived with Him of old in the home of Nazareth, or sailed with Him in the little boat over the crystal waters of Gennesareth. We may be as near to Him at all times—and more than all when we kneel down to pray—as the beloved disciple was when he laid his head upon His breast. The word of God is very nigh us, even in our mouths and in our hearts. To ears that have been closed His voice may seem indeed to sound no longer. The loud noises of War may shake the world; the eager calls of Avarice and of Pleasure may drown the gentle utterance which bids us 'Follow Me.' . . .

"But the secret of the Lord is with them that fear Him, and He will show them His covenant. To all who will listen He still speaks. He promised to be with us always, even to the end of the world, and we have not found [that] His promise[s] fail. It was but for thirty-three years of a short lifetime that He lived on earth; it was but for three broken and troubled years that He preached the Gospel of the Kingdom; but for ever, even until all the Eons have been closed, and the earth itself, with the heavens that now are, have passed away, shall every one of His true and faithful children find peace and hope and forgiveness in His name, and that name shall be called Emmanuel, which is, being interpreted, 'GOD WITH US.' "[2]

Jesus Shall Come Again
(Acts 1:9-11)

There has been a First Coming of Christ, and there shall be a Second Coming of the Son of Man. He came once, born of Mary—to gain his own body, to minister among men, to work out the infinite and eternal atoning sacrifice. He shall come again in all the glory of his Father's kingdom—to live again on earth, to perfect the salvation of his fellows, to deliver the kingdom, in due course, spotless to his Father. After some thirty-three years of mortal life, while angels attended, he ascended up to sit on the right hand of Eternal Power. This same Jesus—living and being as he was, and is, and ever shall be—shall return, accompanied by ten thousands of his angelic saints, to live on earth a thousand years. Then, after a short season, cometh the end, and this earth will attain its celestial destiny.

Hear O Israel, thy King cometh unto thee; he is glorious in his attire and red in his apparel; he rideth upon the clouds and descendeth in his fury. He is just and having salvation; his word is law; and he shall reign forever and ever.

He shall come in a day when many shall say: "There is no Christ, and such a person shall not come. We have no need of another to save us from our sins; God alone has all power, and we have no need for an Advocate or an Intercessor." They will say: "There is no God but Allah and Mohammed is his prophet; Allah has but to speak and a thing is done; he hath no need of a Son." They will say: "Our Messiah will yet come; he will save us; he is our King and our Deliverer; we will wait for him."

But so said they of Jesus when he came of old: "Is not this the carpenter's son; is not his father called Joseph and his mother, Mary; and are not his brothers and sisters with us? Why say ye that he is the Son of God? Does he claim to preach a gospel? His sayings cannot be true; they run counter to our traditions; we will follow Moses instead. Does he pretend to work miracles? What are they but deeds done by Beelzebub the prince of devils. Away with him; crucify him; we have no king but Caesar; his blood be upon us and—God help us!—on our children."

But, no matter, he was God's Son then, and he is God's Son now. He ministered in power and glory then; he proved his divine Sonship by rising from the dead; and he shall come again in a power and glory ten thousand times greater than before. He carried a cross in that day, and he shall wear a crown in this. And they who fight against him and his gospel shall be banished from his presence forever.

He shall come in a day when even those who call themselves Christians shall say: "The Lord delayeth his coming; let us eat, drink, and be merry. If we act amiss, he shall beat us with a few stripes, but eventually we shall be saved in the kingdom of God.''

And so said they of old who bought delicacies and jeweled garments at the bazaars of the sons of Annas; so said they who made His Father's house a den of thieves; so said they who sowed, and reaped, and laid up their harvests in great barns, and who said within themselves, ''Soul take thine ease, for we are rich; we live sumptuously; we have an abundance of this world's goods.''

But, no matter, he came then at the appointed time, and he shall come again when his hour arrives. He came then to destroy their kingdom and leave their house desolate; he said then to those who trusted in riches, ''This night shall thy soul be required of thee; then whose shall all these things be?'' And he shall say when he comes again, ''All those who have laid up treasures on earth and who are not rich unto God, their treasures shall be tried so as by fire, and they only shall abide the day who have laid up treasures in heaven.''

He shall come in a day when many professors of religion shall say: ''He has come already; he dwells in the hearts of his people. The promised era of peace will come when men learn to love one another; then they will beat their swords into plowshares and their spears into pruning hooks. Men will create and usher in their own Millennium by their good works. All these things which the prophets have said about a kingdom of God on earth are spiritual; they cannot be taken literally.''

But, no matter, such men are no different from the Sadducees of old, who believed neither in preexistence, nor in angels, nor in marriage in heaven, nor in the resurrection, nor in eternal glory, nor that He who walked among them was the Son of the living God. What carnal men may think about spiritual things—however much they profess to be religious—is of so little consequence that it scarcely bears repeating. Jesus was the Son of God then, and he is the Son of God now. And to the modern Sadducees, who spiritualize away the prophetic word, we need only say: "Judge ye, for in that fearsome and dread day when he descends, with the trump of God and the shout of the archangel, to take vengeance on all those who know not God and who obey not his gospel—judge ye, for in that great and dreadful day it will be everlastingly too late to prepare for a Second Coming that has passed." When "this same Jesus," who was "taken up . . . into heaven," returns "in like manner" as he went up, then the judgment will be set and the books be opened, and all men shall stand before his bar to be judged according to the deeds done in the flesh.

When first he came—and after he rose from the dead—he walked and talked and ate and drank with his disciples, and he shall do so again in that great day which lies ahead. When—as a symbol of his nation—Thomas doubted and would not believe, except he feel the nail prints in Jesus' hands and in his feet and the spear wound in his side, the troubled apostle was invited to see and feel and know and be not faithless but believing. And so shall it be in the latter days when a troubled people, long in doubt, shall see him again, when they shall look on him whom they have pierced. Then shall these be his words:

Behold the prints of the nails in my hands and in my feet; look upon my riven side; stretch forth thine hands; feel and know; and be not faithless, but believing.

Lo, these are the wounds with which I was wounded in the house of my friends; I am he who was lifted up; I am he who was crucified; I am Jesus of Nazareth of Galilee; I am the Son of God. Come unto me; I died for thee and for all men.

But before the Lord Jesus comes again, all of the promised signs and wonders shall surely come to pass. Ours is the generation in which they are being poured forth. And our need is to learn to read the signs of the times, lest we fail to meet and accept our Promised Messiah as did so many when he came in the meridian of time. We must search the scriptures and heed the Messianic message. The children of light need not be deceived; that day need not come upon them unawares. "And whoso treasureth up my word," he says, "shall not be deceived." (JS-M 1:37.) That day will be one of vengeance for the wicked and of redemption and glory and salvation for the saints. And after he comes, all of the glorious things spoken concerning Israel and Zion and glory and eternal peace shall have their glorious fulfillment.

Arise, O Jerusalem; gather in, O ye dispersed of Judah; hear ye his voice, O scattered ones of Joseph. Let all Israel now rejoice in him who dwells between the cherubim.

Come forth, O Zion, upon the holy mount; let Israel now be gathered home. Come, all ye people; build the city of holiness; let the pure in heart assemble together.

Open thy gates, O Zion, for into thee shall come those of all nations; and the Gentiles shall come to thy light and kings to the brightness of thy rising; and unto thee shall be gathered all those who know the name of the Lord, and who worship the Father in spirit and in truth; and they shall dwell safely within thy walls.

And now what more need we say? We have spoken of him; our message is recorded; our witness is borne.[3] Christ the Lord is God's Almighty Son. He came that man might live, and living, find a place with him where he and his Father dwell eternally. And he shall come again to receive us unto himself.

Ring out ye bells in every belfry of all Christendom. Cry out, ye souls awaiting your redemption. Sing together, ye cherubic hosts; let heaven's dome be filled with anthems of eternal praise.

Ye saints of God, ye holy ones—rejoice. Ye noble souls, ye faithful ones—rejoice. Come now, ye cho-

sen ones—be lifted up: Inherit the kingdom pre-
pared for you from the foundation of the world.

When Will He Come Again?

As we testify of his First Coming and bear record that
he dwelt among men in the meridian of time; as we study
the deeds he did as a mortal and marvel at how wondrous
they were; as our heart burns within us, letting us know of a
surety of his divine Sonship—our thoughts turn to the day
of his return. We long to be with him then, even as the
prophets of old longed to see the day of his mortal ministry.

As we ponder upon these things, it seems clear to us
that we are in an even better position to read the signs of
our times than the Jews were to read the signs of *their*
times. They had the prophetic word telling of his promised
birth; of the words he would speak and the works he would
do; of the atoning sacrifice he would make; of his coming
forth from the grave; and of the consequent resurrection of
all men. Many were the signs and portents then testifying
that the day for all those wondrous works was near even at
their doors. We in like manner have the holy scriptures,
which tell us of the events and describe to us the conditions
that shall precede and attend his triumphal return. We
know he is going to come in the clouds of glory in the midst
of that great era of restoration in which we now live. Many
are the evidences—yea, the infallible proofs—that the hour
of his coming is nigh, even at our doors. Though we do not
know the very day and the very hour of his coming, we do
know the generation; it is our generation, the generation
(dispensation, if you will) of the fulness of times.

Thus saith the Lord; for I am God, and have sent
mine Only Begotten Son into the world for the re-
demption of the world, and have decreed that he
that receiveth him shall be saved, and he that re-
ceiveth him not shall be damned—

And they have done unto the Son of Man even as
they listed; and he has taken his power on the right

423

hand of his glory, and now reigneth in the heavens, and will reign till he descends on the earth to put all enemies under his feet, which time is nigh at hand—

I, the Lord God, have spoken it; but the hour and the day no man knoweth, neither the angels in heaven, nor shall they know until he comes. . . .

And again, verily I say unto you, that the Son of Man cometh not in the form of a woman, neither of a man traveling on the earth.

Wherefore, be not deceived, but continue in steadfastness, looking forth for the heavens to be shaken, and the earth to tremble and to reel to and fro as a drunken man, and for the valleys to be exalted, and for the mountains to be made low, and for the rough places to become smooth—and all this when the angel shall sound his trumpet. (D&C 49:5-7, 22-23.)

But—be it repeated—we are in a better position to read the signs of the times today than our Jewish brethren were in their day. The reason: We have seen the fulfillment of the prophetic word relative to the First Coming and know of a surety that he who then came was the Son of God. We know that he rose from the dead and ascended into heaven. Accordingly, we are bound to believe that he will come again and that the prophetic word relative thereto will come to pass "in like manner" as did the word relative to his ancient ministry.

And yet, no man can know that Jesus is the Lord but by the Holy Ghost, and no man can read the signs of the times except by that same power. As we search the scriptures and seek to know what is destined to happen in our generation we must, above all else, be guided by the Holy Spirit of God. All those who have exercised the power to become, by faith, the sons of God have the right to the constant companionship of that member of the Godhead. Thus the Beloved Disciple said:

Behold, what manner of love the Father hath bestowed upon us, that we should be called the sons of God: therefore the world knoweth us not, because it knew him not.

Beloved, now are we the sons of God, and it doth not yet appear what we shall be: but we know that, when he shall appear, we shall be like him; for we shall see him as he is.

And every man that hath this hope in him purifieth himself, even as he is pure. (1 Jn. 3:1-3.)

NOTES

1. D&C 67:11-13. In this connection, note these words spoken by the Lord to Moses: "Thou canst not see my face at this time, lest mine anger be kindled against thee also, and I destroy thee, and thy people; for there shall no man among them see me at this time, and live, for they are exceeding sinful. And no sinful man hath at any time, neither shall there be any sinful man at any time, that shall see my face and live." (JST, Ex. 33:20.)

2. Farrar, pp. 732-33. These words are used by Farrar to end and climax his *Life of Christ*. Since I have quoted freely from this eminent biblical scholar and recognized literary genius, perhaps I should now append the following. After my first reading of Farrar, I wrote these words on the last page of his work: "In literary craftsmanship—Churchillian in concept and flow; a wondrous witchery of words; a delight to read. In scope and purpose—faith promoting and edifying; written by one who believed, as measured by sectarian standards; and yet much fancy fiction is set forth and much sectarian nonsense and delusion." Manifestly the portions quoted in this work are deemed to be sound and proper; they are, in general, quotations that express the sought-for thought in language seldom equaled and almost never surpassed.

At this point a word about almost all sectarian commentaries and biographies about Christ might not be amiss. It is my judgment that most of the modern publications are far from faith promoting. In most cases it is necessary to go back a hundred years or so to find authors who believed in the divine Sonship with sufficient fervor to accept the New Testament passages as meaning what they say. After all, every "Life of Christ"—this one included—is in large measure a reflection of the faith and knowledge of the author. Providentially, as Latter-day Saints, we have a wealth of sound doctrine available to guide us in all that we write about this or any subject that is not accepted as it should be by the scholars of the world.

3. Edersheim, who devoted seven years of arduous labor and intensive research to his magnum opus, *The Life and Times of Jesus the Messiah*, appended to his work these words of poignant faith and testimony: "*Easter Morning, 1883.*—Our task is ended—and we also worship and look up. And we go back from this sight into a hostile world, to love, and to live, and to work for the Risen Christ. But as earth's day is growing dim, and, with earth's gathering darkness, breaks over it heaven's storm, we ring out—as of old they were wont, from church-tower, to the mariners that hugged a rock-bound coast—our Easter-bells to guide them who are belated, over the storm-tossed sea, beyond the breakers, into the desired haven. Ring out, earth, all thy Easter-chimes; bring your offerings, all ye people; worship in faith, for—'This Jesus, Which was received up from you into heaven, shall so come, in like manner as ye beheld Him going into heaven.' 'Even so, Lord Jesus, come quickly!' " (Edersheim 2:652.)

Chapter 122

"PREPARE YE THE WAY OF THE LORD"

The voice of him
that crieth in the wilderness,
Prepare ye the way of the Lord,
make straight in the desert
a highway for our God.
Every valley shall be exalted,
and every mountain and hill shall be made low:
and the crooked shall be made straight,
and the rough places plain:
And the glory of the Lord
shall be revealed,
and all flesh shall see it together:
for the mouth of the Lord hath spoken it.
(Isa. 40:3-5.)

"This Is My Beloved Son. Hear Him!" [1]

"Behold my Beloved Son, in whom I am well pleased, in whom I have glorified my name—hear ye him." (3 Ne. 11:7.)

On this note we began, on this note we shall end, and the clarion sweetness of this eternal truth shall ring forth forever in all worlds, among all the children of the Eternal Father. The Beloved Son ministered among mortals on planet earth. Jesus our Lord, beloved and chosen from the beginning, came from the Father to do his will, to glorify his name, to save "all the works of his hands, except those sons of perdition who deny the Son after the Father has revealed him." (D&C 76:43.) Then he returned to the glorious Majesty on high. And through the holy accounts we have seen his deeds, learned his law, and felt his Spirit. How glorious is the Word who came down from heaven! What wonders he has shown us, and what spiritual refreshment he has given us!

We saw him make flesh his tabernacle in a stable at Bethlehem of Judea and heard the heavenly choirs acclaim his divine Sonship.

Planted, thus, as a root in dry ground, we saw him grow up as a tender plant in a Jewish home in Nazareth; marveled when he, as a youth, both taught and confounded the wise men in the temple; and rejoiced that he had no need to be taught of men, for God was his Father.

We went with him to Bethabara, where his stern forerunner immersed him in the murky waters of the mighty Jordan; and then, lo, the heavens opened, the Holy Ghost came down in bodily form, serene and calm as a dove, and the Father spoke: "This is my beloved Son, in whom I am well pleased. Hear ye him."

Then we saw him overcome the world when tempted in the wilderness; heard him go forth preaching the gospel of the kingdom of God; gloried as he cleansed his Father's House at the First Passover and again at the Fourth; and heard him say, repeatedly, that he was the Promised Messiah.

We heard him call the Twelve and the Seventy; marveled at the wisdom of his Sermon on the Mount, his discourse on the law of Moses, and then on gospel standards. How we were fed spiritually when he gave the sermon on the bread of life, and the discourse on cleanliness, and on meekness and humility, and on forgiveness and the sealing power, and on the good shepherd, and, then, the

427

sermon on Olivet, and, finally, those in the upper room (the discourse on the two Comforters, and on the law of love, and on the Holy Ghost)! And as to his parables, we need only say, "Never man spake as this Man."

And O the miracles we have seen him work! Before our eyes the lame walked, the blind saw, the deaf heard, paralytics carried their couches, lepers were cleansed, devils were cast out, and the dead were raised. The calm command, "Lazarus, come forth," still echoes in our soul as we remember how he who had been dead four days stood, yet enshrouded in his burial clothes, at the door of his tomb! And all these miracles were as nothing compared to his healing of sin-sick souls; of saying to the sin-encumbered, "Son, thy sins be forgiven thee"; of calling forth the spiritually dead to spiritual life.

We saw him still storms, walk on the tumultuous waves of tempestuous Gennesaret, feed thousands with a few small fishes and a few barley loaves, and walk unharmed through mobs that sought to stone him.

And O the testimonies we have heard! His own: "I am the Son of God"; Peter's: "Thou art the Christ, the Son of the living God"; Martha's: "Thou art the Christ, the Son of God, who should come into the world." Those of believing souls in all walks of life, uttered in unison, ascending as incense to the Father. Thou art the Promised Messiah, the king of Israel, our Deliverer, Savior, and Redeemer. Thou art our God!

And ought we not mention the Mount of Transfiguration, when his face shown with heavenly light and his clothes glistened with celestial brightness, when Moses and Elias came to him, and when Peter, James, and John saw the transfiguration of the earth and received the keys of the kingdom of God on earth?

And then there is Gethsemane, the garden of the olive press, where he sweat great drops of blood from every pore, so great was his suffering and so intense his anguish as he took upon himself the sins of all men on conditions of repentance.

But in nothing have we felt such shame and horror and revulsion as when he was led before Annas and Caiaphas and the Sanhedrin and Pilate and Herod and Pilate again; when the Innocent One was found guilty by the ecclesiastical and civil powers of the world; when he was mocked, derided, spit upon, cursed, smitten, scourged, and led away to be crucified.

There on Calvary we saw Gentile hands drive Roman nails into Jewish flesh; we saw him raised in agony upon the accursed tree; and we wept with his disciples as he drank the dregs of the bitter cup his Father had given him.

But glory be to the Father, he partook. The Beloved One finished his work, voluntarily laid down his life, and then, the third day, took it up again in glorious immortality.

We were with him at the tomb when Mary Magdalene worshipped before him, and when the other women held him by the feet. Then we wept with Peter as the Risen Lord stood gloriously before the Chief Apostle and commissioned him anew to head the earthly kingdom for that day.

And O how our hearts burned within us as we heard him expound the Messianic prophecies on the Emmaus road; as we saw and felt and handled (on two occasions) in the upper room; as we communed and ate on the shore of the Sea of Tiberias; and as we knelt and worshipped on the mountain in Galilee as part of the great congregation.

All these things we saw—and they are not a tithe of it all; nay, they are not a ten thousandth of all that we saw and felt and knew—as he ministered as a mortal among men. And we, therefore, do know and do testify that Jesus of Nazareth was the Son of the living God and that he was crucified for the sins of the world. That the generality of the Jews were not prepared, mentally and spiritually, to receive this knowledge and all that came to the faithful is a matter of sorrow and sadness for them and for their children. And as it was with them, so shall it be with those in all nations in the latter days, unless they prepare themselves to receive this same Jesus at his Second Coming.

As to all these things—and thousands more—what we have written, we have written. For good or for ill, with stumbling words and in halting speech—professing (with Paul) to know nothing among men, save Jesus Christ and him crucified; and yet (we say it humbly) with some inspiration and occasional flights of fluent expression—we have taught and testified of this Jewish Jesus in his Jewish setting. Our work in this respect—meaning with reference to this opus—is ended. And there remaineth but one thing more. We must, for so we have been commanded—it is our divine commission, our sober and sacred duty—we must say to all to whom these words may come: True it is that Jesus ministered among men in the meridian of time, and true it is also that he shall soon come to rule and reign in millennial splendor. And unless our words pertaining to his mortal life prepare and inspire men to make ready for his Second Coming, we have failed indeed.

"My Messenger: . . . He Shall Prepare the Way Before Me"[2]

Isaiah proclaims: "Prepare ye the way of the Lord." (Isa. 40:3.) Our revelations say: "Prepare yourselves for the great day of the Lord." (D&C 133:10.) To prepare the way before the Lord is to bring to pass those things which must be done before he comes. It is to gather Israel, to build Zion, to proclaim the gospel to every nation and people; it is to prepare a people for that dread and glorious day. To prepare ourselves for that great day is to join with the saints, to gather with Israel, to dwell in Zion, to so live that we shall abide the day of his coming. Those who prepare the way before the Lord, by that very process prepare themselves for that which lies ahead. And those who are prepared shall be saved; they shall abide the day;

their seed shall inherit the earth from generation to generation. Those who are not prepared have no such promises.

When Jesus dwelt among men, he chose his friends with care. He preached to all, invited all to believe and obey, called upon all to forsake the world and to join the kingdom. But he chose his friends and close associates from among those who sought to do the things he said. Those who leaned on his bosom, who ate and traveled and lived with him—his friends—were a select and chosen group. In the spirit world he did not even so much as go among the wicked and ungodly; those only who were worthy heard the words of life as they fell from his lips. And so shall it be when he comes again. His voice will be raised among the faithful; his countenance will shine upon the obedient; his friends—those who abide the day—will be the Godfearing and the righteous. Our preparation for that day is fourfold:

1. *We must believe what Jesus believed.*

Repent and believe the gospel. He that believeth shall be saved; he that believeth not shall be damned; signs shall follow those who believe. Believe on the Lord Jesus Christ and thou shalt be saved. Believe in him; believe in his prophets; believe the words of his apostles and elders. Believe and be blessed; disbelieve and be cursed. The first great test of mortality is whether men will believe the everlasting word when it is preached to them. Those who believe the truth can be saved; those who believe a lie shall be damned. At our peril we must choose to believe as Jesus believed, and unless and until we do, we shall never begin the preparation that will qualify us to be his friends. When we believe as he believes; when we gain the mind of Christ; when we think as he thinks; when our desires are harmonious with his—then we will have so much in common that we can be friends. He believed he was the Son of God, and we must believe the same. He believed his Father sent him, and we must have no reservations relative thereto. He believed all the truths of the everlasting gospel, and we must do likewise. No one ever applies eternal truth in his

life until he believes and knows it to be what it everlastingly
is—eternal truth.

2. *We must preach and teach and testify as Jesus did.*

It becometh every man who hath been warned to warn
his neighbor. Every friend of the Lord must tell others of
his Eternal Friend. The gospel cause is to go forth from
mouth to mouth and from heart to heart until the knowledge of God covers the earth as the waters cover the sea.
All who join the Church are under covenant, made in the
waters of baptism, to stand as witnesses of Christ at all
times and in all places and to all people, even unto death. It
does not suffice to believe and do nothing more; every
believer is commanded to take every opportunity to give to
others a reason for the hope which is his.

Thus, Jesus proclaimed the word of truth and salvation
and we must do likewise, and in our day it is the glorious
message of the restoration; of the gathering of Israel; of the
redemption of Zion; of salvation for the dead; of the imminent return of "this same Jesus." We must proclaim—
boldly and without fear—such things as these, for they are
true as God is true:

There has been a famine in the land—not a famine of
bread, nor a thirst for water, but of hearing the word of the
Lord. Now all those who hunger and thirst after righteousness can drink of the waters of life and feast on the good
word of God.

There has been a long night of gloom and darkness and
apostasy. Now the glory of a new day is dawning; darkness
flees; the gospel light shines brightly as before; and the
millennial day is upon us.

The Lord's people have been scattered, spurned,
cursed; they have been a hiss and a byword in all the
nations whither he hath driven them. Now they hear his
voice and heed his cry; now they gather round his gospel
standard in every place where it is raised.

During the long night of darkness—the night when
darkness covered the earth and gross darkness the minds of

432

the people—who has heard the voice of heaven, or seen an angelic face, or gloried in the gifts of the Spirit? But now the ancient powers are restored—the voice of God is heard again: angels minister among us mortals; and signs, gifts, and miracles abound as in olden times.

Once again apostles and prophets mingle among us; they preach and prophesy. Once again the elders of Israel go forth to seek their scattered kin; they preach and minister in power and great glory. Once again the kingdom has been set up on earth in all its glory, beauty, and perfection; its ministers, both male and female, carry forward as did their counterparts among their forebears.

What then say we?

Our voice is one crying in the wilderness—in the wilderness of sin, of apostasy, of worldliness: Repent ye, repent ye, why will ye die O ye nations! Return unto the Lord, O ye people; forsake the world, flee from sin, turn unto the truth. Come unto Christ, and be ye saved.

Our voice is one calling out of the dark, dry deserts of death—out of the waterless waste places of the world: Come, drink of the waters of life; drink deep from the rivers that flow, direct from the great Fountain Head. Come unto him, and drink from the wells of salvation.

Our voice is a voice of joy and gladness—it is one of thanksgiving and the voice of melody: Hear, O ye heavens, and give ear, O earth, for the Lord hath spoken in our day; he hath given again the fulness of his everlasting gospel; every truth, doctrine, power, priesthood, key gift and grace, all things, needed to save and exalt men are now on earth again.

Our voice proclaims—in words of truth and soberness—that the Great God has called his servant, Joseph Smith, Jr., and spoken unto him from heaven, and given him commandments, pursuant to which The Church of Jesus Christ of Latter-day Saints has been set up among men, as the only true and living Church upon the face of the whole earth.

Our voice testifies—by the power and influence of the Holy Spirit of God—that this Church administers the gospel, and that all who come to this ensign, raised anew on the mountains of Israel, can gain peace in this world and eternal life in the world to come.

3. *We must live as Jesus lived.*

Jesus kept the commandments of his Father and thereby worked out his own salvation, and also set an example as to the way and the means whereby all men may be saved. Salvation is available because of his atoning sacrifice and comes by obedience to the laws and ordinances of the gospel. As to how and why and in what manner we must live to gain salvation, we need only quote the teachings of the Prophet Joseph Smith as they are given in the Lectures on Faith.

"Where shall we find a prototype into whose likeness we may be assimilated, in order that we may be made partakers of life and salvation?" the Prophet asked, "or, in other words, where shall we find a saved being? for if we can find a saved being, we may ascertain without much difficulty what all others must be in order to be saved. We think that it will not be a matter of dispute, that two beings who are unlike each other cannot be saved; for whatever constitutes the salvation of one will constitute the salvation of every creature which will be saved; and if we find one saved being in all existence, we may see what others must be, or else not be saved.

"We ask, then, where is the prototype? or where is the saved being? We conclude, as to the answer of this question, there will be no dispute among those who believe the Bible, that it is Christ: all will agree in this, that he is the prototype or standard of salvation; or, in other words, that he is a saved being. And if we should continue our interrogation and ask how it is that he is saved? the answer would be—because he is a just and holy being; and if he were anything different from what he is, he would not be saved; for his salvation depends on his being precisely what he is

434

and nothing else; for if it were possible for him to change, in the least degree, so sure he would fail of salvation and lose all his dominion, power, authority and glory, which constitute salvation; for salvation consists in the glory, authority, majesty, power and dominion which Jehovah possesses and in nothing else; and no being can possess it but himself or one like him."

Then, after quoting various passages of scriptures, the Prophet continued: "These teachings of the Saviour most clearly show unto us the nature of salvation, and what he proposed unto the human family when he proposed to save them—that he proposed to make them like unto himself, and he was like the Father, the great prototype of all saved beings; and for any portion of the human family to be assimilated into their likeness is to be saved; and to be unlike them is to be destroyed; and on this hinge turns the door of salvation." (Lecture 7, cited in *Mormon Doctrine,* 2nd ed., pp. 257–58.)

4. *We must do the things that Jesus did.*

He preached the gospel, performed the ordinances of salvation, wrought miracles, and kept the commandments. So must it be with us. He carried his cross and laid his all upon the altar. So, if called upon, must we do. His promise to us is: "He that believeth on me, the works that I do shall he do also." (John 14:12.) Also: "Ye shall be even as I am, and I am even as the Father; and the Father and I are one." (3 Ne. 28:10.)

"Hosanna in the Highest"[3]

And so we say: He came once and he shall come again. If we have learned well the lessons of his First Coming, we also shall read the signs of the times and be ready for his Second Coming.

> Lo, the mighty God appearing;
> From on high Jehovah speaks!
> Eastern lands the summons hearing,

O'er the west his thunder breaks.
Earth behold him! Earth behold him!
Universal nature shakes.

Zion, all its light unfolding,
God in glory shall display.
Lo! he comes! nor silence holding,
Fire and clouds prepare his way,
Tempests round him! Tempests round him!
Hasten on the dreadful day.

To the heav'ns his voice ascending,
To the earth beneath he cries;
Souls immortal, now descending,
Let their sleeping dust arise!
Rise to judgment; Rise to judgment;
Let thy throne adorn the skies.
—*Hymns,* no. 264

And, now, one thing only remains—the recording of our witness of the divine Sonship of him of whom we have written. To all we have said we append this seal of testimony:

Of Mary's Son, we testify—as God is our witness!—that he is the Holy One of Israel, the Promised Messiah, the Son of God.

As to Jesus of Nazareth we say: He is the God of Israel, the Eternal One, the Great Jehovah, who made flesh his tabernacle and lived as mortals do in a world of sin and sorrow.

As to the Crucified One, him whom they took and by evil hands hanged on a tree, our witness is: He is risen; he came forth from the Arimathean's tomb; he lives; he ascended to his Father; and he reigns on the right hand of the Majesty on high.

Of him who is called Christ, we testify: He is the Redeemer of the world, the Savior of all who believe; he has abolished death and brought life and immortality to light through the gospel; he is the Resurrection and the Life; and in him shall all men have life and that eternally.

And this same Jewish Jesus, whom God hath made both Lord and Christ, shall soon return as the Second David, to rule and reign on the throne of his Father forever.

God grant that we may abide the day. And God grant, further, that our voice shall never cease to speak—in life and in death, in time and in eternity, now and forever—in bearing testimony of Him who has ransomed us from death, hell, the devil, and endless torment.

We write it here; let it also be inscribed in the eternal records; let it be written on earth and in heaven; and let all who read be enlightened by the power of the same Spirit which approves the written word—let all men know (and we so testify) that Jesus Christ is the Son of the living God; that he worked out the infinite and eternal atonement; that he was crucified for the sins of the world; that he rose from death the third day; that he ascended to his Father; that he has restored the fulness of his everlasting gospel in our day; and that he will soon come to reign in power and great glory among those who abide the day and who are not consumed by the brightness of his coming.

He is our King, our Lord, and our God!

Blessed be his great and holy name both now and forever!

Blessed be he that cometh in the name of the Lord. Hosanna in the highest!

NOTES

1. JS-H 1:17.
2. Mal. 3:1.
3. Matt. 21:9.

INDEX

James, 305 n. 1
Jared, brother of, 81 n. 4, 296-97, 370
Jeremiah, 200-202
Jerusalem: sunset over, 27-28; sanctifying
of, 342; splendor of, in last days, 350
Jesus Christ: prepares for his death, 3-4, 6-7;
infuriates Jewish leaders, 12-13; washes
disciples' feet, 37-38; love of, for his
disciples, 47-48; follows his Father's
example, 66 n. 1, 79; prophesies of his
separation from disciples, 69; goes to
prepare place for disciples, 70; is the way,
the truth, and the life, 71; God manifested
himself in, 71-72; as Second Comforter,
75-77; was seen by brother of Jared,
81 n. 4, 296-97; is the true vine, 84-85;
friends of, disciples are called, 87;
rejection of, by world, 90-91; as our
advocate with the Father, 105; is only
accepted mediator, 117 n. 3; in
Gethsemane, 124-28; pain suffered by,
exquisiteness of, 126-27; betrayal of,
by Judas, 130; arrest of, 131; posed
economic threat to Sadducees, 145-46;
trial of, before Annas, 146-47; false
charges against, 150-52; answered
nothing to refute accusations, 152-53;
is found guilty of blasphemy, 155, 158;
is smitten and spit upon, 259-60; looks
upon Peter, after denial, 162-63; is taken
before Pilate, 171; speaks of his kingdom,
176; Pilate finds no fault in, 177, 183;
appears before Herod and remains silent,
180; contrasted with Barabbas, 184-85;
scourging of, 191-92; Pilate delivers, to
will of Jews, 197; stumbles under weight
of cross, 206-7; promises place in paradise
to penitent thief, 222; provides for his
mother, 223-24; calls out for his Father,
226; gives up his life, 228; soldier pierces,
with spear, 235; burial of, 238-40;
ministers to spirits in prison, 241-45;
speaks to Nephites as a spirit, 245-48;
is risen, 251, 261; appears to Mary
Magdalene, 263-65; appears to other
women, 265-67; joins disciples on
Emmaus road, 275-78; appears to
disciples in upper room, 279-82;
appears to Thomas, 284-85; on shore of
Sea of Galilee, 289; instructs Peter to feed
His sheep, 289-90; has all power, 298-99;
did not destroy prophets, but fulfilled
them, 309-10; is the law, 310-11; heals
sick among Nephites, 322; blesses
Nephite children, 322-23; spoke more
plainly to Nephites than to Palestinians,
362-63; work of, is finished, 402-4;
ascension of, 408-9; testimony of, is
spirit of prophecy, 411; belief in,
importance of, 412, 432; testimonies
of, 412-15, 436-37; faithful shall see,
416-17; Second Coming of, 418-22;
summary of work of, 426-30; prepare ye
the way of, 430; example of, men must
follow, 434-35
Jews: factions of, unite to destroy Jesus,
12-13; divisions among, make it difficult
to accuse Jesus, 150; Pilate's encounters
with, 172-73; could not inflict death
penalty, 174; Pilate's fear of, 185-86;
revenges of history upon, 189-90,
202 n. 2-3, 209; latter-day restoration
of, 203 n. 6; taunts of, to Jesus on cross,
217-19; will look upon wounds of Jesus,
235-36, 341, 421; differentiating,
from Gentiles, 314-15; conversion of,
340-43. See also Israel
John the Beloved, 32; gained admittance to
Caiaphas's palace, 160-61; Jesus commits
his mother to care of, 223-24; rushes to
empty tomb, 262; is to tarry until Second
Coming, 291-92
Jonah, sign of, 9
Joseph, son of Jacob, America is land of,
311, 334, 336
Joseph of Arimathea, 237-39
Joy, fulness of, 86-87, 386, 391
Judas: blood money paid to, 14-15;
motives of, for betraying Jesus, 15-18;
modern counterparts of, 17; contention
stirred by, 31-32; sat by Jesus at Last
Supper, 32-33; Jesus washed feet of,
41-42; would be better had he not been
born, 44; receives sop and leaves, 44-45;
departure of, lifts spirits of group, 48;
betrays Jesus with kiss, 129-30; begins
to recognize Jesus' innocence, 197-98;
tries to return the silver, 198-99; death
of, was prophesied, 199-200; hangs
himself, 200
Judgment: inevitability of, 202-3 n. 4, 208-9;
belongs to Christ, 216; all shall undergo,

241; out of records kept, 384-85; hierarchy of, 385
Justice, mercy cannot rob, 211, 215 n. 5

Katalyma, or hostelry, 22-23
King of the Jews, 175, 213-14
Kingdom: eternal, Jesus appoints, unto disciples, 35; of Christ is not of this world, 176
Kiss, Judas betrays Jesus with, 130

Lamb, slaying of, 25
Last Supper: seating arrangement at, 31-33; contention afflicts, 34-35; sadness falls over, 43. *See also* Passover
Law of Moses, Jesus fulfilled, 309-10
Leaven, search for, prior to Passover, 24
Life, laying down, is greatest manifestation of love, 87. *See also* Eternal life
Light, greater, sinning against, 91, 397-99
Lord's Supper. *See* Sacrament
Lots, soldiers cast, for Jesus' robe, 215
Love: of Jesus for the Twelve, 48; is new commandment, 50, 87; showing, by keeping commandments, 74; is of God, 82-83; casteth out fear, 83; of God, 86; manifesting, by laying down life, 87
"Lovest thou me," Jesus asks, of Peter, 289-91
Luke, 275, 278, 285 n. 1

Magdalene, Mary: Jesus appears to, 262-65; is forbidden to touch Jesus, 264, 269-70 n. 1; prominence of, 270 n. 2
Malachi, 367-68
Malchus, Peter wounds, and Jesus heals, 131-32
Mansions, many, Father's house has, 70
Mark, 24
Marred servants, 354
Mary, mother of Jesus, 223-24
Meetings, saints are to hold, 325
Melchizedek, 52-53
Mercy cannot rob justice, 211, 215 n. 5
Messianic prophecies, fulfillment of, 280-81
Micah, 335, 356
Michael, 125
Millennium, prayers of righteous for, 347. *See also* Second Coming
Missionary work: Twelve are called to do,

281-82, 299-300; of John the Beloved, 292
Mob, gathering of, to arrest Jesus, 129
Mockery: Jesus submitted to, 192; of Jesus on cross, 217-19
Mortality, man's limited knowledge in, 392-93
Mosaic law: Passover is not child of, 30; had been fulfilled when Jesus visited Nephites, 309
Moses, Lord commanded, to call Seventy, 164
Mount of Transfiguration, 10
Mountain in Galilee, Jesus' apparance on, 295-305
Mysteries of godliness: Holy Ghost reveals, 99-100; receiving, requires faith, 369-70; many receive, but cannot impart them, 393-94

Nail fastened in sure place, 215 n. 4
Name of Christ: prayers offered in, 73, 102-3; performing works in, 376; true Church must be called in, 376-79; men must take, upon themselves, 378, 387 n. 1
Nephi the Disciple, 300-301
Nephites: sacrament given to, 59, 323-24, 330; twelve disciples among, teach and baptize, 94-95, 326-27; Jesus' prayers among, 106-7, 110-12, 327-28; darkness and destruction among, at Jesus' death, 225-26; Jesus speaks to, as a spirit, 245; righteous among, are spared from destruction, 260; are Jesus' "other sheep," 306, 312; Jesus' work among, 307, 374; were not known to brethren at Jerusalem, 311; are sent home to ponder Jesus' words, 321; Jesus heals sick among, 322; Jesus blesses children of, 322-23; thousands of, gather to meet Jesus, 326; receive Holy Ghost, 327; great faith of, 329; are heirs of Abrahamic covenant, 339; Jesus spoke more plainly to, than to Palestinians, 362-63; Jesus expounds scriptures to, 363-68; the Three, 389-90, 394-96; gospel blessings prevailing among, 397; apostasy of, 397-99
New Jerusalem, 350, 358-59
Nicodemus, 8-9, 75, 239

Officers in Church organization, 411

concerning, 353-54; of kingdom to Israel, disciples ask concerning, 407

Resurrection: Jesus prophesies of his, 101; power of, is bestowed on righteous spirits, 244-45, 273; scriptures celebrating, 255; Jesus is firstfruits of, 257; proves divine Sonship, 257-58; Church's power depended upon, 259; infallible proofs of, 406; effects of, pass upon all men, 411

Revelation: principle of, 104 n. 2; importance of, in determining course of action, 133 n. 1; greater, preparing for, 372-73; to to a few chosen mortals, 393

Revelator, Holy Ghost is, 96, 99-100

Righteousness: peace is reward of, 78; brings joy, 386

Robe, Herod arrayed Jesus in, 180

Rock, being built upon, 62-63

Romans: law of, charges against Jesus must apply under, 151-52; crucified Jesus, but were less guilty than Jews, 204-5; forgiveness for, Jesus pleads for, 211-12; attitude of, toward Jesus, 217; trembled at events following crucifixion, 234

Sabbath, ceremonial pollution of, Jews wished to avoid, 234, 237

Sacrament, 29-30; is message of love, 48; emblems of, 52; prefiguring of, in Abraham's day, 52-53; sketchy scriptural accounts of, 57-58; Jesus gives, to disciples 58-62; prayers of, 59, 61-62; meaning of, and blessings accompanying, 60-61; unworthy partaking of, 63-64, 326; Jesus will partake of, with saints at Second Coming, 65-66; Jesus gives, to Nephites, 323-24, 330

Sacrifice, great and last, 66 n. 4

Sacrifices: offered in similitude, 50-51, 66 n. 3; offering, in last days, 53, 66-67 n. 5; doing away with, 246

Sadducees, hatred of, for Jesus, 145-46

Salvation: is in Christ, 71, 375; Jesus preaches, to spirits in prison, 242; plan of, gospel is, 283, 381

Samuel the Lamanite, Nephites failed to write of, 366

Sanctification, 114; Holy Ghost brings, 96; process of, 383

Sanhedrin: trial of Jesus before, 143, 165-68; meet in Caiaphas's palace to try Jesus,

149; pronounce Jesus worthy of death, 155; were patterned after Moses' Quorum of Seventy, 164; power and role of, 164-65; formal trial of Jesus by, some disclaim, 169 n. 3

Satan: power of, over Judas, 15, 45; men loved, more than God, 18 n. 2; has no power over Jesus, 80; worldly forces belong to, 90; seeks to make all men miserable, 113; sought the soul of Peter, 120; avoiding power of, through prayer, 324

Saul, 92

Scourging of Jesus, 191-92

Scriptures: Jesus expounds, on Emmaus road, 277; fulfillment of, in Christ, 280-81; value of, 362; Jesus expounds, to Nephites, 363-68; withholding of, until faith is proved, 369-71; disciples will believe, 371; men will be judged out of, 384-85

Sea of Galilee, 288-89

Second Comforter, 75-77

Second Coming of Christ, 418-22; men must prepare for, 422; preparing for, steps in, 431-35

Sermon on the Mount, Nephite parallel to, 308-9

Servant is not greater than master, 40-41

Seventy called by Moses, 164

Sheep: Peter is instructed to feed, 289-91; "other," Nephites referred to as, 306, 312

Shepherd, Jesus prophesies smiting of, 122

Sick, Jesus heals, among Nephites, 322

Signs following them that believe, 304-5

Signs of the times: the Lord will give, 347-48; coming forth of Book of Mormon as, 349-50, 351-52; conversion of Israel as, 350; reading, 423-24

Silver, thirty pieces of, 14-15

Simon of Cyrene, 207

Sin: being purified and cleansed from, 85; world to be convicted of, 97; weight of, came upon Jesus, 124; judgment will come for, 202-3 n. 4; remission of, 283, 286 n. 3

Sleep, disciples are overcome by, 125-26

Smith, Joseph, 45 n. 2, 77, 308, 354, 433-34

Sons of God, men are, 425

Sonship, divine: Jesus proclaims his, 154-55; resurrection proves, 257-58